The English Revolution

Advanced History sourcebooks

Barry *Coward*
Chris *Durston*

Series Editor: *Ian Coulson with Andy Harmsworth*

JOHN MURRAY

First published in 1997
by John Murray (Publishers) Ltd
50 Albemarle Street
London W1S 4BD

Reprinted 2002

Layouts by Flying Pig Design
Artwork by Barking Dog Art
Typeset in 10/12pt Gill Sans and Goudy by Wearset Ltd, Boldon, Tyne and Wear
Printed and bound in Great Britain by St Edmundsbury Press, Bury St Edmunds

A catalogue entry for this title is available from the British Library

ISBN 0 7195 7221 5

Contents

Acknowledgements

Cover: Fotomas Index; **p.2** National Trust Photographic Library/Rupert Truman; **p.11** Crown Copyright – published by kind permission of the Historic Royal Palaces; **p.46** Fotomas Index; **p.47** Ashmolean Museum, Oxford; **p.49** *t* & *b* Fotomas Index; **p.55** Houses of Parliament, Westminster, London/ Bridgeman Art Library, London; **p.62** Sir Ralph Verney Bt (photograph: Courtauld Institute of Art); **p.114** By permission of The British Library E411(9); **p.122** Mary Evans Picture Library; **p.124** *t* House of Lords Record Office, reproduced by permission of the Clerk of the Records, *b* Ashmolean Museum, Oxford; **p.128** *l* & *r* Fotomas Index; **p.129** By permission of The British Library E304 (19); **p.131** Worcester College, Oxford; **p.148** The British Library, London/Bridgeman Art Library, London; **p.155** Fotomas Index; **p.163** *c* © Copyright The British Museum, *bl* Image Select, *br* The British Library, London/Bridgeman Art Library, London; **p.164** Fotomas Index; **p.165** *t* Fotomas Index, *b* The British Library, London/Bridgeman Art Library, London; **p.176** Image Select; **p.197** Fotomas Index; **p.202** Mary Evans Picture Library; **p.210** Fotomas Index; **p.218** © Edwin Smith (photograph: Sidney Sussex College, Cambridge)

chapter 1

England before the English Revolution

Introduction

What was England like before the English Revolution? This chapter focuses on that question by describing the main features of the country in the early seventeenth century. The first three sections deal separately with:

- Section A The economy and society
- Section B The government
- Section C Religion and the Church in England.

This chapter also identifies the major problems facing the country's rulers, James I (1603–25) and Charles I after 1625. Section D provides information that will help you investigate how they dealt with those problems, and why, by 1640, the Crown faced a major crisis. You should read the chapter for the first time simply to get some idea of what the country was like before it went through a period of extraordinary crisis and change after 1640. But, later on, you should refer back to it quite often. You will find that you will only be able to make sense of some of the sources in later chapters when you know the answers to questions that are dealt with here, questions such as:

- What was the role of the monarch in government at this time?
- Who were the Puritans and what did they believe?
- What was Laudianism?
- What was the theology of predestination?
- What was ship money?

Section A The economy and society of England before the English Revolution

What was the economic and social life of England like in the early seventeenth century? If people living at the time had been asked that question they would undoubtedly have given very different answers.

The nobility and the gentry

Those born into the wealthy gentry and into noble families who owned large areas of land – a tiny minority of people – would have had every reason to have replied that life for them was comfortable and pleasant. They were brought up in large houses, had plenty to eat (including meat), wore luxurious clothes (made of fine woollen cloth, silks and velvets) and were waited on hand and foot by domestic servants. After being educated at home by tutors or at a local grammar school, the sons would spend some time at a college at the universities of Oxford or Cambridge. This was followed by a spell in London at an Inn of Court, where they were taught enough about the law to enable them to run their estates and carry out their duties as local magistrates (Justices of the Peace – see page 9) and, possibly, as Members of Parliament. Those duties apart, they (women as well as men) had the wealth to enable them spend lots of time in leisure activities.

The 'poorer sort'

In contrast, many of those born into families below the gentry – the vast majority of people – would have had every reason to portray their lives in a much more dismal way. They rarely starved, but their everyday food was basic and dull (usually beans and cheese, not meat). They wore simple clothes made from coarse, hard-wearing woollen cloth, and they worked with their hands from a very early age, for example picking stones out of fields as toddlers, before moving on to more arduous agricultural labouring jobs or domestic service as they got older. There were only limited opportunities for formal education, and leisure time was restricted to a few customary holidays, such as harvest suppers that marked the end of the agricultural year. Life for these people was largely one (at best) of constant work or (at worst) of irregular work and a grim struggle for survival.

● Rich and poor

Here are some examples that illustrate the enormous differences between rich and poor at this time.

In the early seventeenth century an arable farmer with 30 acres had a total annual income of £42. Of this, all but £3–5 was spent on essentials such as seed, rent, and food and clothing for himself and his family.

In contrast, a large landowner like the Earl of Derby, who had thousands of acres of estates in many counties of England and Wales, had a gross income from rents alone of over £5,000 a year. Given the inflation since that time, it is meaningless to try and translate figures like this into modern equivalents. But someone like the Earl of Derby would, today, be in the multi-millionaire class, spending huge sums on buildings, clothes and food. In one week in September 1602, the household of the Earl of Shrewsbury consumed 23 sheep and lambs, 2 bullocks, 1 veal, 59 poultry, 5 pigs, 24 pigeons and 54 rabbits.

In 1582, Elizabeth I's minister Lord Burghley spent £629 on a three-day wedding feast for his daughter, at which the guests drank 1,000 gallons of wine and ate 6 veals, 26 deer, 15 pigs, 14 sheep, 16 lambs, 4 goat kids, 6 hares, 36 swans, 2 storks, 41 turkeys, 49 curlews, 135 mallards, 354 teal, 1,049 plovers, 124 knotts, 280 stints, 109 pheasants, 485 snipe, 840 larks, 21 gulls, 71 rabbits, 23 pigeons and 2 sturgeons.

● Source 1.1

Montacute House in Somerset. The frontispiece shown in this photograph dates from around 1600.

The gulf between rich and poor

In the decades before 1640 it is very likely that the gulf in English society between rich and poor was getting bigger. This raises two important questions:

- Why were the rich getting richer and the poor poorer?
- Did this threaten to undermine the stability of society?

Before we look at those questions, however, some basic features of the economy and society of the country at that time need to be established.

An agrarian society

England was largely an agrarian society in which the vast majority of people earned their living on or from the land.

Although it tends to be an over-simplified view, English landed society at that time can be divided as below.

● The main divisions of landed society

1 *Gentlemen*, who were the nobility and gentry and who got the greater part of their income from rents paid to them by the tenant farmers to whom they let their land. They did not themselves work for a living.
2 *Yeomen*, who were fairly wealthy farmers.
3 *Husbandmen*, who were also farmers, but their landholding and wealth were much smaller than those of yeomen.
4 *Cottagers, labourers and servants*, who held, at the most, smallholdings or allotments and who relied largely on wages (in the form of either money, food or accommodation) for the bulk of their income.

Many of those in the last three groups (who together made up the vast majority of the population) combined work as farmers or farm labourers with part-time employment. This was done in their own homes, and involved producing manufactured goods, in what is often called 'the domestic system of production'.

The main goods produced were made of leather (shoes, gloves, harnesses for horses, etc.), wood (farming tools, fencing, etc.), metal (knives, nails, axes, etc.) and wool. Woolworkers made a wide variety of cloth, from undyed, coarse broadcloths to fine, coloured New Draperies, so called because they were recent innovations brought to the country by Protestant religious refugees from the Netherlands.

As in many present-day Third World countries, economic life was often seriously disrupted by natural disasters, including epidemics of diseases such as plague, or the failure of the harvest because of excessive rainfall or drought. In the later 1640s, which witnessed dramatic political events, the harvests failed due to successive wet summers.

Unlike the situation in many modern underdeveloped countries, most people produced food and manufactured goods for the market, rather than solely for the use of their own families.

Manufacturing

The principal commercial activity apart from agriculture was the manufacture of woollen cloth, which in some parts of the country was very highly organised.

In parts of south-west England and East Anglia, for example, wealthy merchant clothiers controlled huge businesses, putting out raw wool to be spun and woven into cloth by part-time workers in their own homes. They then collected the undyed woollen broadcloth and sold it to merchants in London who, in turn, sold it to merchants in north European cities such as Amsterdam and Hamburg. In the early seventeenth century, however, this industry was suffering from a prolonged crisis which had begun in the mid-sixteenth century. The reasons for this crisis are given below.

Overseas trade

The main activity of English merchants trading overseas was the export of woollen cloth to northern Europe. In return, they imported goods from the Far East brought to Europe by Dutch merchants, and European goods, such as wine, from France and Spain.

Unfortunately, England's woollen cloth trade was disrupted by a series of trade crises for nearly a century after 1550. There were especially severe trade depressions in the early 1620s and also one in the early 1640s. These were caused mainly by the dislocation of markets in northern Europe by warfare: the long Dutch rebellion against Spanish rule in the later sixteenth century and, later on, the Thirty Years War from 1618 to 1648. During that period, English merchants tried to develop alternative trades in the Baltic, the Mediterranean, the East Indies (modern Indonesia) and America (where the first English colonies were beginning to be established). By 1640, however, none of the new trade routes was very profitable. In the Baltic, Mediterranean and East Indies, English merchants faced strong competition from the Dutch. In addition, the trade in tobacco and sugar in the newly founded colonies in Virginia and the West Indies made only a very limited impact on the markets in England and Europe.

Towns

Most people lived in rural villages or small market towns. The only major city was London, which doubled in size during the early seventeenth century (from 200,000 in 1600 to 400,000 by 1640). In England, the only other towns of any size, Bristol and Norwich, could claim at the most 20,000 inhabitants. In 1640 London was the largest city in Europe.

Family life

Most people lived in nuclear families, i.e. families consisting only of parents and unmarried children.

The exceptions were to be found in the large households of the rich landowners and wealthy merchants, which were sometimes sizeable establishments. Outside that small social group, the large extended families (i.e. families consisting of many generations living under one roof) that are sometimes to be found in traditional societies in the underdeveloped parts of the world today, occurred rarely. One of the reasons for this is that it was customary in England (as it was in much of north-west Europe) for people to delay marriage until they were able to set up independent households.

One major consequence of this was that most people (other than members of the small landed and mercantile elites) married (in comparison with later times) very late in life, often in their mid-twenties. It was very common for young people to spend at least ten years before they married working away from home as servants, either domestic servants or so-called 'servants in husbandry', i.e. farm labourers.

This is one explanation for another feature of English society at this time – the high degree of geographical mobility.

Geographical mobility

The view that most people in pre-industrial England lived and died in the parish in which they were born is incorrect. On the contrary, it was very common for people to move about the country. London's rapid growth, for example, was almost entirely dependent on migration to the capital from all parts of rural Britain. Historians who have researched into the social history of this period using parish registers have discovered that those individuals who are registered in the baptismal registers rarely appear in the marriage or burial registers of the same parish. People moved for many reasons but, for the most part, they moved in search of employment in an economy that was very vulnerable to natural disasters and crises. Many of the wealthier members of society also often moved away from home to be educated or to visit London. This high degree of geographical mobility throughout society is a reminder that you should not accept automatically the idea that English people in the early seventeenth century felt a greater loyalty and sense of attachment to their localities than to the nation; nor that news of political events in London rarely reached the provinces. It is unlikely that either of these ideas is valid.

A rising population

By 1640, the population of the country had been rising steadily for at least a century. After a long period of stagnation in the later Middle Ages, between the early 1520s and the early 1650s the population of England and Wales more than doubled from about 2.2 million to 5.2 million.

Why were the rich getting richer and the poor poorer before the English Revolution?

The basic reason for these changes in society was the failure of the English economy to respond adequately to the challenge posed by a steadily rising population. English agriculture also failed to meet fully the increased demand for food.

Changes in agriculture

It would be wrong to give the impression that agriculture failed totally to meet this challenge. It clearly did not. Changes in farming are never rapid, but by 1640 it was clear that the face of English farming had changed greatly during the previous century in three major respects:

● **The main changes in English agriculture in the century before the English Revolution**

1 Much more land was now under cultivation than had been the case in the later Middle Ages. Thousands of acres of land had been brought into cultivation by deforestation and drainage. The most spectacular example is the attempt in the 1630s by a company headed by the Earl of Bedford to drain large areas of marshland in eastern England, employing Dutch engineers such as Cornelius Vermuyden. On a lesser scale, similar schemes were under way in many parts of the country. Even land that had once been considered too difficult to cultivate, such as moorland in parts of Cumberland and Westmorland, was taken in from the waste.

2 New crops were grown and new farming methods were used to try to increase the fertility of the soil. In the absence of artificial, chemical fertilisers, there were two main ways to do this: either to let the land lie fallow to regain its fertility naturally, or to dig animal manure into it. The first took valuable land out of cultivation. The second could only be done on a small scale because of the limited supply of manure caused by a lack of fodder crops, other than hay, to feed animals during the winter.

3 Some regions began to specialise in certain types of farming. Examples of this are the growth of market gardening in regions around London, and the attempt to change parts of the Midlands from traditional grain growing to pasture farming, by enclosing the large, uneconomic, medieval open fields.

However, not all of these changes were completely successful.

• There was an obvious limit to the amount of land that could be brought into cultivation.
• No practical solution had yet been found to the problem of increasing the size of the animal population. As a result the problem of increasing the fertility of the soil and thus increasing agricultural productivity remained unsolved. (It was to be solved in the later seventeenth and early eighteenth centuries by the use of fodder crops such as the turnip.)
• Regional agricultural specialisation involving changes in land use, such as enclosures and fen drainage, sometimes met violent local opposition. Anti-enclosure and anti-drainage riots were common in many parts of England in the early seventeenth century.

● **FIGURE 1.1**

Britain's economy, c. 1600

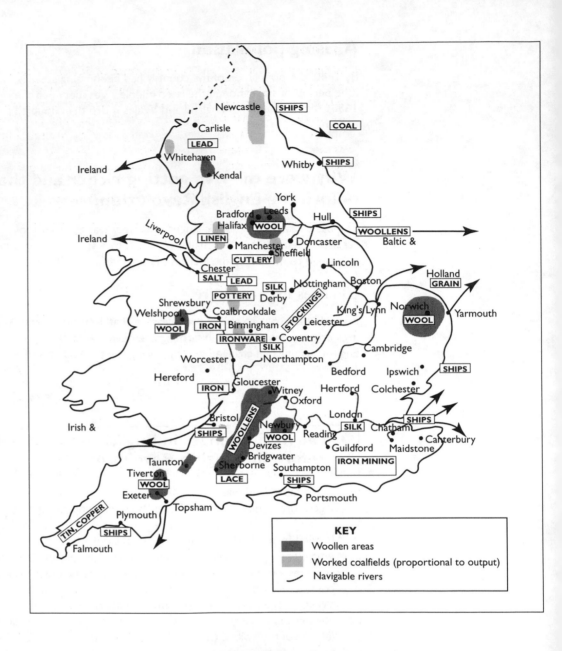

KEY

- Woollen areas
- Worked coalfields (proportional to output)
- Navigable rivers

● **FIGURE 1.2**

Graph of wheat prices, 1500–1620

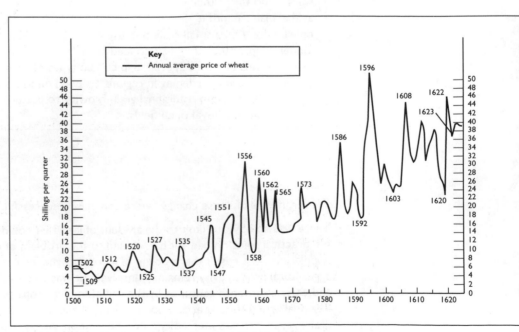

Key
— Annual average price of wheat

The Price Revolution

The clearest indication of the limited success of English agriculture in coping with the demand for food from a rising population is the steady rise in prices during the same period. During the later sixteenth and early seventeenth centuries, the price of all goods rose but food prices rose more rapidly than anything else. Between 1550 and 1640, food prices roughly doubled. In comparison with some twentieth-century examples, this was inflation on a modest scale. It was sandwiched, however, between over a century of stable prices both before the early sixteenth century and after the mid-seventeenth century, so it deserves its common label, the Price Revolution.

This Price Revolution had several social consequences:

● Social consequences of the Price Revolution

The main gainers from rising prices were:

1 landlords, who found it relatively easy to increase their income from rents when there was no shortage of tenants
2 yeomen farmers, who gained from a long period of rising food prices.

The main losers were:

1 small farmers, who did not have the wealth to invest in agricultural improvements or to survive the effects of bad harvests
2 landless labourers, whose money wages failed to rise enough to compensate for the increasing price of essential items such as food.

As a result, poverty was a growing social problem before 1640. Food riots were common in English towns and villages, especially when harvest failures caused bread prices to soar.

How serious were the social tensions caused by population expansion and the Price Revolution?

Some contemporaries believed that popular riots threatened to become serious rebellions against the social and political order. Propertied people began to believe that 'the many-headed monster of the poor' would one day rise up against them.

There are, however, three reasons to believe that these fears were exaggerated:

- Population pressure, which had been increasing since the early 1520s, began to ease off during the 1630s.
- Agricultural output rose sufficiently to avoid the subsistence crises that occurred elsewhere in Europe. English people rarely faced the prospect of starving to death.
- The existence of poor relief schemes cushioned people against the worst effects of poverty, and may have eased social tensions at that time.

● The Elizabethan Poor Law 1601

The Elizabethan Poor Law stated that in each parish the Justices of the Peace were to appoint four overseers, who, together with the churchwardens, would be responsible for the poor of the parish. They were to ensure that the following measures were carried out:

Impotent poor (the deserving poor)
A poor rate was to be collected from all householders.
Poor and orphan children were to be given apprenticeships, girls until they were 21, boys until they were 24.
Stocks of materials were to be made available in the parish for those who were willing to work.
Those unable to work were to be looked after in almshouses.

Sturdy beggars
Begging was forbidden.
Vagabonds were 'whipped until bloody', sent back to the parish of their birth and, if they still refused to work, placed in a House of Correction.

These measures remained in force until the nineteenth century.

● **SOURCE 1.2**

Beggars being punished, from
Holinshed's *Chronicle*, 1577

Look at Source 1.2. Why do you think these punishments were carried out in public?

Section B The government of England before the English Revolution

● **FIGURE 1.3**

The government of England in the
early seventeenth century

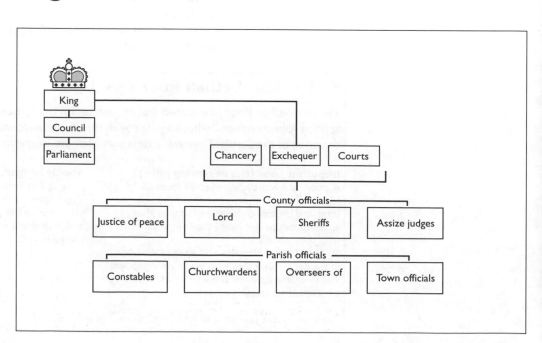

One of the most important questions for anyone studying the English Revolution is: what were the major problems involved in governing the country in the early seventeenth century?

Before you can answer the question, you need to know about the basic features of the government of the country at that time.

Local government

England was an intensively governed country. Anyone living at that time, whether in towns, villages or the countryside, would have come into regular contact with local government officials.

● The main local government officers

1 *Parish officials*, principally *constables* (who were responsible for collecting taxes and arresting criminals), *churchwardens* (who administered the laws regarding compulsory church attendance, as well as looking after the upkeep of church buildings) and *overseers of the poor* (who collected and spent the compulsory poor rates people had to pay for the relief of the poor).

2 *Town officials*. These worked under the *mayors and aldermen* of town councils, and were a vast army of officials, including *scavengers* (road sweepers) and *aleconners* (inspectors responsible for regulating the quality and price of ale). So numerous were they that one in sixteen inhabitants of the London parish of Cornhill in the 1640s held some sort of local office.

3 *County officials*. The main ones were:
a) *Justices of the Peace (JPs)*. These were men appointed by the Crown as commissioners of the peace, local magistrates and law enforcers. This was a highly sought-after post, despite the increasing amount of work put on JPs in this period. They administered a multitude of laws and regulations regarding vagrancy and price- and wage-fixing, as well as acting as judges in criminal cases. This they did in informal petty sessions, often held in their own homes or in the local alehouse, and more formally in quarter sessions, which were held four times a year in the main county towns.
b) *Lord Lieutenants and Deputy Lieutenants* were responsible for supervising the only regular armed force in the country. This was known as *the militia*. It was supposed to consist of every able-bodied man between the ages of sixteen and sixty, who were expected to keep weapons (and horses as well if they were wealthy) and to bring them to annual musters, organised by the Lord Lieutenants and their Deputies. Despite the fact that a proportion of these amateur soldiers were selected for special training in *trained bands* by *muster masters*, the general efficiency of the militia was very poor.
c) *Sheriffs*. By the early seventeenth century they had lost the important position in government that they had held throughout the Middle Ages. Their main function in this period was organising county parliamentary elections, and collecting ship money in the 1630s.
d) *Assize Judges*, who came from London twice a year to hear criminal cases that were too serious to be decided by Justices of the Peace. They were also used by the Crown to pass on royal orders to officials in the localities, as well as to report to the Crown about what was happening in the localities.

Parliament

Parliaments affected the daily lives of people at this time much less than local government officials; they also had a less important role in government than Parliaments today.

There was no doubt that, by the early seventeenth century, laws passed as Acts of Parliament carried more weight than proclamations issued solely by the Crown. Nobody challenged the fact that, following the role of Parliament in the 1530s in bringing about the break with Rome, any future changes regarding the Church had to be approved by Parliament. The right of Parliaments to approve taxation was now well established, as was their role in government. However, kings and queens did not have to call Parliament at all. Clearly, if Parliament was not called then its influence would be limited.

It is important not to exaggerate the role of Parliaments in government in the early seventeenth century. MPs wanted to retain and protect Parliament's place in the constitution, but they showed no signs of wanting to attack the powers of the Crown. They valued meetings of Parliaments as an opportunity to pass laws to deal with local concerns, and to make contacts with the monarch and powerful people around him. Above all, what limited the importance of Parliaments was that they met infrequently. It is often assumed that the fact that Parliament did not meet between 1629 and 1640 was unusual. It was not. For example, during the 45-year reign of Elizabeth I, Parliament only met for a total of 35 months – an average of just three weeks per year.

FIGURE 1.4

Parliament in the early seventeenth century

THE HOUSE OF LORDS

- About 90 hereditary lords
- Bishops and judges – appointed by the Crown

THE HOUSE OF COMMONS

- About 500 members – mostly gentry but also wealthy merchants, lawyers and government officials. They were elected by landowners and the wealthier citizens in towns. The lower classes could not vote.

Parliament met when the King decided, usually at Westminster.
Its main functions were to:

- advise the King
- help the King pass laws. Acts of Parliament needed the majority support of the Lords and Commons and the Royal Assent
- approve the collection of taxes in an emergency.

It was also a useful way for monarchs to measure the opinions of wealthy and influential men who helped enforce law and order in the localities.

The court

The royal court had a more important role in politics and government than Parliaments in this period. It had two important functions in maintaining political stability:

- The royal court was a place where different political views could be expressed and where the Crown could keep in touch with the most influential and important people in the country.
- It was a major source of royal patronage – for example, grants of cash, offices, land and other favours. The distribution of patronage was a normal part of the political process at that time. It was an important method by which the Crown retained the loyalty of its most important subjects. When James I's minister Sir Robert Cecil, Earl of Salisbury, said that 'for a king not to be bountiful were a fault', he was pointing to a major feature of the government system of his day. It was essential that the royal court was used as a means of spreading royal patronage as widely as possible.

The monarchy

Unlike in the present day, the monarchy was the most important part of the government. Kings and queens at that time ruled as well as reigned. They had a Privy Council to advise them. It consisted of men they had chosen, but it was too large a body to make important decisions speedily. Kings and queens often reached decisions outside the formal meetings of the Privy Council, after informal meetings with a handful of advisers. In the last resort all major government decisions were made by the monarch.

The powers of the Crown

The important position of the monarch was strengthened by three main ideas that were not seriously questioned in the early seventeenth century.

The Royal Prerogative

The Crown held wide powers to govern according to the Royal Prerogative and these were used through Royal Prerogative Courts.

● The Royal Prerogative

It consisted of two parts:

1 *'Ordinary' powers* consisted of the monarch's right to choose his own advisers, to command the armed forces, to oversee law and order, to call and dismiss Parliaments whenever he wanted, and to make all the important decisions of government.
2 *'Absolute' powers*. These were given to the monarch to use in times of emergency, when he considered that national security made it necessary to override the law.

● What were the Royal Prerogative Courts?

The main ones were:

1 *The Court of Star Chamber*, which consisted of the Privy Council and major law judges. They heard cases brought to the court by petition.
2 *The Council in the North* (at York) and *The Council in the Marches of Wales* (at Ludlow in Shropshire), which administered royal justice in these outlying areas.

Royal supremacy in the Church

The English Church was under the monarch's control. The monarch was the Supreme Governor of the Church, and chose all archbishops and bishops. The Church strengthened the monarch's power: the bishops acted as royal agents in the localities. Church ministers regularly expressed pro-monarchical views in their sermons.

The Divine Right of Kings

The monarch's prerogative powers were supported by the widespread belief in the Divine Right of Kings.

SOURCE 1.3

The Apotheosis of James I (James joining the gods after his death) by Peter Paul Rubens, a Flemish artist, 1635. This is one of a series of paintings commissioned by Charles I in 1635 to decorate the ceilings of the Royal Banqueting House in Whitehall. They can still be seen there today.

● James and the Divine Right of Kings

When James I made what seems to us nowadays an outrageous statement in a speech to Parliament on 21 March 1610 no one reacted with anything other than approval.

The state of monarchy is the supremest thing on earth; for kings are not only God's lieutenants upon earth and sit upon God's throne, but even by God himself they are called gods … kings are justly called gods for that they exercise a manner or resemblance of divine power upon earth.

Like some other ideas held by people at this time, this might seem so strange to you that you are tempted to underestimate its importance. This is a temptation you should strongly resist. In the early seventeenth century few people questioned the belief in the Divine Right of Kings.

James I was simply asserting the commonly held view that monarchs received their powers from God and that anyone who questioned that fact was guilty of sin against God as well as treason against the monarch. The Bible was frequently used to show that the monarch's powers were ordained by God. Many people accepted this as the natural order of things because the same idea could be used to strengthen the position of everyone who claimed to exercise authority over others: of magistrates over criminals, landlords over tenants, masters over servants, fathers over children and husbands over wives. It came to be seen as the basis for all order in society. If it was removed, it was believed, then society would collapse into anarchy.

Limitation on the powers of the monarch

Monarchs, though, did not have *unlimited* prerogative powers either in theory or in practice. One of the main theoretical limitations on their power was expressed by James I in his speech of 21 March 1610 quoted above. After asserting that kings ruled by divine right, he went on to say that kings were bound to observe the fundamental laws of the kingdom.

● James I's speech to Parliament, 21 March 1610

A king governing in a settled kingdom leaves to be a king [i.e. stops being a king], and degenerates into a tyrant, as soon as he leaves off to rule according to his laws.

In addition, monarchs did not have the resources to exercise unlimited power. As will be seen below, they lacked the finances to maintain a permanent army, state police force or powerful central bureaucracy. These have enabled regimes, at other times and in other countries, to exercise wide dictatorial or absolutist powers.

The last basic feature of government, therefore, is that monarchs at this time had little alternative but to rule with the consent and the co-operation of their most powerful subjects, especially the landowners.

Problems of government

There were three major problems involved in governing the country in the early seventeenth century:

- finances
- multiple kingdoms
- religion.

The first two will be explained next. The problem of religion will be explained in Section C.

The problem of finances

This was not a new problem facing the rulers of England, but it was becoming rapidly more serious during the early seventeenth century.

There are two major reasons for this:

- The government's expenditure was rising, largely due to the inflationary pressures of the Price Revolution.
- Its income was falling, largely due to the failure of Elizabeth I (1558–1603) to reform any of the Crown's four major sources of income.

● The Crown's main sources of income

1 *Income from Crown lands.* This had been increased greatly after the Dissolution of the Monasteries in the 1530s as the Crown took over huge amounts of Church land. This made it very wealthy, but not for long. By 1603, most of these former Church lands had been sold and, by 1640, revenue from the Crown's estates made up only a tiny fraction of its total revenue.

2 *Customs duties* were the money paid by merchants to the Crown for importing and exporting goods. Traditionally, like the Crown estates, these had always been a major source of Crown revenue. However, by the early seventeenth century, they had become less valuable because the Crown, following a practice begun by Elizabeth I, sold its right to collect customs dues to private companies of merchants. In 1604, the vast majority of them were leased in this way in a system they called 'customs farming', which was not unlike what we now call 'privatisation'. Customs farming meant that the Crown gained short-term injections of cash but lost revenue in the long term.

3 *Income from feudal dues.* These dues came from the Crown's ancient feudal rights to land that had been granted by medieval monarchs to their subjects in return for military service. By this time, this service had been changed to ('commuted' is the technical word) money payments. The principal feudal right that the Crown still used was *wardship.* This was demanded when estates of land held by feudal right were inherited by a minor (i.e. someone who was not yet an adult). The Crown then had the right to control the estates until the minor came of age. This, not surprisingly, was a source of fierce opposition from those families affected, and any financial gain to the Crown was made at a great political cost.

4 *Parliamentary taxation.* This was money raised for emergencies. It was not part of the Crown's regular income. The principal tax granted by Parliaments was called a subsidy, based on the principle that taxpayers paid a fixed percentage of their assessed wealth. Unlike modern direct taxes, however, the rate had remained unchanged since the 1520s and the amount individuals had to pay bore no relation to their actual wealth. The result was that in the early years of the seventeenth century the English were the most lightly taxed nation in the whole of Europe, leaving the Crown constantly short of money.

There were two main consequences of the Crown's financial problems:

- It became increasingly difficult for the Crown to govern the country efficiently. The most notable example of this was in foreign affairs. In the early seventeenth century England came to play an insignificant role in European affairs, because the country could not afford to do otherwise.
- The second consequence was potentially more serious. Especially in wartime, the Crown often had no alternative but to devise new means of raising money, for example by raising forced loans. These money-raising schemes had not been approved by Parliaments. As a result, some people began to wonder if the Crown was intent on destroying the right of Parliaments to raise taxes. Thus the Crown's financial weakness threatened to become a serious political problem, because monarchs appeared to be attempting to destroy the traditional rights of Parliaments.

The problem of multiple kingdoms

Before 1603, English monarchs had also been rulers of Wales and claimed to rule Ireland. After 1603, Scotland, an independent and often hostile nation that had traditionally allied with England's enemy, France, was added to the multiple kingdoms over which British monarchs ruled.

The only thing that England, Wales, Scotland and Ireland had in common was that they shared the same monarch; in other respects they were all very different. After James VI of Scotland became James I of England in 1603, Scotland kept its own Parliament, government, law and legal system. Ireland and Scotland were much less prosperous than England. But the most important difference between the kingdoms was religion. Scotland, except for parts of the Highlands, had undergone a far-reaching Protestant Reformation. Ireland, apart from those

England before the English Revolution

areas affected by English and Scottish settlement, had been only slightly touched by the Protestant Reformation. Most Irish people remained Catholic. As will be seen, England's Reformation had not been a clear-cut break with Catholicism.

There are two main reasons why this was a serious problem:

- Since all the countries shared the same monarch, there were bound to be tensions between the different peoples. There were fears that the King would favour the interests of one of his kingdoms more than those of the others.
- All over Europe, in the sixteenth and seventeenth centuries, religious divisions were the source of great political instability. In late sixteenth-century France, religious divisions tore the country apart in a civil war, 'the Wars of Religion'. In the later sixteenth and early seventeenth centuries, Spain was faced with serious rebellions in the dependent kingdoms and provinces of Portugal, Catalonia, parts of Italy and the Netherlands. The revolt of the Protestant Netherlands against the colonial Catholic rule of Spain weakened Spanish power greatly from the 1560s to the early 1600s. The lesson to be drawn from these European experiences by British monarchs was that any attempt to try to impose religious uniformity on their multiple kingdoms would be fraught with danger.

1 You are a leading member of the Privy Council in 1603, when James VI of Scotland arrives in London to become James I of England. Prepare an information pack for the new King containing the following:

a) his powers as king
b) restrictions on his powers
c) problems with the system of government
d) your recommendations to solve these problems.

2 You are a leading member of the gentry in the countryside in 1603. Write an entry in your diary to record your feelings about the new King and what you hope he will do in your area.

3 You are a farm worker in 1603 meeting with your friends in the local tavern. Explain to them what you feel about the new King and what you hope he will do for your area.

4 'The system of government in the early seventeenth century was on the brink of collapse.'

a) What evidence can you find to support this statement?
b) What evidence can you find to oppose this statement?
c) Weighing up the evidence for and against, do you agree with this statement?

Section C Religion and the Church in England before the English Revolution

Religion was a third problem that threatened to disrupt life in early seventeenth-century England. Before you can appreciate how serious this problem was you need to know about the main features of religion and the Church in England at that time.

In 1640 England had been officially a Protestant country for about 80 years, since the Elizabethan religious settlement of 1559.

There are a number of key questions that need to be answered:

- What were the main features of the reformed Protestant Church?
- In what ways had the Reformation changed the English Church?
- How widely was the new Church accepted before the English Revolution?

● **FIGURE 1.5**

The structure of the Church of England

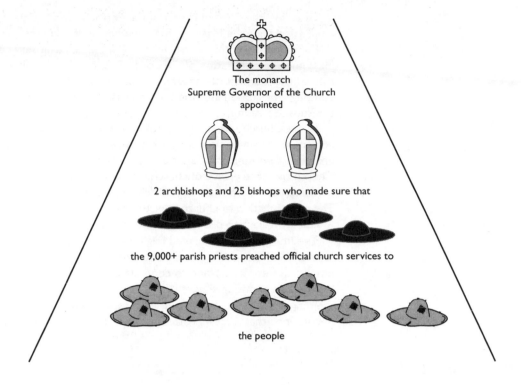

Legislation

The Act of Supremacy, 1559	The Act of Uniformity, 1559
• The monarch was the Supreme Governor of the Church. • All judges, members of the government, JPs and mayors had to take an oath approving the Royal Supremacy. • Those refusing to do so would be imprisoned – or, for a third refusal, executed.	• A moderate Protestant prayer book was introduced. • All clergy had to swear an oath to use it. • All clergy were to wear vestments. • Ornaments were permitted in churches. • Anyone who refused to attend (recusants)church would be fined 1 shilling (5p) per week.

In what ways had the Reformation changed the English Church?

Church attendance

The Reformation did *not* change the fact that there was only one national Church to which everyone was forced to belong.

Church attendance was compulsory and those who refused to attend (recusants) were fined and imprisoned. Those who wrote and preached against the State Church were liable to even harsher penalties, such as torture and execution.

Church government

What did change, though, is that the head of the English Church was no longer the Pope but the monarch. Ever since the Act of Supremacy of 1559 English monarchs were called (and still are) the Supreme Governor of the English Church.

That, however, was the only major change in the way the English Church was governed. Unlike some other countries which were affected by the Reformation, the English Church retained an episcopal form of government (i.e. a church with archbishops and bishops; *episcopus* is the Latin word for bishop).

Before 1640 the English Church did not become a Presbyterian Church (a church in which archbishops and bishops were replaced by a hierarchical system of national and provincial synods, with local classes replacing parishes).

Gradually the form of church services (the liturgy) of the English Church changed, emphasising not the Mass but the importance of sermons, preaching and Bible study.

For generations the centrepiece of Catholic church services had been the ceremony of the Mass and the celebration of the Lord's Supper (Communion or the Eucharist). It was believed that, at the moment of consecration by the priest, the bread and wine given to the congregation turned into the body and blood of Christ. (This is known as the miracle of transubstantiation.)

In the Church of England's Book of Common Prayer of 1559, however, the Eucharist became merely a commemorative service. The communion table was moved from its prominent position as an altar at the east end of the church into the nave. In the English Church the centrepiece of church services became the sermon. This represented a fundamental shift in the new Church towards the study of the Bible by individuals themselves. The main function of church ministers was to help them do this. Catechisms (simple guides to the Bible) were also produced, to be distributed by ministers with the same intent.

The liturgy of the reformed English Church, though, did not break with the past entirely. Church ministers were still allowed by the Book of Common Prayer to wear elaborate robes (known as vestments), and to continue to use Catholic practices such as using the sign of the cross when baptising children, bowing when Jesus's name was mentioned and using the ring in the marriage service. Some churches, too, retained candles and other traditional church decorations that radical Protestants thought unnecessary, superstitious and popish.

● **Figure 1.6**

Plan of a parish church

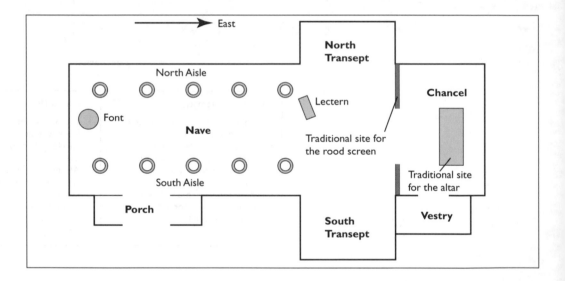

The appearance of churches

By the early seventeenth century, however, many outward signs of the old faith, for example interior decorations, had been stripped out of many parish churches in a process known as iconoclasm.

From the mid-sixteenth century onwards churchwardens destroyed altars, paintings and statues of the saints and the Virgin Mary, whitewashed over medieval wall paintings, smashed stained-glass windows and dismantled rood screens (which divided the eastern end of churches from the nave). The typical parish church interior was now very simple, emphasising the prominence of the pulpit and lectern from where sermons and lessons were delivered.

Religious festivals

By the early seventeenth century, too, some (though not all) of the traditional festivals associated with the old Church had gone.

These included performances of mystery plays, Corpus Christi processions and saints' day holidays. These were replaced by celebrations of Protestant events, such as the accession day of Elizabeth I (17 November) and the discovery of the Gunpowder Plot (5 November).

The Reformation, though, did not wipe away all traditional Church festivals. The Church year was still marked by the celebration of festivals such as Christmas and Easter.

Religious beliefs

The post-Reformation English Church adopted a different theology from the Catholic Church.

For centuries the Catholic Church had taught that men and women would receive God's salvation after they died as a reward for faith and the good works they had done on earth.

The theology that was commonly accepted in the English Church was very different. It is known as the Calvinist doctrine of predestination. This is the belief that people are divided by God into those who after death will be saved (the Elect) and those who will not (the Damned) and that people's actions on earth cannot affect that decision.

The last major feature of the reformed Church was an intense anti-Catholicism: the belief that Catholicism was the most evil force present in the world.

● The fear of popery and millenarianism

It is difficult to exaggerate the fear and loathing of Catholicism felt by most Protestants in the early seventeenth century. The Pope and Catholics were commonly referred to as Antichrist. In one of the most influential books of this period, John Foxe's *Book of Martyrs* (first published in 1565 and reprinted many times), this idea was extended and fitted into a general explanation of how the world had developed in the past and how it would develop in the future. This became known as millenarianism.

This was the belief, prophesied in the Bible, that one day Jesus Christ would return to earth and rule for one thousand years (the Millennium). Foxe and others argued that this would only happen when the forces of Antichrist that were at work in the world had been defeated. They argued that Antichrist was represented by the Pope and popery and that episodes like the cruel persecution of Protestants in Mary Tudor's reign (which Foxe recounted in lurid detail) were just a part of a global battle for world supremacy. So they demanded that Protestant English people should work to defeat the Antichrist. Foxe even argued that the English were the Elect Nation chosen by God to lead that campaign.

● FIGURE 1.7

Religious beliefs in early seventeenth-century England

	ROMAN CATHOLICS	PROTESTANTS Conformists or moderate Protestants	Puritans ('the hotter type of Protestant')
Head of Church	The Pope in Rome	The king or queen	The king or queen
Government of Church	Cardinals, archbishops and bishops, priests	Archbishops and bishops, priests	Archbishops and bishops, ministers
Clergy	Unmarried priests	Married or single clergy	Married or single clergy and lay preachers
Dress	Vestments – highly decorative robes	Vestments – decorative robes	Plain, simple black or brown clothes
Church services	Latin Mass Bread and wine become body and blood of Christ by a miracle	Communion in English Bread and wine taken in remembrance of Christ	Communion in English Bread and wine taken in remembrance, simple service: sermons
Bible	Bible in Latin for priest to interpret	Bible in English for all to read	Bible in English for all to read
Music	Hymns and organs	Hymns and organs	No musical instruments; only chanting of psalms
Decoration	Highly decorated churches – wall paintings, stained glass, statues, rich altar cloths	Decorated churches – stained-glass windows, statues, altar cloths, royal coat of arms	Very plain chapels: whitewashed walls, plain windows, no statues, plain table and benches
Support in England in 1640	Very small minority, mainly in the north and west	Growing throughout the country – in the majority by 1640	Growing, especially in London and the south-east of England, but still a minority

How widely was the reformed English Church accepted before the English Revolution?

Roman Catholics and Protestants

English Catholics certainly did not accept the post-Reformation English Church, but how extensively Catholicism survived in post-Reformation England is a subject of some historical debate. It is possible to exaggerate the speed of Catholicism's decline in the later sixteenth and early seventeenth centuries. Yet there is little doubt that, by 1640, popular Catholicism had greatly dwindled. It only survived in the households of a few wealthy noblemen and gentry, who kept the old faith alive despite the persecution meted out to active Catholics in this period. Committed Catholics probably made up only 1–2 per cent of the total population in 1640.

As before the Reformation, it is probable that a percentage of the population remained ignorant or sceptical of, or indifferent to, organised religion.

How large a part of the population this was at this time it is impossible to estimate. But there is no reason to think that it was any greater than at other times.

Although there is a danger of exaggerating the speed with which the English became converted to Protestantism, it is probable that, by the early seventeenth century, it had become generally accepted in most English parishes. Support for the national Church established in and after 1559 grew.

The best evidence for this comes from the period of the English Revolution. At that time, attempts by successive regimes to outlaw the Book of Common Prayer and the kind of Church that had been developed during James I's reign, 'half-reformed' though it might be, with a Book of Common Prayer and festivals such as Christmas and Easter, were met with strong resistance at the grass-roots parochial level.

Yet within the English Church there were people who did not believe that the Church as it had developed during James I's reign was perfect. Two groups were most vocal in demanding changes: the Puritans and the anti-Calvinists.

Puritans and anti-Calvinists

● Who were the Puritans and what did they believe?

The Puritans were not a group outside the Church who were trying to destroy it. Puritans worked within the English Church. Before 1640 they accepted the government of the Church by bishops. They were not Presbyterians (see page 15) or Independents (those who wanted either to extend toleration to individual congregations within the national Church or to abolish the national Church altogether, although both of these ideas grew significantly in popularity during the 1640s).

Yet Puritans (they called themselves 'the godly') wanted to reform the Church. They believed that the Reformation of the mid-sixteenth century had not gone far enough. Their principal aim was to bring about what they called 'a further reformation' of the Church. They considered that the Church, by the early seventeenth century, was (in their own words) only 'halfly reformed'. They wanted to get rid of most of the popish practices in the Church that had not yet been abolished.

Puritans also had a constructive, as well as a destructive, aim. The phrase they used to describe this was 'a reformation of manners'. This was a campaign to bring about a full reformation in popular behaviour. They wanted to stop drunkenness, fornication, adultery, swearing and other sinful behaviour. Alehouses were especially singled out for closure as breeding grounds of sin. Sundays (the Sabbath) were to be set aside for religious worship and education, not popular sports.

Those who depict seventeenth-century Puritans as people who were against fun and enjoyment for its own sake do them an injustice. Fun and enjoyment were permissible so long as they did not get in the way of what Puritans considered to be a morally pure life.

Although Puritans worked within the Church, they clearly had views that distinguished them from other Protestants. Patrick Collinson's description of them as 'a militant tendency within the Church' is particularly good.

19

How did James I and Charles I deal with the major problems facing them before the English Revolution!

● Who were the anti-Calvinists and what did they believe?

Unlike Puritans, anti-Calvinists believed that the Reformation had gone too far.

They attacked the Calvinist predestinarian beliefs of the English Church and they began to claim that salvation was open to all and could be earned by people's good works on earth.

They also wanted a return to church services that emphasised ceremony and the celebration of the Eucharist rather than sermons. Many Protestants, and especially Puritans, feared that anti-Calvinists were really secret Catholics, who were plotting to destroy the Protestant Church of England and pave the way for a return of the Catholic Church and the Pope.

They are often known as Arminians because they are thought to have followed the teaching of the Dutch theologian Arminius.

Why did this religious situation present a potentially serious problem before the English Revolution?

In a country in which only one national Church was allowed and in which the head of the State was also head of the Church, religion was bound to be a major political issue. Indeed, religion and politics were so interwoven that they could not be separated.

In these circumstances it was essential that differences about the nature of the Church, especially the differences between Puritans and anti-Calvinists, should not be allowed to get out of hand. Both groups had to be kept within the Church. If they were not and if any religious group felt that it had to oppose the Church from outside, then this would inevitably become a political attack on the Crown as well.

It is 1603 and James I has just arrived in London:

a) Catholics want him to be more tolerant towards them, relax laws against them and allow them to worship freely. James I's mother, Mary Queen of Scots, was a Catholic.
b) Moderate Protestants want James to keep the Church of England established by Elizabeth I in 1559.
c) The Puritans want changes in the Church; Presbyterians want the abolition of bishops and a Presbyterian Church structure; Separatists want the freedom to worship as they please.
d) James himself has been brought up under a Presbyterian Church in Scotland but disliked the fact that he had so little control over it.

You are an adviser to the King on Church affairs. Discuss the advantages and disadvantages of following each course of action outlined above, and explain what kind of Church you recommend James to have in England.

Section D How did James I and Charles I deal with the major problems facing them before the English Revolution?

You will notice that this question is not 'how *well* did they deal with the problems?' That is a question that you will investigate in Chapter 2.

What follows is a summary of how James I and Charles I dealt with the main problems they faced in governing the country. You will need to look at one or two textbooks about this period to add to this information.

The early Stuarts and the problem of finance

James I

The King's financial extravagance

Immediately he became King of England James I ignored all advice to reduce his expenditure. He continued to make generous grants of lands, money and gifts of all kinds to friends and courtiers throughout his reign.

> ● **The Great Contract**
>
> This was the first serious attempt at fundamental reform of the government's finances in the seventeenth century. It was a proposal made to Parliament in 1610 by James I's principal minister at this time, Robert Cecil, Earl of Salisbury. In return for the abolition of the Crown's feudal revenue, including wardships, Parliament was to guarantee to provide the King with regular taxes of £200,000 a year. After lengthy discussions MPs rejected the scheme, fearing that it would enable the Crown to rule without calling Parliament again.

James I tried various methods of raising money to supplement parliamentary taxation. All met with opposition from Parliaments.

> ● **James I's efforts to raise money without Parliament's help**
>
> 1 *Monopolies* were granted simply to raise money (a monopoly gives an individual or organisation the exclusive control of the supply of a product or service).
> 2 *Sale of honours*, i.e. the sale of titles, such as baronetcies (created in 1611), which were sold for £1,095 each.
> 3 *Impositions* were additional customs dues. These were collected from 1608 onwards and not approved by Parliament.

An inexpensive foreign policy

After the Treaty of London (1604), which ended England's long war with Spain, the country was at peace throughout James I's reign. The King's main interventions in foreign affairs were diplomatic (including an attempt to arrange a marriage alliance between his son Charles and the Spanish King's daughter). James I's refusal to abandon that attempt and to support the Protestant cause of his son-in-law, the Elector Palatine, in the Thirty Years War in Europe, which began in 1618, was criticised by some MPs in the Parliaments of 1621 and 1624. But it was a cheap foreign policy that the country could afford.

Charles I

An expensive foreign policy

Very soon after he became King in 1625, Charles I took his country into war in Europe, against Spain in 1625 and, after 1627, against France as well. The disastrous English war effort (largely run by Charles I's chief minister George Villiers, Duke of Buckingham) increased the Crown's financial problems.

From 1626 Charles began to raise money by *forced loans*. He also began to use martial law to force householders to house and feed (i.e. to billet) seamen and soldiers who were on their way to the war.

Earlier monarchs, including Elizabeth I, had forced certain wealthy people to lend them money. The forced loans that Charles I announced in September 1626 were different. All people who normally paid parliamentary taxes were liable to pay forced loans. No attempt was made to disguise the fact that the intention was to collect a tax without the approval of Parliament. In these circumstances it is surprising that over 70 per cent of the amount to be paid by forced loans was collected. But there was opposition: in the Five Knights Case in 1627, five gentlemen who had refused to pay forced loans were imprisoned. What increased the opposition was that the judges in the case decided that the King had a right to imprison them without bringing them to trial. The main grievances felt at these policies were set out in the Petition of Right, passed by Parliament in 1628 and eventually approved by Charles I.

> ● **The main demands made in the Petition of Right, 1628**
>
> 1 The King should not levy taxes without Parliament's approval.
> 2 People should not be imprisoned without either the cause being given or them being brought to trial.
> 3 Billeting of soldiers and sailors by martial law should be forbidden.

Charles I did not call Parliaments during the 1630s but continued to collect money without their approval.

● **Charles I's principal methods of raising money during the period of Personal Rule (1629–40)**

1 *Distraint of knighthood*: these were fines on landowners who were eligible to be knights but who had not attended the King's coronation in 1625 in order to be knighted.
2 *Forest fines*: these were collected by resurrecting an ancient royal right that had not been exercised for centuries. Forest courts administering royal rights in the ancient forests began to meet again, primarily to fine anyone who held land within the ancient forest boundaries on a charge of trespass. Fines could be large. The Earl of Salisbury was fined £20,000 for trespassing in Rockingham Forest.
3 *Ship money*. This was the most important money-raising expedient of the 1630s. Writs demanding ship money (a traditional tax paid by coastal counties to finance the navy) were issued in 1634. From 1635 onwards annual writs were sent to every county of England, including those inland. The amounts demanded from each county were stated and were much higher than those collected by parliamentary taxation. Until the very end of the 1630s, the only major evidence of opposition to ship money was the trial of John Hampden in 1637–8 for non-payment of ship money. He was found guilty but five of the twelve judges refused to support the verdict. However, until 1639, 90 per cent of the ship money demanded was paid. Yields only fell off drastically in 1639–40.

The early Stuarts and the problem of multiple kingdoms

James I and Scotland

James I put forward a proposal for uniting Scotland and England.

● **James I's proposal for 'perfect union of England and Scotland'**

This was a proposal that James tried unsuccessfully to persuade English MPs to agree to between 1604 and 1607. He wanted to unite his two kingdoms under a common government, parliament and laws. So hostile were MPs to the idea that James dropped it.

Although James abandoned this scheme to promote a full union of his two kingdoms, he continued to try to bring about greater uniformity between the Scottish Kirk and the English Church. Two events were especially significant in this respect:
• the Scottish Kirk's agreement to accept the royal appointment and authority of Scottish bishops in 1612
• the Article of Perth, 1618, which allowed church practices, such as private baptism, that had been abolished in Scotland at the Reformation.
   When these provoked an outcry in Scotland, James slowed down his drive towards Anglo-Scottish religious uniformity.

James I and Ireland

During the reign of James I English and Scottish colonisation of Ireland made rapid progress.

● **The plantation of Ulster**

This was the planned colonisation of the province of Ulster in northern Ireland, which began in 1608. The plan was remove Irish landlords and tenants from large areas of land and 'plant' (settle) it with English and Scottish settlers. It was not carried out fully. Some land remained in the hands of Irish landlords and tenants.

Charles I and Scotland

One of Charles I's first decisions regarding Scotland was his announcement in 1625 that he intended to cancel the grants of land given by the Crown and Kirk (the Scottish Church) to Scottish landowners since 1540.

In 1633 Charles decided to impose the English Prayer Book on the Scottish Kirk. When he tried to put that decision into effect in the later 1630s, it provoked a national uprising which is often known as the Scottish Revolution.

● The Scottish Revolution and the outbreak of the Bishops' Wars

This began with riots in Scottish churches when ministers, acting on the orders of Scottish bishops, tried to use the English Prayer Book. Organised resistance followed, culminating in the calling of a Scottish National Assembly in 1638. In defiance of Charles I's authority, it abolished the Prayer Book and bishops. There then followed two Anglo-Scottish wars, called 'the Bishops' Wars'. The first lasted from November 1638 to June 1639 and the second from August to October 1640. Both ended in humiliating defeats for the English.

Charles I and Ireland

● Thomas Wentworth, Earl of Strafford

Wentworth was a wealthy Yorkshire landowner, who first came to national prominence in the later 1620s for his opposition to forced loans. He was imprisoned in 1627 for refusing to pay a forced loan. He also took part in organising the Petition of Right in 1628. From that point onwards, however, he became a firm supporter of Charles I. In 1629 he was appointed President of the Council of the North, one of the Royal Prerogative Courts, and from 1632 he was the King's Lord Deputy in Ireland. He was created Earl of Strafford in 1640. Wentworth was so hated and feared by Parliamentarians that his downfall and death were demanded by the Parliamentary leaders in 1640–1. He was executed in May 1641.

Thomas Wentworth's rule of Ireland in the 1630s was characterised by a sustained attack on:

• the rights and property of Catholic landowners in Ireland, who were called 'the old English' (the descendants of those who had settled in Ireland *before* the Reformation)
• 'the new English', i.e. Protestant landowners and their descendants who had settled in Ireland *after* the Reformation. Wentworth began to force them to give up ex-Church lands.

He also built up a powerful army in Ireland, consisting largely of Catholics, which was greatly feared in England.

The early Stuarts and the problem of religion

James I

James I's religious policies are characterised by two events, the Hampton Court Conference and the appointment of George Abbott as Archbishop of Canterbury.

● The Hampton Court Conference, 1604

This Church conference was held to discuss the state of the Church at the start of the new reign. Contrary to what was once thought, the conference was not a confrontation between two sides, Puritans and bishops, but a 'round table conference' representing many views. James acted as arbitrator, preventing differences that arose from getting out of hand. The conference agreed on several moderate Church reforms, easily the most important of which was the production of a new translation of the Bible. This was completed in 1611. It is known as the Authorised Version or King James' Bible.

● Appointment of George Abbott as Archbishop of Canterbury in 1611

Abbott was a representative of mainstream thinking within the English Church. He was an ideal partner to James I in his aim of overseeing a Church that could contain a fairly wide range of Protestant views.

Charles I

The rise of William Laud, who became Archbishop of Canterbury in 1633, indicates the change in royal religious policies after the accession of Charles I in 1625.

● William Laud

Laud came from fairly humble origins. He was born in 1573, the son of a clothier, in Reading, Berkshire. Like others from similar backgrounds, he found that a career in the Church enabled him to rise in wealth and status. He was promoted by Charles I to the position of Bishop of London and then Archbishop of Canterbury. He had long been a supporter of anti-Calvinist views (see page 19) and he used his position of influence to promote those views within the Church. Whether he or Charles I was the main influence on royal religious policies in the 1630s is uncertain. They shared similar views. Many, at the time, thought he was primarily responsible for the policies, and he was widely suspected of being a secret Catholic. This accounted for the fact that, in 1640, hatred for Laud among Parliamentarians was secondary only to their hatred for Strafford. He was impeached and imprisoned in 1640. He remained in the Tower until he was executed in 1645.

Royal ecclesiastical policies in the 1630s are often known as 'Laudianism'.

● What was Laudianism?

Laudians wanted:

1 the emphasis in church services to be on sacraments and ceremony, with church ministers wearing elaborate vestments, and less emphasis on preaching and sermons
2 statues and stained-glass windows to be restored to churches, and altars to be re-positioned at the eastern end of churches and often railed off from the congregation in the nave
3 the clergy and Church courts to be given a greater role in lay affairs
4 less stress on the Calvinist theory of predestination, and more stress on the idea of free will – that God's salvation was open to all and could be earned by good works on earth.

● Summary Task

1 What would the following groups of people have thought about James I:

   a) English landlords
   b) The Scots
   c) The Irish Catholics
   d) Catholics
   e) The Puritans?

2 What would these same people have thought about Charles I's reign by 1640?

3 Was Charles I facing serious problems in 1640?

Why did Charles I face a crisis in 1640–1?

Introduction

The first major historical question that confronts anyone who begins to study the English Revolution is why did it begin: why did Charles I face the most serious crisis of any English monarch since Henry VI in the middle of the fifteenth century? As will be seen, this is a question to which historians nowadays give greatly differing answers and about which they disagree violently. This chapter will explain the ways in which historians have tackled this question.

When I (Barry Coward) began to study the history of seventeenth-century England as an A-level student and then as an undergraduate in the 1960s, 'Why did Charles I face a crisis in 1640–1?' was a historical question which was relatively straightforward to answer. Historians of the period generally agreed about what caused Charles I to become very unpopular in the country by 1640. Most historians believed that the answer was to be found in long-term developments that had been under way since the mid-sixteenth century and that made the appearance of opposition to the monarchy inevitable. When I was in the sixth form and then at university this meant that I was able to base my term-time and examination essays to this question on long-term explanations that everyone, by and large, accepted.

During the later 1970s and early 1980s, however, the validity of many of these explanations was questioned by historians in a process that has become known as 'revisionism', so called simply because historians began to *revise* traditional historical interpretations of early seventeenth-century English history in roughly similar ways. From a personal point of view, what was especially fascinating about 'revisionism' was that it coincided with a period when I was writing a general book on seventeenth-century England, *The Stuart Age 1603–1714*, which was published by Longman in 1980. While I was writing the first half of the book I read many 'revisionist' books and articles on the early Stuart period. These new views persuaded me to change many of the ideas about the period I had held since my school and university days and which I had used in my early teaching career at the University of London. In the light of what I read it seemed to me that the explanation of why the country was plunged into a deep political crisis in 1640–1 lay not in long-term factors that made it inevitable but in short-term events and accidents of personality.

A few years after that book appeared, however, the historical debate about early Stuart England took another dramatic turn to a new phase in which many 'revisionist' assumptions, in turn, came to be questioned. This coincided with a time in the early 1990s when I began to write a new edition of *The Stuart Age*. As I read sections of the first edition I was amazed to find in it views about the early part of the period that I no longer held. When the book was completed and published in 1994, it was the chapters on the early Stuart period that were most changed (in some cases quite drastically) from the first edition. I realised that I no longer held some of the opinions I had formed under the influence of revisionism a decade or so earlier. I felt it necessary to emphasise that my view now was that the crisis of 1640–1 was, in part at least, rooted in long-term developments and ideological conflicts. But these were *different* developments and conflicts from those that in pre-revisionist days had seemed to me and many others to have been such powerful influences in shaping the crisis of 1640–1.

The way in which historians' views about why the English Revolution began in 1640 have changed dramatically and rapidly during the last 30 years is exceptional, making the period an exciting, intellectually challenging and also sometimes a confusing one to study. But what is *not* exceptional is that historical interpretations of the period have changed and are still changing. The historiography (i.e. the writing of history) of *all* historical periods and topics changes as each generation of historians reinterpret them in the light of new evidence or new approaches. These interpretations are influenced by the intellectual and political climate in which they live. Indeed, the fact that historians' interpretations of the past are shaped by their views in the present is one that you should get used to. It means that there are no 'correct' answers to most historical questions and problems. In common with those of many other historians, my view of what seems to me to have been the 'correct' explanation of why the English Revolution began in 1640 has often changed (and will no doubt keep changing).

This chapter looks at the question of why the English Revolution began, through the eyes of different historians who have written about it in recent years. The historiography of the topic has gone through three broad phases. This chapter is divided into three parts that will enable you to examine the ways historians' views have changed in each phase:

- Phase A Before revisionism
- Phase B Revisionism during the late 1970s and 1980s
- Phase C After revisionism.

Read the views of the historians in each phase. As you read, your principal concern should be to understand the views that are being expressed. As you go along you will be asked to put these views into your own words and also to explain how the views of historians in each phase differ from those at other times.

This will be useful preparation for your final task in this chapter, which will be to come to *your own* conclusion about why Charles I faced massive opposition in the country in 1640–1.

Phase A Before revisionism

Until the early 1970s, explanations of why Charles I faced a major crisis in 1640–1 came from two different types of historians, who can be labelled 'Marxist' and 'Whig'. These are words that carry lots of different meanings, most of which are irrelevant in this context. Here they are used with the following simple meanings:

1 'Marxist' historians are those whose approaches to history are influenced by the work of Karl Marx, who believed that the principal explanations of historical developments are to be found in economic and social changes.
2 'Whig' historians are those (from S. R. Gardiner, who wrote in the late nineteenth century, onwards) whose writings are influenced by two major ideas:
   - that political and religious change ought to be the central concern of historians
   - that historical development is one of progress from 'inferior' forms of government and attitudes, principally absolutism and religious intolerance, to 'superior' ones, especially parliamentary democracy and religious toleration.

By far the best book that incorporates both 'Marxist' and 'Whig' explanations for the outbreak of the English Revolution is the one by Lawrence Stone, from which all the extracts (Sources 2.1–2.5) in this section are taken. In the words of one revisionist (John Morrill), this was 'the book that sparked off the revisionist revolt from the mid 1970s'. Note the date when it was published (this is something you should get used to doing whenever you use a source).

Stone's description of the nature of the crisis faced by Charles in 1640–1 in Source 2.1 is typical of many historians' views in and before 1972.

● **SOURCE 2.1**

From Lawrence Stone, *The Causes of the English Revolution* (1972)

Laud: *William Laud, Archbishop of Canterbury from 1633. (See the profile on page 23.)*

By the time the government collapsed in 1640 there existed among very large numbers of normally conservative noblemen and gentlemen a strong desire for widespread change ... They arrived at Westminster full of talk of a Reformed Church, a Godly Commonwealth, Magna Carta, the Ancient Constitution, and the Country. But these were slogans rather than a concrete programme, and it would be foolish to suggest that the opposition in 1640 had much more in mind than a desire to preserve and increase the political influence of Parliament, to establish the supremacy of the common law as a bulwark of property, to rid the Church of the popish innovations introduced by LAUD, to put domestic and foreign policy on a forthrightly Protestant track, and to reduce the political influence of the bishops. But to achieve these objectives they had to tear down institutions like the prerogative courts, which were over 150 years old, to arrogate to themselves the power of determining the term of their own dissolution, to execute one leading minister of the Crown and drive another into exile, and to throw the Archbishop of Canterbury into the Tower.

In only one respect is the book untypical of widely held views at that time about the period before 1640. This is the way in which (as you can see in this second extract) it includes a 'Marxist' assumption that social and economic changes had a key role in bringing about the crisis of 1640–1. Source 2.2 describes one of the 'preconditions' that Stone believed led to the Revolution: social change.

● **SOURCE 2.2**

From Lawrence Stone, *The Causes of the English Revolution* (1972)

homogeneous: *united*

What happened between 1540 and 1640 was a massive shift of relative wealth away from Church and Crown, and away from both the very rich and the very poor towards the upper middle and middle classes … This changing socio-economic balance … meant that there was bound to be friction between the traditional wielders of power, the Crown, courtiers, higher clergy and aristocracy, and the growing but, as yet, far from HOMOGENEOUS forces of gentry, lawyers, merchants, yeomen and small tradesmen. The problem that faced the state was how to bring the latter into fruitful and co-operative participation in the political process.

One of Stone's other 'preconditions' that led to revolution was much more typical of the views of most historians in the early 1970s and before. This can best be described as 'the Rise of Parliament', the belief that Parliament, and especially the House of Commons, had been steadily growing in constitutional importance since the Tudors had brought about the Reformation by Parliamentary means. Many historians, principally J. E. Neale (in his books on Elizabethan Parliaments) and Wallace Notestein (writing on early Stuart Parliaments) assumed that MPs sought, with some success, to force the Crown to give them a greater say in government than ever before. They described, as does Stone in Source 2.3, politics in the later sixteenth and early seventeenth centuries as a constant running battle between the Crown and a Parliamentary 'opposition'.

● **SOURCE 2.3**

From Lawrence Stone, *The Causes of the English Revolution* (1972)

It was in Parliament, and particularly in the House of Commons, that the opposition built its institutional base … Men actually fought and even paid to be members of it, instead of having to be paid their expenses as an inducement to serve. With its control over taxation, especially for war, and its control over legislation, especially concerning religion, it was strategically placed to demand redress of grievances. During the course of the middle and late sixteenth century many things happened to increase Parliament's powers and to diminish the capacity of the Crown to control it. The House of Commons grew from about 300 to 500, and the gentry component in it rose from about 50 per cent to about 75 per cent, despite the fact that most new seats were borough seats. The members gained experience and a sense of continuity owing to the enhanced frequency of Parliamentary sessions between 1590 and 1614. They developed an efficient committee system, which freed them from manipulation by a Crown-appointed Speaker, and by the early seventeenth century Parliamentary leaders were beginning to emerge, men who built their careers on playing a key role in debates and on committees in the House. The Crown had serious trouble with this body at all times in the late sixteenth and early seventeenth centuries, but slowly the nature of the trouble changed and became far more menacing. In the early years of Elizabeth's reign, there were quarrels over specific issues – religion or taxation or foreign policy – but by the early seventeenth century there is the visible beginning of a formal opposition, men who came up to Parliament with a set determination to challenge the Crown on a wide range of issues. Loosely calling themselves 'the Patriots' or 'the Country', they developed their own distinct ideology and tactics.

In Source 2.4 Stone describes the third 'precondition' of revolution that most historians would have found quite acceptable in 1972: 'the Rise of Puritanism' as a revolutionary ideology. This was a view that was shared by 'Marxist' historians such as Christopher Hill and 'Whig' historians such as J. E. Neale, who portrayed Puritanism as ideas that were:

• totally different from the moderate Protestantism of the post-Reformation English Church
• held generally by 'the middling sort' in society
• subversive of the *status quo* in Church and State.

● **SOURCE 2.4**

From Lawrence Stone, *The Causes of the English Revolution* (1972)

Hobbes: *Thomas Hobbes was one of the greatest political thinkers who emerged during the English Revolution. His major work was Leviathan (1651).*

vernacular Bible: *the English translation of the Bible. The first official version of the Bible in English was authorised by Henry VIII and Thomas Cromwell in the 1530s. Thereafter, the vernacular Bible had a prominent place in the post-Reformation English Church.*

A true revolution needs ideas to fuel it – without them there is only a rebellion or a coup d'état – and the ideological underpinnings of the opposition to the government are therefore of the first importance …

The most far-reaching in its influence on men's minds, although very difficult to pin down in precise detail, was Puritanism, here interpreted to mean no more than a generalised conviction of the need for independent judgement based on conscience and Bible reading …

It provided an essential element in the Revolution, the feeling of certainty in the rectitude of the opposition cause, and of moral indignation at the wickedness of the established authorities.

This independence of moral judgement about the religious and political hierarchy … arose from the process of individual interpretation of the VERNACULAR BIBLE, the free access to which was regarded by HOBBES as one of the principal causes of the Revolution. He complained that 'after the Bible was translated into English, every man, nay every boy and wench, that could read English, thought they spoke with God almighty and understood what he said' …

Apart from the working of these subversive ideas, the second major contribution of the Puritans was to provide an embryo organisation out of which grew true radicalism …

Finally, Puritanism provided the opposition with the necessary leadership. The Puritan lobby in the House of Commons in the days of Elizabeth has been described as the first political party in English history … They led the attack on Buckingham's character and policies in the 1620s … It was through their associations … that their leaders could assemble in private to lay the plans for the overthrow of Charles's government in the 1630s. It is as safe as any broad generalisation in history can be to say that without the ideas, the organisation and the leadership supplied by Puritanism there would have been no revolution at all.

Source 2.5 illustrates a fourth 'precondition' that Stone argued made the situation that developed in the 1640s inevitable. This is what he called a 'crisis of confidence' in the leaders of the political system. Like many other historians before him, Stone singled out James I for blame. He emphasised James's poor reputation: the widely held view that he was 'the Wisest Fool in Christendom' who did not have the political ability or charisma necessary to withstand the dangerous forces of rising Parliamentarianism and Puritanism and who therefore accelerated England's rapid and inevitable progress along the historical 'high road to Civil War'.

● **SOURCE 2.5**

From Lawrence Stone, *The Causes of the English Revolution* (1972)

As a hated Scot, James was suspect to the English from the beginning, and his ungainly presence, mumbling speech and dirty ways did not inspire respect. Reports of his blatantly homosexual attachments and his alcoholic excesses were diligently spread back to a horrified countryside … It was reported that when hunting the king did not dismount in order to relieve himself, and so habitually ended the day in a filthy and stinking condition. In the light of these stories it was clear that the sanctity of monarchy itself would soon be called into question.

1 Make notes summarising the Whig–Marxist explanation for the crisis of 1640–1 using the following headings:

- social and economic changes
- the rise of Parliament
- the rise of Puritanism
- the failure of James I.

2 What links does Stone make between social changes and growing political conflict in the early seventeenth century?

3 Why does Stone believe that Parliament grew in power in the sixteenth century, causing it to come into serious conflict with the Crown in the early seventeenth century? (See Source 2.3.)

4 Why did Stone believe that Puritanism was a set of revolutionary ideas? (See Source 2.4.)

Phase B **Revisionism**

Historians in the mid-1970s began to attack some of the foundations on which the Whig–Marxist view of the origins of the crisis of 1640–1 rested. Several of these deny that they are part of a 'revisionist school'. It is true that the historians from whose writings extracts have been chosen for this section are not in agreement about everything. But, as you read these extracts, you should ask yourself whether you agree with me that there is a great deal that they have in common.

The first extract is from Conrad Russell, now Professor of History at King's College, London. The youngest son of the philosopher Bertrand Russell, he has fairly recently inherited the title Earl Russell and is therefore one of the premier English Whig aristocrats. It is not without some irony therefore that Russell played a major part (as he continues to do) in leading the revisionist charge against the Whig interpretation of early Stuart history. In this extract he complements the criticisms made, also in the 1970s, by Geoffrey Elton in a series of lectures and articles (see Further reading, page 40). These challenge the ideas of J. E. Neale, that Parliament 'rose' in the later sixteenth and early seventeenth centuries and that there was a 'high road to Civil War'. The lecture by Elton that I remember most vividly is the one that was published in *The Historical Journal* in 1979. It was delivered in December 1978 as the J. E. Neale Memorial Lecture in Neale's old college, University College London, and with Neale's widow, Lady Neale, present in the audience.

● **SOURCE 2.6**

From Conrad Russell's article 'Parliamentary history in perspective, 1604–29', *History*, vol. 61 (1976)

---

denouement: *the end of the story when the person guilty of the crime is revealed*

A historian is like a man who sits down to read a detective story after beginning with the last chapter. The clues pointing to the ultimate DENOUEMENT then appear to him in such embarrassing abundance that he wonders how anyone can ever have been in doubt about the ultimate outcome. Much of the historian's working life, then, is spent in drawing attention to those clues which point towards the solution which he knows ultimately emerged. Usually, this is a useful process, but there is one important difference between life and detective fiction: life is not a story written by an author who had decided on the ultimate solution before the story began. A historian must always run the risk of letting hindsight lead him to see the evidence out of perspective. Those who write the story remembering the ultimate conclusion may miss many of the twists and turns which gave it suspense along the way. They may even forget that the result ever was in suspense.

This risk is particularly tempting for historians who describe the years before revolutions. In particular, the study of English Parliamentary history of the years 1604–29 has been so dominated by the knowledge that it preceded a Civil War that it is dangerously easy to treat it as a mere preface, and not as a story in its own right. It is dangerously easy to believe, because the story ended with Parliament in a position to challenge the King for supremacy, that it was bound to end in this way, and that it was the direction in which most of the evidence points. In particular, the use of the word 'opposition' to describe the type of criticism the Crown faced during these Parliaments can easily suggest that the criticisms uttered during these years were such as to lead on logically to Civil War against the Crown …

The conventional belief that the Parliaments of 1604–29 were a 'high road to Civil War' logically implies two … beliefs. One is the belief that Parliament was a powerful institution … The other logical necessity to the belief that this period was a high road to Civil War is the belief that the Parliaments of these years witnessed a constitutional struggle between two 'sides', government and opposition, or, in modern language, court and country. Two sides are an essential precondition of a Civil War, and where there are not two sides, there cannot be a high road to Civil War …

There was only one thing which could give Parliament power in a situation in which the King did not wish to be persuaded, and that was control of supply. A monopoly of the power of extraordinary taxation was the only means by which Parliament could, in a situation of conflict, hope to force its will on a reluctant Crown. What use did Parliament make of its power to give or withhold supply, and what were the effects of its use? [Russell then proceeds to answer his questions by saying that between 1604 and 1629 Parliaments used the threat not to vote taxes until grievances were redressed on only four occasions and that on each occasion the threat failed] … The conclusion appears irresistible that the withholding of supply was not a powerful bargaining counter.

If Parliament had so little coercive power, its members were dependent, not on coercion, but on persuasion. If Parliament could not, by withholding supply, force the King to do what it wished, its members all had to engage in a process of lobbying designed to persuade the King, of his own free will, to do what they wished …

If Parliamentary critics of the Crown were entirely dependent on persuasion, it must give us pause before describing them as an 'opposition'. An opposition, as we know the term, can hope to force changes of policy, either by changing the government, or by appealing so eloquently to the public that the government is forced to change its ground. In this sense, opposition as we know the term was impossible. It is also a characteristic of an 'opposition' that it is united by some common body of beliefs, which it does not share with members of the government. This ideological gulf between 'government' and 'opposition' is impossible to find in Parliament before 1640. There were many disagreements on policy, often profound ones, but these were divisions which split the Council itself. On none of the great issues or the great questions of the day did Parliamentary leaders hold any opinions not shared by members of the Council.

There appear to have been no important issues of principle which divided members of the so-called opposition from their friends in the Council … The English gentry in the 1620s were not a divided society: all the important political disagreements were such that those on both sides could work together with the same Council. Where there is not a divided society, there is not the fuel to sustain a division into two parties. All the leading MPs of the 1620s were legitimately entitled to hope for office. Since they could accept office without abandoning any of the principles for which they pressed while in Parliament, those, like WENTWORTH … who accepted office, do not deserve any strictures for 'changing sides'. They saw no sides to change. Cases like these should be regarded not as the exception, but as the rule.

Wentworth: *Thomas Wentworth, Earl of Strafford (see the profile on page 22)*

What are Russell's main arguments against the idea that Parliament was becoming more powerful, bringing about a clash with the Crown?

Source 2.7 is from another article that has been very influential in casting doubt on traditional accounts of later sixteenth- and early seventeenth-century English history. In it Tyacke attacks the Whig–Marxist idea of a 'rise of Puritanism'.

● **SOURCE 2.7**

From Nicholas Tyacke's article 'Puritanism, Arminianism and counter-revolution', Conrad Russell (ed.), *The Origins of the English Civil War* (1973)

Historians of the English Civil War all agree that Puritanism had a role to play in its origins. Beyond this, however, agreement ceases. For some, particularly the Marxists, Puritanism was the ideology of the newly emergent middle classes, or bourgeoisie, as they are sometimes called. Puritan ideas, it is argued, complemented and encouraged the capitalist activities of 'progressive' gentry, merchants and artisans alike. On the assumption, again made by those under the influence of Marxism, that the English Civil War was a 'bourgeois revolution' the Puritans are naturally found to be fighting against King Charles and his old-world followers. An alternative and widely held interpretation sees Puritanism as a religious fifth column within the Church of England, and one whose members dramatically increased during the first decades of the seventeenth century; by the early 1640s, with the collapse of the central government and its repressive system of church courts, the Puritans were thus able to take over at least in the religious sphere …

In the following essay, however, a different view will be put forward.

First, however, something needs saying about the definition of a Puritan.

Indeed the point needs making that it is extremely artificial to start drawing hard and fast lines between Puritans and 'Anglicans' in the Elizabethan and Jacobean periods. There are far too many cases which defy categorisation. [Tyacke then argues that even George Abbott, Archbishop of Canterbury between 1611 and 1633, was a 'Puritan', i.e. someone who believed in a PREDESTINARIAN theology, wanted further reform of the Church to purify it of any popish remnant, and supported concentrating church services on preaching and not on ceremonies.] …

Hindsight is often the curse of the historian, and none more so in attempting to reconstruct the religious history of the pre-Civil War era. The battle lines of 1640–2 were not drawn up by the early 1620s in this any more than in other spheres.

predestinarian: *see the doctrine of predestination on page 17*

> Summarise Tyacke's case that there was no religious divide between Anglicans and Puritans in the early seventeenth century.

Another significant revisionist onslaught has been on the notion that James I was an incompetent monarch. Source 2.8 is from an article by Jenny Wormald which has been very influential in rehabilitating James's reputation. It is not coincidental that Wormald is a Scottish historian of Scotland, a point which is brought out at the very beginning of this extract.

● **SOURCE 2.8**

From Jenny Wormald's article 'James VI and I; two kings or one?', *History*, vol. 68 (1983)

transmogrification: *not just a simple transformation but one that is very surprising*

In 1603 something happened which is so well known that its startling and dramatic nature is forgotten: England and Scotland, actively or passively hostile since the late thirteenth century, were forced into conjunction because of the stubborn refusal of Elizabeth to fulfil an essential function of monarchy by providing an heir of her body … King James's southern and northern subjects shared one attitude: both treated this man, who embarked on his dual role three months short of his thirty-seventh birthday, as *their* king, dividing him as far as possible into two separate individuals. In so doing, they set the scene for a historiographical tradition which has lasted to the present day.

The difference between the two kings is remarkable. [She then quotes Lawrence Stone's description of James I which we have already seen in Source 2.5.]

In stark contrast, Gordon Donaldson [a historian of Scotland] writes of James VI as:

a man of very remarkable political ability and sagacity in deciding on policy and of conspicuous tenacity in having it carried out. He may not have been the ablest of the Stuarts, but he was assuredly the most successful of his line in governing Scotland and bending it to his will …

These violently conflicting views can hardly both be right.

What lies behind the TRANSMOGRIFICATION of James VI to James I?

[Wormald goes on to argue that the answer to her question lies in English fear and hatred of the Scots, which was reflected in *A Perfect Description of the People and Country of Scotland*, written by Anthony Weldon, a minor royal household official, who went with James to Scotland in 1617. She finds in Weldon's 'masterly and malicious wit' the source of many of the legends of James's unsavoury reputation. In *A Perfect Description* he poured out scurrilous abuse about a country 'too good for those that possess it, and too bad for others to be at the charge to conquer it. The aire might be wholesome but for the stinking people that inhabit it … There is a great store of fowl too, as foul houses, foul sheets, foul linen, foul dishes and pots, foul trenchers and napkins …' Not surprisingly, after reading this account of his native country James sacked Weldon, who now turned his venomous pen against the king in another book, *The Court and Character of King James*.]

It is to Weldon that the traditional picture – even the famous tag 'the Wisest Fool in Christendom' – can be traced. Here is the James who wore padded clothes because of his fear of the assassin's knife, whose tongue, too large for his mouth, caused him to dribble disgustingly when he drank, the vain pedantic buffoon who never washed … Weldon's brilliant and deeply biased character sketch has never quite failed to influence later attitudes to James I, even for those who have never even heard of Weldon …

[Wormald then sets out a fairly comprehensive reassessment of James, showing him to have been a much more politically skilful and successful monarch of England than he has often been thought to have been.]

> How does Wormald account for the reasons why English (and American) historians have portrayed James I in a very different way from that in which Scottish historians have written about James VI?

Perhaps the most extreme example of revisionism is the work of Kevin Sharpe on the Personal Rule of the 1630s. Like Russell, who denies that there was an 'opposition' in the 1620s, Sharpe seeks to play down the seriousness of the criticism of the Crown in the 1630s. He even denies that Charles I's and Archbishop Laud's ecclesiastical policies were novel and so seen by a conservative nation as dangerous. Sharpe's article, from which Source 2.9 is taken, puts a strident revisionist case.

● **SOURCE 2.9**

From Kevin Sharpe's article 'The Personal Rule of Charles I', H. Tomlinson (ed.), *Before the English Civil War* (1983)

A study of the Personal Rule is … essential for an understanding of the crisis which led to civil war. To some, perhaps, the place of that decade in the story of civil war is clear: the period of government without Parliament intensified the conflicts between Crown and subjects which had been set in motion since the succession of James I; accelerated, that is, the fateful journey towards civil war past many a milestone of divisive controversy. As Professor Rabb has recently put it, 'the attempt to do without Parliament in the 1630s was in the long run untenable … Resistance to Charles's policy was inevitable'.

But was it? To those on the road during the 1630s the journey seemed far from a headlong rush towards conflict. Even looking backward from a knowledge of later events, Edward Hyde, no uncritical flatterer of Charles I, recalled … the Personal Rule as a decade of calm and felicity …

What were the ideals and purposes, for ideals and purposes there were, which underlay the directives and proclamations issued and published by king and Council during the decade of Personal Rule? … Central to all his directives was an obsessive concern with order – in matters both large and small … it was an obsession most visible in the Royal Court and Household. In the Memoirs of her husband, Lucy Hutchinson recalled vividly the change of style from King James to King Charles: 'The face of the Court was much changed in the King, for King Charles was temperate, chaste and serious, so that the fools and bawds, mimics and catamites of the former Court grew out of fashion' … The style of Charles's court reflected the image of the king, formal and reserved. But it was not only in the sphere of morality and manners that the concern for order was revealed. Charles instigated a programme of reform and retrenchment at Court, a programme which, if never very successful, at least curtailed the curve of rising extravagances …

The concern with order was not confined to the Court. Indeed it is important to understand that for Charles the Court was not to be, as some historians have maintained, a retreat from the world of reality, but rather a model for the reformed government of Church and state. Fear of the collapse of all authority and the dislocation of society directed the king's attention to the reordering of society and government. Where there were no laws, the Council was to tackle problems, where statutes had already prescribed measures, the Council was to ensure that they were enforced.

It is in the context of these concerns, of this looking back to an (idealised) society of harmony and deference, that we should understand Charles's religious policy. If order was Charles's private religion, then it behoved all the more that the religion of the realm be ordered … Throughout the 1630s royal letters reflect the king's personal concern with the Church, with the proper maintenance of the clergy and episcopacy, and with due observance of the forms of worship established by the Book of Common Prayer. Charles determined to end theological controversy, to reform and to re-establish respect for the hierarchy of the Church and to order its service with a view to uniting the realm in a liturgy common to every parish. It was an ideal close to that of Elizabeth in 1559. It was now an ideal which embraced not only England, but all three kingdoms, and even the PLANTATIONS …

Were the aims and ideals of Charles I ANATHEMA to the gentry rulers of the counties?

Such questions are hard to answer qualitatively. Silence, or even letters of support from the localities, could conceal diligent activity, grudging compliance, at times even outright resistance … On the other hand, few … questioned the legality of KNIGHTHOOD FINES. For all the evasions, … the compositions for knighthood brought £173,537 into the Exchequer. If there was opposition, it did not in the end prevent payment …

The great success story, however, was SHIP MONEY. Ship money was a rate, not a tax, collected at first from the maritime counties, but after 1635 from the whole country. It owed its origins to royal diplomacy, and especially the King's negotiations with Spain. It was never a source of ordinary revenue and was received not into the Exchequer, but into the Treasury of the Navy. It is important to bear in mind that ship money was not, and was never, demanded (whatever was intended) as a regular or permanent levy. Each writ was a separate request for aid in time of a national emergency; the preface to each writ explained and justified the need to equip a fleet for the year. It may be that the early responses of the country reflected a genuine recognition (after the debacle of 1628) of the need for a strong navy in a war-torn Europe. It is significant certainly that when the writ was extended from the maritime counties to the country at large, the point at which the legality might have been questioned, only 2.5 per cent of the sum requested failed to come in, and the amount raised, £194,864, was never exceeded. The success story continued … and it was not until 1639 and 1640 that the collection of ship money collapsed …

anathema: *something that is thought to be absolutely evil*

knighthood fines: *see page 21*

plantations: *the seventeenth-century word for colonies*

ship money: *see page 21*

Hampden: *John Hampden was the defendant in the Ship Money case in 1637–8 (see page 21)*

Before HAMPDEN there are almost no recorded instances of objection to the levy on legal or constitutional grounds. Complaints were confined to rating disputes; protests were limited to unfair assessments … Purses were more in evidence than principles … It was Hampden who raised the issue of principle and so took ship money to law … But whatever his place in the portrait gallery of martyrs for English constitutionalism, Hampden should not loom too large on the canvas of Personal Rule … In the year of Hampden's case more than 90 per cent was collected. If the trial delayed payments, and raised the question of legality, the final decision, unwelcome though it was, may have resolved more legal doubts than it aroused …

And so we come to the fundamental question … Could Charles have succeeded, could the Personal Rule have continued without the rebellion of the northern kingdom? … The early 1630s were marked by calm and quiet at Court and throughout the country … Peace brought the expansion of trade … The calm and peace continued. The ordinary budget was better balanced … Tensions and grievances never stymied government nor threatened revolt … In the many volumes of correspondence, public and private, we find few demands for a Parliament … Nor should that surprise us … In 1629 Parliament was still an event; it was not an institution.

> **What are the main reasons why Sharpe describes the 1630s as a decade of relative harmony?**

Sources 2.6–2.9 show the *destructive* aspect of the revisionist case. This argues that:

- there were *no* long-term developments (such as the Rise of Parliament or the Rise of Puritanism) corroding the structure of the State and Church before 1640
- James I was *not* an incompetent king
- the political stability of the country was *not* threatened for much of the 1630s.

How then did revisionist historians explain why Charles I was faced with a major political crisis at the end of the decade? In other words, what explanations did revisionist historians in the late 1970s and 1980s put in the place of 'Marxist' and 'Whig' long-term explanations?

One of the most important ideas used by many revisionists to construct new explanations was the concept of 'the county community', i.e. the idea that England consisted at this time of semi-independent local and urban communities whose inhabitants put loyalty to locality before allegiance to the nation. This was developed first by Alan Everitt in studies of Suffolk and Kent that were published in the late 1960s. Here he explains his idea in an article (Source 2.10), that was originally broadcast by BBC Radio in 1966.

● **SOURCE 2.10**

Alan Everitt, 'The county community', E. W. Ives (ed.), *The English Revolution* (1968)

Levellers: *a radical group discussed in Chapter 7*

sublimate: *a scientific term, meaning to convert from solid state to vapour, used here to mean 'transform'*

When the Long Parliament, the Parliament of the English Revolution, met in 1640, it did not meet as a body of revolutionaries. It met first and foremost as a body of angry countrymen … There was nothing revolutionary in this attitude of mind. What was new was the Country's lack of confidence in the Court, and the absence of anything at the centre which could SUBLIMATE local loyalty into loyalty to the state … And as its [i.e. the Court's] influence over the nation as a whole declined, each region, each county, became more than ever before a little self-centred kingdom on its own … There is nothing surprising in the localism of provincial people which … brought the king's government to a grinding halt in 1640 … it seems surprising only because so much of our history, until recent years, has been written from the viewpoint of Westminster, or the stance of untypical minorities like the LEVELLERS and Laudians. As soon as one begins to study the history of any provincial community … one finds that even during the Civil War the shouting and the tumult of these minorities played only a small part in its history. Most towns and counties were far more interested in living a life of their own, in which politics played merely an intermittent part, than in supporting either roundheads or cavaliers … Beyond a radius of fifteen miles [24 kilometres] from the city [of London], the vast majority of Kentish people were dyed-in-the-wool countrymen: living, marrying, farming, buying, selling, governing, hunting, and visiting within a very limited circle of local manor houses and market towns.

In these key passages in Source 2.11, the revisionist historian Conrad Russell makes clear his intellectual debt to Everitt's idea that there was a fundamental local–national tension within early seventeenth-century English society. The importance of Russell's book lies in the fact that it locates the causes of political tensions in the 1620s not in ideological differences, but in 'functional' (i.e. non-ideological) reasons.

● **SOURCE 2.11**

From Conrad Russell, *Parliaments and English Politics, 1621–29* (1979)

The object of this book is to reconstruct the Parliamentary history of the 1620s using a set of analytical tools which owe more to local studies than to previous Parliamentary studies. Its central contention is that the sort of men who assembled at Westminster were not widely different in character and outlook from the same men as they have become familiar to us as Justices of the Peace. The Justices of the Peace were not an opposition; they were, within certain partly self-imposed limits, loyal and hard-working servants of the Crown. Their service to the Crown, however, normally took third place behind their own concern for the welfare of their counties and for their own pockets … they almost always put concern for their own counties above any concept of the national interest …

What … was all the trouble about? If the Parliaments of the 1620s were not the scene of a power struggle between 'government' and 'opposition', if they were not polarised by ideological disputes, and if they were full of members who wished to preserve good relations with the court, why did they generate so much ill-will?

There appear to be three important answers to this question. The first and fundamental reason is … the 'functional breakdown' of English administration; the straining of the links between central and local government, which meant the King was constantly unable to collect an adequate revenue. He was therefore forced to resort to methods of revenue collection which only increased the collectors' unpopularity. The second was the complex and rapid political manoeuvring of the Duke of Buckingham … The third reason, bred from the other two, is the pressure of war on the English local administration. Because the wars of the 1620s were so unsuccessful, it is too readily forgotten that they were seriously intended, and prepared for on such a scale as to create a serious administrative burden. It was this burden of war, imposed on an administration already in a state of functional breakdown by the Duke of Buckingham whose purposes, and even whose enemy, appeared unidentifiable, that brought relations between central and local government, and hence between King and Parliament, to the point of collapse. The crisis of 1626–8, like the crisis of 1640, was the result of England's administrative inability to fight a war.

This is an argument that is fully supported by Kevin Sharpe in his work on the Personal Rule. In Source 2.12 he explains why, despite his picture of a period of successful rule, it collapsed in the late 1630s.

● **SOURCE 2.12**

From Kevin Sharpe's article 'The Personal Rule of Charles I', H. Tomlinson (ed.), *Before the English Civil War* (1983)

coat and conduct money:
a tax ordered by the King to be collected to pay for the English army that fought the Scots in the Bishops' Wars

In the end we come back to the Bishops' Wars … War revived the problems and grievances of 1628. The demand for COAT AND CONDUCT MONEY raised legal, administrative and fiscal problems. In many counties the cost of equipping soldiers equalled (and at times surpassed) the amount of ship money which was still demanded … Central policy now threatened local order. It was impossible to preserve them both. The issues at stake were not constitutional. 'What had changed between 1634 and 1639 was not the gentry's opinion of Charles's constitutional arguments, but the breakdown of peace, quiet and order in the local communities' [J. S. Morrill, *The Revolt of the Provinces*, p. 29] … War undoubtedly provided the opportunity for the expression of discontents. But more significantly, because on a wider plain, it created problems and grievances not in evidence before. At court, the decision to fight the Scots meant the end of domestic reform, a crash from financial stability, and the distraction of the Council from the business of normal government. In the counties, that decision, like the years of the 1620s, strained the fabric of local government and threatened the peace of local society. The problems which faced Charles I from 1638 to 1640 … were … rooted less in the constitution than in the structure of English government. Charles was too conservative ever to seek to change that structure. It was his achievement to have governed so ambitiously and so successfully within it.

In Sources 2.11 and 2.12, Russell and Sharpe identified the effects of war as the main cause of the political tensions of the early seventeenth century. In Source 2.13, Tyacke concentrates on religious reasons why Charles became deeply unpopular. Unlike previous accounts, however, he finds the answer not in the fact that Puritanism was a revolutionary force. For Tyacke it was *Charles I and his archbishop* who were the real revolutionaries.

● **SOURCE 2.13**

From Nicholas Tyacke's article 'Puritanism, Arminianism and counter-revolution', Conrad Russell (ed.), *Origins of the English Civil War* (1983)

Arminianism: *another word often used to describe Laudianism*

Congregationalism: *unlike most other Protestants, including Presbyterians, Congregationalists did not believe that there should be only one national Church, but that individual congregations should decide for themselves what form their church government and worship should take.*

Declaration of Sports: *a declaration allowing people to play games and take part in other recreational activities on Sundays*

predestinated: *decided beforehand. Tyacke uses this unusual word to remind his readers that he is referring to the Calvinist theology of predestination.*

Presbyterianism: *the central feature of Presbyterianism is the replacement of bishops in the national Church by a hierarchy of synods and classes.*

Religion became an issue in the Civil War crisis due primarily to the rise of ARMINIANISM in the 1620s. The essence of Arminianism was a belief in God's universal grace and the freewill of all men to obtain salvation. Therefore, Arminians rejected the teaching of Calvinism that the world was divided into elect and reprobate whom God had arbitrarily PREDESTINATED the one to Heaven and the other to Hell. It is difficult for us to grasp how great a revolution this involved for a society steeped in Calvinist theology as was England before the Civil War …

English Arminians came to balance their rejection of the arbitrary grace of predestination with a new-found source of grace freely available in the sacraments, which Calvinists had belittled. Hence the preoccupation under Archbishop Laud with altars and private confession before receiving communion … Such a view involved the replacement of preaching as the normal vehicle of saving grace, and one restricted in its application to the elect saints, by sacraments which conferred grace indiscriminately …

Theory went hand in hand with practice. In November 1633, three months after Laud became Archbishop of Canterbury, King Charles by act of Privy Council established the precedent that all parochial churches should follow the by then general cathedral practice of placing communion tables altar-wise at the east end of chancels … On the basis of this Privy Council ruling, Arminianism during the 1630s was made manifest through every parish in England …

This change in attitude extended to nonconformity in general, and not only did the breaking of the Calvinist theological bond lead to stricter enforcement of conformity: nonconformity itself acquired a much wider definition. Nonconformist offences now included … any form of predestinarian preaching, objecting to the new ceremonies associated with the transformation of communion tables into altars, and refusal to implement the DECLARATION OF SPORTS, which was reissued by Charles in 1633. The surviving Calvinist bishops found themselves in an alien world, and were distrusted by their colleagues … Hardly surprisingly the 1630s as a whole saw a great increase in the number of persecutions for Puritanism, an indirect measure of this being the large scale emigration to New England. In addition to creating widespread resentment of the episcopal hierarchy, these persecuting activities generated a Puritan militancy which in the early 1640s was to erupt in the shape of PRESBYTERIANISM and CONGREGATIONALISM …

In terms of English Protestant history the charge in 1640 that King Charles and Archbishop Laud were religious innovators is irrefutable.

In Source 2.14 John Morrill developed Tyacke's views in a very persuasive way, by including reference to ideology with the other characteristics of the revisionists' work. But, as Morrill makes clear in these powerfully argued passages, it was in *religious* ideology that he found the real origins of the crisis of the early 1640s.

● **SOURCE 2.14**

From John Morrill's article 'The religious context of the English Civil War', *Transactions of the Royal Historical Society*, 5th series, vol. 34 (1984)

My argument will be that there was in 1640 an ideological crisis as well as a FUNCTIONAL crisis. But I wish to argue that, however jumbled together they were in the hectic early days of the Long Parliament, there were three quite distinct and separable perceptions of misgovernment or modes of opposition – what will be called the *localist*, the *legal-constitutionalist*, and the *religious*. *The* argument of this paper will be that the localist and legal-constitutionalist perceptions of misgovernment lacked the momentum, the passion, to bring about the kind of civil war which England experienced after 1642. It was the force of religion that drove minorities to fight, and forced majorities to make reluctant choices …

The legal-constitutionalist perception of misgovernment was … one of limited tyranny, and it led to an unhurried and largely uncontroversial programme of remedial legislation consciously intended to restore a lost balance, to conserve the ancient constitution. There was no recognition either that the old system was unworkable or intrinsically tyrannical, or that the remedial legislation was making it unworkable or intrinsically unstable. There was no intellectual ferment in the period November 1640 to August 1641 creating new theories of government and new constitutional imperatives. If the king's behaviour left many unsatisfied with the achievements of the first session, there was no new rhetoric of popular or Parliamentary sovereignty spurring members on to self-confident constitutional demands. All this is in stark contrast to the progress of religious concerns …

I believe that it is almost impossible to overestimate the damage caused by the Laudians. I see no reason to doubt that most 'hotter sort of Protestants' were integrated into the Jacobean church and state. Puritan magistrates and churchwardens abound and can be found arguing for and working for an evangelical drive to instruct the ignorant, and an alliance of minister and magistrate to impose godly discipline. There was no incompatibility between serving God and the Crown … While they saw James I as moving too slowly but in the right direction, they found in Charles I a negligent king who was oblivious to the threat of popery at home, abroad, and within the church of which he was the supreme governor … The programme of Charles and Laud was profoundly offensive to most lay and clerical opinion … Whatever they thought they were doing, by 1640 their programme had aroused disenchantment amongst its [the Church's] committed and its critical members, a disenchantment which gave rise to a debate more passionate than a debate on the constitution. In November 1640, Wentworth was the most feared man in England; but Laud was the most detested – 'the sty of all pestilential filth', according to HARBOTTLE GRIMSTON, 'like a busie angry wasp, his sting in the tayl of everything' …

The widespread belief in a Popish Plot about the king's person … was seen as the only credible explanation of his behaviour. It was not claimed that Charles I was a papist; but it was believed that he had ceased to be responsible for his actions, had ceased to govern. It was, in modern parlance, as though he had been got at by the Moonies, had been brainwashed, programmed; or in a metaphor more appropriate to the seventeenth century, that he had been insidiously and deliberately poisoned, so that he had gradually become disoriented, distracted …

Talk of 'popery' is not a form of 'white noise', a constant fuzzy background in the rhetoric and argument of the time against which significant changes in secular thought were taking place. This has been a fundamental error in the intellectual historians of the English Revolution. This falsifies the passionate belief … that is the ground of action, that England was in the process of being subjected to the forces of ANTICHRIST, that the prospects were of anarchy, chaos, the dissolution of government and liberties …

Have we been so confused in seeking parallels between the British Crisis of the 1640s and the wave of rebellions on the continent (brought on by war and the centralising imperatives of war), or between the English Revolution and the events of 1789 and 1917, that we have missed an obvious point? The English Civil War was not the first European revolution: it was the last of the Wars of Religion.

Antichrist: *the identification of Antichrist with Catholicism by many English Protestants is explained on page 17*

functional: *for the distinction between functional and ideological explanations, refer to Source 2.11*

Harbottle Grimston: *an MP in the Long Parliament*

In his works in the late 1980s and early 1990s, Conrad Russell has focused on another explanation for political tensions in the early seventeenth century, including the crisis of 1640–1: the British Problem.

● **SOURCE 2.15**

From Conrad Russell's article 'The British Problem and the English Civil War', *History*, vol. 72 (1987)

Lady Bracknell: *a character in a famous play by Oscar Wilde,* The Importance of Being Earnest

The English Civil War is regularly discussed as if it were a unique event, but it was not: between 1639 and 1642, Charles I faced armed resistance in all three of his kingdoms … When three kingdoms under one ruler all take to armed resistance within three years, it seems sensible to investigate the possibility that their actions may have had some common causes … There are two obvious types of cause which are common to all three kingdoms. One is that they were all ruled by Charles I. It is perhaps fair to paraphrase LADY BRACKNELL and to say that 'to lose one kingdom might happen to any king, but to lose three savours of carelessness' … The other thing all three kingdoms have in common is that they are all parts of a multiple monarchy of three kingdoms. We now know … that the relations between multiple kingdoms were among the main causes of instability in continental Europe … The normal cause of trouble within multiple kingdoms [was] religion … The most famous case of multiple kingdoms with different religions is that of Spain and the Netherlands, and that produced disturbances on the same scale as the British … Moreover, Britain appears to be a unique case of multiple kingdoms all of which were internally divided in religion, and in all of which there existed a powerful group which preferred the religion of one of the others to their own … Charles, at some date not later than 1633 … decided to drop a match into this powder keg by setting out to achieve one uniform order of religion within the three kingdoms.

The final extract in this section on revisionism illustrates another major revisionist explanation for the outbreak of the English Revolution: the character and political ability of Charles I. For revisionist historians, Charles I replaced James I as the individual who must bear most blame for the dire predicament in which the monarchy found itself in the early 1640s. Derek Hirst summarises this view in Source 2.16.

● **Source 2.16**

Derek Hirst, *Authority and Conflict: England 1603–58* (1985)

connoisseurship: *a connoisseur is someone who is a good judge in matters of taste. Charles was a particularly good connoisseur of paintings; he spent large sums of money collecting (as well as commissioning) paintings by famous artists of the day such as Van Dyck and Rubens. Much of his collection was dispersed during the English Revolution.*

Charles I was ill-suited to cope with his plight, and must rank amongst the most inept of all English kings. Possessing none of the subtlety of his father, he shared to the full James's views on the divinity of kingship; he also had a total conviction of his own rectitude. While it would be foolish to conclude that the Civil War occurred simply *because* Charles was king, it would be equally foolish to underestimate the part played by his personality … Charles was brought up in an authoritarian fashion, very much in the shadow of his glamorous elder brother Henry [who died in 1612]. The diffidence of his youth may have been intensified by a habitual stutter. Whatever the case, Clarendon was later to blame the King's notorious proneness to vacillation – which proved a major handicap to the royal cause in the 1640s – on his 'not trusting himself enough'. That awkwardness may also help account for Charles's insistence on the dignity of kingship …

Charles's attitude had immediate political consequences. He failed to appreciate the need to explain his actions – never one of James's failings. His terse speeches from the throne to his Parliaments reveal not only his awkwardness but also his vision of rule: the proper course was conformity, not argument. Charles's incomprehension that any could honestly differ from their King led him to mistake the functions of his councillors and to turn his Scottish councillors in particular into a body of yes-men. As Laud once despairingly concluded, Charles was 'more willing not to hear than to hear' … Charles far preferred the private worlds of CONNOISSEURSHIP, hunting and family life. The King's character traits led him, under stress, into what sometimes looked uncomfortably like sheer dishonesty …

Charles can be accorded few accolades for statesmanship, and the distrust with which many of his subjects later viewed him is readily comprehensible. As disaster loomed even Laud sadly concluded that the King 'neither knows how to be, nor to be made, great'.

1 What new explanations have revisionist historians found for Charles I's troubles with Parliaments in the later 1620s and in 1640–1?

2 Note the references in the extracts from Russell, Tyacke and Sharpe to the dangers of historians using hindsight. Explain these dangers in your own words.

3 Who do revisionist historians blame for the crisis of 1640–1? Who do they think were 'the revolutionaries' and who were 'the conservatives' in that crisis?

Phase C **After revisionism**

How satisfactory do you find these revisionist explanations for the beginning of the English Revolution? The third part of this chapter includes sources written by historians who have not been totally convinced by them.

Before looking at what they have written, it is important to note that none of these historians defends many of the Whig–Marxist explanations for the crisis of 1640–1 that have been seen in Sources 2.1–2.5. Few would now argue that there was a 'Rise of Parliament' or 'Rise of Puritanism' as described by Stone. None of them assumes that James I was 'the wisest fool in Christendom' or that there was a 'high road to Civil War' stretching back to 1603 or even earlier.

Most historians would also concede that revisionists have successfully highlighted the major weaknesses in the structure of the country's Church and State that were identified in the first chapter of this book, on England before the English Revolution: the inadequacies of its public finance system, the partially reformed nature of the English Church and the problem of one monarch ruling three kingdoms, each with different political, social and (especially) religious traditions. Nor would many historians deny that the revisionists have successfully identified the incapacity of Charles I to deal with these problems.

What then are the major criticisms of revisionism that are emerging in recent writing? At least three are identified in the following extracts. The first is put by Anne Hughes in Source 2.17.

● **SOURCE 2.17**

From Anne Hughes, *The Causes of the English Civil War* (1991)

knights of the shire: MPs who *represented county (not borough) constituencies*

The Grand Remonstrance: *one of the principal documents issued in the early years of the Long Parliament (see page 50)*

Examining these [the nature of central–local relationships] in a European perspective suggests that the notion of an English 'county community' and the view that there were sharp and inevitable conflicts in England between local and national concerns are both improbable …

Compared to the rest of Europe, England had a highly integrated and centralised political system, deriving in large part from the early strength of the English monarchy, both Anglo-Saxon and Norman. Seventeenth-century England was made up of various local communities within which people experienced the different aspects of their lives: the village, the parish, the market town, the farming region and the diocese all mattered for personal, economic and religious affairs. The county too was important; the Court of Quarter Sessions was vital for the maintenance of order, the punishment of crime, and the regulation of local administration; the election or selection of KNIGHTS OF THE SHIRE to sit in Parliament meant that the county was a vital political focus. But the county was not the sole or even a prime focus of loyalty for most of the population including the gentry, and all local communities were conceived of as a part of a national polity; it was rarely assumed that local and national concerns were inevitably contradictory. Between the separate kingdoms of Spain, and the highly autonomous provinces of France … there were great variations in the legal system, in the privileges and procedures under which taxation was levied, and in administrative practices. Some kingdoms and provinces had powerful representative assemblies with proud traditions; others weak bodies, or none at all. England had one common law … it had a national framework for local administration … and, most important of all, it had one national representative body which voted taxation for the whole kingdom …

England was a centralised, but not a bureaucratised country; monarchs were therefore dependent on co-operation of local elites to raise taxes and soldiers, and enforce order … These local elites were in turn, however, dependent on the Crown and the central government for their appointment to local office, and often for help against local rivals … Again compared to continental Europe, England had a comparatively uniform national culture and system of higher education, accessible mainly to the upper classes, but open to some members of those middling groups who were also part of the 'political nation' …

Indeed the centre and the localities were so inextricably intertwined in English politics that even using the separate terms can suggest a polarity that contemporaries did not recognise. This close interrelationship was a vital element in political culture and practice, and in the nature of opposition to Charles I. There was an almost insatiable hunger for news of rivalries at court or factions in the Privy Council, and a wide interest in international affairs … Local communities were capable of sustained lobbying and petitioning over a wide variety of issues … From the 1580s and 1590s … to the petitioning campaign over episcopacy and the GRAND REMONSTRANCE, in the first years of the Long Parliament, we can see local communities involved in general issues and using local pressure to influence national alignments … Hence the opposition to Charles was not particularist, concerned only with a variety of local or privileged interests, but general, concerned with the nature and direction of one central government.

Sources 2.18 and 2.19 question another feature of the revisionist case, by arguing that all the political conflicts of the early seventeenth century, including the crisis of 1640–1, were brought about by much more deeply rooted and serious causes than a 'functional breakdown' of government resulting from the accidental impact of war.

● **SOURCE 2.18**

From Johann Sommerville's article 'Ideology, property and the constitution', Richard Cust and Anne Hughes (eds.), *Conflict in Early Stuart England: Studies in Religion and Politics, 1603–42* (1989)

The main purpose of this paper is to challenge the claim that broad unity on constitutional questions prevailed in early Stuart England … At least two markedly different constitutional theories were voiced throughout the period. Of course, some men were confused, or apathetic, or ill-informed on constitutional questions. Others attempted to tone down their claims for the sake of preserving harmony. Nevertheless differences of constitutional principle contributed to political conflict, especially when they were applied to issues involving property or taxation … It was in connection with such issues that the King or his ministers were usually accused of attempting to introduce arbitrary government. The King's extra-Parliamentary levies became contentious not merely because of their local effects but also because of their constitutional implications ... From the late sixteenth century onwards a number of men claimed that the King could tax without consent in what he regarded as emergencies ... This claim was frequently associated with the contentions that kings derived their powers not from the people, nor from the law of the land, but from God alone, and that kings could issue binding commands which contradicted the law ... Many Englishmen rejected these views and argued that the King's powers were derived from the people or from the laws of the realm, and that the King did not have to be obeyed if his orders conflicted with law.

● **SOURCE 2.19**

From Richard Cust, *The Forced Loan and English Politics, 1626–28* (1987)

Although war created the conditions in which the King's concern with disloyalty came to the fore, it alone was not responsible for this. A more profound cause was the ideological division [of the kind identified by Sommerville above] which explains his difference of perspective ... There can be little doubt that the memories of opposing and defying the Crown's servants in 1626 and 1627 carried into the later period and helped to undermine ... the collection of knighthood fines and Ship Money ... There were also important tactical developments emerging out of the resistance to the loan. A pattern was established whereby – in the absence of a Parliament – the Crown's opponents first of all tried to obstruct the process of raising money in the shires and then, if this failed to dissuade the Council, sought to bring about a political trial which would mobilise political opinion ... The progression ... whereby opponents of the Crown moved away from the Council and the Court towards stirring up dissent among the wider public, was maintained and extended; and this was to lead to the methods employed by Pym and his allies during the Long Parliament, culminating in the Grand Remonstrance ...

The response to the loan often provided the best indication of ultimate political allegiance prior to the Civil War, especially among those who had no aspirations for royal office. This is a measure of the extent to which the later lines were already drawn. Although there were not yet, or perhaps ever, two clearly defined 'sides', many of the basic principles had emerged and some had been obliged to declare where they stood in relation to these. These principles related to the broad issues which had been brought to the fore between 1626 and 1628. For the Crown the main concern was with preserving royal authority against what were seen as the assaults of the 'ill-affected' and the 'popular'. Amongst its critics there was distrust of the King's intentions, anxiety about the future of Parliaments and unease at the influence of 'evil counsellors' ... The same issues re-emerged time and again and were still causing division on the eve of the Civil War. Indeed in this sense the causes of the Civil War can be said to have extended back beyond the immediate situation out of which it arose. This is not to argue that earlier conflicts of principle made it inevitable, but they did ensure that where differences arose it was much harder to find common ground and reach a mutually acceptable settlement.

Source 2.20 examines revisionist interpretations of Puritanism and Arminianism and questions the assumption of some revisionist historians that religious ideas can easily be separated from constitutional and political debates in the early seventeenth century.

● **SOURCE 2.20**

From Richard Cust and Anne Hughes (eds.), 'Introduction: after revisionism' in *Conflict in Early Stuart England: Studies in Religion and Politics, 1603–42* (1989)

The notion that there was a clearly defined 'Puritan opposition' in England has been effectively countered by both sixteenth- and seventeenth-century historians. Puritans were not necessarily conformists from the English Church, still less 'alienated' from the political establishment. On the range of matters from the basics of Calvinist theology to the importance of preaching and of an unceasing struggle against popery, they had much in common with key members of the political and ecclesiastical establishment. However, we do not accept recent work which argues in effect that Puritanism did not exist, that it was part of a broad and indistinguishable Calvinist consensus. At the very least Puritans were the 'vanguards' of English Protestants, the most concerned to eliminate popery from the Church, and to evangelise a population which had not yet satisfactorily absorbed the essentials of Protestantism. As individuals, Puritans emphasised an active, individual understanding or internalisation of the fundamentals of faith as revealed in scripture and expounded through preaching ... On a personal level this produced a tendency towards introspection, assiduous scriptural study, attendance at sermons, and conscientious attempts to live all aspects of life according to God's word. More broadly Puritans sought out like-minded Christians, to form communities of the godly, and distinguished themselves from those who complacently accepted an ungodly world. They also tended to confirm and demonstrate their inner assurance of salvation by an external, activist programme of reform in the world. Thus they attempted to root out popery and establish a godly, moral regime in the Church and in society as a whole ...

Seen in this light it is clear that there was a great, and often realised, potential for Puritanism to become a disruptive influence in local communities and in the realm as a whole. Puritans were not inevitably 'opponents' of the monarchy. A godly prince who headed the struggle against the popish Antichrist would receive the support of staunch Protestants. But ... this support was conditional on the monarch actually fulfilling his expected role, something which Charles I manifestly failed to do. In the circumstances of 1641–2, this enabled Puritans to tap a wider constituency committed temporarily to the fight against popery, and mount a remarkably effective challenge to the King ...

Puritanism ... included elements which were far from conservative or supportive of the status quo; and it is as misleading to cast the Puritan–Arminian polarity as a progressive–conservative divide, as it is to categorise conflict in early-Stuart England generally. Both were in many senses innovative attempts to deal ... with new problems deriving from the Reformation ... Arminianism did not emerge from nowhere, and ... Charles's support for Arminians is consistent with his general attitudes. In other words ... these developments are explicable in the context of fundamental tensions and problems in the English polity; they are not the random accidents they appear in some revisionist accounts ...

We agree with some revisionists, notably Morrill, that religion was crucial to the divisions which brought about the Civil War, but we do not share the tendency to see religion as a phenomenon hermetically sealed from other aspects of life ... The need to combat popery in all its guises led to an emphasis on freely elected Parliaments which were seen as the means to uphold true religion and protect the King from popish counsellors at the same time as defending property and law. Those who were more fearful of the popular implications of Puritan activism tended to support an authoritarian monarchy.

● Summary Task

1   What are the principal criticisms made by these 'post-revisionist' historians of revisionist explanations for the crisis of 1640–1?

2   What are the post-revisionists' principal explanations for the political tensions of the early seventeenth century between Crown and Parliamentarians, including the crisis of 1640–1?

3   What do you think were the causes of the crisis of 1640–1?
    Write an essay answering this question. The one clear thing that comes out of the historical debate you have just examined is that there is no single cause for the crisis of 1640–1. You will therefore need to organise your answer under different headings that enable you to discuss various possible causes, before you decide which ones you think are the most important.
    Before answering the question read the following extracts from a speech made by an MP in the first week of the Long Parliament in November 1640, which is typical of many that were made at this time.

● **SOURCE 2.21**

Sir John Culpepper's speech in the House of Commons, 9 November 1640. He was an MP for Kent and from 1641–2 became a firm supporter of the King and a Royalist in the Civil War.

divers: *many*

Mr. Speaker, I stand not up with a petition in my hand, I have it in my mouth; and have it in charge from them that sent me hither, humbly to present to the consideration of this House the grievances of the county of Kent. I shall only sum them up; they are these:

First, the great increase of Papists, by the remiss execution of those laws which were made to suppress them ...

The second is the obtruding and countenancing of DIVERS new ceremonies in matters of religion, as placing the communion table altar-wise, and bowing and cringing too, towards it; the refusing the Holy Sacrament to such as refuse to come up to the rails. These carry with them some scandal and much offence.

The third is military charges ... The last summer was twelve month 1000 of our best arms taken from their owners and sent unto Scotland ...

The fourth is the canons [new Laudian regulation for the running of the Church drawn up by a body representing the Church, called Convocation] ... The clergy without confirmation of a Parliament have assumed to themselves power to make laws … This is a grievance of a high nature.

The next is the great decay of clothing, and fall of our wools. These are the golden mines of England … I will not trouble you with more than one cause of it, which I dare affirm to be the greatest. It is the great customs and impositions laid upon our cloth [taxes on the export of cloth not granted by Parliament] …

I have but one grievance more to offer to you, but this one comprises many; it is a nest of wasps or swarm of vermin, which have over-crept the land. I mean the monopolists … These like the frogs of Egypt have gotten the possession of our dwellings, and we have scarce a room free from them: they sup in our cup, they dip in our dish, they sit by our fire … These are the leeches that have sucked the Commonwealth … Mr. Speaker, I have echoed to you the cries of the kingdom. I will tell you their hopes. They look to heaven for a blessing upon this Parliament … It is the wise conduct of this whereby the other great affairs of this kingdom and this of our grievances of no less importance may go hand in hand in preparation and resolution. Then by the blessing of God we shall return home with an olive branch in our mouths, and a full confirmation of the privileges which we received from our ancestors, and owe to our posterity, and which every free-born Englishman hath received with the air he breathes in. These are our hopes. These are our prayers.

The following class activity will be useful as a preparation for writing the essay.

Divide into two groups to debate the following question:
Was the crisis of 1640–1 the accidental result of short-term factors?
The first group should argue that it was so; the second group should argue that it was not.

● Further reading

The best brief introductions to many of the debates touched on in this chapter are Richard Cust and Anne Hughes, 'Introduction: after revisionism' in Richard Cust and Anne Hughes, (eds.), *Conflict in Early Stuart England: Studies in Religion and Politics 1603–42* (Longman, 1989) and Richard Cust and Anne Hughes, 'Introduction: continuities and discontinuities in the English Civil War' in Richard Cust and Anne Hughes (eds.) *The English Civil War* (Edward Arnold, 1997). Read also the full versions of the books and articles from which extracts, in this chapter, have been taken.

chapter **3**

1640–2: Why did the political crisis of 1640 become civil war?

1640
April 13: The Short Parliament opens at Westminster.
May 5: Charles I dissolves the Short Parliament after its refusal to give him financial support for the Scots War.
August 28: The Scots defeat the English at Newburn, near Newcastle.
November 3: The Long Parliament opens at Westminster.
December 11: The Root and Branch Petition is presented to Parliament.

1641
March 22: The opening of impeachment proceedings against the Earl of Strafford.
April 10: A Bill of Attainder against Strafford is introduced in the House of Commons.
April 21: The House of Commons passes Bill of Attainder against Strafford.
May 7: The House of Lords passes Bill of Attainder against Strafford.
May 10: Charles I gives royal assent to Strafford's Attainder.
May 12: The Earl of Strafford executed on Tower Hill.
late October: The Irish Rebellion breaks out.
November 8: The Grand Remonstrance is introduced to the House of Commons.
November 22: The House of Commons narrowly approves the Grand Remonstrance.

1642
January 4: Charles I attempts to arrest five MPs in the House of Commons.
January 10: Charles I leaves London.
March 5: Parliament passes the Militia Ordinance.
early June: Parliament's Nineteen Propositions for peace are sent to Charles I.
June 11: Charles issues Commissions of Array for the raising of a Royalist army.
mid-June: Charles rejects the Nineteen Propositions. Parliament issues the Militia Ordinance, ordering a Parliamentary army to be raised.
August 22: Charles I raises his standard at Nottingham Castle.

Introduction

The MPs of the Long Parliament met for the first time at Westminster on 3 November 1640. If they had been told then that, within two years, a full-scale civil war would have broken out in England, most of them would have been astonished and horrified. The overwhelming majority of MPs were determined to change the recent government policies of Charles I's Personal Rule. Most of them were moderate, wealthy and conservative men, who looked to achieve their ends through discussion and persuasion. They were united on all the main issues.

Within a few weeks they had begun on an ambitious programme of legislative reform. By the end of 1641 they seemed to have achieved their aims:

• Charles I's chief advisers, William Laud and Thomas Wentworth, Earl of Strafford, had been removed from power.
• Ship money had been declared illegal.

- The Prerogative Courts of Star Chamber and High Commission had been abolished.
- A Triennial Act had guaranteed the regular meeting of future Parliaments.

Despite all this apparent progress, however, by early 1642 many MPs were very troubled. The House of Commons, which had appeared so united at first, was now seriously divided. The fierce controversies of the previous eighteen months had deeply divided the moderate MPs from their more radical colleagues, led by John Pym. Pym and his supporters were prepared to use methods such as popular demonstrations to pressurise Charles into granting their demands, which many of their fellow MPs found unacceptable. In addition, although Charles had given his approval to the major legislative changes demanded by Parliament, many MPs still deeply distrusted the King's ministers and were extremely suspicious of their motives.

From the end of 1640 onwards, it was increasingly clear that, while the MPs were virtually unanimous in their opposition to the religious policies introduced by William Laud and his fellow bishops during the 1630s, they were deeply divided over the future of the English Church. Moderate Protestants wanted the Laudian bishops to be replaced by bishops who were more acceptable, but Presbyterians and Independents wanted the complete abolition of bishops. By August 1642, the Long Parliament was split down the middle into Royalists and Parliamentarians, the two sides which were to fight the Civil War.

In the following primary sources, we will investigate why the MPs of the Long Parliament became so deeply divided and why civil war broke out in 1642. At the end of the chapter you will be asked to explain why the King and his opponents failed to find a peaceful settlement of their differences during this period.

Section A Demands for religious reform: the Root and Branch Petition, December 1640

In December 1640, a petition signed by several thousand Londoners which called for the 'root and branch' abolition of the bishops was presented to Parliament. For the first time since they had met two months before, the MPs had strongly opposing views, some welcoming the petition, but others objecting strongly to it. In 1641, a Root and Branch Bill for the abolition of episcopacy (government of the Church by bishops) came before Parliament, but it again provoked serious divisions and was taken no further. Episcopacy remained for the time being.

● **SOURCE 3.1**

The Root and Branch petition, December 1640

Attached to the petition was an annexe entitled, *A particular of the manifold evils, pressures and grievances caused, practised and occasioned by the prelates and their dependants.* It gave a detailed list of the damaging consequences of the activities of William Laud and the bishops during the 1630s. Below and opposite are some of the items.

Jesuits: *an order of Roman Catholic priests*

ministrations: *administration*

Papist: *Roman Catholic*

prelates: *bishops*

profanation: *violation*

Romish party: *Roman Catholics*

The humble petition of many of his Majesty's subjects in and about the City of London, and several counties of the kingdom, Showeth

That whereas the government of archbishops and lord bishops, deans and archdeacons etc., with their courts and MINISTRATIONS in them, have proved prejudicial and very dangerous both to the Church and Commonwealth … And whereas the said government is found by woeful experience to be the main cause and occasion of many foul evils, pressures, and grievances of a very high nature unto His Majesty's subjects in their own consciences, liberties and estates … We therefore most humbly beseech this honourable assembly, that the said government, with all its dependencies, roots and branches, may be abolished and all laws in their behalf made void, and the government according to God's Word may be rightly placed amongst us: and we your humble SUPPLIANTS, as in duty we are bound, will daily pray for the prosperous success of this high and honourable Court of Parliament …

the faint-heartedness of ministers to preach the truth of God lest they should displease the PRELATES …

the encouragement of ministers to despise the TEMPORAL MAGISTRACY, the nobles and gentry of the land …

the restraint of many godly and able men from the ministry, and thrusting out of many congregations their faithful, diligent, and powerful ministers …

the great increase of idle, lewd and dissolute, ignorant and erroneous men in the ministry, which swarm like the locusts of Egypt over the whole kingdom …

the discouragement of many from bringing up their children in learning; the many SCHISMS, errors, and strange opinions which are in the Church; great corruptions which are in the universities; the gross and lamentable ignorance almost everywhere among the people; the want of preaching ministers in very many places both of England and Wales; the loathing of

profaneness: *wickedness*

schism: *religious division*

suppliants: *petitioners*

temporal magistracy: *civil government*

vestures: *dress*

the ministry, and the general defection to all manner of PROFANENESS

the growth of popery and increase of PAPISTS, priests and JESUITS in sundry places

the great conformity and likeness both continued and increased of our Church to the Church of Rome, in VESTURES, postures, ceremonies and administrations

PROFANATION of the Lord's Day, pleading for it and enjoining ministers to read a Declaration … for tolerating sports upon that day

the general hope and expectation of the ROMISH PARTY, that their superstitious religion will ere long be fully planted in this kingdom again …

1   What corrupt practices of the parish clergy did the petitioners accuse the bishops of having encouraged?

2   What sort of activities did the petitioners believe the parish clergy should be engaged in?

3   How according to the petitioners had the Laudian bishops encouraged the people to mis-spend their Sundays during the 1630s?

4   How according to the petitioners had the Laudian bishops encouraged the spread of popery?

5   Comment on the language and tone of the petition and its annexe. How would the following types of MPs have reacted to this petition and why:

   a) Moderate Protestant
   b) Presbyterian
   c) Independent?

Section B Revenge for the Personal Rule: the attack on the Earl of Strafford, 1640–1

Thomas Wentworth, Earl of Strafford, was one of the King's closest advisers during the 1630s. He was particularly loathed and feared by Charles I's opponents, who saw him as one of the chief architects of the hated policies of the Personal Rule. Several weeks after the Long Parliament assembled, therefore, the House of Commons began impeachment proceedings against him. Impeachment was a long-standing judicial process whereby the Commons presented charges against a government minister who they believed was abusing his power. The accused was then tried by the House of Lords.

● **SOURCE 3.2**

John Pym, Charles I's most able and powerful critic in the House of Commons, launched the impeachment in a speech to the House of Lords on 24 November 1640. In it, he accused Strafford of committing treason.

abridgement: *reduction*

arbitrary: *unregulated*

distemper: *illness*

intercourse: *relationship*

prerogative: *personal power*

restoratives: *remedies*

[He has committed] … a great and dangerous treason, such a one as is advanced to the highest degree of malice and mischief. It is enlarged beyond the limits of any description or definition … treason against God, betraying his truth and worship; against the King, obscuring the glory and weakening the foundations of his throne; against the Commonwealth, by destroying the principles of safety and prosperity. Other treasons are against the rule of law: this is against the being of law. It is the law that unites the King and his people, and the author of this treason hath endeavoured to dissolve that union, even to break the mutual, irreversible, indissoluble bond of protection and allegiance whereby they are, and I hope ever will be, bound together.

If this treason had taken effect our souls had been enthralled to the spiritual tyranny of Satan, our consciences to the ecclesiastical tyranny of the Pope, our lives, our persons and estates to the civil tyranny of an ARBITRARY, unlimited, confused government.

Treason in the least degree is an odious and horrid crime. [But] other treasons are particular: if a fort be betrayed or an army, or any other treasonable act committed, the kingdom may outlive any of these. This treason would have dissolved the frame and being of the Commonwealth; it is a universal, a Catholic treason; the venom and malignity of all other treasons are abstracted, digested, sublimated into this …

The laws of this kingdom have invested the royal crown with power sufficient for the manifestation of his goodness and of his greatness; if more be required it is like to have no other effects but poverty, weakness and misery, whereof of late we have had very woeful

44

1640–2: Why did the political crisis of 1640 become civil war?

experience. It is far from the Commons to desire any ABRIDGEMENT of those great PREROGATIVES which belong to the King; they know that their own liberty and peace are preserved and secured by his prerogative … A King and his people make one body: the inferior parts confer nourishment and strength, the superior, sense and motion. If there be an interruption of this necessary INTERCOURSE of blood and spirits, the whole body must needs be subject to decay and DISTEMPER. Therefore obstructions must be removed before RESTORATIVES can be applied. This, my lords, is the end of this accusation, whereby the Commons seek to remove this person, whom they conceive to have been a great cause of the obstructions between his Majesty and his people; for the effecting whereof they have commanded me to desire your lordships that your proceedings against him may be put into as speedy a way of despatch as the courses of Parliament will allow …

1 Why according to Pym had Strafford's actions been so dangerous?

2 Pym compares the state to a body. How did this help him to call for Strafford's removal?

3 What is Pym's attitude to the King in this speech? Explain the likely reasons for this.

4 Which of Pym's arguments would have been most convincing to the members of the House of Lords?

● **SOURCE 3.3**

At the beginning of 1641 more specific charges were levelled against Strafford. They included the following accusations.

annexed: *attached*

assizes: *courts which dealt with serious crimes*

liege people: *those obliged to offer the King support*

loins: *weight*

pretext: *excuse*

procure: *persuade*

reposed: *placed*

… that shortly after obtaining the said commission [as Lord President of the Council in the North in 1633] … he the said earl (to bring his Majesty's LIEGE PEOPLE into a dislike of his Majesty and of his government, and to terrify the justices of the peace from executing the laws) … did publicly at the ASSIZES held for the county of York … declare and publish … that some of the justices were all for law, and nothing would please them but law, but they would find that the King's little finger should be heavier than the LOINS of the law;

That the realm of Ireland having been time out of mind ANNEXED to the imperial crown of this his Majesty's realm of England, and governed by the same laws, the said earl being Lord Deputy of that realm … did upon the 30th day of September in the ninth year of his Majesty's reign [1633] in the city of Dublin … declare and publish that Ireland was a conquered nation, and that the King might do with them what he pleased …

That the said earl hath in the 15th and 16th years of his Majesty's reign 1639–40, and divers years past, laboured and endeavoured to breed in his Majesty an ill opinion of his subjects, namely, those of the Scotch nation, and divers and sundry times … he the said earl did labour and endeavour to persuade, incite, and provoke his Majesty to an offensive war against the said subjects of the Scotch nation …

And having incited his Majesty to an offensive war against his subjects of Scotland by sea and land, and by PRETEXT thereof to raise forces for the maintenance of that war, he counselled his Majesty to call a Parliament in England. Yet the said earl intended that if the said proceedings of that Parliament should not be such as would stand with the said Earl of Strafford's mischievous designs he would then procure his Majesty to break the same;

That upon the 13th day of April last the Parliament of England met, and the Commons House … did accordingly to the trust REPOSED in them enter into debate and consideration of the great grievances of this kingdom, both in respect of religion and the public liberty of the kingdom … and while the Commons then assembled were in debate and consideration of some supply, before any resolution by them made, he the said earl of Strafford, with the help and assistance of the said archbishop [William Laud], did PROCURE his Majesty to dissolve the said Parliament upon the 5th day of May last

All and every which words, counsels and actions of the said Earl of Strafford were spoken, given and done … traitorously, and contrary to his allegiance to our sovereign lord the King, and with an intention and endeavour to alienate and withdraw the hearts and affections of the King's liege people of all his realms from his Majesty … for which they do further impeach him … of high treason against our sovereign lord the King, his Crown and Dignity.

1   Make a list of the specific actions of which Strafford was accused. Use the following headings:

    a) the North of England
    b) Ireland
    c) Scotland
    d) the Short Parliament of April 1640.

2   Why, according to Pym, did these actions amount to treason?

● Source 3.4

Strafford responded to the charges in Source 3.3 in a speech he made in the House of Lords in April 1641.

---

accumulative: *piece by piece*

circumspection: *caution*

confederacy: *association*

eschew: *avoid*

inculcate: *maintain*

omnipotency: *complete power*

probation: *proof*

propriety: *property*

statute: *Act of Parliament*

My Lords, I have all along watched to see that poisoned arrow of treason that some would have to be feathered in my breast, and that deadly cup of wine that hath so intoxicated some petty misalleged errors as to put them in the elevation of high treason … They tell me of a twofold treason, one against the STATUTE, another by the Common Law; this direct, that constructive; this individual, that ACCUMULATIVE; this in itself, that by way of construction … To make up this constructive treason, or treason by accumulation, many articles are brought against me, as if in a heap of felonies or misdemeanours – for in their own conceit they reach no higher – some prolific seed apt to produce what is treasonable could lurk.

Here I am charged to have designed the overthrow both of religion and the State. The first seemeth to me to have been used rather for making me odious than guilty, for there is not the least PROBATION alleged concerning my CONFEDERACY with the Popish faction, nor could there be any indeed … never a servant in authority beneath the King my master who was more hated and maligned, and am still, by these men than myself, and that for a strict and impartial execution of the laws against them. Hence your Lordships may observe that the greater number of the witnesses used against me either from Ireland or Yorkshire are men of that religion; and for my own resolution I thank God I am ready every minute of the day to seal my disaffection to the Church of Rome with my dearest blood …

As to my designs about the State, I dare plead as much innocency here as in the matter of my religion. I have ever admired the wisdom of our ancestors, who have so fixed the pillars of this monarchy that each of them keeps due measure and proportion with [the] other … The prerogative of the Crown and the PROPRIETY of the subject have such mutual relations that this took protection from that, that foundation and nourishment from this … the excess of prerogative is oppression, of a pretended liberty in the subject, disorder and anarchy. The prerogative must be used, as God doth his OMNIPOTENCY at extraordinary occasions. The propriety of the subject is ever to be maintained if it go in equal pace with this; they are fellows and companions that have been and ever must be inseparable in a well governed kingdom; and no way so fitting, so natural to nourish … both as the frequent use of Parliaments. By this a commerce and acquaintance is kept between the King and the subject; this thought has gone along with me these fourteen years of my public employments, and shall, God willing, to my grave. God, his Majesty and my own conscience, yea, all who have been accessory to my most inward thoughts and opinions, can bear me witness I ever did INCULCATE this: the happiness of a kingdom consists in [the] just poise of the King's prerogative and the subject's liberty, and that things should never be well till these went hand in hand together …

These gentlemen tell me they speak in defence of the commonweal against my arbitrary laws; give me leave to say that I speak in defence of the commonweal against their arbitrary treason. For if this latitude be admitted, what prejudice shall follow to the King, to the country, if you and your posterity be disabled by the same from the great affairs of the kingdom. And whether judgement in my case – I wish it were not the case of you all – be it life or death, it shall be righteous in mine eyes …

1   How does Strafford reply to the accusations made by John Pym in Source 3.3?

2   Strafford argued that treason could not be 'accumulative'. What did he mean by this?

3   How did Strafford believe the English constitution should work?

4   Strafford tried to persuade his fellow peers to find him not guilty by suggesting that if they condemned him they would later regret it. What arguments does he use to support this claim?

46

1640–2: Why did the political crisis of 1640 become civil war?

This clever and emotional defence had a real impact upon the House of Lords. Realising that the impeachment might be rejected, his opponents withdrew it and instead introduced a Bill of Attainder into the Commons. This Bill simply declared Strafford to be a traitor by Act of Parliament and it did not require the same proof as impeachment. Some MPs opposed this course of action for its dubious legality. Around 50 later voted against the Bill, on the grounds that to condemn Strafford in this way was to adopt the same high-handed tactics as he had used in the 1630s. Most members of the Commons, however, agreed with the MP Oliver St John, who argued that 'it was never accounted either cruelty or foul play to knock foxes and wolves on the head … because they be beasts of prey'. The Bill subsequently passed through both Houses of Parliament and, in early May, Charles, under intense pressure from violent demonstrations outside Whitehall Palace, gave it his royal assent. On hearing of this, William Laud, who, like Strafford, was a prisoner in the Tower of London, commented that Charles 'knew not how to be, or to be made great'. The Earl of Strafford was beheaded outside the Tower on 12 May 1641; the event was witnessed by a huge crowd, the great majority of whom were delighted by his death. Charles I on the other hand never forgave himself for abandoning the earl to his enemies.

1 Why were Pym and his followers so determined to remove Strafford from power?

2 What impact do you think the death of Strafford had on relations between Charles and his opponents?

● **SOURCE 3.5**

A contemporary view of Strafford's execution

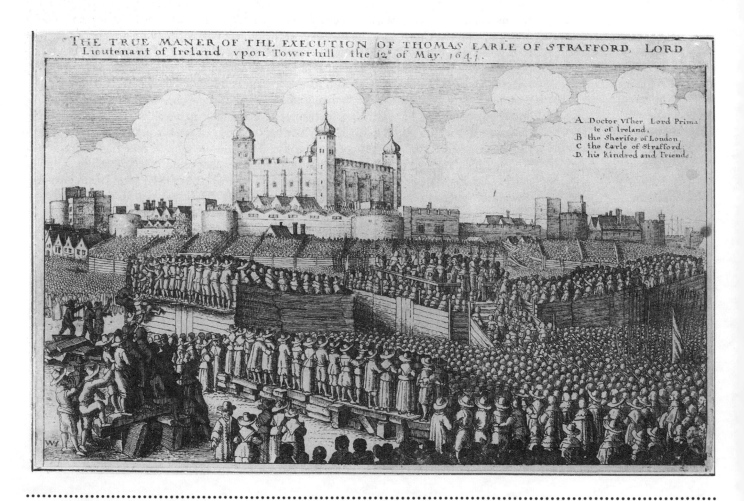

THE TRUE MANER OF THE EXECUTION OF THOMAS EARLE OF STRAFFORD, LORD Lieutenant of Ireland, vpon Tower-hill the 12ᵗʰ of May 1641.

A Doctor Vſher Lord Primate of Ireland.
B the Sherifes of London
C the Earle of Strafford
D his kindred and Friends.

THOMAS *Graaf van Straffort, Onder Koning van Ierland, Binnen Londen Onthalst, Den 22 van May 1641.*

I.L

1 What can a historian learn about Strafford's execution from Source 3.5?

2 What differences can you identify between Sources 3.5 and 3.6?

3 Which do you think is likely to be the more reliable source? Give reasons for your choice.

48

1640–2: Why did the political crisis of 1640 become civil war?

Section C Fears of a Papist massacre: the Irish Rebellion, October 1641

At the end of October 1641, some of the native Catholic population of Ulster rose up in armed rebellion against the Protestant landowners. (Protestants had settled in Ulster over the previous 30 years on land which had previously belonged to the native Irish.) A great deal of violence followed. Both Catholics and Protestants massacred their opponents. These dramatic and bloody events affected the political crisis in England in two main ways. While Charles and his MPs were agreed that the raising of an English army to crush the rebellion was essential, they were divided about who should control it. The King believed that control of the army was an essential part of the royal prerogative. Pym and his supporters, however, feared that the army could be used to close Parliament and return to the hated policies of the 1630s. The rising also confirmed the fears of many English Protestants that a similar rebellion by English Catholics was imminent, and that the atrocities that had occurred in Ulster could soon be repeated in England. For these reasons the Irish Rebellion heightened the political crisis and raised the politically explosive issue of who should control the army.

A particularly lurid account of events in Ireland during the first few weeks of the rebellion was given in a letter which Thomas Partington sent to a friend in England at the end of November 1641. The letter was subsequently published and circulated widely in various printed versions. It was also read to the House of Commons in December.

● **SOURCE 3.7**

Thomas Partington's letter to a friend in England

---

expedition: *speed*

exquisite: *skilful*

munitions: *weapons*

privy members: *genitals*

ravishing: *raping*

travel: *childbirth*

All I can tell you is the miserable estate we continue under, for the Rebels daily increase in men and MUNITIONS in all parts except the Province of Munster, exercising all manner of cruelties, and striving who can be most barbarously EXQUISITE in tormenting the poor Protestants wheresoever they come, cutting off their PRIVY MEMBERS, ears, fingers and hands, plucking out their eyes, boiling the heads of little children before their Mothers' faces, and then ripping up their Mothers' bowels; stripping women naked, and standing by them being naked whilst they are in TRAVEL, killing the children as soon as they are born, and ripping up their Mothers' bellies as soon as they are delivered; driving men, women and children by hundreds together upon Bridges and from thence cast them down into Rivers, such as drowned not they knocked their brains out with poles or shoot them with Muskets that endeavour to escape by swimming out; RAVISHING wives before their Husbands' faces and Virgins before their Parents' faces; after they have abused their bodies making them renounce their religion and then marry them to the basest of their fellows.

Oh, that the Lord, who hath moved the kingdoms of England and Scotland to send relief to these afflicted Protestants, would likewise stir them to effect their undertaking with all possible EXPEDITION, lest it be too late. Some of the persons particularly mentioned to have suffered who are known to you are Master Jerome, minister of Brides, his body mangled and his members cut off; Master Fullerton, minister of Lughall; Simon Hastings, his ears cut off; Master Blandry, Minister, hanged, his flesh pulled off from his bones, in the presence of his wife, in small pieces, he being hanged two days before her in the place where she is now prisoner; Abraham James of Newtown in the Diocese of Clohor cut in pieces, and it is reported that the Bishop of Clohor is turned to the Rebels. Thus moving pardon in presuming to trouble you at this time in your public employments, do with humble remembrance of his best respects to you and your virtuous lady, remain

Your Servant to command

Thomas Partington

---

1 What impact was this letter designed to have upon its English readers?

2 How reliable a guide do you think this letter is of events in Ireland in 1641?

● **SOURCE 3.8**

A Protestant artist's view of the
Massacre of Portadown Bridge in
1641

Driuinge Men Women & children by hund: reds vpon Briges & casting them into Riuers, who drowned not were killed with poles & shot with muskets.

● **SOURCE 3.9**

Extract fom a Protestant account of
the Irish Rebellion of 1641

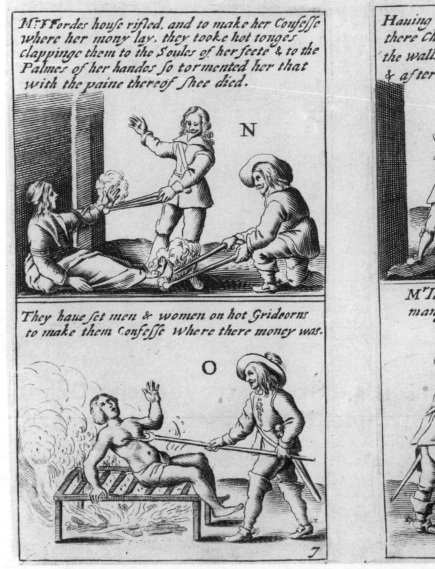

Mr Ffordes house rifled, and to make her Confesse where her mony lay, they tooke hot tonges clapping them to the Soules of her feete & to the Palmes of her handes so tormented her that with the paine thereof shee died.

They haue set men & women on hot Grideorns to make them Confesse Where there money was.

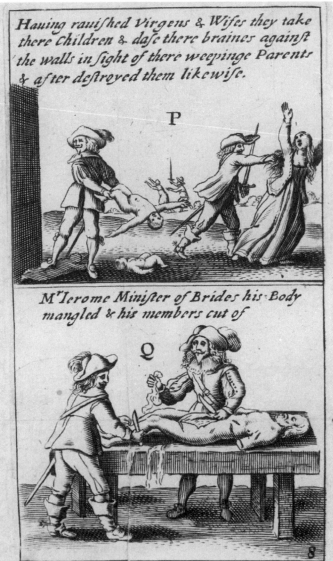

Hauing rauished Virgens & Wifes they take there Children & dase there braines against the walls in sight of there weeping Parents & after destroyed them likewise.

Mr Ierome Minister of Brides his Body mangled & his members cut of

50

1640–2: Why did the political crisis of 1640 become civil war?

1 How reliable are Sources 3.8–3.9 as evidence of the behaviour of Catholics during the rebellion?

2 In the light of your answer, assess the usefulness of these sources for a historian studying the Irish Rebellion.

● **FIGURE 3.1**

Map showing Tudor and Stuart Plantations in Ireland

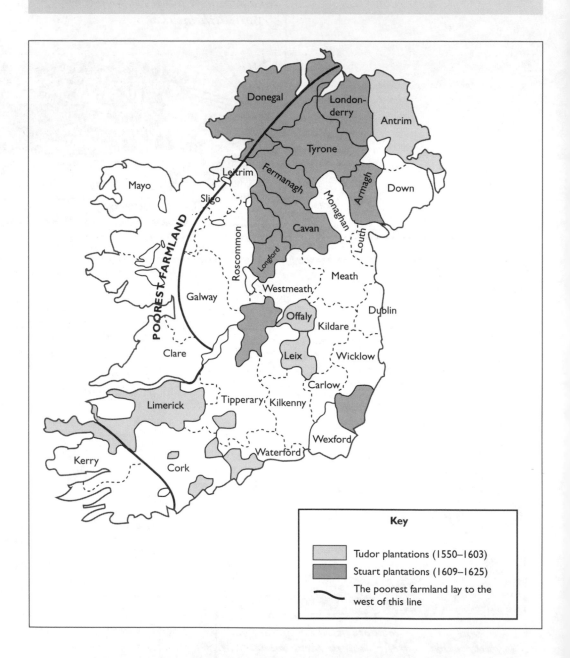

Key

Tudor plantations (1550–1603)

Stuart plantations (1609–1625)

The poorest farmland lay to the west of this line

Section D Parliament's unity destroyed: the Grand Remonstrance, November–December 1641

At the end of 1641, the King's leading critics in Parliament were aware that they were losing support. They decided to make a direct appeal to the people to support their cause. They outlined their demands in the Grand Remonstrance, a lengthy document, which they presented to the King and circulated throughout the country. It described the abuses of government during the 1630s and early 1640s and listed the various reforms that had already been achieved; it also identified those who had obstructed the reform work during the preceding year and pointed out what still needed to be done. When the Grand Remonstrance was introduced to the House of Commons, in November 1641, it split MPs right down the middle; 159 MPs voted for it and 148 against, while another third of the members stayed away from Westminster altogether. In a subsequent, equally narrow, vote the MPs agreed to print copies of the Remonstrance and publish it throughout the kingdom. These debates revealed that by the end of 1641 the MPs of the Long Parliament who had previously been united, were now divided into Royalist, Parliamentarian and neutralist parties.

● **SOURCE 3.10**

In a petition attached to the Grand REMONSTRANCE, those who had drawn it up made a number of points to Charles.

The duty which we owe to your Majesty and our country cannot but make us very sensible and apprehensive, that the multiplicity, sharpness and MALIGNITY of those evils under which we have now many years suffered, are fomented and cherished by a corrupt and ill-affected party, who amongst others their mischievous devices for the alteration of religion and government, have sought by many false scandals and IMPUTATIONS, cunningly INSINUATED and dispersed amongst the people to blemish and disgrace our proceedings in this Parliament, and to get themselves a party and faction amongst your subjects, for the better strengthening themselves in their wicked courses, and hindering those provisions and remedies which might, by the wisdom of your Majesty and counsel of Parliament, be opposed against them.

For preventing whereof, and the better information of Your Majesty, your Peers and all other loyal subjects, we have been necessitated to make a declaration of the state of the kingdom, both before and since the assembly of this Parliament, unto this time, which we do humbly present to your Majesty, without the least intention to lay any blemish upon your royal person, but only to represent how your royal authority and trust have been abused, to the great prejudice and danger of your Majesty, and of all your good subjects.

And because we have reason to believe that those malignant parties whose proceedings evidently appear to be mainly for the advantage and increase of Popery … We your most humble and obedient servants, do with all faithfulness and humility beseech your Majesty:

That you will be graciously pleased to concur with the humble desires of your people in a Parliamentary way, for the preserving the peace and safety of the kingdom from the malicious designs of the Popish party:

For depriving the bishops of their votes in Parliament, and abridging their immoderate power usurped over the clergy …

For the taking away such oppressions in religion, church government and discipline, as have been brought in and fomented by them.

That your Majesty will likewise be pleased to remove from your council all such as persist to favour or promote any of those pressures and corruptions wherewith your people have been grieved; and that for the future your Majesty will VOUCHSAFE to employ such persons in your great and public affairs, and to take such near you in places of trust, as your Parliament may have cause to confide in …

We confess our intention is, and our endeavours have been, to reduce within bounds that exorbitant power which the prelates have assumed to themselves, so contrary both to the Word of God, and to the laws of the land, to which end we passed the Bill removing them from the temporal power and employments …

And the better to effect the intended reformation, we desire there may be a general synod of the most grave, pious, learned and judicious divines of this island; assisted with some from foreign parts, professing the same religion with us, who may consider of all things necessary for the peace and good government of the Church …

That his Majesty be humbly petitioned by both Houses to employ such councillors, ambassadors and other ministers, in managing his business at home and abroad as the Parliament may have cause to confide in, without which we cannot give his Majesty such supplies for support of his own estate, nor such assistance to the Protestant party beyond the sea, as is desired …

That all Councillors of State may be sworn to observe those laws which concern the subject of his liberty, that they may likewise take an oath not to receive or give reward or pension from any foreign prince, but such as they shall within some reasonable time discover to the Lords of his Majesty's Council.

imputations: *suggestions*

insinuated: *introduced*

malignity: *wickedness*

Remonstrance: *protest*

vouchsafe: *agree*

● **SOURCE 3.11**

This reaction of a Royalist to the Remonstrance was published in 1701.

Upon the King's return out of Scotland, the City of London's splendid entertainment of him and the discourses that flew in all parts of the ample satisfaction the King had given (both which they foresaw before it was put on execution), make them prepare so foul a

Remonstrance to give the King his first entertainment amongst them, that a blacker libel could not be framed either against his person or government; and it passed so tumultuously two or three nights before the King came to town, that at three of the clock in the morning, when they voted it, I thought we had all sat in the valley of the shadow of death, for we, like Joab's and Abner's young men, had catched each other's locks, and sheathed our swords in each other's bowels, had not the sagacity and great calmness of Mr Hampden by a short speech prevented it, and led us to defer our angry debate until the next morning.

1 Who did the compilers of the Remonstrance accuse of obstructing their reform work?

2 Describe the attitude towards the King in the Remonstrance. What do you think are the likely reasons for this?

3 Summarise the main political and religious demands contained in the Grand Remonstrance.

4 Were the authors of the Remonstrance more worried about recent political developments or religious innovations?

5 Prepare a speech against the Grand Remonstrance that might have been made by one of the 148 MPs who voted against it.

● **SOURCE 3.12**

At the end of December 1641, after several delays, Charles responded to the Remonstrance.

abridging: *reducing*

innovations: *novelties*

inordinate: *excessive*

preamble: *preface*

premises: *principles*

schismatics and **separatists:** *those who wished to break away from the national Church*

To the petition we say that ... there are divers things in the PREAMBLE of it which we are so far from admitting that we profess we cannot at all understand them ... so that the prayers of your petition are grounded upon such PREMISES as we must in no wise admit; yet notwithstanding, we are pleased to give this answer to you.

To the first, concerning religion ... we say that, for preserving the peace and safety of this kingdom from the designs of the Popish party, we have, and will still, concur with all the just desires of our people in a Parliamentary way: [but] that, for the depriving the bishops of their votes in Parliament, we would have you consider that their right is grounded upon the fundamental law of the kingdom and constitution of Parliament ...

As for the ABRIDGING of the INORDINATE power of the clergy, we conceive that the taking away of the High Commission Court hath well moderated that ...

Unto that clause which concerneth corruptions (as you style them) in religion ... for any illegal INNOVATIONS which may have crept in, we shall willingly concur in the removal of them ... But we are very sorry to hear, in such general terms, corruption in religion objected, since we are persuaded in our conscience that no Church can be found upon earth that professeth the true religion with more purity of doctrine than the Church of England doth, nor where the government and discipline are jointly more beautified and free from superstition than as they are here established by law, which, by the grace of God, we will with constancy maintain (while we live) in their purity and glory, not only against all invasions of Popery, but also from the irreverence of those many SCHISMATICS and SEPARATISTS, wherewith of late this kingdom and city abounds ...

To the second prayer of the petition, concerning the removal and choice of councillors, we know not any of our Council to whom the character set forth in the petition can belong ... it is the undoubted right of the Crown of England to call such persons to our secret counsels, to public employment and our particular service as we shall think fit ...

1 What was Charles I's reply to the demands for further reforms contained in the Grand Remonstrance?

2 How did Charles I defend his government against the accusations in the Remonstrance?

3 How do you think the supporters of the Remonstrance would have reacted to Charles I's reply?

Clear evidence of the divisive nature of the Grand Remonstrance, and the way it drove a wedge between the moderates and radicals in Parliament, is provided by the debate on the document in the House of Commons. John Pym spoke strongly in favour of its acceptance.

● **SOURCE 3.13**

Notes made by Sir Ralph Verney MP on Pym's speech on the Grand Remonstrance

enjoined: *ordered*

idolatry: *worship of idols*

prophesy: *predict the future*

The honour of the King lies in the safety of the people, and we must tell the truth; the plots have been very near the King, all driven home to the court and the popish party.

Nothing but a declaration can take away the accusations that lie upon us.

We have suffered so much by councillors of the King's choosing, that we desire him to advise with us about it, and many of his servants move him about them, and why may not Parliament?

Altar-worship is IDOLATRY, and that was ENJOINED by the bishops in all their cathedrals.

The matter of the declaration is not fit for the Lords, for the matters were only agitated in this House, and again many of them are accused by it.

The declaration doth not PROPHESY, but says what is fit, and may easily be done.

Remonstrances are not directed either to the King or the people, but show the acts of this House.

This declaration will bind the people's hearts to us, when they see how we have been used.

1   Why did Pym believe the Remonstrance should be approved?

2   Why does he not want it to be considered by the House of Lords?

3   What questions would you want to ask about this source in order to decide whether it provides reliable evidence of Pym's speech – and why?

● **SOURCE 3.14**

Sir Edward Dering, the moderate MP for Kent, viewed the Remonstrance very differently. He was deeply disturbed by both its contents and the decision to publish it. The following is an extract from Dering's speech.

affirmative: *supportive*

descension: *spreading downwards*

pernicious: *evil*

presently: *immediately*

represent: *point out*

wherefore: *why*

This Remonstrance is now in progress upon its last foot in this House; I must give a vote unto it, one way or other. My conscience bids me not to dare to be AFFIRMATIVE: so sings the bird in my breast and I do cheerfully believe the tune to be good.

This Remonstrance, whensoever it passeth, will make such an impression and leave such a character behind, both of his Majesty, the people, the Parliament and of his present church and state, as no time shall ever eat it out whilst histories are written and men have eyes to read them …

WHEREFORE is this DESCENSION from a Parliament to a people? …

I did never look for it of my predecessors in this place, nor shall do from my successors. I do here profess that I do not know any one soul in all that country [Kent], for which I have the honour to serve, who looks for this at your hands. They do humbly and heartily thank you for so many good laws and statutes already enacted, and pray for more; that is the language best understood of them and most welcome to them. They do not expect to hear any other stories of what you have done, much less promises of what you will do.

Mr Speaker, when I first heard of a Remonstrance, I PRESENTLY imagined that like faithful councillors, we should hold up a glass unto his Majesty: I thought to REPRESENT unto the King the wicked counsels of PERNICIOUS councillors; the restless turbulency of practical Papists; the treachery of false judges; the bold innovations and some superstition brought in by some pragmatical bishops and the rotten part of the clergy.

I did not dream that we should remonstrate downward, tell stories to the people and talk of the King as a third person.

The use and end of such [a] Remonstrance I understand not; a least, I hope I do not.

1   In what ways does Dering agree with the authors of the Remonstrance?

2   What was Sir Edward Dering's main objection to the Grand Remonstrance?

3   What do you think he is referring to when he thanks Parliament for 'the many good laws and statutes already enacted'?

4   How do you think Dering voted for:

a) the Remonstrance

b) the printing of it?

54

1640–2: Why did the political crisis of 1640 become civil war?

Section E The King raises the stakes: Charles I's attempted arrest of the Five Members in January 1642

In December 1641, Parliament began discussing the Militia Bill, a measure to give it control of the army. There were serious protests in London when Charles attempted to replace a popular commander of the Tower of London. In addition, Pym's supporters won control of London City Council and, at the end of the month, Parliament ordered the imprisonment of twelve bishops.

In January 1642, Charles I came under intense pressure from some of his advisers, and particularly from his Queen, Henrietta Maria, to strike against his principal enemies in Parliament. On 3 January, he instructed the Lord Keeper to draw up charges of treason against five MPs – John Pym, John Hampden, William Strode, Denzil Holles and Sir Arthur Haselrig – and one peer, Lord Kimbolton. The charges are set out in Source 3.15.

● **SOURCE 3.15**

The charges against the Five Members

aspersions: *attacks*

countenanced: *planned*

endeavoured: *tried*

tumults: *disturbances*

1 That they have traitorously ENDEAVOURED to subvert the fundamental laws and government of the kingdom of England, to deprive the King of his regal power, and to place in subjects an arbitrary and tyrannical power over the lives, liberties and estates of his Majesty's liege people.

2 That they have traitorously endeavoured, by many foul ASPERSIONS upon his Majesty and his government, to alienate the affections of his people, and to make his Majesty odious unto them.

3 That they have endeavoured to draw his Majesty's late army to disobedience to his Majesty's commands, and to side with them in their traitorous designs.

4 That they have traitorously invited and encouraged a foreign power to invade his Majesty's kingdom of England.

5 That they have traitorously endeavoured to subvert the rights and very being of Parliament.

6 That for the completing of their traitorous designs they have endeavoured … by force and terror to compel the Parliament to join with them in their traitorous designs, and to that end have actually raised and COUNTENANCED TUMULTS against the King and Parliament.

7 And they have traitorously conspired to levy, and actually have levied war against the King.

---

1   What evidence could the King have used to support his accusations that the MPs had:

   a) tried 'to deprive the King of his regal powers'
   b) made 'many foul aspersions upon his Majesty'
   c) 'invited and encouraged a foreign power to invade'
   d) 'endeavoured to subvert the rights and very being of Parliament'
   e) 'raised and countenanced tumults'
   f) 'levied war against the King'?

2   Prepare a speech by one of the five MPs in which he defends himself against these accusations.

On the next day, 4 January, Charles went to Westminster with an armed guard and burst into the House of Commons to arrest the five MPs. They had already been warned of his intentions, however, and had gone into hiding in the City of London. This serious breach of Parliamentary privilege horrified the MPs and destroyed the last remains of trust between the King and his opponents in Parliament.

The next four sources are accounts of the incident.

● **SOURCE 3.16**

The Attempted Arrest of the Five Members, a nineteenth-century painting

● **SOURCE 3.17**

The version of the King's adviser, Edward Hyde, from his *History of the Rebellion,* published in 1702–4

---

privilege: *Parliamentary protection*

thither: *there*

The next day in the afternoon, the King, attended only by his own guard and some few gentlemen, who put themselves into their company in the way came to the house of commons; and commanding all his attendants to wait at the door and to give offence to no man, himself with his nephew, the prince elector [Charles Louis], went into the house, to the great amazement of all: and the speaker leaving the chair, the King went into it and told the house 'he was sorry for that occasion of coming to them; that yesterday he had sent his sergeant at arms to apprehend some that by his command were accused of high treason, whereunto he expected obedience, but instead thereof he had received a message. He declared to them that no King of England had ever been, or should be, more careful to maintain their PRIVILEGES, than he would be; but that in cases of treason no man had privilege; and therefore he came to see if any of those persons, whom he had accused, were there; for he was resolved to have them, wheresoever he should find them: and looking then about, and asking the speaker whether they were in the house, and he making no answer, he [Charles] said he perceived the birds were all flown, but expected they should be sent to him as soon as they returned THITHER; and assured them in the word of a King, that he never intended any force, but would proceed against them in a fair and legal way'; and so returned to Whitehall.

● **SOURCE 3.18**

The account of one of the MPs, Sir Simonds D'Ewes

---

espy: *see*

issue: *event, outcome*

uncovered our heads: *took off our hats*

About three of the clock we had notice that His Majesty was coming from Whitehall to Westminster with a great company of armed men, but it proved otherwise in the ISSUE that there were only some of the officers who served in His Majesty's late army and some other loose persons to the number of about some 400.

Mr Pym and the other four members of our house who stood accused by His Majesty's authority of high treason, knowing that His Majesty was coming to the House of Commons, did withdraw out of it, the house leaving it to their own liberty whether they would withdraw or stay within, and it was a pretty while before Mr Strode could be persuaded to it. His Majesty came into the house with Charles, Prince Elector Palatine with him a little after three of the clock in the afternoon, who all stood up and UNCOVERED OUR HEADS and the Speaker stood up just before his chair. His Majesty as he came up along the house came for the most part of the way uncovered, also bowing to either side of the house, and we all bowed again towards him, and so he went to the Speaker's chair on the left hand of it, coming up close by the place

1640–2: Why did the political crisis of 1640 become civil war?

56

where I sat, between the south end of the clerk's table and me. He first spake to the Speaker, saying 'Mr Speaker, I must for a time make bold with your chair', the rest of what passage doth here follow at large as it was taken in characters by Mr Rushworth, the clerk's assistant. The speech itself is the greatest part of it printed by His Majesty's command out of the said Mr Rushworth's notes, but the King caused all that to be left out, viz. when he asked for Mr Pym whether he were present or not, and when there followed a general silence that nobody would answer him, and he then asked for Mr Holles whether he was present, and when nobody answered him, he pressed the speaker to tell him, who kneeling down did very wisely desire His Majesty to pardon him, saying that he could neither see nor speak but by command of the house, to which the King answered 'Well 'tis no matter, I think my eyes are as good as another's', and he then looked round about the house a pretty whiles to see if he could ESPY any of them … After he had ended his speech he went out of the house in a more discontented and angry passion than when he came in … the Speaker having adjourned the house … we rose about half an hour after three of the clock in the afternoon, little imagining for the present, at least the greater part of us, the extreme danger we had escaped through God's providence.

For the design was to have taken out of our house by force and violence the said five members, if we had refused to have delivered them up peaceably and willingly, which for the preservation of the privileges of our house we must have refused. And in the taking of them away, they were to have set upon us all, if we had resisted in an hostile manner. It is very true that the plot was so contrived as that the King should have withdrawn out of the house … but 'tis most likely that those ruffians being about 80 in number who were gotten into the said lobby, being armed all of them with swords and some of them with pistols ready charged, were so thirsty after innocent blood as they would scarce have stayed the watchword if those members had been there, but would have begun their violence as soon as they had understood of our denial, to the hazard of the persons of the King and Prince Elector as well as us …

● SOURCE 3.19

The official account of Parliament

… the next day His Majesty in his royal person came to the said House, attended with a great multitude of men armed in a warlike manner with HALBERDS, swords and pistols, who came up to the very door of the House … and His Majesty, having placed himself in the Speaker's chair demanded of them the persons of the said members to be delivered unto him, which is a high breach of the rights and privileges of Parliament, and inconsistent with the liberties and freedoms thereof … Many soldiers, Papists and others, to the number of about five hundred, came with his Majesty … armed with swords, pistols and other weapons, and divers of them pressed to the door of the said House, thrust away the door-keepers … some holding up their pistols ready cocked near the said door and saying 'I am a good marksman; I can hit right, I warrant you' … and when several members of the House of Commons were coming in the House, their attendants desiring that room might be made for them, some of the said soldiers answered, 'A pox of God confound them' and others said 'A pox take the House of Commons, let them come and be hanged'; … and upon the king's return out of the said House, many of them by wicked oaths and otherwise expressed much discontent that some members of the said House for whom they came were not there … afterwards some of them being demanded what they thought the said company intended to have done, answered that, QUESTIONLESS, in the posture they were set, if the word had been given, they should have fallen upon the House of Commons and have cut all their throats.

halberd: *combined spear and battle-axe*

questionless: *without a doubt*

1 What treasonable activities did Charles accuse the five MPs of having committed?

2 How did Charles I's actions violate the privileges of the House of Commons?

3 How reliable is Source 3.16 as evidence of the attempted arrest?

4 In what ways do the three written accounts agree about what happened?

5 In what ways do they disagree?

6 How would you explain the differences?

7 Edward Hyde was a Royalist in the Civil War. Did he support the arrest of the Five Members?

8 Comment on the tone and language of these three written descriptions of what happened.

9 Many historians have suggested that the attempted arrest of the Five Members made a civil war much more likely. Do you agree?

Section F Calls to arms: the King and Parliament raise their armies

Shortly after this unsuccessful attempt to arrest the five MPs, Charles decided to leave London. After spending some time at Windsor, he journeyed north and, by the early summer, he had established his court at York. By this time both he and his opponents, realising that armed conflict was becoming increasingly unavoidable, had begun to raise troops. Although Parliament had no legal right to do so, in early March 1642 it passed the Militia Ordinance which set out detailed instructions for the raising of a Parliamentary army.

● **SOURCE 3.20**

Parliament's ORDINANCE of March 1642

arrayed: *drawn up*

effect: *result*

Lieutenant: *Lord Lieutenant or chief military commander*

meet: *ready*

Ordinance: *a declaration of Parliament approved by Lords and Commons and issued as a law but without the King's approval*

take muster: *gather together and inspect*

singular: *every*

Whereas there hath been of late a most dangerous and desperate design upon the House of Commons, which we have just cause to believe to be an EFFECT of the bloody counsels of the Papists and other ill-affected persons who have already raised a rebellion in the kingdom of Ireland; and by reason of many discoveries we cannot but fear they will proceed not only to stir up the like rebellion and insurrections in this kingdom of England, but also to back them with forces from abroad.

For the safety of His Majesty's person, the Parliament and kingdom in this time of imminent danger: It is ordained by the Lords and Commons now in Parliament assembled that Henry, Earl of Holland, shall be LIEUTENANT of the County of Berks, Oliver, Earl of Bolingbroke, shall be Lieutenant of the County of Bedford [the lieutenants of all the other counties are then listed] … And shall severally and respectively have power to assemble and call together all and SINGULAR His Majesty's subjects within the said several and respective counties and places … that are MEET and fit for wars, and them to train and exercise and put in readiness, and them after their abilities and faculties well and sufficiently from time to time cause to be ARRAYED and weaponed, and to TAKE MUSTER of them in places most fit for that purpose … And it is further ordained, that any such persons as shall not obey [the lieutenants] in any of the premises, shall answer their neglect and contempt to the Lords and Commons in a Parliamentary way …

1 How did Parliament justify the raising of an army?

2 To what were they referring when they claimed 'there hath been of late a most dangerous and desperate design upon the House of Commons'?

3 Whom do the MPs blame for this 'design'?

4 Why did they claim to be raising their army to protect the King?

5 Why would the King and his supporters in Parliament have been so opposed to the Militia Ordinance?

● **SOURCE 3.21**

Charles responded in late May 1642 with a royal proclamation that condemned the Militia Ordinance.

levy: *raise*

trained band: *military reserve force*

… We do, therefore, by this our Proclamation expressly charge and command all our sheriffs, and all colonels, sergeant-majors, captains, officers and soldiers, belonging to the TRAINED BANDS of this kingdom, and likewise all high and petty constables, and all other officers and subjects whatsoever, upon their allegiance, and as they tender the peace of this our kingdom, not to muster, LEVY, raise or march, or to summon or warn, upon any warrant, order or ordinance from one or both of our Houses of Parliament … any of our trained bands or other forces … and in case any of our trained bands shall rise or gather together contrary to this our command, we shall then call them in due time to a strict account, and proceed legally against them as violators of the laws and disturbers of the peace of this kingdom.

Commission of Array: *the traditional method of raising the country's army*

A few days later Charles issued a COMMISSION OF ARRAY, which called on the leading inhabitants of each county to raise troops for him. On 12 June he sent a letter to the commissioners in Leicestershire.

58

1640–2: Why did the political crisis of 1640 become civil war?

● **SOURCE 3.22**

A letter from Charles I to the commissioners in Leicestershire

… We, therefore, considering that by the laws of the realm it belongeth to us to order and govern the militia of the kingdom, have thereupon by our Proclamation of 27 May last, prohibited all manner of persons whatsoever upon their allegiance to muster, levy or summon upon any warrant, order or ordinance from one or both Houses of Parliament … we have thought fit to refer it to that ancient legal way of disposing the power of the militia … authorising you … to array and train our people, and to apportion and assess such persons as have estates and are not able to bear arms, to find arms for other men in a reasonable and moderate proportion; and to conduct them so arrayed, as well to the coasts as to other places, for the opposition and destruction of our enemies in case of danger …

The issuing of these contradictory orders put many individuals in a serious dilemma. This is illustrated in Source 3.23.

● **SOURCE 3.23**

A letter written by the Norfolk MP Sir Thomas Knyvett to his wife in the early summer of 1642

advise upon: *consider*

in great straits: *very undecided*

musterings: *gatherings of troops*

trenches: *touches*

I cannot let any opportunity pass without telling of thee how I do … I would to God I could write thee any good news, but that is impossible so long as the spirit of contradiction reigns between King and Parliament higher still than ever, and 'tis to be feared this threatening storm will not be allayed without some showers (I pray God, not a deluge) of blood. The one party now grows as resolute as the other is obstinate … Oh, sweetheart, I am now IN GREAT STRAITS what to do. Walking this morning at Westminster, Sir John Potts [another Norfolk MP] saluted me with a commission from the Lord of Warwick to take upon me, by virtue of an Ordinance of Parliament, my company and command again. I was surprised what to do, whether to take or refuse. 'Twas no place to dispute, so I took it and desired some time to ADVISE UPON it. I had not received this many hours, but I met with a Declaration point blank against it by the King. This distraction made me to advise with some understanding men what condition I stand in, which is no other than a great many men of quality do. What further commands we shall receive to put this ordinance in execution, if they run in a way that TRENCHES upon my obedience against [to] the King, I shall do according to my conscience; and this is the resolution of all honest men that I can speak with. In the meantime I hold it good wisdom and security to keep my company as close to me as I can in these dangerous times, and to stay out of the way of new masters till these first MUSTERINGS be over.

---

1 Explain why Thomas Knyvett was in a serious dilemma in the summer of 1642.

2 What do you think he did decide to do in the end:

   a) support the King
   b) support Parliament
   c) remain neutral?

3 Until recently, historians thought that the country was divided down the middle for King or Parliament in 1642. In the light of this, do you think that Source 3.23 is an important source?

4 Why did Charles stress that the Commission of Array was the 'ancient, legal' way of raising an army?

5 What considerations did individuals like Knyvett have to take into account before deciding whether to raise troops for one side or the other?

Section G Could war against the King be justified? The arguments over resistance

Following the passing of the Militia Ordinance, many of those sympathetic to Parliament began to search their consciences over the difficult question of whether it could ever be justifiable to take up arms against a sovereign, who had not only a legal but also a divine right to rule. One way Parliament attempted to justify publicly its decision to raise an army against the King was by claiming that it would actually be fighting on behalf of Charles to rescue him from the influence of evil councillors who had corrupted him. For this reason, many of Parliament's declarations from this period state that it has taken up arms in support of 'King and Parliament'. While some of the MPs genuinely believed this theory, others merely saw it as the most acceptable way of presenting their cause.

A number of writers tackled the question of resistance to authority more directly. Among them were the fiery Puritan preacher Stephen Marshall and the conservative lawyer Sir John Spelman, both of whom drew upon examples from the Bible to support their views.

Stephen Marshall viewed the imminent war as a struggle between the true religion of the Puritans and the Satanic forces of evil in the form of the King and his supporters. For him, resistance was not only a right but a duty.

● **SOURCE 3.24**

This is an extract from Stephen Marshall's sermon MEROZ Cursed, which he preached to Parliament at the end of February 1642 and which was printed soon after.

like: *likely*

Meroz: *the city mentioned in the Old Testament that had been cursed by God for refusing to take up his cause*

Nehemiah: *a Hebrew prophet*

… It may be that some of you may be called as soldiers to spend your blood in the Church's cause. If you knew the honour and the reward that belongs to such a service, you would say, as the martyr once, Had every hair on your head a life, you would venture them all in the Church's cause. It may be others of you may with NEHEMIAH be called from your own ease and honour to some wearisome task, embrace it readily. It is LIKE your collections and contributions will be more frequent … Only remember this, that what you give in this cause is interpreted by Christ as given to his own person … And whatsoever else the Lord and his church may have any need of you, remember that God's blessing is upon them that come to help him and that all are cursed who come not to the help of the Lord.

● **SOURCE 3.25**

A few months later Sir John Spelman outlined his case in his *Certain Considerations upon the Duties of Princes and People.* He referred to the story of David and Saul.

sacrilege: *the abuse of sacred things or people*

strangers: *foreigners*

… Saul was king, but misgoverning himself and his kingdom … was deposed, and David was by God's express command anointed to be king. All which notwithstanding, neither David nor the people ever sought to depose him, to renounce obedience unto him, to combine against him, question his government, or so much meddle with the ordering of any of the affairs that belonged to the king … Now whatsoever Saul was, or whatsoever he had done, neither his falling from God, nor God's declaring him rejected … could dissolve the duty of his subjects, nor make it lawful for them to lay their hands on him, no not [even] when he was in wicked hostility against them. But Saul, in David's account, was still the Lord's anointed, still a sacred person, still David's master … Neither is the anointing of kings a thing sacred as to their own subjects only, but the regard thereof is required at the hands of STRANGERS also, because of the profanation and SACRILEGE that in the violation of their persons is committed even against God … And therefore all actions of subjects that in the progress of them tend or by way threaten to arrive at that upshot are unlawful, foul and wicked, and not only [are] the actors themselves wicked but their assistants, favourers and those that wish them well [too].

1 Whom did Marshall (Source 3.24) and Spelman (Source 3.25) decide to support and why?

2 Why was it so important at that time to find arguments in the Bible to support people's views?

Section H The last chance for peace: the Nineteen Propositions, June 1642

At the beginning of June 1642, Parliament made one last public attempt to avoid war by sending the King the Nineteen Propositions. Some historians have argued that these propositions demanded large concessions and were less concerned to reach a peaceful settlement than to win support from the population at large. Charles I's answer to the Nineteen Propositions was carefully constructed with public opinion in mind, and attempted to portray him as a moderate man faced by a group of dangerous, revolutionary and

60

1640–2: Why did the political crisis of 1640 become civil war?

unreasonable opponents. Soon afterwards, 23 MPs left Westminster to join Charles in York. This left 300 MPs in Parliament.

There were now two rival centres of authority in England, each claiming the obedience of the rest of the population.

● **SOURCE 3.26**

Extracts from the Nineteen Propositions, June 1642

adherents: supporters

approbation: approval

clear: clear the name of

liturgy: worship, services

United Provinces: Holland

1 That the Lords and others of your Majesty's Privy Council and such great officers and ministers of state … may be put from your Privy Council and from those offices and employments, excepting such as shall be approved of by both Houses of Parliament …

2 That the great affairs of the kingdom may not be concluded or transacted by the advice of private men, or by unknown or unsworn councillors, but that such matters as concern the public … may be debated, resolved and transacted only in Parliament …

4 That he or they unto whom the government and education of the King's children shall be committed shall be approved of by both Houses of Parliament …

5 That no marriage shall be concluded or treated for any of the King's children, with any foreign prince … without the consent of Parliament …

6 That the laws in force against Jesuits, priests, and Popish recusants be strictly put in execution, without any toleration or dispensation to the contrary …

7 That the votes of Popish Lords in the House of Peers may be taken away.

8 That your Majesty would be pleased to consent that such reformation be made of the Church government and LITURGY as both Houses of Parliament shall advise …

9 That your Majesty will be pleased to rest satisfied with the course that the Lords and Commons have appointed for ordering the militia, until the same shall be further settled by a bill …

15 That the forts and castles of this kingdom may be put under the command and custody of such persons as your Majesty shall appoint with the APPROBATION of your Parliament …

16 That the extraordinary guards and military forces now attending your Majesty may be removed and discharged …

17 That your Majesty will be pleased to enter into a more strict alliance with the States of the UNITED PROVINCES, and other neighbouring princes and states of the Protestant religion, for the defence and maintenance thereof, against all designs and attempts of the Pope and his ADHERENTS to subvert and suppress it.

18 That your Majesty will be pleased, by Act of Parliament, to CLEAR the Lord Kimbolton, and the Five Members of the House of Commons, in such manner that future Parliaments may be secured from the consequences thereof.

1 List the demands of the Nineteen Propositions under the following headings:

  a) government/political
  b) military
  c) religious
  d) foreign policy
  e) other.

2 'A genuine attempt to reach a peaceful settlement with the King'.
  'A propaganda exercise to win support with no apparent willingness to compromise. It required the King's complete surrender.'
  Which of these two statements about the Nineteen Propositions do you find more acceptable? Explain your reasons.

3 Is it likely that Charles would agree to these demands?

4 Why were many moderate MPs horrified by these demands?

● **SOURCE 3.27**

Charles I's reply to the Nineteen Propositions, 18 June 1642

democracy: here this means the people represented by a property-owning House of Commons of gentry, merchants and lawyers.

There being three kinds of government among men: absolute monarchy, aristocracy and DEMOCRACY … [all these are efficient] as long as the balance hangs even between the three estates … [Each on its own]: the ill of the absolute monarchy is tyranny, the ill of the aristocracy is faction and division, the ills of the democracy are tumults, violence and licentiousness.

In this kingdom laws are made jointly by a king, by a House of Lords and by a House of Commons … The government according to these laws is trusted to the King … The prince may not make use of this high and perpetual power to the hurt of those for whose good he hath it … The House of Commons (an excellent convener of liberty, but never intended for any share in government, or in choosing of them that govern) is solely entrusted with the levy of money, and impeaching of those who for their own ends have violated the law … The Lords, being entrusted with the judiciary power, are an excellent screen between the prince and the people, to assist each against the encroachments of the other.

1 What according to Charles were the proper functions of:

a) the King
b) the House of Commons
c) the House of Lords
d) all three together?

2 What does he suggest would be the consequences of any one of these gaining supreme power?

3 In the light of your study of Charles I's reign since 1625, how convincing do you find his reply to be as evidence of his real beliefs about how the country should be governed?

4 Suggest reasons why Charles made his reply in the way he did.

5 Which do you think was more likely to win support, the Nineteen Propositions or Charles I's reply? Explain the reasons for your choice.

Section I   For King or Parliament: taking sides

By the middle of the summer of 1642 both King and Parliament were busy raising men for their armies. All over the country, individuals were having to decide whether to give active support to one side or the other. We will now consider some sources that give an insight into why individuals decided to fight for one side or the other.

Royalists

Some of the King's supporters, especially the younger ones, were particularly eager to take up arms. During the summer, hundreds of young 'cavaliers' flocked to York to join Charles. One man who would probably have been amongst them, had he not already been imprisoned by Parliament in London, was the handsome and wealthy young poet Richard Lovelace.

● **SOURCE 3.28**

One of the poems Lovelace wrote around this time, *To Lucasta, Going to the Warres,* outlines a view of the approaching war that was shared by many of these cavaliers.

Tell me not (Sweet) I am unkind
that from the Nunnery
Of thy chaste breast and quiet mind
To War and Arms I fly

True; a new Mistress now I chase
The first foe in the field
And with a stronger Faith Embrace
A Sword, A Horse, a Shield

Yet this Inconstancy is such
As you too shall adore
I could not love thee (Dear) so much
Loved I not Honour more

1 What according to the poem seem to have been Lovelace's main reasons for supporting Charles?

2 What was Lovelace's view of the approaching war?

3 What image of the cavalier does the poem convey?

Some other Royalists viewed the conflict in a far less romantic light, and supported the King more reluctantly. One such was the courtier Sir Edmund Verney of Claydon in Buckinghamshire.

● **SOURCE 3.29**

Sir Edmund Verney and his tomb, painted by Anthony Van Dyck

● **SOURCE 3.30**

In his *History of the Rebellion*, Edward Hyde recounted the following words that Verney had spoken to him in the summer of 1642.

… for my part I do not like the quarrel, and do heartily wish that the King would yield and consent to what they [Parliament] desire; so that my conscience is only concerned in honour and in gratitude to follow my master. I have eaten his bread, and served him near thirty years, and will not do so base a thing as to forsake him; and choose rather to lose my life (which I am sure I shall do) to preserve and defend those things which are against my conscience to preserve and defend: for I will deal freely with you, I have no reverence for the bishops, for whom this quarrel [subsists] …

1 In what ways did Verney agree with Parliament?

2 In what ways did he agree with the King?

3 What was the main deciding factor for Verney to support the King?

4 What does Verney believe is the most important issue over which the war was fought?

Parliamentarians

Among the more enthusiastic supporters of Parliament were Nehemiah Wharton and Brilliana, Lady Harley. Wharton was a London apprentice who joined the Parliamentary forces in the summer of 1642 and marched with them into the Midlands. During the autumn he sent a series of letters to his old master in London in which he described the activities of the troops. A few weeks after writing these letters he was killed at the Battle of Edgehill.

● **SOURCE 3.31**

Extracts from letters sent by Nehemiah Wharton

16 August: On 8th August we marched to Acton … The next day, Tuesday, several of our soldiers sallied out to the house of one Penruddock a Papist and, being basely affronted by him and his dog, entered his house and pillaged him to the purpose. This day also the soldiers got into the church, defaced the ancient and sacred glazed pictures and burned the holy rails. Wednesday Mr Love gave us a famous sermon, this day also the soldiers brought the holy rails from Chiswick and burned them in the town …

13 September: Sabbath day morning, Mr [Stephen] Marshall, that worthy champion of Christ, preached to us; in the afternoon Mr Ash ...

30 September: [from Worcester, after a skirmish with some Royalists] They boast wonderfully and swear most hellishly that the next time they meet us they will make but a mouthful of us. But I am persuaded the Lord hath given them this small victory that they may in the day of battle come on more presumptuously to their own destruction; in which battle though I and many thousands more may be cut off, yet I am confident the LORD OF HOSTS will in the end triumph gloriously over these horses and their cursed riders ... Our army did little think ever to have seen Worcester, but the providence of God hath brought us hither and, had it not, the city is so vile and the country so base, so papistical and ATHEISTICAL, and abominable, that it resembles SODOM and is the very emblem of GOMORRAH ... But we have handsomely handled some of them and do cull out the rest as fast as we can.

7 October: [from Hereford] The inhabitants are totally ignorant in the ways of God and much addicted to drunkenness and other vices, but principally to swearing, so that the children that have scarce learned to speak do universally swear stoutly ... Sabbath day about the time of morning prayer we went to the MINSTER, where [organ] pipes played and PUPPETS sang so sweetly that some of our soldiers could not forbear dancing in the holy choir ... The anthem ended, they fell to prayers and prayed devoutly for King, the Bishops, etc., and one of our soldiers with a loud voice said 'What never a bit for Parliament?', which offended them much more. Not satisfied with this human service, we went to divine, and passing by found some shops open and men at work, to which we gave some plain DEHORTATIONS, and went to hear Mr Sedgewick who gave us two famous sermons, which much affected the poor inhabitants who wondering said they had never heard the like before. And I believe them. The Lord move your hearts to commiserate their distresses and to send them some faithful and PAINFUL ministers ...

atheistical: *unbelieving in God*

dehortations: *criticisms*

Lord of Hosts: *God*

Minster: *cathedral*

painful: *painstaking*

puppets: *choristers*

Sodom and **Gomorrah:** *pagan cities destroyed by God in the Bible*

---

1 Why do you think Wharton joined the Parliamentary forces?

2 What does he find shocking about Worcester and Hereford?

3 Why does he disapprove of people working on Sunday?

● **SOURCE 3.32**

In July 1642, Brilliana, Lady Harley, wife of Sir Edward Harley of Brampton Bryan in Herefordshire, whose family was one of the few who supported Parliament in that largely Royalist county, wrote to her son about the impending conflict.

iniquities: *sins*

Pharaoh: *the ruler in ancient Egypt*

My dear Ned, I thank God I am not afraid. It is the Lord's cause that we have stood for and I trust, though our INIQUITIES testify against us, yet the Lord will work for his own name's sake and that He will now show the men of the world that it is hard fighting against heaven. And for comfort I think never any laid plot to root out all God's children at once but that the Lord did show Himself mightily in saving His servants and confounding his enemies as He did PHARAOH when he thought to have destroyed all Israel ... Now the intention is to root out all that fear God and surely the Lord will arise to help us.

---

1 Why is Brilliana Harley so confident that Parliament will win the Civil War?

2 On the basis of the sources you have studied in this section, what appear to have been the main differences, if any, between Royalists and Parliamentarians?

Section J **Why did some people remain neutral?**

To take up arms either for the King or for Parliament was not, however, the only option available to people in the summer of 1642. Many individuals declined to come out firmly for one side or the other. Some individuals were also reluctant to part with their money to finance the war.

64

1640–2: Why did the political crisis of 1640 become civil war?

● **SOURCE 3.33**

In his *History of the Rebellion*, Edward Hyde, Earl of Clarendon, related an amusing story about the unsuccessful attempts of the King to persuade two Nottinghamshire lords, the Earl of Kingston and Lord Deincourt, to lend him money in the summer of 1642.

administered some mirth: *caused some amusement*

parsimony: *meanness*

There was a pleasant story then much spoken of in the court which ADMINISTERED SOME MIRTH. There were two great men who lived near Nottingham, both men of great fortunes and of great PARSIMONY and known to have much money lying by them, Pierrepont, Earl of Kingston, and Leake, Lord Deincourt. To the former the Lord Capel was sent, to the latter John Ashburnham … each of them with a letter all written in the King's hand to borrow of each ten or five thousand pounds. Capel was very civilly received by the earl and entertained as well as the ill accommodation in the house and his manner of living would admit. He expressed with wonderful civil expressions of duty the great trouble he sustained in not being able to comply with his Majesty's commands. He said 'all men knew that he neither had nor could have money because he had every year of ten or a dozen past purchased a thousand pounds' land a year; and therefore he could not be imagined to have any money lying by him, which he never loved to have'. But he said he had a neighbour who lived within a few miles of him, the lord Deincourt, who was good for nothing and lived like a hog, not allowing himself necessaries, and who could not have so little as 20,000 pounds in the scurvy house in which he lived, and advised that he might be sent to, who could not deny the having of money … Ashburnham got no more money nor half so many good words … [Deincourt] told him that, though he had no money himself but was in extreme want of it, he would tell him where he might have money enough; that he had a neighbour who lived within four or five miles, the Earl of Kingston, that never did good to anybody and loved nobody but himself, who had a world of money and could furnish the King with as much as he had need of; and, if he should deny that he had money when the King sent to him, he knew where he had one trunk full and would discover it; and that he was so ill beloved and had so few friends that nobody would care how the King used him …

In some parts of the country, groups of individuals came together to make a public declaration of neutrality.

● **SOURCE 3.34**

The neutralist declaration which was drawn up in Cheshire in August 1642

fiat: *decree or order*

Hippocrates' twins: *Siamese twins*

vizt: *that is to say*

The declaration then listed a number of 'Articles to be considered of for the peace and quiet of the county'. The most important are listed here.

A Remonstrance, or declaration of us the inhabitants of the county palatine of Chester … that we owe our laws, liberties, ourselves and what else we can style ours (next to God's infinite mercies) to the goodness of his Majesty and to the great care and indefatigable pains of the honourable Parliament. To the one for discovering the variety of oppressions that had almost overwhelmed us, and preparing and advising apt remedies; To the other for crowning those wholesome counsels with a blessed FIAT, wherein the joint acts of a good king and a faithful council have so apparently concurred to the general good that we cannot but look upon all such as unworthy of future happiness who do admit for current that dangerous and disloyal distinction (which rings too loud in our ears) VIZT 'For the King' [or] 'For the Parliament'. Our loyal affections and judgements will not permit us to style them true patriots and lovers of their country that are not cordially affected to our gracious sovereign, nor them good subjects that disaffect Parliament. The King and Parliament, being like HIPPOCRATES' TWINS, they must laugh and cry, live and die together; and both are so rooted in our loyal hearts that we cannot disjoint them.

First that the commission of array and order or ordinance of Parliament for the Militia be wholly suspended in the county until such time as some course be agreed upon for the ordering of the Militia for the King and Parliament and this without disputing the legality or illegality of either but as finding of neither of them so necessary at this time as for setting them on foot to involve this county in blood …

Thirdly that no ammunition, [or] forces whatsoever shall be suffered to enter the county in a hostile manner … and whatsoever and they that shall attempt to do it, the whole county shall rise against them as enemies against the peace to be suppressed …

Sixthly, that none shall be arrested in this county as delinquents for either party but [by] a legal peaceable and quiet way, that is by the legal officers and their assistants only, and not by armed men and soldiers who may be an occasion to bring fire amongst us …

1	Why did those who drew up this declaration not wish to take sides?
2	Why were they so anxious to keep soldiers and weapons out of Cheshire?
3	How different are the reasons for neutralism given in Source 3.33 from those given in Source 3.34?

Section K Raising the standard: how did the Civil War begin?

After many months of preparation, the official beginning of the Civil War came on 22 August 1642, when Charles raised his standard at Nottingham Castle.

● **SOURCE 3.35**

Edward Hyde, Earl of Clarendon, later gave an account of this day in his *History of the Rebellion.*

conflux: *coming together*

melancholic: *sad or depressed*

presages: *signs*

regiment of foot: *a unit of foot soldiers*

… the standard was erected about six o'clock in the evening of a very stormy and tempestuous day. The King himself with a small train rode to the top of the Castle Hill, [Sir Edmund] Verney the knight marshal who was standard bearer carrying the standard which was then erected in that place with little other ceremony than the sound of drums and trumpets. MELANCHOLIC men observed many ill PRESAGES about that time. There was not one REGIMENT OF FOOT yet levied and brought thither so that the trained bands which the sheriff had drawn thither was all the strength the King had for his person and the guard of the standard. There appeared no CONFLUX of men in obedience to the proclamation; the arms and ammunition were not yet come from York and a general sadness covered the whole town, and the King himself appeared more melancholic than he used to be. The standard itself was blown down the same night it had been set up by very strong and unruly wind and could not be fixed again in a day or two till the tempest was allayed … And this was the melancholic state of the King's affairs when the standard was set up.

1   Does Clarendon believe that Charles was in a strong position to fight the Civil War in August 1642?

2   How might many people at the time have explained the blowing down of the standard?

3   What does Clarendon's account reveal about the atmosphere in which the country embarked upon the Civil War?

4   Clarendon wrote this account in the 1650s. How might this affect the accuracy of the source?

● **Summary Task**

1   In November 1640 MPs were united in their opposition to Charles I's government. Why did they become increasingly divided over the next eighteen months?

2   Does the fact that Parliament divided into Royalists and Parliamentarians provide a sufficient explanation for the outbreak of the Civil War in 1642?

3   Several events could be called 'turning points' in the drift towards Civil War:

   a) the execution of Strafford
   b) the Irish Rebellion
   c) the Grand Remonstrance
   d) the attempted arrest of the Five Members
   e) the passing of the Military Ordinance
   f) the Nineteen Propositions.

   Which do you think was the most important turning point and why?

4   The motives and actions of individuals can play an important role in causing events to happen. Referring to both their motives and their actions, do you think that Charles I or John Pym was to blame for the outbreak of the Civil War?

5   Divide into groups of Royalists, Parliamentarians and Neutrals and compare your reasons for taking the stand you have chosen. Nominate two people to argue the justice of your case against two representatives of the opposing sides.

● **Further reading**

Anthony Fletcher, *The Outbreak of the English Civil War* (Edward Arnold, 1981); Conrad Russell, *The Fall of the British Monarchies* (OUP, 1991).

These two long and very detailed accounts of events in the late 1630s and early 1640s are the most authoritative modern studies of the descent into civil war.

   For a less exhaustive but more accessible approach see Christopher Durston, 'Phoney War: England, Summer 1642', *History Today*, (June 1992).

chapter 4

How did the Civil War affect people's lives?

1642
August 22: Charles I raises his standard at Nottingham.

October 23: The inconclusive Battle of Edgehill is fought.

mid-November: Charles abandons his attempt to retake London at Turnham Green and establishes his headquarters at Oxford.

1643
February 24: Parliament introduces the weekly assessment.

March: Parliamentary Ordinance imposing sequestrations is issued.

July 5: The Royalists win the Battle of Lansdown.

July 13: The Royalists win the Battle of Roundway Down.

July 22: The excise is introduced by Parliament.

July 26: Royalists under Prince Rupert capture Bristol.

August 10: Charles lays siege to Gloucester.

September 5: The siege of Gloucester is ended by the Earl of Essex.

mid-September: An alliance is made between the English Parliament and the Scots: the Solemn League and Covenant.

September 20: The inconclusive first Battle of Newbury is fought.

December 8: John Pym dies.

1644
January 19: A Scottish army enters northern England to fight for Parliament.

July 2: Parliament and Scots victorious at the Battle of Marston Moor.

July 16: York surrenders to Parliament.

late August: Essex's Parliamentary army surrenders to Charles I in Cornwall.

October 27: The inconclusive second Battle of Newbury is fought.

1645
January 10: Archbishop William Laud is executed by Parliament.

February 15: Parliament passes the New Model Ordinance which authorises the raising of the New Model Army.

April 3: Parliament passes the Self-Denying Ordinance which excludes all Members of Parliament from serving in the New Model Army.

April and May: The New Model Army is organised.

June 14: The New Model Army wins a decisive victory against Charles I at Naseby in Northamptonshire.

July 10: The New Model Army defeats Lord Goring's Royalist army at Langport in Somerset.

September 11: Prince Rupert surrenders Bristol to the New Model Army.

October 14: Cromwell storms and sacks Basing House in Hampshire.

1646
April 27: Charles I leaves Oxford in disguise.

May 5: Charles I surrenders to the Scots in Nottinghamshire.

May 11: The New Model Army lays siege to Oxford.

June 24: Oxford surrenders to the New Model Army.

Introduction to the English Civil War

The English Civil War officially began on 22 August 1642 when Charles I raised his standard at Nottingham Castle. Following this declaration of war, he marched west to the borders of Wales and raised troops in the strongly Royalist counties of Hereford and Shropshire. By October, he was marching towards London. A Parliamentary army under the Earl of Essex was sent out of the capital to oppose him. These two armies fought out the first major pitched battle of the Civil War at Edgehill on the border of Oxfordshire and Warwickshire on 23 October 1642. Following this bloody but inconclusive encounter, Charles continued on his progress towards London, arriving at Brentford in Middlesex in mid-November. At Turnham Green, near Brentford, his advance on the capital was blocked by a force of London trained bands. Charles subsequently retreated to Oxford, which became his headquarters for the remainder of the war. As military operations were impossible in the depths of winter, fighting was not resumed until the early spring of 1643.

During the 1643 campaigning season, Royalist generals won several major victories in the West Country and captured the important city of Bristol. The Royalist Duke of Newcastle, meanwhile, was enjoying considerable success in Yorkshire. As a result, by the early autumn of 1643 the Royalists appeared to be gaining the upper hand; Charles's armies were besieging Parliament's important strategic strongholds of Gloucester and Hull and the King intended to follow their capture with a combined attack on London. Parliament, however, survived this period of crisis; the siege of Gloucester was lifted by Essex's army and Charles's subsequent advance on London was blocked by Essex and his London soldiers at the Battle of Newbury in Berkshire, which ended in stalemate.

From the beginning of 1644 the tide began to turn in Parliament's favour. At the start of the year a Scots army of 20,000 men marched into northern England to fight for the English Parliament. On 2 July the Scots and their English allies won a major victory against the King at Marston Moor near York, which gave Parliament control of northern England. This success, however, was partly offset by the disastrous defeat of Essex in Cornwall several weeks later and by the Parliamentary failure to defeat a much smaller Royalist force at the second Battle of Newbury in late October. At the end of the 1644 campaigning season, neither side had gained the decisive advantage but it was clear that Parliament possessed the greater resources. The longer the fighting continued the more likely it was to end in Parliament's favour.

During the following winter, Parliament decided to undertake a complete reorganisation of its military forces. The best units of the existing regiments were now brought together in a new national and centrally controlled force known as the New Model Army, under the command of Sir Thomas Fairfax. In addition, the commanders of Parliament's forces, especially the Earl of Essex, who was frequently criticised for his half-heartedness, were forced to resign by the Self-Denying Ordinance. Within weeks of this new army being formed, in the early summer of 1645, it had inflicted two crushing defeats on the King at the Battles of Naseby and Langport. These defeats destroyed the last Royalist armies and, in the next year, Parliamentary forces crushed any surviving centres of Royalist resistance. The Royalist headquarters at Oxford was besieged at the beginning of May 1646 and surrendered to Sir Thomas Fairfax in June. Charles had left Oxford in disguise shortly before the siege began and surrendered to the Scots at Newark in Nottinghamshire.

All wars are unpleasant experiences for those who are forced to live through them, but civil wars can be particularly divisive and barbaric. A civil war is always fought 'at home' and the enemy is not a foreign nation against which a people can unite. Often members of families find themselves fighting on opposing sides. While the English Civil War of the 1640s may not have been fought with the same level of hatred and vindictiveness as witnessed recently in Bosnia and other areas of the former Yugoslavia, it was a widespread and lengthy conflict. It exacted a heavy toll of death and injury among the combatants, and disease, malnourishment and financial ruin among the civilian population.

The first Civil War lasted four years, from the raising of the King's standard at Nottingham in August 1642 to the surrender of Oxford in the summer of 1646. Two years later, in 1648, another full-scale conflict – the second Civil War – broke out in England. From then onwards English troops continued to be involved in bitter fighting in Scotland and Ireland well into the 1650s. As a result, the 1640s was arguably the most disastrous decade in the entire history both of England and of the British Isles as a whole. The fighting brought disruption and dislocation to the whole of England, but the scale of its impact varied greatly. Those areas which were considered of most strategic importance suffered especially badly, while other regions of less military significance escaped more lightly.

The following sources will consider the impact the Civil War had on some of those who lived through it under the following headings:

- Section A What was the fighting like?
- Section B How did the armies affect local communities?
- Section C How heavy were the financial burdens of the war?

Section A **What was the fighting like?**

Battles

Between 1642 and 1651, 22 battles, each involving more than 5,000 soldiers, were fought in England. Historians have estimated that as many as 80,000 men may have been killed in these battles. If they are right, this would represent a higher proportion of the population than died during the First World War. In addition, the Civil War also involved hundreds of smaller skirmishes, and numerous attacks on, and sieges of, towns and garrisons.

Civil War battles were crude, terrifying events, involving cavalry charges and hand-to-hand fighting by the crowds of infantry, all of which resulted in a heavy toll of death and injury. Perhaps the most shocking and disturbing of these battles, if only because it was the first, was that fought at Edgehill in Warwickshire on Sunday, 23 October 1642. During three hours of intense combat, nearly 30,000 men fought themselves to an inconclusive standstill; by the evening some 1,500 men were dead and several thousand seriously injured.

● **SOURCE 4.1**

Shortly after the Battle of Edgehill, one of the participants, Captain Edward Knightley, sent this account of his experiences to a relative in London.

---

entreated: *asked*

pieces of ordnance: *cannons*

regiments of horse: *units of soldiers on horseback*

Loving cousin, I shall make so near as I can a true, though long, relation of the battle fought between the king's army and our army … On Sunday 23 October about one o'clock in the afternoon the battle did begin and continued until it was very dark; the field was very great and large and the king's forces came down a great and long hill, he had the advantage of ground and wind, and they gave a brave charge and did fight very valiantly; they were 15 Regiments of Foot and 60 REGIMENTS OF HORSE, our Horse were under 40 Regiments and our Foot 11 Regiments: my Lord General [the Earl of Essex] did give first charge, presenting them with two PIECES OF ORDNANCE which killed many of their men, and then the enemy did shoot one to us which fell 20 yards short in ploughed land and did no harm; our soldiers did many of them run away, to wit blue coats and grey coats being 2 Regiments, and there did run away 600 horse … and when I was entering the field I think 200 horse came by me with all the speed they could out of the battle, saying that the King hath the victory and that every man cried God and King Charles. I ENTREATED, prayed and persuaded them to stay and draw up in a body with our Troops, for we saw them fighting and the Field was not lost, but no persuasions would serve, and then turning to our three troops, two of them were run away [and] of my troop I had not six and thirty men left … I stayed with those men I had, being in a little field, and there was a way through, and divers of the enemy did run that way, both horse and foot. I took away about ten or twelve horse, swords and armour. I could have killed 40 of the enemy [but] I let them pass, disarming them and giving spoil to my Troopers … The armies were both in confusion … The Enemy ran away as well as our men …

---

1 For which army did Captain Knightley fight – the King's or Parliament's?

2 Explain the comment made by the soldiers, 'For God and King Charles'.

3 What impression of a Civil War battle does this source provide?

● **SOURCE 4.2**

Many of those involved in later battles had similar experiences. Captain Richard Atkins wrote an account of the Battle of Lansdown, in Somerset, in June 1643.

> **volleys:** *discharging of guns and cannons*
>
> **whither:** *where*

The air was so darkened with smoke of powder that for a quarter of an hour together (I dare say), there was no light seen, but what the fire of the VOLLEYS gave: and 'twas the greatest storm that I ever saw, in which I thought I knew not WHITHER to go, nor what to do, my horse had two or three musket bullets in him, which made him tremble under me at that rate, and I could hardly with my spurs keep him from lying down, and he did me the service to carry me off … and then died.

> Does Source 4.2 give a similar or a different impression of Civil War battles to that given in Source 4.1?

● **SOURCE 4.3**

Sir Arthur Trevor meanwhile described his part in the Battle of Marston Moor, outside York, in July 1644.

> **shoal:** *group*
>
> **whither to incline:** *which way to go*

In the fire, smoke and confusion of that day I knew not for my soul WHITHER TO INCLINE; the runaways on both sides were so many, so breathless, so speechless, and so full of fears that I should not have taken them for men, but by their very motions which still served them well: not a man of them being able to give me the least hint where the Prince was to be found, both armies both mingled, both horse and foot, no side keeping to their posts.

In this horrible distraction did I court the centre, here meeting with a SHOAL of Scots crying out 'Weys [Woe is] us, we are all undone', and so full of lamentations and mourning, as if their day of doom had overtaken them, and from which they knew not [where] to fly …

> How does the impression given of a Civil War battle in Source 4.3 compare with the impressions given in Sources 4.1 and 4.2?

Sackings and sieges

In addition to such set-piece battles, the Civil War also saw frequent attacks and sieges of towns, castles and fortified houses.

Sackings

● **SOURCE 4.4**

A description of the sacking of Birmingham in the spring of 1643 by a Royalist force under the command of Charles I's nephew, Prince Rupert

> **Bedlams:** *madmen*
>
> **conceived:** *believed*
>
> **Furies:** *avenging spirits*
>
> **healthing:** *drinking toasts*
>
> **hewed:** *cut*
>
> **malignants:** *enemies*
>
> **vaults:** *cellars*

The Cavaliers rode up into the town like so many FURIES or BEDLAMS, the Earl of Denbigh being in the front, singing as he rode, they shot at every door or window where they could spy any looking out, then hacked, HEWED or pistolled all they met without distinction, blaspheming, cursing and damning themselves most hideously … Having thus possessed themselves of the Town, they ran into every house, cursing and damning, threatening and terrifying the poor women most terribly, setting naked swords and pistols to their breasts; they fell to plundering all the town before them, as well MALIGNANTS as others, picking purses and pockets, searching in holes and corners, tiles of houses, wells, pools, VAULTS, gardens and every place they could suspect for money or goods, forcing people to deliver all the money they had … It is CONCEIVED they had £2,000 in money from the town. They beastly assaulted many women's chastity and impudently made their brags afterwards how many they had ravished, glorying in their shame … That night few or none of them went to bed, but stayed up revelling, robbing and tyrannising over poor affrighted women and prisoners, drinking [until] drunk, HEALTHING upon their knees, yea drinking healths to Prince Rupert's dog.

Nor did their rage here cease, but when on the next day they were to march out of town, they used all possible diligence in every street to kindle fire in the town … The houses burned were about 87, besides multitudes of barns, stables and their back buildings … And yet for all this, the soldiers told the inhabitants that Prince Rupert had dealt mercifully with them, but when they came back with the Queen's army they would leave neither man, woman, nor child alive.

---

1   List the main ways in which Birmingham was affected by this attack.

2   What can you tell from this account about its author? What reasons might he have had for writing this account – and how could they affect its reliability as historical evidence of these events?

Sieges

Sieges usually caused acute hunger and other difficulties, as well as serious danger of death and injury if the besieged site was eventually stormed. One of the bitterest sieges of the 1640s occurred at Colchester in 1648, when a Royalist garrison was surrounded by the New Model Army under the command of Sir Thomas Fairfax. Shortly before its capture, a group of starving women and children left the town and tried to cross the Parliamentarian lines; they were not allowed through and many of them died in the 'no-man's-land' between the two forces.

● SOURCE 4.5

A vivid picture of Colchester at the end of the siege was given in the pamphlet *Colchester's Tears*, which appeared at the time.

---

countenances: *faces*

shifting: *struggling*

How sad a spectacle it is to see goodly buildings, well furnished houses and whole streets to be nothing but ruinous heaps of ashes, and both poor and rich now brought almost to the same woeful state; to see sick people scarce able to stand upon their legs and women, some presently upon the delivery, some ready to be delivered, and infants in their mothers' laps and some hanging on their mothers' breasts, all turned out of harbour and left helpless to lie on the cold ground; to see poor and rich men lately of good quality now equal to the meanest, toiling and sweating in carrying some mean bed or other away, or some inconsiderable household stuff out of the burning; all of them with wailing and weeping ghastly COUNTENANCES, and meagre thin faces, SHIFTING and flying in distraction of mind they scarce know whither; to hear the lamentable cries of the people come from the town, old and young, women and children, poor and rich … crying unto the General's guards to pass …

---

1   What can you tell from this source about the sympathies of its author?

2   In the light of its tone and content, why do you think it was written?

The bloodshed that could result from the storming of a besieged stronghold is recorded in the following two sources.

● SOURCE 4.6

A letter written by a Scottish soldier who witnessed a Parliamentarian attack on Newcastle in July 1644

---

assailants: *attackers*

batteries: *gun positions*

defendants: *defenders*

untrailed: *raised*

Truly it was more than admirable to behold the desperate courage both of the ASSAILANTS and DEFENDANTS, the thundering cannons roaring from our BATTERIES without, and theirs roaring from the castle within; the thousands of musket balls flying at each others' faces, like driving hailstones …; the clangor and carvings of naked and unsheathed swords; the pushing of UNTRAILED pikes, crying for blood, and the pitiful clamour of heart-fainting women imploring for mercy for their husbands, themselves and their children … the carcasses of men to be like dead dogs upon the groaning streets, and man against man to be the object of homicidal and barbarous cruelty.

The Scots were allies of Parliament during the war. In the light of this and the content of the source, would you regard this as a reliable account?

● **SOURCE 4.7**

Sir Anthony Ashley Cooper described the storming of a fortified house by his Parliamentarian troops at Abbotsbury, in Dorset, in October 1644.

> **furze faggots:** *bundles of gorse used to start a fire*
> **grenadiers:** *soldiers armed with grenades*
> **hot:** *fierce*
> **quarter:** *mercy*

The business was extreme HOT for above six hours, we were forced to burn down an outgate to a court before we could get to the house, and then our men rushed in through the fire and got into the hall porch where with FURZE FAGGOTS they set fire on it, and plied the windows so hard with small shot, that the enemy durst not appear in the low rooms. In the meantime one of our guns played on the other side of the house, and the gunners with fire balls and the GRENADIERS with scaling ladders endeavoured to fire the second storey, but that not taking effect our soldiers were forced to wrench open the window with iron balls, and forcing in faggots of furze fire, set the whole house in a flaming fire, so that it was not possible to be quenched. And then they cried for QUARTER, but having beat diverse men before it, and considering how many garrisons of the same nature we had to deal with, I gave command that there should be none given.

1 Do you think Ashley Cooper gives an accurate account of these events?

2 How did he justify his decision to kill all the inhabitants of this house?

3 What do Sources 4.4–4.7 reveal about the nature of warfare during this period?

4 How reliable do you think these accounts are for historians trying to find out about the Civil War?

Section B How did the armies affect local communities?

While such fighting was often deeply traumatic for those who were involved in it or witnessed it, a worse feature of the war for many people was the presence of large numbers of soldiers in their communities for long periods. Even when they were not engaged in fighting, these men were unruly, ill-disciplined and dangerous and likely to resort to violence if they did not get their way. Many civilians were forced to give free quarter (food and lodging) to the troops and many others had their horses, food stocks and other goods taken away without payment.

Below are several accounts of the widespread looting and pillaging that occurred during the Civil War.

● **SOURCE 4.8**

In September 1642, when the war was only a few weeks old, a party of Parliamentarian soldiers from Gloucester, under the command of Captain Scriven, looted the house of Rowland Bartlett of Castlemorton, in Worcestershire.

> **garrets:** *attic rooms*
> **hanging presses:** *large shelved cupboards*
> **loose:** *chase*
> **lumber:** *old and disused furniture*
> **offer:** *search*
> **perry:** *alcoholic drink made from pears, similar to cider*
> **pewter:** *kitchen utensils of little value*
> **thence:** *there*
> **tumult:** *unruly crowd*
> **wearing apparel:** *clothes*

… in a confused TUMULT they rush into the house; and, as eager hounds at a LOOSE OFFER here and there and know not well where to fasten, so these hunt from the parlour to the kitchen, from THENCE by the chambers to the GARRETS … besides Mr Bartlett's, his wife's and children's WEARING APPAREL, they rob the servants of their clothes; with the butt ends of muskets they break open the HANGING PRESSES, cupboards and chests: no place was free from this ragged regiment … except bedding, PEWTER and LUMBER, they left nothing behind them, for besides two horses laden with the best things (Scriven's own plunder) there being a hundred and fifty rebels, each rebel returned with a pack on his back. As for his beer and PERRY, what they could not devour they spoiled, the earth drinking what the rebels could not.

1   List in your own words the damage done to this house.

2   What possible reasons can you suggest for soldiers behaving in this way?

3   What is the author's attitude to these events?

● **SOURCE 4.9**

The account of a Parliamentarian lawyer, Bulstrode Whitelocke. He was outraged by the behaviour of a group of Royalist troops who stayed at his house, Fawley Court, near Henley in Oxfordshire, in November 1642.

There was no insolence or outrage usually committed by common soldiers on a reputed enemy which was omitted by these brutish fellows at my house. They had their whores with them, they spent and consumed a £200 load of corn and hay, littered their horses with sheaves of good wheat and gave them all sorts of corn in the straw. Divers writing[s] of consequence and books which were left in my study, some of them they tore in pieces, others were burnt to light their tobacco, and some they carried away with them.

1   What damage was done at Bulstrode Whitelocke's house?

2   What reasons can you suggest for the behaviour of these soldiers?

● **SOURCE 4.10**

William Davenport, of Cheshire, another individual who suffered at the hands of the soldiers, recorded his experiences in his COMMONPLACE BOOK.

bushel: *measure of grain, approximately eight gallons*

commonplace book: *journal or diary*

cornet: *junior officer*

fowling piece and **cocking piece:** *guns for hunting*

victuals: *foodstuffs*

About which time Sir William Brereton sending his CORNET with part of his troop to be quartered with me overnight, next morning came to Bramhall himself, attended with his whole troop … and then he disarmed me of all the arms I had in my house …

On New Year's day 1644 … Captain Sankey, Captain Francis Duckenfield with two or three troops came to Bramhall and went into my stable and took out all my horses, then drove all they could find out of the park taking them quite away with them, above 20 in all, afterwards searched my house for arms again, took my FOWLING PIECE, COCKING PIECE and drum which Sir William [Brereton] had left me with divers other things; and although by means my wife made to Sir William Brereton, we had a warrant from him to have all my goods restored and had my young horse (which died within a while after) with some other horses again, yet we lost them both horses and other goods, which we could never after get …

In May 1644 … came Prince Rupert and his army, by whom I lost better than 100 pounds in Linens and other goods at Milesend, besides the rifling and pulling in pieces of my house. By them and my Lord Goring's army, I lost eight horses and besides VICTUALS and other provision, they ate me three score [20] BUSHELS of oats. No sooner was the prince gone but Stanley's cornet, one Lely, and 20 of his troop hastened their return to plunder me of my horses which the prince had left me, which he did …

1   Do you think the soldiers described by Davenport were Royalists or Parliamentarians?

2   Why did the soldiers take Davenport's horses, and why was it so serious for him to lose them?

3   What other types of plunder were seized from Davenport and why?

4   On the basis of your study of Sources 4.8–4.10, was the behaviour of the Royalist troops any better or worse than that of the Parliamentarian soldiers?

By the later part of the war, relations between the soldiers and the civilian population in many parts of the country were extremely bad. In a number of counties neutralist or 'Clubmen' movements were set up to protect their local area from soldiers of both sides.

● **SOURCE 4.11**

In March 1645, the Parliamentarian Sir Thomas Myddleton wrote to the Speaker of the House of Commons to complain about the behaviour of one group of soldiers in the Welsh borders.

The LICENTIOUSNESS of the soldiers in plundering and wasting the country make most people that have no relation to arms to hate the very name of a soldier, and drives the country to catch at any invention or new design which may seem to tend to the curbing of those EXORBITANCES; and this hath BEGOT a great party in ADJACENT parts of Shropshire, Hereford, Radnor and Montgomeryshire, who call themselves neutrals, and have armed themselves to withstand plunderings, and although the ringleaders of them be known to be dangerous persons, yet I conceive the generality of them, and of the common people in all COUNTRIES, would very suddenly be gained to our side, if there were some severe declaration of both houses against plundering, and against all commanders that should connive at, or neglect to punish the same …

adjacent: *neighbouring*

begot: *created*

countries: *counties*

exorbitances: *excesses*

licentiousness: *wickedness*

● **SOURCE 4.12**

The state to which Newcastle and the surrounding countryside were reduced by the soldiers was graphically described in a remonstrance sent to Parliament from the Northern Association shortly after the end of the war.

alleavement and retardation: *lessening*

insaturate: *unable to be satisfied*

rapine: *plundering*

We daily groan under the unsupportable weight of oppressive taxes, free-quarter (besides murder, RAPINE, robberies, not mentioning the deep exhaustings during the late time of war and since both by English and Scottish forces no part of the kingdom being so infested) we humbly desire a speedy ALLEAVEMENT and RETARDATION thereof, that yet (if it be possible) we may have bread to sustain the lives of our poor wives and children; many thousands being ready to perish through want, and unable to supply themselves, much less of power to supply the rigid desires and demands of an useless and INSATURATE soldiery; else we shall be enforced through necessity (heaven knows our unwillingness) to acquit ourselves (by the readiest way) of our [not] any longer tolerable calamities, and purchase freedom, though with the sacrifice of our dearest blood.

1   What problems were being faced by civilians in the areas referred to in Sources 4.5–4.8?

2   What advice does Sir Thomas Myddleton offer MPs and why?

3   What threat do the authors of Source 4.12 make to Parliament?

4   Did the issues raised in the sources present any problems to the leaders of the Royalists and Parliamentarians?

5   Who do you think would have been more seriously affected by these protests in 1645–6 – the King or Parliament? Explain the reasons for your answer.

Section C How heavy were the financial burdens of the war?

Taxes

Those who were lucky enough to escape direct involvement in the dramatic military events described in Sections A and B were not left completely untouched by the war. All over the country individuals were forced to pay heavy taxes, and faced the threat of losing their homes and livelihoods.

Before the Civil War, the English people had paid only occasional and relatively light taxes. The main tax they had to pay was the subsidy. This was collected only when approved by Parliament. It required the wealthy gentry and aristocracy to make only very modest contributions towards government expenses. Levels of taxation increased significantly during the 1630s, particularly as a result of Charles I's decision to collect ship money throughout the country for five consecutive years. As we have seen, this tax produced a storm of protest and helped to cause the crisis of the early 1640s. Even so, in 1640, the English were still an undertaxed people. They found the demands for taxes during the Civil War to be a very unpleasant shock.

The two main taxes imposed by Parliament during the Civil War were the assessment and the excise. The assessment was a direct tax on income and wealth, particularly land. The excise was duty on a range of goods, including beer and wine.

The assessment

● **SOURCE 4.13**

The assessment was established by this ordinance of 24 February 1643.

The Lords and Commons now assembled in Parliament, being fully satisfied and resolved in their consciences that they have lawfully taken up arms, and may and ought to continue the same for the necessary defence of themselves and the Parliament from violence and destruction, and of this kingdom from foreign invasion, and for the bringing of notorious offenders to … punishment, which are the only causes for which they have raised an army which cannot possibly be maintained … without the speedy raising of large and considerable sums of money proportionable to the great expenses which now this kingdom is at for the supporting of the said army, and for the saving of the whole kingdom, our religion, laws and liberties from utter ruin and destruction … the said Lords and Commons do ordain … that for the intents and purposes aforesaid the several and weekly sums of money hereafter in this ordinance mentioned shall be charged, rated, taxed and levied upon all and every the several counties, cities, towns, liberties, places and persons hereafter mentioned, according to the proportions, rates and distributions in this present ordinance expressed, the same to be paid weekly to the several collectors appointed by this ordinance for the receiving hereof …

1 How does Parliament justify the introduction of this new tax?

2 Why do you think MPs felt it was necessary to make this justification?

3 How regularly was the assessment to be collected?

4 Explain why taxation was so important for both sides during the Civil War.

● **FIGURE 4.1**

Table showing the assessment charged on London and the English counties (along with the ship money they had been expected to pay in the 1630s)

Place	Yearly assessment charge	Yearly ship money charge
Bedfordshire	£13,000	£3,000
Berkshire	£28,600	£4,000
Buckinghamshire	£21,840	£4,500
Cambridgeshire	£19,500	£3,500
Cheshire	£9,110	£3,500
Cornwall	£32,500	£6,500
Cumberland	£1,950	£1,000*
Derbyshire	£9,100	£3,500
Devon	£96,226	£9,000
Dorset	£22,984	£5,000
Durham	£3,250	£2,000
Essex	£58,500	£8,000
Gloucestershire	£42,250	£5,500
Hampshire	£39,000	£6,000
Herefordshire	£22,750	£4,000
Hertfordshire	£23,400	£4,000
Huntingdonshire	£11,440	£2,000
Kent	£65,000	£8,000
Lancashire	£26,000	£3,500
Leicestershire	£9,750	£4,500
Lincolnshire	£42,250	£8,000
London	£520,000	£1,600
Middlesex	£39,000	£5,500
Norfolk	£65,000	£8,000
Northamptonshire	£22,100	£6,000
Northumberland	£2,600	£3,000
Nottinghamshire	£9,750	£3,500
Oxfordshire	£33,800	£3,500
Rutland	£3,250	£1,000
Shropshire	£19,500	£4,500
Somerset	£54,600	£8,000
Staffordshire	£11,050	£2,000
Suffolk	£65,000	£8,000

Surrey	£20,800	£4,000
Sussex	£32,500	£5,000
Warwickshire	£29,250	£4,000
Westmorland	£1,417	£1,000**
Wiltshire	£37,700	£7,000
Worcestershire	£28,600	£4,000
Yorkshire	£55,250	£12,000

* Shared with Westmorland
** Shared with Cumberland

1 How do the levels of assessment taxation compare with those of ship money?

2 On average how much higher was the amount of assessment imposed on the counties during the Civil War than ship money?

3 Can we learn anything from these figures about the distribution of wealth in England at the beginning of the Civil War?

4 What do the figures reveal about London's wealth and its importance to the Parliamentary cause?

5 These figures show how much tax was ordered to be collected at these different times. What further questions would you want to ask about them and why?

● **SOURCE 4.14**

Some idea of the impact of the assessment at the local and individual level can be gauged by the comments made by the Isle of Wight Royalist Sir John Oglander in his commonplace book.

Christendom: *Christian Europe*

Parliament lays a tax on the kingdom of £90,000 for the army. Of which the Isle of Wight pays every month £305, and the parish of Brading pays every month £21 10s, and of this Sir John Oglander payeth £3 10s, and every week 18s. I believe few princes in CHRISTENDOM have such coming in …

1 What is Sir John Oglander's main complaint about the assessment?

2 How reliable is his account as evidence of typical attitudes towards this new tax?

The excise

● **SOURCE 4.15**

The excise was established by a Parliamentary Ordinance of 22 July 1643 and contained these provisions.

Commonwealth: *state*

levies: *taxes*

… Forasmuch as many great LEVIES have already been made … and the malignants of this kingdom have hitherto practised by all cunning ways and means how to evade and elude the payment of any part thereof, by reason whereof the Lords and Commons do hold it fit that some constant and equal way for the levying of monies for the future maintenance of the Parliament forces … may be had and established, whereby the said malignants and neutrals may be compelled to pay their proportionable parts of the aforesaid charge …

I Be it therefore ordered, ordained and declared by the said Lords and Commons that the several rates and charges in the schedule hereunto annexed and contained shall be set and laid, and are hereby set and laid, charged and imposed upon all and every the commodities in the said schedule particularly expressed …

II And be it further ordained by the said Lords and Commons that for the better levying of the monies hereby to be raised, that an office from henceforth by force and virtue of these present shall be, and is hereby erected, made and appointed in the city of London, called or known by the name of the Office of excise or New Impost, whereof there shall be eight commissioners to govern the same …

XI That if any sellers of the said commodities shall refuse or neglect to make a true entry of the said commodities … he or they so refusing, neglecting or doing contrary to the said article, shall forfeit to the use of the COMMONWEALTH four times the true value or worth of the goods or commodities so by him or them neglected to be entered or delivered …

XII That if any common brewer, alehouse keeper, cider or perry maker, in the country or in any city town or place therein, which doth brew ale or beer, or make cider and perry in their houses or elsewhere, do not make a true entry in manner aforesaid … then they shall incur the like penalty as aforesaid …

XIII That all and every person and persons whatsoever that keep or shall keep private houses and families … which brew … their own ale and beer for the sustenance of their families … shall monthly cause the like entries to be made … or the like penalties to be levied on the offenders herein …

XX That the said commissioners … shall have power and authority to call before them any persons or persons whom they shall think fit … for the better discovery of fraud or guile in the not entering, or not payment, of the rates of excise or the new impost herein mentioned …

XXI That the said commissioners … shall from time to time appoint any officer or officers belonging to the said office to enter into cellars, shops, warehouses, storehouses, or other places of every person that selleth, buyeth or spendeth any of the said commodities, to search and see what quantities of any of the said commodities every such hath on his hands …

---

1   On which commodities was the new excise tax to be paid?

2   Did MPs think that it was adequate simply to order that this new tax should be paid?

3   Do you think this was a *fair* method of raising money for Parliament's armies?

The excise was particularly resented and as they went about their business the excise collectors encountered frequent hostility and occasionally even open violence.

● **SOURCE 4.16**

A report of an excise riot which took place in Haverfordwest in Pembrokeshire in 1644

warrants: *written orders*

On Monday last the commissioners for the excise came to this town and having shown us their commission we yielded obedience unto it, and thereupon they sent out their WARRANTS for the summoning of the inhabitants before them. And having sat yesterday in the afternoon on it there came to the town hall a company of the poorest sort of women of this town, and there made a mutiny and forced the commissioners thence to their lodgings. And having complained unto us … we … entreated the commissioners to sit again this day and that we would assist them therein. And we and the said commissioners being in the town hall thinking to proceed on the service, the said women came again and would have forced into the hall, whereupon we committed some of them to the sheriff, thinking they would have yielded obedience thereunto, but they fell again into such a mutiny that for safeguard of the commissioners we were forced to leave the hall, and having repaired with them to their lodging with an intent to see them safe out of town, the said women followed us thither and would have forced on them [the commissioners] in their chamber in such manner as for the space of six hours we could not pacify them …

---

1   What does this source suggest about the role of women in the Civil War?

2   What reasons can you suggest for their hostility to the excise?

3   What can you tell from this source about the author's attitude to:

a) the excise
b) the women?

The contribution

Charles I raised a tax known as the contribution from those counties that he controlled.

● **SOURCE 4.17**

The declaration was issued by Charles I, in January 1643, for the contribution to be collected in Worcestershire.

sessions: *Quarter Sessions*

… the King's Majesty's most gracious letters agreed that there should be raised forth of the County of Worcester, the sum of three thousand pounds of lawful English money a month, towards the payment of his Majesty's forces, sent and raised for the defence of this said county and city of Worcester. The first payment to be for this present month of January, and the said sum or sums, which should be raised, to be paid unto the several High Constables of the County of Worcester, and to be paid by them unto John Bacon Gent., to be disposed of by Sir William Russell, Baronet, High Sheriff of the County of Worcester, and Governor of the said city, upon account to be given by him to the King's Majesty's Justices of the Peace of the county … which first monthly payment shall be paid before the second day of February next coming, and so to continue as long as Sir William Russell and the King's Majesty's Justices of the Peace of the County of Worcester assembled at this present SESSIONS, should think fit. And that the money should be assessed by four or more of the sufficient inhabitants of every parish or village in the said county of Worcester, according to the usual rates of payment within the said county.

> 1 How regularly was the contribution to be collected?
>
> 2 In what ways did the King try to make it acceptable to the population?

● **FIGURE 4.2**

A table comparing the assessment and contribution charged on four counties

County	Yearly assessment	Yearly contribution
Berkshire	£28,600	£67,200
Gloucestershire	£42,250	£72,000
Oxfordshire	£33,800	£76,800
Worcestershire	£28,600	£36,000

> 1 How do the assessment and contribution taxes for these counties compare?
>
> 2 What reasons can you suggest to explain these differences?
>
> 3 Do you think that the inhabitants of these counties paid both of these taxes?
>
> 4 What would actually decide whether a county paid its taxes to the King or Parliament?

Sequestration

The King and Parliament also sequestered (confiscated) any property that belonged to their opponents in areas they controlled. Parliament declared its intention to do this by an ordinance passed in March 1643.

● **SOURCE 4.18**

Extract from the ordinance passed by Parliament in March 1643 which declared its intention to sequester property

arrearages: *arrears*
hereditaments: *inheritances*
personal estate: *other property*
plate: *silver*
tenements: *houses*

Be it therefore ordained by the said Lords and Commons that the estates … of … all such bishops, deans, deans and chapters … archdeacons, and of all other person or persons, ecclesiastical or temporal, as have raised or shall raise arms against the Parliament, or have been, are or shall be in actual war against the same, or have voluntarily contributed, or shall voluntarily contribute … any money, horse, PLATE, arms, munition … or other assistance, for or towards the maintenance of any forces raised against the Parliament … shall be forthwith seized and sequestered into the hands of the sequestrators and committees hereafter in the ordinance named … Which said sequestrators and committees … are hereby authorised and required by themselves, their agents and deputies, to take and seize into their hands and custodies as well all the money, goods, chattels, debts and PERSONAL ESTATE, as also all and every the manors, lands, TENEMENTS and HEREDITAMENTS, rents, ARREARAGES of rents, revenues and profits of all and every the said delinquents … and also two parts of all the money, goods, chattels, debts, and personal estate, and two parts of all and every the manors, lands, tenements and hereditaments, rents, arrearages of rents, revenues and profits of all and every Papist …

1   Make a list of the activities that rendered an individual liable to have property sequestered by Parliament.

2   On the basis of this source whom did Parliament regard as its most dangerous enemies?

In 1644, the lands of William Davenport of Bramhall in Cheshire were threatened with sequestration by the Parliamentary authorities in that county. He avoided the loss of his estates only by paying a large composition fine.

● SOURCE 4.19

In this account from his commonplace book, William Davenport of Bramhall relates how the process of sequestration was carried out.

commissioners of array: *those who had raised forces for the King in 1642*

composition: *fine*

delinquency: *Royalism*

deputed: *appointed*

detain: *withhold*

inventory: *list*

leases: *rental agreements*

matches lighted: *weapons ready to fire*

National Covenant: *Solemn League and Covenant of 1643*

respite: *delay*

withal: *as well*

On Friday, 9th August 1644, information was brought into the sequestrators against me for DELINQUENCY … but by whose malicious instigation I could not yet come to know, but certainly by my own tenants. On Monday following, being the 12th of the said month … there came to Bramhall, William Barret, Captain Edmund Shelmerdine, Richard Button, George Newton, Gerard Hayes, Robert Ridgeway, John Wharmby, William Thomson, my own tenant Daniel of the Lane, William Smith, commissioners DEPUTED by the sequestrators of Macclesfield Hundred … with a commission directed to them from the … sequestrators to take an INVENTORY of all my goods both within the house and without, which they in a most strict and severe manner performed, going into every room in the house, narrowly searching every corner, causing all boxes and chests to be opened which otherwise they threatened to break up, being in the mean time guarded with a company of musketeers who stood in the park and all about the house with their MATCHES LIGHTED.

On Thursday next … they began their examination of witnesses to prove me a delinquent … wherein some of my own tenants showed themselves forward to give evidence against me, but I must not know who they were. About three weeks after I received a warrant from the sequestrators to appear at Stockport in person to answer such objections as they had framed against me, which I accordingly did, where they alleged against me that I had joined with the COMMISSIONERS OF ARRAY at Hoo Heath at Knutsford and at Macclesfield, whereunto I affirmatively answered that I was there, and … gave them such reasons for my being there as might have satisfied them, yet nevertheless I did conceive that my COMPOSITION made with Sir William Brereton, Sir George Booth and Colonel Duckenfield since then, and my restraint from arms might free me from delinquency in that point, if thereby I had incurred the penalty thereof. With these and other allegations in defence of myself at that time, I thought I had given them such satisfaction as I should have heard no more from them, till above a month afterwards that I received another warrant to appear before them at Stockport again, where they said they had more to charge me WITHAL concerning my delinquency. I accordingly came before them the second time, Colonel Duckenfield being there, and then they demanded if I had taken the NATIONAL COVENANT and pressed me with it, whereunto I desired to have time given me in such weighty matter to advise with some of my friends about it, and at length got ten days' RESPITE to answer it at Nantwich … [but they] neglecting my just allegations in defence of my innocency, proceeded further against me in renewing their commands to my tenants to DETAIN their rents from me, and commanding them to bring their LEASES before them in viewing and rating all my lands; and in conclusion, unless I would agree to give them five hundred pounds in COMPOSITION they intended to proceed against me as a delinquent in all rigour and extremity …

1   Who, according to this source, was to blame for the author's difficulties?

2   What reasons may these people have had for informing on him?

3   What objections did Davenport have to the way the sequestration commissioners behaved?

4   Why was Davenport accused of being a delinquent?
5   In what ways did he try to defend himself?
6   What was the decision of the commissioners?
7   For what reasons would you want to study other sources about these events before reaching any firm conclusions about what happened?

● **Source 4.20**

This Royalist account records how the Parliamentarian Sequestration Committee in Kent dealt with one Royalist family in their county.

pillaged: *plundered*

want of accommodation: *lack of a home*

… [the Royalist] was so plundered, chased and vexed that, being 80 years old, with the removal and WANT OF ACCOMMODATION it shortened his life … Before his death [he] was sent to by the Kentish Committee … for a tax of £2,000 … His nephew (who was heir) went to the committee desiring the sequestration might be taken off his estate, showing them they had been so deeply PILLAGED that 'twas impossible to raise one, much less £2,000 … The noble knight Sir Anthony Weldon replied … that he should not think to get his estate unsequestered; 'and whereas', quoth he, 'you say you are unable to pay one thousand pounds, you shall pay two, and ought to pay three, for we have killed your uncle for you, and caused you to be heir' …

1   In what ways does the author of this passage try to encourage sympathy for this family?
2   From the evidence in this source, who do you think Sir Anthony Weldon was and what is the author's opinion of him?
3   From the evidence you have studied in Sources 4.13–4.20, which side organised their war effort more effectively: the Royalists or the Parliamentarians?

Section D Case Study: What was the Civil War like in Berkshire?

Introduction

This section examines the impact of the Civil War on one particular county, Berkshire. It lay directly between Parliament's headquarters in London and Charles I's in Oxford, so it was one of the main theatres of the war and one of the worst affected counties in England. Berkshire experienced two major pitched battles (the first and second Battles of Newbury), several major sieges of its towns and castles (Reading and Donnington) and the constant presence of large numbers of both Royalist and Parliamentarian soldiers. An idea of the effects of this military presence can be gained from the fact that during the winter of 1643–4 the town of Reading, which had a normal peacetime population of around 3,000 inhabitants, had about 3,000 Royalist soldiers stationed there.

From 1642–3 most of Berkshire was controlled by the Royalists, who established garrisons at Reading, Wallingford, Abingdon and Donnington Castle near Newbury. Parliament's influence during this period was restricted to a small area in the extreme east of the county around Windsor Castle. In the summer of 1644, following a Royalist decision to withdraw from the area around Oxford, the Parliamentarians set up garrisons in Reading and Abingdon. For the next twelve months the two sides fought for control of the county. While the Royalists established a new garrison at Faringdon and attempted to hold on to the Vale of the White Horse in the west of Berkshire, the Parliamentarians, who now controlled the east of the county, tried to extend their influence towards Oxford to link up with their isolated garrison at Abingdon. Following Charles I's crushing defeat at the Battle of Naseby in the Midlands in June 1645, the final year of fighting in Berkshire saw a gradual Parliamentary advance on Oxford. Donnington Castle was captured in March 1646 and, soon afterwards, the Parliamentarians laid siege to Faringdon, Wallingford and Oxford itself. Oxford and Faringdon surrendered together in June 1646, but the garrison at Wallingford held out until the end of July and was one of the last places in the country to fall to the victorious Parliament.

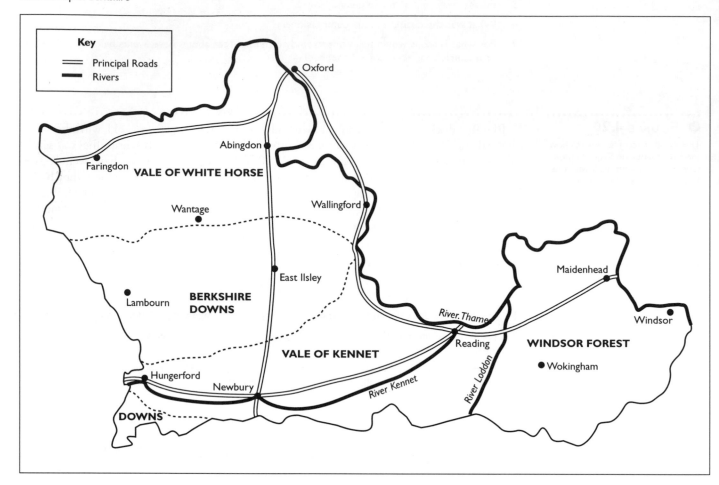

Make four copies of your own of this outline map of Berkshire. Using the information on page 79, mark on your maps the Royalist and Parliamentary garrisons for the war years 1643, 1644, 1645 and 1646. Then shade in on each map the areas of the county controlled by the Royalists and Parliamentarians.

⬤ **Note on sources**

Source material for the impact of the Civil War on the English counties can normally be found in the local county records office. Each English county has such an office, usually situated in the county town near the county council headquarters. They are open to anyone who wishes to consult the archives. Much additional information can be found in the collections held by the Public Record Office in London and the major national libraries, in particular the British Library in London and the Bodleian Library at Oxford. The British Library possesses a remarkable collection of 22,000 tracts and pamphlets collected by a London bookseller, George Thomason, between 1641 and 1660. These Thomason Tracts are also available in a number of other libraries on microfilm. A great many document collections have also been published by organisations such as the Historic Manuscripts Commission, and are available in larger libraries. The Berkshire material above is taken exclusively from national records collections; this is because much of the local archive material for seventeenth-century Berkshire was destroyed in a fire in 1707.

Below are some contemporary accounts of the effect of the Civil War on Berkshire. Read them and answer the questions that follow.

SOURCE 4.21

A petition of inhabitants of Berkshire to Charles I, January 1643

apparel: clothes

assuaged: lessened

clandestinely: secretly

derivative from: caused by

enormities: wrongs

execrable: horrible

insatiate: unable to be satisfied

licentious: immoral

manifested: shown

The increasing miseries and continued mass of tumultuous troubles that, since the sad beginning of these civil wars, having run like lightning through all Your Majesty's dominions, have not fixed so long and with so destroying a hand in any one Province of the kingdom as in this county of Berkshire, which hath been for some months and so is like to continue during Your Majesty's abode at Oxford, the very theatre where all the tragedies which are DERIVATIVE FROM the cruelty and barbarism of such a war as this must be acted, since we are exposed as it were in the very middest betwixt both armies, which surely cannot but bring the certain estate of destruction into our borders. The fertility and wealth of the county, the main blessing which heaven's bounty hath conferred upon it, being the immediate cause of its ruin and destruction, those ministers of God's wrath, the soldiers, sparing nothing of our estates that may anyway satisfy the greedy humours of their INSATIATE desires which extend to all that we have of value or precious, as is MANIFESTED by the frequent plundering of towns and houses by cavaliers at their first arrival in these quarters; And though Your Sacred Majesty hath by the severity of your laws, enacted and proclaimed against such riotous disturbers of the public peace, somewhat ASSUAGED the inhumanity of their proceedings so that they dare not with such open and LICENTIOUS practice either plunder houses or pillage travellers, yet CLANDESTINELY and by the by they commit many ENORMITIES and EXECRABLE outrages, robbing all those they can conveniently seize upon of their money, APPAREL, or anything … that will yield any profit … For our corn and cattle, the chief support of our subsistence, we cannot affirm that we possess them but, according to the occasion, the soldiers have of them, who make no great scruple of taking away without payment meat for themselves and their horses.

1 On what activity, according to this petition, was the wealth of Berkshire mainly based?

2 Which aspects of the soldiers' behaviour were the petitioners most upset about?

3 Why did the petitioners think that the King's presence at Oxford was the cause of their problems?

4 What did the authors of this petition hope to achieve by sending it to the King?

SOURCE 4.22

A NEWSBOOK account of a Royalist attack on Wokingham in 1643

newsbook: an early form of newspaper, in this case one which supported Parliament

well affected: supporter

His Majesty's forces invaded Ockingham [Wokingham] and practised the most barbarous cruelty which malice or fury could invent, so that what the sword left untouched, the rage of flame devoured. There was no moderation observed in the estates of poor or rich, WELL AFFECTED or malignant, they distinguish not between friend and foe, but whatever goods did come into their hands it was accounted lawful plunder. They have made the inhabitants the unparalleled subjects of distress and turned the town into a wilderness.

1 How was Wokingham affected by this Royalist attack?

2 What appears to have been the motive behind this Royalist attack?

3 Why might the above account not be entirely reliable?

4 What in particular does the author appear to be most upset about and why?

SOURCE 4.23

Petition of the mayor and aldermen of Reading (probably December 1644)

constrained: forced

insolency: rudeness

redress: remedy

Since the time the two armies came into this town your petitioners have had their sufferings so multiplied upon them, the soldiers growing to that height of INSOLENCY that they break down our houses and burn them, take away our goods and sell them, rob our markets and spoil them, threaten our magistrates and beat them, so that without a speedy REDRESS we shall be CONSTRAINED, though to our utter undoing, yet for the preservation of our lives, to forsake our goods and habitation, and leave the town to the will of the soldiers, who cry out they have no pay, they have no beds, they have no fire, and they must and will have it by force or they will burn down all the houses in the town, whatever become of them.

1 List the main complaints of the petitioners against the soldiers in Reading.

2 Can you tell from the document whether it is referring to Royalist or Parliamentarian soldiers?

3 What clue is contained in this petition which might help explain why the soldiers behaved in these ways?

● **SOURCE 4.24**

A letter from George Varney to Reading Town Council (undated)

threescore: *sixty*

vapour: *make idle talk*

We cannot enjoy our land we rent of you because the armies of both sides lie so near us, consuming the profits of our grounds. Besides taxes are so hard we are not able to pay them; there is but THREESCORE and eight yard lands within the parish which comes at £10 a yard land [to] £680 a year, but the taxes that are laid upon us by both armies is above £1200 a year, besides quartering with us. Yet notwithstanding I will plough it so long as I can, and so soon as I can I will send you money. I had eleven horses taken away by the King's soldiers and four of those eleven were well worth £40: I rode after the eleven horses and bought nine of them again and brought them home; then riding after the other two, while I was abroad the King's soldiers took the other nine away again, and I could never have them more. Since again this last winter going to market with a load of corn, the Earl of Manchester's [Parliamentarian] soldiers met with my men and took away my whole team of horses letting my cart stand in the field four miles from home; never had them more. You know by ordinance of Parliament landlords should pay their taxes for their tenants. Besides all this, when the King's soldiers come to us the[y] call me Roundheaded Rogue, and say I pay rent to the Parliament's garrisons and they will take it away from me. And likewise when the Parliament soldiers [come], they VAPOUR with me and tell me I pay rent to [the Marquis of] Worcester and [the Marquis of] Winchester, therefore the Parliament's soldiers say they will have the rent.

1 What can you tell from this source about the way the author made a living?

2 List the main ways in which George Varney was affected by the war.

3 Would you regard this letter as a reliable source for this purpose?

4 Why had George Varney found himself in a particularly difficult situation during the war?

5 What can you tell from this source about its author's attitude to the two sides?

By the summer of 1645 the inhabitants of the county had become desperate to see an end to the fighting. Several thousand of them held a mass protest meeting on the Berkshire Downs near Compton, where they drew up a statement or petition.

● **SOURCE 4.25**

The petition of the Berkshire Clubmen, 1645

conscionable: *reasonable*

distractions: *problems*

effusion: *spilling*

execution of the premises: *carrying out our agreement*

We the miserable inhabitants of the county of Berks … foreseeing famine and utter desolation will inevitably fall upon us, our wives and children, unless God of his infinite mercy shall … be graciously pleased to put a period to these sad DISTRACTIONS, are unanimously resolved to join in petitioning His Majesty and the two Houses of Parliament for a happy peace and accommodation of the present differences without further EFFUSION of Christian blood … In the meantime we with one heart and mind declare that we really intend to the utmost hazard of our lives and fortunes:

1 to defend and maintain the true Reformed Protestant religion;
2 to join with and assist one another in the mutual defence of our laws, liberties and properties against all plunderers and all other unlawful violence whatsoever;
3 we do hereby resolve and faithfully promise to each other that if any person or persons whatsoever, who shall concur with and assist us in these our resolutions, happen to suffer in his person or estate in EXECUTION OF THE PREMISES, it shall be as the suffering according to his damage, and in the case of loss of life, provision shall be made for his wife and children, and all this to be done at a CONSCIONABLE rate and allowance to the uttermost ability of all the associates;
4 lastly, we do declare all such men unworthy of our assistance as shall refuse to join with us in the prosecution of these our just intentions.

1   Why had the Berkshire Clubmen felt it necessary to draw up this declaration?

2   What did the supporters of this petition promise to do?

3   What was the main purpose of their movement?

● **SOURCE 4.26**

A letter from a Berkshire MP, William Ball, to William Lenthall, Speaker of House of Commons, March 1646

discover unto you: let you know

freeholder: small landowner

secure: take control of

Some of the soldiers were driving away the sheep of Andrew Pottinger of Woolhampton, a FREEHOLDER of £60 p.a., a very considerable man for Parliament, having a wife and six young children, who, endeavouring to SECURE his sheep, the soldiers struck him on the head so that he became presently speechless and dead within a few hours, to the great grief and sorrow of the neighbourhood. Another party of nine soldiers armed with muskets came yesterday to the house of Mr Ilsley of Beenham and broke open his door, to the great affright of his wife; he being absent and learning of it, got together his neighbours and so beat the soldiers that they were all wounded and not able to return to their quarters. I will give you many more instances were it necessary, but this I thought fit to DISCOVER UNTO YOU, that the soldiers and the country people are all grown desperate and continue one against the other, that we are like to have little other than killing and robbery if there be not a speedy supply of money for the soldiers. I beseech you to take the opportunity to acquaint the House with the condition of these parts which under the most terrible time of the enemy was nothing so bad.

1   About what activities does William Ball complain in this letter?

2   Do you think he is complaining about Royalist or Parliamentarian soldiers?

3   What does the author believe would help to solve these problems?

4   What does this letter reveal about relations between the soldiers and the civilian population at the end of the war?

5   Why did Ball feel it was necessary to inform Lenthall about these incidents?

6   Use Sources 4.21–4.26 to explain the impact of the Civil War in Berkshire.

7   Assess the usefulness and limitations of a detailed study of Berkshire to a historian seeking to understand the impact of the Civil War in England and Wales between 1642 and 1646.

Section E Case Study: How did the Civil War affect family life?

Introduction

In the following section you will investigate the impact of the Civil War not on large communities such as counties, towns and villages, but at the grassroots level of family life. The Civil War had major effects on families; many found themselves 'by the sword divided', with fathers, sons and brothers fighting on different sides, and large numbers were adversely affected by the death, injury or absence of husbands, wives and parents. On the other hand, some women found that the Civil War years brought them increased freedom and opportunities and some married couples drew closer together in the face of threats and disturbances produced by the war and its aftermath.

In a considerable number of families, close relatives found themselves to be political enemies; in a few instances this caused deep and long-lasting divisions, but within many other families every effort was made to minimise the damage caused to personal relationships. Two of the families that you will study suffered particularly badly in this respect. They were the Feildings of Newnham Paddox in Warwickshire and the Verneys of Claydon in Buckinghamshire.

The Feilding family

During the summer of 1642, as King and Parliament both prepared for a war which seemed increasingly unavoidable, William Feilding, Earl of Denbigh, decided to give his support to Charles I. It was soon reported, however, that his eldest son Basil intended to support Parliament.

● **Source 4.27**

A letter written by Susanna, Countess of Denbigh, to her son Basil, when she heard rumours that he was to fight for Parliament

travail: *labour, struggle*

I am much troubled to hear the King lay any marks of disfavour upon you, for I desire you should prosper in all things; but at this time, I do more TRAVAIL with sorrow for the grief I suffer for the ways you take, that the King doth believe you are against him, than ever I did to bring you into the world … and now give me leave to tell you, you have broke promise, for you did assure me that you would never be against the King.

1 For what reasons does the Countess feel sorrow and grief about her son's behaviour?
2 What can you tell from this letter about the reasons it was written?
3 What does this letter reveal about issues affecting side-taking at the beginning of the Civil War?

Despite this and subsequent letters from his mother and sister, Basil Feilding continued to back Parliament and, in the autumn of 1642, he fought against his father at the Battle of Edgehill. The following spring, William Feilding was seriously wounded whilst taking part in the Royalist attack on Birmingham (see page 69). Several days later, Basil was granted permission to visit his dying father but arrived too late. The widowed Susanna Feilding now increased her efforts to persuade her son to abandon Parliament, sending him a stream of letters from The Hague, in Holland, where she was in attendance upon Charles I's Queen, Henrietta Maria.

● **Source 4.28**

A letter written by Susanna, Countess of Denbigh, to her son Basil from Holland after the death of her husband in the fighting

I beg of you, my first born, to give me the satisfaction which you owe me now, which is to leave those that murdered your dear father … O, my dear Jesus, put it into my dear son's heart to leave that merciless company that was the death of his father, for now I think of it with horror, before with sorrow … Before you were carried away with error, but now it is hideous and monstrous … Let your dying father and unfortunate mother make your heart relent; let my great sorrow receive some comfort.

● **Source 4.29**

The Countess wrote a further letter begging Basil to comply with her wishes.

abstain: *stop*
soliciting: *requesting*

I have so often written to you to alter your course that I am out of all hope of prevailing; yet my tender and motherly care cannot ABSTAIN from SOLICITING of you to go to the King before it be too late … have pity upon me, your poor mother. I have so great a part in you, that you are too cruel to deny me any longer. Look up to Heaven, the great God of heaven commands you obey me in this my just desire.

Basil Feilding refused, however, to respond to any of these emotional pleas and remained in arms for Parliament throughout the Civil War.

1 Compare the content and tone of these letters with those of Source 4.26.
2 What reasons can you suggest for the differences?
3 Why did Susanna Feilding believe that her son should fight for the Royalists?
4 What arguments did Basil Feilding's mother use to attempt to persuade him to join the King's side?

The Verney family

Sir Edmund Verney, the head of the Verney family of Claydon, Buckinghamshire, who had very reluctantly supported Charles at the outbreak of the Civil War (see page 62), was killed while acting as his standard-bearer at the Battle of Edgehill in October 1642. During the last few months of his life he had been deeply distressed to learn that his eldest son, Sir Ralph Verney, had decided to support Parliament, and as a result had broken off all contact with him. Sir Ralph's Royalist younger brother, Edmund, was also upset about his decision, but he was anxious that their political differences should not end all contact between them and lead to a lasting hatred.

● **SOURCE 4.30**

A letter written by Edmund Verney to his brother, Ralph, at the beginning of the war

Brother, what I feared is proved too true, which is your being against the King; give me leave to tell you, in my opinion it is most unhandsomely done and it grieves my heart to think that my father already, and I who so dearly love and esteem you should be bound in conscience (because in duty to our King) to be your enemy …

> 1   For what reason does Edmund Verney think that his brother should change sides?
>
> 2   What light does this source shed on the general issue of side-taking in 1642?

● **SOURCE 4.31**

Having received no reply from his elder brother, a few months later, in early 1643, Edmund wrote again.

I beseech you, let not our unfortunate silence breed the least distrust of each other's affections. Although I would willingly lose my right hand that you had gone the other way, yet I will never consent that this dispute shall make a quarrel between us, there be too many to fight with besides ourselves … Though I am tooth and nail for the King's cause and shall endure so to the death, whatsoever his fortune be, yet, sweet brother, let not this my opinion (for it is guided by conscience), nor any other report which you can hear of me, cause any diffidence of my true love to you.

> In what ways is this letter similar to and different from Source 4.30?

Sir Ralph now wrote back explaining that because Edmund's first letter had been 'so full of sharpness' he had 'chose to forbear answering it'. Thereafter, the brothers continued to correspond.

● **SOURCE 4.32**

This is an extract from a later letter written by Sir Ralph.

… though perhaps in some things we may differ in judgement and opinion, yet nothing of that kind shall ever prevail with me to break that knot of true affection that ought to be betwixt us, there are too many others to contend with …

They remained on good terms until Edmund was killed later in the Civil War.

> 1   How did their political differences affect the relationship between Sir Ralph Verney and his brother?
>
> 2   Did the Feilding and Verney families react to political division in similar ways or in different ways?

The Harley family

The Civil War also disrupted personal relationships by forcing friends and relatives to endure the prolonged absences of their loved ones. For most of the first two years of the war, Sir Robert Harley of Brampton Bryan in Herefordshire was away from home serving as an MP at

Westminster. In his absence his wife Brilliana, Lady Harley took charge of the family estates. She found her isolation in a largely Royalist county increasingly frustrating, and in March 1643 she wrote a letter to her son Edward.

● **SOURCE 4.33**

Letter from Brilliana, Lady Harley to her son, Edward, in 1643

---

cessation of arms: *truce*

remove: *move*

stay: *stop*

My dear Ned, I should have been very glad to have received a letter from you by Mr Taylor; and dear Ned, find some way or other to write to me that I may know how the world goes and how it is with your father and yourself; for it is a death to be amongst my enemies, and not to hear from those I love so dearly ... I wish with all my heart that everyone would take notice what way they [the Royalists] take; that if I do not give them my house, and what they would have, I shall be proceeded against as a traitor. It may be everyone's case to be made traitors; for I believe everyone will be as unwilling to part with their houses as I am. I desire your father would seriously think what I had best do; whether stay at Brampton or REMOVE to some other place. I hear there are 600 soldiers appointed to come against me. I know not whether this CESSATION OF ARMS will STAY them. I cannot tell what to think that I hear nothing of your sister Brilliana's son, nor that you did not write me word that he was to come to you.

---

1   What were Brilliana's main worries in the spring of 1643?

2   What would Brilliana have liked to have done?

3   How did Brilliana intend to come to a decision about what she should do?

Lady Harley was subsequently placed under even more stress when she was forced to defend her house against Royalist attacks. These difficulties taxed her both physically and mentally and probably contributed to her premature death in 1644.

Dorothy Denne and William Taylor

Similar stresses were placed on the relationships of those who wished to marry but were forced to separate by the war.

● **SOURCE 4.34**

In this letter a young gentlewoman, Dorothy Denne, writes to her sweetheart, William Taylor.

---

cornet: *junior officer*

rhetoric: *praise*

Dear love, you write in such strains of RHETORIC I know not well how to answer them. Your compliments term me a goddess; I know you are sensible of my frailties and imperfections, which will witness that I am not divine but a poor mortal creature subject to all kinds of miseries, and I account myself the more miserable in losing thy sweet company, which is more pleasing to me than anyone else in the world. I do deplore thy absence now, but if thou should go to the wars, I should be in continual fears for thee ... I hear you are a CORNET to Sir Timothy Thornell ... if you could get some friend that were acquainted with ships for to get thee some place there, for I think 'tis safer there than in the wars ... but if you have no remedy but to go to the wars, then my prayers shall attend thee while I live.

---

1   How had the war affected Dorothy Denne?

2   What advice did Dorothy Denne give William Taylor about the best way to protect himself while fighting?

3   How useful is this source to historians studying this period?

Anne Harrison

While the Civil War clearly caused real distress and dislocation within some families, members of other families found that it brought them more excitement, freedom and opportunities than they could possibly have expected in peacetime. One young woman whose life was transformed by the Civil War was Anne Harrison, who in 1643 was only seventeen.

She left her comfortable family house in Hertfordshire and joined her father in the Royalist headquarters in Oxford. While she found the living conditions in Oxford to be very basic, the discomfort was compensated for by the exciting atmosphere of the garrison town, and she soon met, fell in love with and married a young Royalist, Richard Fanshawe.

● SOURCE 4.35

Anne Harrison later described her wartime experiences in a memoir of her life which she wrote for her eldest son.

discourse: talk

garret: attic room

portion: dowry

preferred: promoted

rack: storm

stock: money

My father commanded my sister and myself to come to him at Oxford where the court then was; but we, that had till that hour lived in great plenty and great order, found ourselves like fishes out of water and the scene so changed that we knew not at all how to act any part but obedience; for from as good house as any gentleman of England had we come to a baker's house in an obscure street, and from rooms well furnished to lie in a very bad bed in a GARRET, to one dish of meat and that not the best ordered; no money, for we were as poor as Job, nor clothes more than a man or two brought in their clothes bags. We had the perpetual DISCOURSE of the losing and gaining of towns and men; at the windows the sad spectacle of war, sometimes plague, sometimes sicknesses of other kind, by reason of so many people being packed together, as I believe there never was before of that quality; always want, yet I must needs say most bore it with a martyrlike cheerfulness. For my own part I began to think we should all like Abraham live in tents all the days of our lives … But as in a rack the turbulence of the waves disperses the splinters of the rock, so it was my lot; for having buried my dear brother Will Harrison in Exeter College Chapel, I then married your dear father in [16]44 in Wolvercote Church, two miles from Oxford, upon the 18th day of May. None was at our wedding but my dear father (who by my [deceased] mother's desire gave me her wedding ring, with which I was married), and my sister Margaret, and my brother and sister Butler, Sir Edward Hyde, afterwards Lord Chancellor, and Sir Geoffrey Palmer, the King's attorney. Before I was married my husband was sworn Secretary of War to the Prince, now our King [Charles II], with a promise from Charles the First to be PREFERRED so soon as occasion offered it, but both his fortune and my promised PORTION, which was made £10,000, were both at that time in expectation, and we might be truly called merchant adventurers, for the STOCK we set up our trading with did not amount to £20 betwixt us. But, however, it was to us as a little piece of armour is against a bullet, which if it be right placed, though no bigger than a shilling serves as well as a whole suit of arms; so by our stock [we] bought pens, ink, and paper, which was your father's trade, and by it I assure you we lived better than those that were born to £12,000 a year as long as he had his liberty …

1   What can you tell from this source about when it was written?

2   In what ways did the Civil War cause problems for Anne Harrison?

3   In what ways did the Civil War bring added excitement and opportunities to Anne Harrison?

4   What does the source reveal about the issues affecting side-taking at the beginning of the war?

5   What are the advantages and disadvantages of memoirs as sources for historians?

6   Use Sources 4.30–4.35 to explain the impact of the Civil War upon families, and in particular upon women's lives.

7   Assess the limitations and usefulness of a study of these families to a historian investigating the impact of the Civil War.

● **Summary Task**

1   'How much were ordinary people really affected by the events of the Great Rebellion? The present writer is gradually coming to the conclusion that we may have exaggerated the impact of the war on daily life … it would be misleading to suppose that daily life was continuously interrupted by fighting, even in the Midlands. The Great Rebellion was far from being a total war …' (Alan Everitt, *The Local Community and the Great Rebellion*, 1969)
    On the basis of your study of the sources in this chapter and any other research you may have done, do you agree or disagree with this author's conclusions about the impact of the Civil War? Explain your answer fully.

2   Why do you think historians have reached different conclusions about the impact of the Civil War upon the civilian population?

● Further Reading

Charles Carlton, *Going to the Wars* (Routledge, 1992) paints a colourful picture of the realities of the Civil War conflict for both soldiers and civilians.

The impact of the war on the English counties can also be studied through the publications of John Morrill, especially *The Revolt of the Provinces* (Longman, 1976), *Reactions to the English Civil War* (Macmillan, 1982), and *The Impact of the English Civil War* (Collins and Brown, 1991). There are also a number of important studies of individual counties: John Morrill, *Cheshire 1630–1660* (OUP, 1974); Anthony Fletcher, *A County Community in Peace and War: Sussex 1600–1660* (Longman, 1975); Alan Everitt, *The Community of Kent and the Great Rebellion* (Leicester University Press, 1966); Anne Hughes, *Religion, Society and Civil War in Warwickshire* (CUP, 1994).

For the damage caused by the fighting see Stephen Porter, *Destruction in the English Civil Wars* (Alan Sutton, Stroud, 1994), and for the effect of the war on families see Christopher Durston, *The Family in the English Revolution* (Blackwell, 1989).

chapter 5

Why did Parliament win the Civil War?

Introduction

When the Civil War broke out in 1642 the King's defeat was far from certain. At first the Royalist and Parliamentarian forces seemed to be quite evenly matched. In the early stages of the war Charles appeared to gain the upper hand, but he failed to achieve an early victory. Fortunes swayed during 1643 and 1644 and there were lengthy periods of deadlock. Not until the second half of 1644 did the war begin to swing in Parliament's favour, but it still took another two years to complete the victory. The outcome of the war remained in doubt until the summer of 1645. Then, as you have seen, the King's forces were decisively defeated at the Battles of Naseby and Langport by Parliament's recently formed New Model Army. The Civil War finally ended with Charles I's surrender to the Scots in June 1646.

The main aim of this chapter is to investigate why Parliament, rather than the King, won the Civil War of 1642–6. It is also intended to help you to develop your essay-writing skills. It contains three sections:

- Section A Guidance on writing an essay
- Section B A selection of extracts from historians' writings about the causes of Parliament's victory
- Section C An end of chapter exercise in which you will be asked to compare two sample essays.

In your previous study of history you will have come across several wars. Discuss some of these wars and the reasons why the eventual winners were able to defeat their opponents. This activity will provide a useful starting point for analysing the factors that help explain why Parliament won the Civil War.

Section A Writing a history essay

Essays are an important part of your A Level History course. An essay is essentially an answer to a question, in the form of a piece of extended writing (consisting of several paragraphs). It should be concerned with explaining rather than just describing historical events. A successful history essay should demonstrate:

- good understanding of the issues raised by the question and ideas to answer it
- knowledge: accurate facts and details to support the ideas
- skills: of selecting, organising and presenting information and ideas.

Effort, thought and regular practice will help you to improve your essay-writing technique during the course. The main stages in writing a history essay are summarised in the diagram on page 90.

Essay writing

The question:

Why did Parliament win the Civil War?

Read the question carefully. Make sure that you understand exactly what you are being asked to explain. Your teacher will tell you how long your essay should be and if it is to be written in study time or under test conditions.

First thoughts

Parliament was bound to win. The New Model Army was a much better army than the King's.

You should already have some ideas to answer the question. To answer it fully you will need to find out more information and ideas. Be prepared to change or even discard some of your first ideas if necessary.

Research

There were more causes of Parliament's victory than I first thought.

You will need to study a range of sources. Primary sources can provide you with information about events and what people at the time thought about them. You must consider their reliability; for example, a lot of propaganda was issued during the Civil War. You should read what several historians have written about the question. Their accounts will provide you with new ideas as well as different conclusions for you to consider.

Making notes

Make notes as you carry out your research. They will become the raw material for your essay. Concentrate on material which is relevant for answering the question. Use sub-headings regularly – they will help you to find information and organise facts and ideas later on.

Planning

There was much more to Parliament's victory than just the New Model Army.

Select the most important points and information from your notes. Then plan your essay in rough. It should consist of:

- a short introduction
- five or six main paragraphs; each one should contain a major point to answer the question and detailed information to support it
- a conclusion to draw your main points together and present an overall answer to the question; for example, you could explain which you think was the most important reason for Parliament's victory.

Make sure that your essay will have a good balance between argument (points to answer the question) and supporting detail.

Writing your essay

Now you can write your answer to the question. When you have finished, check your work for:

- factual errors
- spelling mistakes
- inaccurate grammar
- punctuation.

Evaluation

How can I do better next time?

Your tutor's comments will help you identify your strengths and weaknesses. This will help you to improve your essay-writing technique as the course progresses.

Section B Investigating the causes of Parliament's victory

The following sources have been selected to help answer the question, 'Why did Parliament win the Civil War?' They have not been supplemented with any tasks. This will allow you to make your own selection and decide on which points are most significant in your view. Make notes as you study the sources and then plan your essay using the planning sheet on page 94. There are suggestions for further reading at the end of this chapter.

● **SOURCE 5.1**

From Christopher Hill, *The Century of Revolution* (1961)

Support for Parliament came from the economically advanced south and east of England, the King's support came from the economically backward areas of the north and west. In Yorkshire, Lancashire and Sussex there was a clear division between Parliamentarian industrial areas and Royalist agricultural areas. Many towns in areas controlled by the King held out for Parliament. The ports were all for Parliament. So was the navy. The defection by the fleet and the ports meant that the King could neither end the war by blockading London nor obtain the foreign help he tried so hard for. The London trained bands, or militia, were the most reliable Parliamentary troops in the early stages of the war.

As the war went on, two parties appeared in each of the counties held for Parliament. A conservative group of higher rank favoured a defensive war and a negotiated peace; whereas the win-the-war party found that its main support came from lower social groups … They wanted appointment by merit, irrespective of social rank, and the full mobilisation of Parliament's vastly superior resources in men and money.

Promotion by merit went together with religious toleration; people must be appointed for efficiency irrespective of their views. Cromwell selected his own officers and men regardless of labels; it was one reason for his early military success. Those who were most convinced that they were fighting God's battles proved the most effective fighters; because they trusted God they took the very greatest care to keep their powder dry, and were ready to accept a discipline that was effective because self-imposed.

● **SOURCE 5.2**

From Charles Wilson's article 'Economics and Politics in the Seventeenth Century' in *Historical Journal* V, No. 1 (1962)

The picture that emerges from Mr Hill's account is simple but unsatisfying: an England divided geographically between an advanced economic region attached to advanced political causes, producing a valorous, volunteer army, against a retarded region led by reluctant, semi-feudal commanders. He writes, for example, 'The ports were all for Parliament.' Were they? London, of course; Hull also, but loyalties of the citizens were evenly divided. At Bristol, Parliamentary sympathies were uppermost but there was strong support for the King, and Bristol served the Royal cause well from its capture by Rupert early in the war to its surrender in September 1645. So did Falmouth and Chester. Exeter, with its small but useful port of Topsham, was a Royalist centre. Newcastle was the funnel through which the northern Cavaliers got valuable foreign help, which Mr Hill says they were denied. The defection of the fleet was not the social revolt of professional captains: naval loyalty had been badly strained by Charles' unpopular pro-Spanish policy. That the loss of London, Hull and the fleet was a grievous blow to Charles is true, but these events do not of themselves explain his failure. Even less is to be explained in terms of the other military factor to which Mr Hill attaches great importance: the performance of the London trained bands who were 'the most reliable Parliamentary troops in the early stages of the war'; which in turn presumably reflects his belief that Calvinism turned out the 'most effective fighters'. Twice he credits them with 'checking the Royalist advance at Turnham Green and preserving the army at Newbury'. But did they? The Battle of Turnham Green was never fought. It was not valour, but numbers, that frightened the impressionable Charles, who promptly retired to Hounslow. At Newbury it seems more than likely that the trained bands were preserved by the efficient deployment of the Parliamentary artillery.

Closely related to the theory that the Civil War was a class struggle is the theory that resources inevitably determined the victory: that the unequal distribution of resources and support doomed the Cavaliers to inevitable failure. Economic resources do not, by themselves, however, win wars. It was the failure in leadership, the dissensions and intrigues in the high command, that prevented the King from exploiting the considerable tactical victories he won, and dispersed and dissipated his resources. Only this gave the Parliamentary command time to organise itself. Slowly the superior potential available to Parliament was made actual. In the interval while that was being done, Charles lost the war.

● **SOURCE 5.3**

From Sir Charles Firth, *Cromwell's Army* (1902)

The issue of the war depended upon the question of whether King or Parliament could soonest organise an effective army ... To organise an effective army, to feed it, to clothe it, to pay it, and to recruit it, so as to maintain its fighting power and its numbers for any length of time, seemed beyond the skill of either.

Parliament perceived the necessity for such an army ... It was not till April 1645, however, that the organisation of the new army was completed, and not till May that the New Model could set forth on its career of conquest.

● **SOURCE 5.4**

From Mark Kishlansky, *The Rise of the New Model Army* (1979)

The formation of the New Model Army marked no great break with Parliament's past, no ascendancy of a 'win-the-war' policy, and no feat of administrative genius. It was organised almost entirely ... from the old armies, financed through the old assessment scheme, and run by Parliament's administrative committees, and its triumph was as unexpected as it was puzzling.

The New Model had begun as an amalgamation of the old armies, and nothing in the first fifteen months of its history substantially changed its composition, character or conduct. The presupposition that the New Model was radical at its creation, dominated by those who supported radical religion and politics, cannot be supported. Only after Parliament's failure to secure the peace that the New Model's victories made possible, was the New Model transformed into a truly radical army.

● **SOURCE 5.5**

From Ronald Hutton, *The Royalist War Effort, 1642–1646* (1982)

By late 1644 any piece of Royalist territory was in the hands of military men who were with one exception either younger sons or gentry from districts distant from those placed under their rule. The local populations had to be squeezed and squeezed again without mercy until they were forced to disgorge the money and provisions which the war effort needed. Local gentry would hesitate to ruin their neighbours; outsiders would not. The most important of the new commanders, Rupert, raised and equipped an army which may have come near to winning the war at Marston Moor. During the following winter the new military men met with a considerably hostile reaction from the communities they governed, resulting not merely from growing war weariness, but recent Royalist defeats, and eventually overcame this challenge. By the summer of 1645 they put a formidable army in the field.

At Naseby, however, that army was destroyed. This forced the King to appeal for fresh sacrifices while depriving him of the means to coerce the communities which chose instead to ally with Parliament in evicting the King's forces. In the last resort it was the local community that defeated Charles I, not from hatred of his cause but from hatred of the war itself.

● **SOURCE 5.6**

From John Morrill, 'The Stuarts', in K. Morgan (ed.), *The Oxford History of Britain* (1984)

The King had several initial advantages – the support of personally wealthy men, a naturally unified command structure ... a simpler military objective (to capture London). But Parliament had greater long-term advantages: the wealth and manpower of London, crucial for the provision of credit; the control of the navy and of the trade routes with the result that hard-headed businessmen preferred to deal with them rather than the King; a greater compactness of territory less vulnerable to invasion than the Royalist hinterlands; and the limited but important help afforded by the invasion of 20,000 Scots in 1644 ...

It was always likely that the Parliamentary side would wear down the Royalists in a long war. So it proved. Purely military factors played little part in the outcome. Both sides deployed the same tactics and used similar weapons; both had large numbers of experienced officers who had served in ... the Thirty Years' War. In 1645 both sides 'new modelled' their military organisations ... Parliament's bringing together three separate armies ... This New Model Army was put under the command of ... Sir Thomas Fairfax ... and all MPs were recalled from their commands to serve in the Houses. The New Model was not, by origin, designed to radicalise the Parliamentary cause and it was not dominated by radical officers.

Professionalisation, not radicalisation, was the key; the army's later reputation for religious zeal and for representing a career open to the talents was not a feature of its creation. The great string of victories beginning at Naseby in June 1645 was not the product of its zeal, but of regular pay. In the last eighteen months of the war, the unpaid Royalist armies simply dissolved. The Civil War was won by attrition.

To win the war Parliament had imposed massive taxation on the people. Direct taxation was itself set at a level of 15–20 per cent of the income of the rich and of the middling sort. Excise duties were imposed on basic commodities such as beer and salt. Several thousand gentry and many thousands of others whose property lay in an area controlled by their opponents had their estates confiscated.

In order to win the Civil War, Parliament had to grant extensive powers, even arbitrary powers, to its agents. The war was administered by a series of committees in London who oversaw the activities of committees in each county. Committees at each level were granted powers … to assess people's wealth and impose their assessments; to search premises and to distrain goods; to imprison those who obstructed them without trial. Only thus had the resources to win the Civil War been secured.

● **SOURCE 5.7**

From Angela Anderson, *The Civil Wars, 1640–49* (1995)

It is clear that Parliamentary control of the south-east and London provided superior resources, and that the possession of the navy and the major ports of the kingdom enabled the Parliament to stop the King from redressing the balance with supplies from abroad. Thus one factor in Parliament's success was its underlying superiority of resources. Time was required, however, to access these resources fully, and the initial advantage lay with the King. Hence the Royalist failures of 1642–3 were also crucial. Determined resistance by pockets of Parliamentary support – in particular, the London trained bands after Edgehill and the ports of Hull, Plymouth and Gloucester in 1643 – contributed to these, but the rivalries among the Royalist commanders were equally, if not more, important. Newcastle's failure to march south in the summer of 1643 prevented an attack on London when Parliamentarian fortunes were at their lowest ebb, and the continuing disputes between Prince Rupert and Lord Digby meant that strategic decisions were often influenced by personal considerations. Ultimately this failure of leadership must rest with the King, who had an authority denied to the Parliamentary leaders. His hesitations and uncertainties, as well as the lack of judgement in choosing his advisers that he had shown all his life, contributed in no small measure to the Royalist failure.

If Royalist errors prevented an early Royalist victory, they did not ensure Parliamentary success. Without effective leadership, Parliament would have been unable to use the breathing space provided. Thus the skill of John Pym in balancing the opposing parties within the Commons, in persuading members to adopt new and unpopular methods of administration, and to accept a Scottish alliance was essential. As a result the balance swung in favour of Parliament, and it can be argued that the factors outlined so far created the probability, or likelihood, that the Parliamentary forces would win the war, but this was by no means certain. The failure of Essex in Cornwall showed how easily mistakes could be made, and resources drained. The final condition necessary for Parliament's victory came with the military reorganisation of 1644–5, the emergence of leaders who sought victory as the prerequisite of peace, and the establishment of the New Model Army. Thereafter, it is difficult to see that a Royalist victory could have been possible.

If Parliamentary victory was now inevitable at some time, it was by no means certain that it would be quick or complete. It was Charles' tactical error in fighting the Battle of Naseby, and the re-emergence of neutralism, that brought Royalist collapse within little more than a year. These contingent factors did much to speed up the process, but with resources already stretched and rivalries continuing, it is difficult to believe that the Royalists were capable of matching the effectiveness of the New Model Army, or of reorganising themselves to become so. By 1645 the combination of superior resources, superior leadership and superior military organisation had established the essential conditions for Parliamentary victory.

● **SOURCE 5.8**

From Barry Williams, *Elusive Settlement* (1984)

The reasons for this military victory, overwhelming and inevitable as it seemed from the vantage point of 1646, lay in the slow emergence of three factors: first, the Royalist failure to solve the problem of provincialism; secondly, Parliament's political and military leadership; and thirdly, the effective Parliamentary marshalling of resources.

Provincialism struck twice at the Royalist military effort. The abortive execution of the 1643 plan was serious enough, but over the next two years a more insidious form of localism affected the Royalists. The preservation of county interests bedevilled attempts to establish a well-paid national force commanded from the King's headquarters at Oxford. As the war proceeded Charles acquiesced and allowed local control of parts of his army. Its impact on the King's forces was soon apparent: the money required from the counties to maintain field armies slumped. Parliament, of course, faced the same problems. But in the political arena the leadership until his death in 1643 of John Pym, and then of Fairfax and Cromwell on the battlefield, brought sufficient energy, ruthlessness and centralised direction to the cause to allow an effective use of Parliament's considerable resources. Parliament controlled London with its 'supply' of men, its city monies, its great port attracting trade like a magnet, and its Tower armoury; the fleet, in fair shape ironically because of ship money, declared for Parliament in July 1642; the economically prosperous East Anglian and Yorkshire woollen areas gave Parliament much support.

Only one more factor emerges as fundamental and undisputed in an evaluation of Parliament's victory: financial organisation. It was Pym's achievement to lay the foundation in 1643 for the centralised and often ruthless acquisition of enough money to feed the war machine. County committees of leading Parliamentary gentry were set up to supervise the collection of the Weekly Pay (later called the Monthly Assessment).

Sequestrations were also supervised by the county committees, enabling them to seize estates and personal effects of 'delinquents'. Another device of Pym's was the Excise, a kind of sales tax on goods like tobacco and beer. The provision of cash for the Parliamentary cause was a great achievement. Over a million pounds a year was the lifeline which kept the armies in being. The architect of it all was John Pym, whose ghost presided in magisterial fashion over Parliament's eventual victory in 1646.

ESSAY PLANNING

Question: Why did Parliament win the Civil War?

Introduction

Paragraph 1   Main point
                     Supporting evidence

Paragraph 2   Main point
                     Supporting evidence

Paragraph 3   Main point
                     Supporting evidence

Paragraph 4   Main point
                     Supporting evidence

Paragraph 5   Main point
                     Supporting evidence

Conclusion

Section C Two sample essays

Now that you have planned your essay, you should compare it with the two sample essays provided below. After you have read them, discuss:

- the strengths and weaknesses of each essay
- which you think is the best essay and why.

Comments about each of these essays by an examiner are provided at the end of this section.

Essay 1

1   Charles I came to the throne in 1625 and faced serious problems from the start. During the late 1620s and 1630s he went to war with Spain and France and his soldiers came off very badly in these. He also promoted William Laud and his Armenian beliefs which angered many Puritains. In 1629 he decided to call no

5   more Parliaments; he began an 11-year period without Parliaments which is known as the Eleven Years' Tyranny.

What happened during these years upset people greatly, especially Ship Money, and Charles was forced to recall Parliament in 1640. Charles, therefore, governed the country very badly for 11 years, taxing the people far too much. It is not

10   surprising that he and his people were on the verge of Civil War in 1640. Between 1640 and 1642 there were various attempts to avoid war but they all failed. Charles should therefore bear most of the responsibility for causing the war.

After the Civil War had started and he had set up his standard at Nottingham, Charles moved west towards the Welsh border to raise troops and many Welsh

15   men flocked to join his army. It is not clear why Wales was such a strong royalist area. In the autumn of 1642 the first major battle of the Civil War took place at Edgehill in Warwickshire. Both sides thought they could win, but after a long and bloody battle it was clear that neither had done so and that the war would go on much longer than they had expected.

20   After the battle Charles marched on towards London in an attempt to end the war by retaking his capital city. He was halted at Turnham Green by forces of the London militia and after a short battle he moved back to Oxford where he established his headquarters. Some writers have said that he should have tried harder to capture London at this stage and that if he had managed to do this he

25   would probably have won the war. It is difficult to decide why Charles did turn back at Turnham Green but some people say that this was probably a bad mistake.

Charles was based at Oxford for the remainder of the war and had a lot of support in the town. He also had some very good generals, particularly Prince Rupert and Prince Maurice who were his uncles, and the royalists won several

30   important battles in the early stages of the war. The parliamentarians also had good generals, particularly Oliver Cromwell, who later became the ruler in the 1650s. The royalists controlled the north and west of the country and they captured Bristol in 1643, which was one of the most important ports in the kingdom. In the summer of 1643 the king laid siege to Gloucester, although he

35   might have been better advised to have tried to capture London again at this stage. By now Charles was becoming short of money and he was forced to raise extra taxes from parts of the country he controlled. Parliament too needed to raise money but were able to do this more quickly.

By the middle of the war Parliament was gaining the upper hand. In 1644 Prince

40   Rupert was defeated at Marston More, near York, by Oliver Cromwell and a Scottish army, but a few weeks later the Earl of Essex's parliamentary army was defeated by the King at Lostwithiel in Cornwall. Later that year Parliament decided to form a new army called the new model army. It was led by Sir Thomas Fairfax and no member of Parliament, except Oliver Cromwell, was allowed to be

45   part of it. This army was full of Puritans who had volunteered to fight against Charles I who they thought was a Catholic. They were paid regularly and they could become officers if they showed they were good soldiers. The new model army helped greatly to win the war for Parliament by winning a number of

important victories. By 1645 Charles was losing many battles, especially Naseby,
50 where many of his troops were captured.

After Naseby, Parliament was just too strong for him. Parliament was now
getting a lot more money and this helped their war effort greatly. Charles was not
strong enough any more.

Thus we can see that the defeat of Charles I in the Civil War was inevitable
55 once Parliament had defeated him at Naseby. After the end of the war Charles
was offered a number of chances to reach a compromise with his enemies but for
two-and-a-half years he tried to regain power without making any concessions.

In the end he left Parliament with no option but to execute him on 30 January
1649.

60 A few years later Cromwell was offered the Crown. Thus we can see that
Charles lost the Civil War because the Parliamentarians were just too strong for
him.

Essay 2

1 In order to explain why, after four years of bitter and intense fighting in England in
the 1640s, it was the Parliamentarians rather than Charles I who were victorious
in the English Civil War, it is necessary to consider a range of factors. Some of
them were purely military but others were to do with the back-up that was
5 provided to the soldiers by their civilian supporters.

The more direct military issues which will be considered first include the
question of the quality of leadership, the organisation of the various armies and
the supply of soldiers. Both sides could boast generals of some considerable
ability. Prince Rupert, the King's nephew, who had considerable experience of
10 warfare on the continent before 1642, was the ablest military strategist on either
side, and most of the other experienced veterans were found among the ranks of
the royalists. Nonetheless, although most of the parliamentary officers were less
experienced than the royalists, some of them, like Oliver Cromwell, proved to
have an aptitude for fighting and were more than a match for their foes.
15 Furthermore, the leadership of the royalist forces was fatally weakened by Charles
I's decision to take overall control of strategy into his own hands. Mistakenly
believing that he was a highly skilled tactician himself, Charles frequently ignored
the advice of his more experienced officers and persisted in policies which only he
could see the wisdom of. In this sense, Charles himself was personally responsible
20 for weakening the royalist war effort.

In the early stages of the war, the fighting strength of both sides was roughly
equal, and both had their resources divided up into two or three main armies. In
the spring of 1645, however, Parliament decided to reorganise its soldiers into a
single, unified force, the New Model Army. The New Model was a national army
25 raised for service throughout the country; it was well disciplined and regularly
paid, and a substantial proportion of its members were volunteers, who could be
relied upon not to desert at any opportunity. As promotion to senior rank in the
New Model was on the basis of military expertise, it was soon led by its most
dedicated and able members. Some historians like John Morrill (in the introduction
30 to *Reactions to the English Civil War*) and Ronald Hutton (in the *Royalist War Effort*)
have tried to play down the part played by the New Model in Parliament's victory,
but the fact remains that within a few months of it taking the field it had won
crucial victories at Naseby and Langport. In doing so it had effectively broken the
back of the king's war effort. The main royalist army was decimated at Naseby and
35 never recovered. It is difficult not to conclude that the formation of the New
Model Army was a vitally important factor in Parliament's victory.

Another reason for the weakness of the royalist effort in the last year of the
war was the problem the king had in replacing the losses to his forces through
death, injury and desertion. While Parliament had a fair degree of success
40 recruiting replacement soldiers, by the last months of the war the king was unable
to find sufficient men to serve in his infantry. Whether this was the result of
defects in his recruitment procedures or because of the reluctance of individuals

to come to his aid, this problem worsened Charles' already serious problems in the aftermath of Naseby.

45 The remaining purely military factors which need to be considered are the involvement of the Scots and the navy. Both sides in the conflict were keen to acquire foreign aid. Charles sent his wife, Henrietta Maria, to France in an attempt to enlist French support, but her mission was a failure. In 1643 it was Parliament which gained a foreign ally – the Scots Covenanters. The Scots agreed to fight on
50 Parliament's side in the expectation that a parliamentary victory would be followed by the establishment of a Presbyterian church in England. They marched into northern England in early 1644 and fought there until the end of the war. Their presence added significantly to Parliament's strength and was particularly important at the Battle of Marston Moor in 1644.

55 At the beginning of the war the English navy came out for Parliament. This made it that much more difficult for the king to obtain help from abroad. It was also important in military operations on the coast as it allowed Parliament to relieve its own besieged operations on the coast and to blockade royalist ports from the sea.

60 Armies can only fight effectively when they are properly supplied and supported. In this area too it is clear that Parliament gradually gained a big advantage. Parliament was at its weakest in the early months of the war when it was creating from scratch a wartime administrative structure. Charles' best chance of victory came at this stage. The fact that he did not take it is explained
65 partly by his own mistakes and partly by the efforts of John Pym, whose leadership was of enormous benefit to Parliament. Realising that the war could not be fought without plentiful supplies of money, Pym introduced the assessment tax, the excise and the confiscation of royalist estates. County committees were established to ensure that taxes were collected. Pym also saw the importance of a
70 foreign ally and he was largely responsible for the Scottish alliance. Pym died in December 1643, but during the first eighteen months of the war he had done a great deal to ensure both Parliament's early survival and eventual victory.

Perhaps one of the most important reasons of all, however, for Parliament's eventual success was their possession of the capital. London was by far the biggest
75 and wealthiest city in the country. Its population paid a large proportion of Parliament's taxes and its men provided a large pool from which Parliament's soldiers could be drawn. The London trained bands were the best trained militia in the country. Possession of the Tower of London meant access to a large arsenal.

80 London was by far the most important port in the country which enabled Parliament to collect customs duties. It contained the country's wealthiest merchants from whom Parliament was able to borrow large sums. Parliament's possession of London meant that by the latter stages of the war it was able to lay its hands on cash far more readily than Charles.

85 Parliament's victory was secured by a combination of these factors but of crucial importance was the contribution of the New Model Army and Parliament's ability to exploit the resources of London. These advantages did not make a victory inevitable, but they meant that the longer the war went on the less likely it was that Charles would be able to sustain his war effort at the same level as his
90 enemies.

Examiner's comments

Essay 1

This is not a very successful essay. Its most serious weakness is its failure to concentrate upon answering the question. Most of this essay just describes events and it is able to offer only a few simplistic points to answer the question, such as 'the Parliamentarians were just too strong ...' (line 61). Several important points are ignored and some irrelevant material is included. Lines 1–11 refer to Charles's reign before the Civil War and are more concerned with explaining, unconvincingly, why the war broke out rather than why Parliament won it. Lines 55–60 deal with the period after the war.

In several places important points are touched upon. Some of Charles's tactical mistakes are referred to. Parliament's finances (lines **37–8** and **51–2**), the involvement of the Scots (line **41**) and the New Model Army are all mentioned but there is little explanation of how and why these factors helped Parliament win the war.

There are several factual errors and inaccuracies. Charles I's wars with France and Spain had ended by 1630 (line **2**). Few historians today accept that Charles I's government during the 1630s was a 'tyranny' (line **6**); it is now more commonly referred to as the period of 'Personal Rule'. The claim that it 'upset people greatly' (line **7**) is also highly questionable (see Chapter 1). The statement that this supposed unpopularity 'forced Charles to recall Parliament in 1640' (line **8**) ignores the role of Charles I's defeat by the Scots in precipitating his decision to recall Parliament. The statement 'he and his people were on the verge of Civil War in 1640' (line **10**) shows weak understanding of the situation in 1640 and the use of the term 'people' is too imprecise. Prince Rupert and Prince Maurice were Charles I's nephews, not uncles (line **29**). The soldiers in the New Model Army were *not* all volunteers – many of them were forced to fight (line **45**). The reference to 'some writers' (line **23**) is too imprecise; their names and the titles of their books should be given.

This essay is written in generally accurate English but there are several spelling mistakes. 'Armenian' should be 'Arminian' and 'Puritains' should be 'Puritans' (line **4**). 'Marston More' (line **40**) should be Marston Moor. Capital letters should be used for technical terms such as the 'New Model Army'.

Essay 2

This is a much more convincing essay. Unlike Essay 1 it concentrates throughout upon answering the question and irrelevant material is avoided. Rather than treating the Civil War chronologically, it is organised around seven main points:

- Charles's defects as a military strategist
- the New Model Army
- the recruitment problem of the Royalists by 1645
- the Scottish alliance
- the support of the navy for Parliament
- the political leadership of John Pym
- Parliament's possession of London.

This essay is clearly argued, accurate and generally well supported with facts, although the first point would have benefited from some examples. The points are effectively presented as 'military' and 'non-military' factors. Other ways of categorising these factors which could have been used are long- and short-term causes, or necessary and contingent factors. There is a clear attempt to evaluate the causes of Parliament's victory. Parliament's possession of London is described as 'one of the most important reasons' (line **73**) and the New Model Army is referred to as 'a vitally important factor' (line **36**); both points are explained and followed up in the conclusion. There are some direct references to the work of historians (lines **29–31**).

Other points which could have been considered include Parliament's possession of the wealthier south and east of the country throughout the war, Oliver Cromwell's qualities as a cavalry commander and the role of Puritanism in Parliament's armies, especially the New Model Army.

The conclusions about the importance of the New Model Army are, as the essay recognises, open to debate. Several recent historians have argued that, by 1645, following his defeat at Marston Moor and the loss of northern England, the King's resources were rapidly running out. In addition, the New Model Army was still in its infancy and largely dependent on generals and soldiers from Parliament's earlier county armies when it won the decisive battles of Naseby and Langport. Furthermore, its superiority in numbers has often been cited as an important factor in its victories; for example, at Naseby it outnumbered the Royalists by almost two to one. This again brings us back to the issue of resources. Therefore the New Model Army can be seen as the catalyst of Parliament's victory rather than a major cause. If we follow this line of argument, the most important causes of Parliament's victory appear to be longer-term factors: its superior resources for fighting a long war, of which London was undoubtedly the most valuable, and the methods MPs, especially John Pym, created to exploit them.

● Further reading

Chapter 5 in *The Civil Wars, 1640–49* by Angela Anderson (Hodder and Stoughton, 1995) from which Source 5.7 is taken, is highly recommended as a recent, detailed, thorough and accessible analysis. It also has useful advice on making notes and answering both essay and source-based questions on the Civil War. G. E. Aylmer's analysis on pages 116–29 in *The Struggle for the Constitution* (Blandford, 1963), although dated, is still useful.

chapter 6

Why was Charles I executed in 1649?

1646
May 5: Charles I surrenders to Scots.

July 13: Parliament issues the Propositions of Newcastle.

1647
January 30: The Scots hand over Charles I to Parliament.

February 18–19: Parliament proposes to reduce the New Model Army.

March 30: Parliament condemns the Army's petition for redress of grievances.

April: From the early part of the month soldiers in the New Model Army begin to elect agitators.

May 12: Charles I issues his third answer to the Propositions of Newcastle.

June 4: Charles I is seized by Cornet Joyce and taken to Hampton Court.

June 5, 14: The army issues The Solemn Engagement of the Army and A Representation of the Army.

July 16–17: The Army Debates take place at Reading.

August 1: The Heads of Proposals is published.

August 6: The army occupies London and purges Parliament of eleven MPs.

October 18: *The Case of the Army Truly Stated* is issued.

October 28: *The Agreement of the People* is issued by the Levellers and army agitators. The Putney Debates between the army and the Levellers begin (until 15 November).

November 11: Charles I escapes from Hampton Court.

November 15: Cromwell suppresses an army mutiny at Corkbush Field, in Hertfordshire.

December 25: Riots occur in Canterbury on Christmas Day.

December 26: Charles I, now on the Isle of Wight, signs the Engagement with the Scots.

December 28: Charles I rejects the Four Bills presented to him by Parliament.

1648
January 3: The Vote of No Addresses is passed by the House of Commons (approved by the Lords on 17 January).

March: A revolt breaks out in South Wales.

April 28–30: The Army Prayer Meeting is held at Windsor.

May: Revolts begin in Kent and Essex.

July 8: The Scottish army invades England.

August 17–20: Cromwell defeats the Scots near Preston.

August 24: The Vote of No Addresses is revoked by Parliament.

August 27: The surrender of Colchester marks the end of the Second Civil War.

September 18: The Newport negotiations on the Isle of Wight between Charles I and Parliament begin.

November 27: Parliament rejects The Remonstrance of the Army.

December 1: Charles I is seized by the army and is removed to Hurst Castle.

December 5: The Commons vote to continue negotiating with Charles I.

December 6: Pride's Purge reduces Parliament to a 'Rump' of 154 MPs.

1649
January 6: The Rump passes an Act establishing a High Court of Justice to try the King.

January 20–27: The trial of Charles I takes place in Westminster Hall.

January 30: Charles I is executed.

Introduction: revolution and counter-revolution, 1646–9

The period from the end of the Civil War in May 1646 until the trial and execution of the King in January 1649 could claim to be the most extraordinary period in British history. The year 1647 saw the victorious Parliamentary New Model Army explode in a major revolt, during which it developed its own political programme for a post-war settlement. In the summer of 1647 the army occupied London, and there the Army Council (which included agitators, elected representatives of junior officers and ordinary soldiers, as well as senior officers) debated fundamental political principles, including democracy and people's rights. Outside the army an even more wide-ranging and revolutionary programme of change was publicised by civilian radicals, whom contemporaries were beginning to nickname 'Levellers'.

If 1647 was a year of revolution, most of 1648 was one of counter-revolution, marked by provincial risings against the New Model Army, a revolt in the navy and a Scottish invasion designed to restore Charles I to power. These events are often called the Second Civil War. By the end of 1648, the New Model Army emerged victorious from the Second Civil War as it had from the first. It then embarked on what is often known as the English Revolution. In December 1648 and January 1649, it forcibly expelled its enemies from Parliament, put the King on trial and then executed him. What was left of the House of Commons after the army's purge (the Rump Parliament) abolished the monarchy and the House of Lords and established an English republic.

The most important task for historians of this exciting period is to explain why all this happened and, specifically, to explain why all attempts to reach a post-war settlement with Charles I failed. Why did the King end his life on the scaffold on 30 January 1649? There are no easy or obvious answers to these questions, primarily because, until the end of 1648, hardly anyone seems to have wanted the King's execution. On the contrary, after the end of the Civil War most people in Britain wanted a settlement that would have restored the King to power. Even the minority of men who brought the King to trial early in January 1649 had, for much of the previous two-and-a-half years, worked hard to reach such a settlement.

You will be asked at the end of this chapter to explain why no settlement was made at the end of the Civil War in 1646 and why, only three years later, Charles I was executed.

The sources in this chapter are designed to help you work out your own answers to these questions.

The sources are grouped in three sections:

- Section A From the end of the Civil War to July 1647
- Section B From July 1647 to January 1648
- Section C From January 1648 to January 1649.

Each section consists of extracts from primary sources, questions on the sources and a concluding task.

Section A From the end of the Civil War to July 1647: why did the New Model Army become politicised?

This period is dominated by the development of the New Model Army into a force as powerful in British politics as it had been on the Civil War battlefields. The politicisation of the New Model Army did not end the chances of a settlement with the King, since the centrepiece of the army's blueprint for a settlement was the restoration of Charles I to power. But one major result of the army's appearance on the political stage was to frustrate the intentions of some conservative Parliamentarians to bring about a speedy settlement with the King.

An essential first step when tackling the central investigation of this chapter is, therefore, to explain why the New Model Army emerged as a political force. Keep that question in mind as you read the sources.

The attitude of the King to settlement proposals: the Propositions of Newcastle, July 1646

There was very little agreement among the victors in the Civil War about what kind of peace settlement there should be. There were two major factions among English Parliamentarians: *Political Presbyterians* and *Political Independents*. The Political Presbyterians, who were anxious to disband the New Model Army, would have been content to see Charles I return with very few conditions imposed on him (notably the acceptance of a Presbyterian Church); while the Political Independents were anxious to secure greater concessions from the King before disbanding the army. The Scots, to whom Charles had surrendered in May 1646, were also divided. Out of this complex political situation came, in the early summer of 1646, a set of peace proposals from the English Parliament, the Propositions of Newcastle.

The main terms of the Newcastle Propositions were as follows:

- Parliament was to nominate thirteen key officers of state.
- Parliament was to control the militia for 20 years.
- Bishops were to be abolished and a Presbyterian Church established for three years.
- 58 Royalists were to be exempted from pardon.

Charles I's *public* response was to produce several evasive replies. Clues to his real attitude to the Newcastle Propositions are contained in his *private* letters to his wife, Henrietta Maria.

● **SOURCE 6.1**

Charles wrote these letters from Newcastle, where he was in the custody of the Scottish army, to his wife, who was at the French court at St Germain-en-Laye in France, awaiting the arrival of their eldest son, Prince Charles, from Jersey.

perfidies: *treacherous behaviour*

Newcastle, 17 June 1646.

Dear Heart, I think it fit … to give thee a particular account of the several humours of the Scots. I divide them into four factions, Montroses, the neutrals, the Hamiltons, and the Campbells … They all seem to court me, and I behave myself as evenly to all as I can … My opinion upon the whole business is, that these divisions will either serve to make them all join with me, or else God hath prepared this way to punish them for their many rebellions and PERFIDIES … So longing to hear from thee, and that Pr. Charles is safe with thee, I rest eternally thine, Charles R.

Newcastle, 1 July 1646.

Dear Heart, I had the contentment to receive thine of the 28th of June upon Saturday last. The same day I got a true copy of the London propositions, which ('tis said) will be here within ten days, and now do assure thee that they are such as I cannot grasp without loss of my conscience, crown, and honour; to which, as I can no way consent, so in my opinion a flat denial is to be delayed as long as may be, and how to make an handsome denying answer is all the difficulty … Charles R.

What do these letters tell you about Charles I's attitude to:

a) the Propositions of Newcastle
b) any kind of settlement proposal?

● **SOURCE 6.2**

The King's third answer to the Propositions of Newcastle. In May 1647, Charles I responded to the proposals presented by Parliament.

In answer to all the Propositions concerning religion, His Majesty proposes that he will confirm the Presbyterian government, the Assembly of Divines at Westminster, and the Directory, for three years (being the time set down by the two Houses), so that His Majesty and his household be not hindered from using the form of God's service which they have formerly; and also that a free consultation and debate be had with the Divines at Westminster 20 of His Majesty's nomination being added unto them), whereby it may be determined by His Majesty, and the two Houses, how the Church shall be governed after the said three years, or sooner if the differences may be agreed.

Touching the Covenant, His Majesty is not therein yet satisfied, and desires to respite his particular answer thereunto until his coming to London: because, it being a matter of conscience, he cannot give a resolution therein till he may be assisted with the device of some of his own chaplains (which have hitherto been denied him), and such other divines as shall be most proper to inform him therein.

   As to the Proposition touching the militia: though His Majesty cannot consent unto it as it is proposed (because thereby, he conceives, he wholly parts with the power of the sword intrusted to him by God and the laws of the land for the protection and government of his people, thereby at once divesting himself, and disinheriting his posterity of that right and prerogative of the Crown which is absolutely necessary to kingly office, and so weakening monarchy in this kingdom that little more than the name and shadow of it will remain), yet, if it be only security for the preservation of the peace of this kingdom after these unhappy troubles, and the due performance of all the agreements which are now to be concluded, which is desired (which His Majesty always understood to be the case, and hopes herein that he is not mistaken), His Majesty will give abundant satisfaction; to which end he is willing to consent, by Act of Parliament, that the power of the militia, both by sea and land, for the space of ten years, be in such persons as the two Houses of Parliament shall nominate (giving them power, during the said term, to change the said persons, and to substitute others in their places at pleasure), and afterwards to return to the proper channel again, as it was in the times of Queen Elizabeth and King James of blessed memory.

1   Which of Parliament's proposals was Charles prepared to accept?

2   Which of them did he not accept?

3   How did Charles I's approach in this source differ from that shown in Source 6.1? Explain the likely reasons for this difference.

4   Charles had lost the Civil War. Why then did he not accept all of Parliament's proposals?

The hostility of the Political Presbyterians to the New Model Army

In January 1647 the political situation was transformed. As a result of a treaty between the Scots and the English Parliament, the Scottish army withdrew from northern England and the King was handed over to the English Parliamentary guards at Holdenby [Holmby] House in Northamptonshire. This placed the Political Presbyterians and their leaders, Denzil Holles and Philip Stapleton, in a strong position to push ahead with their plan to get rid of the New Model Army. From February to May 1647, instead of voting the £200,000 that was necessary to settle the New Model Army's arrears of pay, Holles and Stapleton led a campaign in Parliament to break up the army without paying the soldiers what they were owed. The main events in that campaign are as follows.

February 18–19:	Parliament proposes to reduce the New Model Army in size.
March 8:	Parliament votes that only Presbyterians should be officers in the reduced army, which is to be sent to Ireland.
March 30:	Parliament condemns an army petition for redress of grievances (see Source 6.4) as treasonable (The Declaration of Dislike).
April 16:	Parliament passes an ordinance establishing a City Militia Committee to form an alternative army, using non-New Model Army regiments.
May 18:	Parliament votes that all New Model Army regiments that refuse to go to Ireland should be disbanded.
May 25–7:	Parliament votes to disband the New Model Army, giving the soldiers only eight weeks' arrears of pay.

Source 6.3 helps to explain why the Political Presbyterians singled out the New Model Army for such hostile treatment.

● SOURCE 6.3

These are extracts from *Gangraena, or a New Higher Discovery of the Errors, Heresies, Blasphemies, and Insolent Proceedings of the Sectaries of This Time*, published in December 1646. The author, Thomas Edwards, was a prominent London Presbyterian preacher, who had been persecuted in the 1620s and 1630s for protesting against Laudian 'innovations'. In the 1640s, he conducted a militant campaign from the pulpit and in the press against religious Independents. For Edwards, and many like him, religious toleration was a direct threat not only to the existing religious order but also to the traditional social and political order.

sectaries: a word used at this time to describe members of religious groups (sects) with whom the writer disagreed. In this case, those who opposed the idea of one national church.

… I acknowledge the New Model under Sir Thomas Fairfax hath done gallant service against the enemy, and did the greatest and best service when it had not so many SECTARIES as it hath now, and my interest is not in the least to cast dirt upon the Army, but only to relate errors and insolencies of a part of the army …

July the third 1646. Two citizens, honest men related to me this story in the hearing of another minister, and that with a great deal of confidence (one of them having lain in the town where the fact was committed, and having spoken with many Inhabitants about it). That summer was two years Captain Beamant and his company quartered at Yakely in Huntingdonshire, there being a child in the town to be baptised, some of the soldiers would not suffer the child to be carried to the church to be baptised, and the lieutenant of the troop drew out a part of the troop to hinder it, guarding the church that they should not bring the child to be baptised. In contempt of baptism, some of the soldiers got into the church, pissed in the font, and went to a gentleman's stable in the town, and took out a horse, and brought it into the church, and there baptised it.

A godly young man of Somersetshire, or Dorsetshire, at whose house a lieutenant of a company of Sir Thomas Fairfax's army quartered, told me, that this lieutenant maintained these opinions; 1) That women might preach, and would have a gentlewoman in the house (this young man's sister) to have exercised her gifts, telling her he knew she had gifts and had been alone a meditating. 2) That if a woman's husband was asleep or absent from her, she might lie with another man, and it was lawful; for sleep was a death; and pressed it upon a young gentlewoman in the house, whose husband was then in London. 3) That it was unlawful to kneel in prayer, which was maintained by him, or some others of his company; and when they prayed, they prayed leaning.

A godly minister of this city told me June 12, 1646, that he discoursing with a major belonging to the army about the government of the Church, he told him plainly that they were not so much against Presbyterian government (though many thought them so) as against the being tied to any government at all … They held liberty of conscience, that no man shall be bound, or tied to any thing, but every man left free to hold what they pleased; that was the judgment and true genius of that sort of men in the army, called Independents, that in all matters of religion no man should be bound, but every one left to follow his own conscience.

1   How consistent are Edwards's comments about the New Model Army in the first paragraph with the comments in the rest of this source?

2   What were the major reasons why Edwards hated and feared the New Model Army? What were his main allegations against its soldiers?

3   Why was he appalled at the claim that women should be allowed to preach?

4   Why did Edwards condemn claims for liberty of conscience and those who spoke against orthodox godly ministers?

5   What might lead you to be sceptical about accepting Edwards's allegations at face value?

6   How valuable do you think *Gangraena* is as a historical source for understanding why many people hated the New Model Army at the end of 1646?

The politicisation of the New Model Army

Sources 6.4–6.7 are taken from just a few of the multitude of petitions, declarations and remonstrances which were produced by the New Model Army in the first six months of 1647. They should be read with the following questions in mind:

- What light do they throw on the reasons for and the timing of the emergence of the New Model Army as a political force?
- Did the aims of the soldiers change during the spring and early summer of 1647?

105

From the end of the Civil War to July 1647: why did the New Model Army become politicised?

The petition of the New Model Army, c. 21 March 1647. This was circulated among the soldiers of the New Model Army in and around its headquarters at Saffron Walden in Essex. It came into the possession of the three parliamentary commissioners who had been sent there to organise the break-up of the army and to despatch 12,600 of its soldiers to Ireland. They produced it in the Commons on their return on 27 March. Three days later a parliamentary motion was passed, condemning the petitioners as 'enemies of the state, and disturbers of the public peace' (The Declaration of Dislike).

indemnity: *exemption from legal prosecution*

press: *compulsory enlistment for military service; conscription*

1 First, whereas the necessity … of the War hath put us upon many actions, which the Law would not warrant, nor we have acted in a time of settled peace; we humbly desire, that before our disbanding, a full and sufficient provision may be made by Ordinance of Parliament (to which the royal assent may be desired) for our INDEMNITY and security in all such cases.

2 … that before the disbanding of the army, satisfaction may be given to the petitioners for their arrears …

3 That those who have voluntarily served the Parliament in the late wars may not hereafter be compelled by PRESS or otherwise to serve as soldiers out of this kingdom.

[The fourth and fifth demands were for pensions and compensation for war veterans and their widows and dependants and for money so that the army could pay for its own upkeep and not be 'oppressive to the country'.]

1 What is being demanded in the first clause of the petition (it occurs in many army petitions at that time)? Why should the soldiers put this demand at the top of their list of grievances?

2 What else do the soldiers demand?

3 What specific overseas service might the petitioners be referring to in the third clause?

4 Why did such an apparently moderate petition prompt the Commons to react so violently?

A Second Apologie of All the Private Soldiers, 3 May 1647. This was attached to *The Apologie of the Common Soldiers of Sir Thomas Fairfax's Army,* which was presented to Fairfax by three leading agitators, Edward Sexby, William Allen and Thomas Shepherd, on 28 April 1647. The two were printed and published together on 3 May 1647.

Sirs: We your soldiers, who have served under your commands, with all readiness, to free this our native land and nation from all tyranny and oppressions whatsoever, and that by virtue and power derived from this present Parliament, given not only to his Excellency Sir Thomas Fairfax, our now present General, but likewise under all the late generals, his predecessors, under whom we, even the whole soldiery, have served both the state and you faithfully and diligently; by which means God hath been pleased to crown us with victory in dispersing our common adversaries, so that we hoped to put an end to all tyranny and oppressions, so that justice and equity, according to the law of this land, should have been done to the people, and that the meanest subject should fully enjoy his right, liberty and properties, in all things … But instead of it, to the great grief and saddening of our hearts, we see that the oppression is as great as ever, if not greater, yea, and that upon the cordial friends to the Parliament and us, and to the just rights and liberties of this nation … Therefore brave commanders, the Lord put a spirit of courage into your hearts, that you may stand fast in your integrity that you have manifested to us your soldiers; and we do declare to you that if any of you shall not, he shall be marked with a brand of infamy for ever as a traitor to this country and an enemy to this Army.

Is it not better to die like men than to be enslaved and hanged like dogs? Which must and will be your and our portion if not now looked into, even before our disbanding … We have been quiet and peaceable in obeying all orders and commands, yet not, we have a just cause to tell you, if we be not relieved in our grievances. We shall be forced to that which we pray God to divert, and keep your and our hearts upright, desiring you to present these things to the General as our desires:

fomenters: *those who instigated the 'Declaration of Dislike'*

1 That the honour of this Army may be vindicated in every particular, especially about the late petition, and reparations given, and justice done upon the FOMENTERS.

2 That an Act of Indemnity may be made for all things done in time and place of war.

3 That the wives and children of those that have been slain in the service, and maimed soldiers, may be provided for.

4 Our arrears, under this General, to be paid us; our arrears under other generals to be audited and stated, and security given for the payments.

5 That we that have served the Parliament freely may not be pressed out of the kingdom.

6 That the liberty of the subject may no longer be enslaved, but that justice and judgements may be dealt with to the meanest subject according to the old law. Now unless all these humble requests be by you for us your soldiers and yourselves stood for to be granted, it had [been] better we had never been born, or at least we had never been in arms, but we had by the sword been cut off from the misery we and you are like to undergo. So we rest in hopes of your faithfulness.

Your soldiers.

---

1 What differences in language and tone do you detect between this document and Source 6.4?

2 Do the aims of the soldiers expressed in this document differ from those in Source 6.4?

3 Why do you think that the petitioners felt that the army's honour needed to be vindicated?

● **SOURCE 6.6**

Extracts from the grievances of New Model Army regiments, 13–14 May 1647. These were presented to four new parliamentary commissioners (Henry Ireton, Oliver Cromwell, Philip Skippon and Charles Fleetwood), all officer–MPs, sent to the army headquarters at Saffron Walden in May 1647. The demands of eleven regiments survive (those of Nathaniel Rich, John Desborough, Henry Ireton, Edward Whalley, Thomas Boteler, Sir Thomas Fairfax, James Hewson, Hardress Waller, Robert Lilburne, Edward Harley, John Lambert). Dr John Morrill's analysis of them (see 'The army revolt of 1647' in John Morrill, *The Nature of the English Revolution* (1993)) includes the following eleven grievances (the number of regiments mentioning each grievance is inserted in brackets): arrears of pay (11), resistance to service in Ireland (5), indemnity (5), freedom from conscription (6), vindication of the soldiers' right to petition (11), demand for a purge of ex-Royalists from office (7), regulation of free quarter (7), demand for investigation of corruption by civilians (4), demand for army pensions (4), demand for soldiers who were ex-apprentices to be given freedom of their trades or crafts (5), demand for freedom of worship (3), law reform (2).

[Whalley's regiment]

That such rigour is already exercised that we are denied the liberty which Christ hath purchased for us, and abridged of our freedom to serve God according to our proportion of faith, and like to be imprisoned, yea, beaten and persecuted, to enforce us to a human conformity never enjoined to Christ.

[Harley's regiment]

That notwithstanding we have engaged our lives for you, ourselves, [and] posterity, that we might be free from the yoke of Episcopal tyranny, yet we fear that the conscience of man shall be pressed beyond the light they have received from the rule of the Word in things appertaining to the worship of God, a thing wholly contrary to the Word of God [and] the best Reformed Churches.

[Lambert's regiment. Christopher Love was, like Thomas Edwards, a prominent religious Presbyterian.]

That the ministers in their public labour by all means do make us odious to the kingdom, that they might take off their affections from us lest the world should think too well of us, and not only so but have printed many scandalous books against us, as Mr Edwards's *Gangraena* and Mr Love's *Sermons*.

[Hewson's regiment]

That we who have engaged for our country's liberties and freedom, are denied the liberty to petition in case of grievance, notwithstanding the Parliament have declared (in their Declaration, 2nd November) … that it is the liberty of the people to petition unto them in case of grievances, and we humbly conceive that we have the liberty.

That the freemen of England are so much deprived of their liberties and freedom (as many of them are at this day) as to be imprisoned so long together for they know not what, and cannot be brought to a legal trial according to the laws of this land, for their just condemnation or justification, although both themselves and their friends have so often petitioned to the Parliament for it; which we know not how soon may be our case.

That the laws of this land by which we are governed, are in such unknown tongue, so that we may be guilty of the breach of them unknown to us, and come into condemnation.

---

1 In your own words briefly list the grievances of these four regiments.

2 What specific event might have prompted Hewson's regiment to demand the liberty to petition?

3 In the light of Dr Morrill's analysis of all the grievances, how representative of them all are the ones contained in these extracts?

During June the army began to march slowly from Saffron Walden towards London. On 5 June, at a rendezvous near Newmarket, in Cambridgeshire, it issued The Solemn Engagement of the Army, announcing the establishment of a General Council of the Army consisting of senior officers and representatives of junior officers and rank-and-file soldiers. Source 6.7 consists of extracts from a second major manifesto of the army issued at another rendezvous, Thriplow Heath, near Cambridge. This is the first comprehensive statement of the army's political programme. It followed it up on the following day by announcing the impeachment of Holles and ten other Political Presbyterians ('The Eleven Members') and by continuing to march towards London via St Albans, Berkhamsted and Uxbridge.

● **SOURCE 6.7**

A Representation of the Army, 14 June 1647. It was probably drafted by Ireton, before being approved by the new General Council of the Army.

There then followed other demands, including those for regular elections according to the Triennial Act of 1641, for the abolition of royal power to adjourn and dissolve Parliaments, for a redistribution of parliamentary seats according to the taxation contribution of areas, for the people's right to petition Parliament, and for an Act of Indemnity to cover all but a few Royalist delinquents.

Nor will it now, we hope, seem strange or unseasonable to rational and honest men ... if ... we shall, before disbanding, proceed in our and the kingdom's behalf to propound and plead for some provision for our and the kingdom's satisfaction and future security ... Especially considering that we were not a mere mercenary army, hired to serve any arbitrary power of a state, but called forth and conjured by the several declarations of Parliament to the defence of our own and the people's just rights and liberties. And so we took up arms in judgement and conscience to those ends ... And truly such kingdoms as have, according both to the law of nature and nations, appeared to the vindications and defences of their just rights and liberties, have proceeded much higher; as our brethren of Scotland, who in the first beginning of these late differences associated in covenant from the same principles and grounds, having no visible form either of Parliament or King to countenance them – and as they were therein justified and protected by their own and this kingdom also, so we justly shall expect to be ... Now, having thus cleared our way in this business, we shall proceed to propound such things as we do humbly desire for the settling and securing of our own and the kingdom's right, freedom, peace and safety, as followeth:

I   That the House may be speedily purged of such members as for their delinquency, or for corruption, or abuse to the state, or undue election, ought not to sit there ...

II That those persons who have, in the late unjust and high proceedings against the Army, appeared to have the will, the confidence, credit, and power to abuse the Parliament and the Army, and endanger the kingdom in carrying on such things against us while an army, may be some way speedily disabled from doing the like or worse to us, when disbanded or dispersed, and in the condition of private men, or to other free-born people of England in the same condition with us.

There are, besides these, many particular things which we could wish to be done, and some to be undone, all in order still to the same end of common right, freedom, peace and safety; but these proposals aforegoing being the principal things we bottom and insist upon, we shall, as we have said before, for our parts acquiesce for other particulars in the wisdom and justice of Parliament. And whereas it has been suggested, or suspected, that in our late and present proceedings our design is to overthrow Presbytery, or hinder the settlement thereof, and to have the Independent government set up, we do clearly disclaim and disavow any such design. We only desire that, according to the declarations promising a privilege for tender consciences, there may be some effectual course taken, according to the intent thereof, and that such who upon conscientious grounds may differ from the established forms, may not for that be debarred from the common rights, liberties, or benefits belonging equally to all as men and members of the commonwealth, while they live soberly, honestly, inoffensively towards others, and peacefully and faithfully towards the state.

1   In what ways do the army's demands in this document differ from the ones in Sources 6.4, 6.5 and 6.6?

2   What is meant by the claim that 'we were not a mere mercenary army'?

3   Who are 'those persons' referred to in the second of the army's demands?

4   Four days earlier, Fairfax and the Council of War had assured the City of London that they sought 'no alteration in the civil government'. In what ways does this document make this claim suspect?

5   Why was the army now making more comprehensive demands than it had done before?

107

From the end of the Civil War to July 1647: why did the New Model Army become politicised?

The politicisation of the New Model Army: who took the lead, officers or agitators?

Sources 6.8–6.12 relate to another major historical question about developments within the New Model Army at that time: who led the politicisation of the army?

At least three different answers to that question have been put forward by contemporaries and historians:

- that senior army officers (including Oliver Cromwell) manipulated the soldiers' grievances for their own ends
- that it was the agitators who took a leading role, pushing their conservative superiors into taking radical political action
- that, at this stage, the views of senior officers and agitators were broadly the same.

Which, if any, of these three answers seems the most valid to you in the light of your reading on this period, together with the information in the following sources: Sources 6.8–6.10 (the army's seizure of the King, 4 June 1647)?

Parliament made many concessions to the army as it marched menacingly towards the capital. For example, on 3 June the Commons voted to pay all its arrears. Yet many in the New Model Army still mistrusted the Political Presbyterians, fearing that they planned to move the King from Holdenby House and use him to lead an army against them. Cornet George Joyce's seizure of the King from his Parliamentary guards was designed to prevent that.

● SOURCE 6.8

Joyce's own account of the seizure of the King. It relates what Joyce and his troop of about 500 cavalry did on 2 June, when they confronted Charles I and the parliamentary commissioners who held him at Holdenby House. Note that Joyce refers to himself as both 'Joyce' and 'I'.

Further for the security of the King's person, the party marched towards Holdenby, and when they came to the house, the commissioners sent one Captain Middleton to know of us what we came for, and what we would have, and who commanded? Answer was made him. All commanded. Then Captain Middleton replied, if you have any thing to do here, the commissioners would know what it is, and desired they would send in to the commissioners one or more to certify what was the intent of coming thither. Whereupon Cornet Joyce, by unanimous consent of the party, went into the commissioners, and told them the truth of their coming thither, which was to secure his Majesty's person, and to protect them; there being a secret design, as they were informed, to convey or steal away the king, and to raise another army to suppress this under his excellency Sir Thomas Fairfax. Likewise he said, he knew no other way to keep this kingdom from blood, or another war, but by the present security of the King's person, and that he may be no more misled; and if he were, that the kingdom was utterly undone for ever.

At the end of the following day, 3 June, the King was told that he would be removed early next morning by Joyce and his comrades. At 6 am on 4 June, as the King and soldiers prepared to leave, Charles asked:

What commission I had for doing what I did? I told his Majesty, the soldiery of the army; or else I should not have dared to have done what I have; and conceiving it to be the only way to bring peace to England, and justice with mercy, which is the thing all honest men will desire, and none will hinder but some guilty consciences, who by their will seek to destroy both king and people, to set up themselves. Yet the King was not satisfied with this, but asked, whether I had nothing in writing from Sir Thomas Fairfax our general, to do what I did? The cornet desired the king he would not ask him such questions, for he did conceive he had sufficiently answered him before. Then said the King, I pray Mr Joyce deal ingeniously with me, and tell me what commission you have? The cornet's answer was here is my commission. Where, said the king? He answered, behind me; pointing to the soldiers that were mounted; and desired his Majesty that might satisfy him. Whereupon the king smiled, and said, it is as fair a commission, and as well written as he had seen a commission in his life; a company of handsome proper gentlemen as he had seen a great while. But what if I should refuse yet to go with you? I hope you would not force me? I am your king, and you ought not to lay violent hands on your king; for I acknowledge none to be above me here but God. Then said Mr Joyce, our desires are not to force your Majesty, but have humbly entreated your Majesty to go with us.

● **SOURCE 6.9**

Joyce's letter sent to Oliver Cromwell, 4 June 1647. There was no name or address attached to it, but most historians assume it was sent to Cromwell. Colonel Richard Graves was in charge of one of the two regiments that guarded the King for the Parliamentarians at Holdenby.

Sir, we have secured the king. Graves is run away. He got out about one o'clock in the morning and so went his way. It is suspected he is gone to London; you may imagine what he will do there. You must hasten an answer to us, and let us know what we shall do. We are resolved to obey no orders but the general's; we shall follow the commissioner's directions while we are here, if just in our eyes. I humbly entreat you to consider what is done and act accordingly with all the haste you can. We shall not rest night nor day till we hear from you.

Yours and the kingdom's faithful servant till death.

GEORGE JOYCE

Holdenby this 4th of June at 8 of the clock in the morning.

● **SOURCE 6.10**

On 4 June 1647, Joyce wrote a second letter. The recipient of the letter is not known. It was written after Joyce had arrived at Huntingdon, where he had taken the King on 4 June.

There hath been a party of horse, about 500, at Holdenby, who have secured and taken his majesty into their custody, and the king who doth desire to speak with Sir Thomas Fairfax. The king is now at Huntingdon town, and will be at Newmarket tomorrow. Persuade all your friends you can to come and meet him, and endeavour to do for the best. Certainly God hath appeared in a mighty manner, and therefore I shall wholly rely on you for what I desire, which is a party to do that which may be justifiable before god and man. Haste, think on me.

I rest

GEORGE JOYCE, Cornet.

Read this enclosed, seal it up, and deliver it what ever you do, that so we may not perish for want of your assistance.

Huntingdon at 11 of the clock at night the 4th of June 1647.

[The enclosure reads]

Let the agitators know once more we have done nothing in our own name, but what we have done hath been in the name of the whole army, and we should not have dared to have done what we have, if we had not been sure that you and my best old friend had consented hereunto, and know that I speak nothing but truth.

1   What reasons does Joyce give for seizing the King?

2   What authority does Joyce claim for his actions in Sources 6.8, 6.9 and 6.10?

3   What conclusions do you draw from Source 6.9 about the extent and nature of Cromwell's implication in the capture of the King?

● **SOURCE 6.11**

Payments to agitators by Fairfax's warrant: an extract from the accounts of the New Model Army, July 1647. A book of accounts authorised by Fairfax has survived. It lists sums of money paid by the army leadership. Among the accounts is an entry for a payment to Cornet Joyce.

10 July 1647. To Cornet Joyce for extraordinary charges – £100

● **SOURCE 6.12**

The army debates at Reading, July 1647. When it reached Uxbridge the New Model Army halted its march on London and moved with the King to Reading, 35 miles west of London. There, on 16 and 17 July, there took place the first recorded debates of the full Army Council, including officers and agitators. These extracts are from the first day of the debate.

[Cromwell's speech] Your zeal hath been much stirred up to express in your paper that there is a necessity of a speedy marching towards London to accomplish all these things. Truly I think that possibly that may be that we shall be necessitated to do [in the end]. Possibly it may be so; but yet I think it will be for our honour and our honesty to do what we can to accomplish this work in the way of a treaty; and if I were able to give you all those reasons that lie in this case, I think it would satisfy any rational man here. For certainly that is the most desirable ... we shall avoid that way and the other a way of necessity, and truly, instead of all means let this [one] serve: that whatsoever we get by a treaty, whatsoever comes to be settled upon us in that way, it will be firm and durable, it will be conveyed over to posterity ... we shall avoid that great objection that will lie against us, that we have got things of the Parliament by force; and we know what it is to have that stain lie upon us.

[The speech of Captain John Clarke, one of the officer–agitators who had signed a petition urging an immediate march on London] And whereas the Lieutenant General was pleased to move, that it was the best way to compose the differences between the parliament and the army by way of a treaty, I presume to say in the name of these gentlemen, they likewise wish it might be so, but truly, sir, we have great fears and jealousies that these treaties, managed by a power so adverse to us, will prove rather destructive and delusive to us than any ways certain for our security and [for] the settlement of the kingdom.

1   In Source 6.11 what might the payment to Joyce have been for?

2   Look at Source 6.12.

   a) Why did Cromwell (and his fellow senior officers) resist the agitators' demands on this issue?
   b) Why did the agitators want the army to occupy London immediately?

3   After reading Sources 6.8–6.12, what views have you formed on the questions of:

   a) who was controlling the army at this crucial time: officers or agitators?
   b) were there any major disagreements between officers and agitators by July 1647?

4   For what reasons did the army become a political force in the period 1646–7?

5   Divide into two groups.
  One group should consider the views of the soldiers of the New Model Army as they marched through Cambridgeshire in June 1647. Their task is to draw up a press release of no more than 250 words explaining the army's position.
  The other group should consider the views of Political Presbyterian MPs in London, such as Denzil Holles. Their task is to draw up a press release of similar length, explaining the MPs' reactions to what was happening in the army.

Section B July 1647–January 1648: why did the New Model Army's negotiations with the King fail?

The main themes that run through the fast-moving events of this period are:

- the concerted attempt by the leaders of the New Model Army to reach an agreement with the King on the Heads of the Proposals, the terms of which were decided in July, when the army was camped at Reading
- the collapse of that attempt, marked in January 1648 by a Parliamentary decision (taken with the support of the army) never again to negotiate with the King (the Vote of No Addresses).

You should use the sources in Section B to help you understand why the negotiations on the Heads of the Proposals failed. Here are two possible theories you should be thinking about as you read the sources. At the end of Section B you will be asked to decide which, if either, seems to offer the better explanation:

- Theory A: The main reason the Heads of the Proposals failed was the King's obstinate refusal to negotiate seriously with the army.

- Theory B: Even if the King had proved more co-operative in his negotiations with the army, the Heads of the Proposals never stood a chance of becoming the basis of a successful settlement.

The King's attitude to the settlement proposals: the Heads of the Proposals

It is essential to begin Section B (like Section A) by considering Charles I's attitude to a settlement.

The Heads of the Proposals were probably drafted by Henry Ireton, after consultation with the army's civilian Political Independent allies and (perhaps) Leveller representatives. The main terms of the Heads of the Proposals were as follows:

● The Heads of the Proposals

- The chief officers of state were to be nominated by Parliament.
- Parliament was to control the militia for ten years. — *less than Propositions of Newcastle*
- <u>Bishops were not to be abolished</u>, although they were to lose their powers to force everyone to attend the national Church, i.e. religious toleration should be established.
- Seven Royalists were to be exempted from pardon.
- There should be biennial Parliaments with seats redistributed according to the localities' wealth.
- Parliament should take measures, demanded by the Levellers, to remedy grievances such as the excise, the cost and length of legal proceedings and the unjust treatment of debtors.

---

1 Were the Heads of the Proposals any more favourable to the King than Parliament's Propositions of Newcastle? (You will find it helpful to refer to pages 102–3.)

2 How do you think Charles I would have reacted to these proposals?

Negotiations between senior army officers, civilian Political Independents and the King began at Reading in July and continued throughout the summer. Despite the relative leniency of the army's proposals, Charles I's *public* response was to prevaricate, while ensuring that the negotiations did not collapse. Source 6.13 is the only major contemporary account of Charles I's *private* attitude to these negotiations.

● SOURCE 6.13

Sir John Berkeley's account of the King's negotiations with the army, July–August 1647. Sir John, who had been a Royalist general in the south west of England during the Civil War, was sent by Queen Henrietta Maria and her advisers to help promote an agreement between the King and the army. He arrived at Reading on 12 July 1647.

narrow maxims: fixed, rigid principles

When I came to Reading, I found many of the agitators jealous that Cromwell was not sincere for the King, and they desired me, if I found him false to their engagement, that I would let them know it, and they did not doubt to set him right, either with, or against his will. But, in all my conferences with him, I found no man, in appearances, so zealous for a speedy blow as he; sometimes wishing the King was more frank, and would not tie himself so strictly to NARROW MAXIMS; sometimes complaining of his son [in law] Ireton's slowness in perfecting the proposals, and not accommodating more to his Majesty's sense; always doubting that the army would not preserve their good inclinations for the King. I met with him about three days after I came to Reading, as he was coming from the King, then at Caversham [just across the river Thames from Reading]: He told me, that he had lately seen the tenderest sight that ever his eyes beheld, which was the interview between the King and his children, and wept plentifully at the remembrance of it, saying, that never man was so abused as he, in his sinister opinions of the King, who, he thought, was the uprightest and most conscientious man of his three kingdoms; that they, of the Independent party (as they are called) had infinite obligations to him, for not consenting to the Scots' Propositions at Newcastle, which would have totally ruined them, and which his Majesty's interest seemed to invite him to; and concluded with me, by wishing, that God would be pleased to look upon him according to the sincerity of his heart towards his Majesty. I immediately acquainted his Majesty with this passage; who seemed not well edified by it, and did believe, that all proceeded out of the use Cromwell and the army had of his Majesty, without whom, he thought, they could do nothing …

What with the encouraging messages, which his Majesty had (by my Lord Lauderdale, and others) from the Presbyterian party and the City of London, who pretended to despise the army, and to oppose them to death, his Majesty seemed very much erected; insomuch, that, when the proposals were solemnly sent to him, and his concurrence most humbly and earnestly desired, his Majesty not only to the astonishment of Ireton and the rest, but even to mine entertained them with very tart and bitter discourses; saying sometimes that he would have no man to suffer for his sake, and that he repented of nothing so much as the Bill against the Lord Strafford; (which, though most true, was unpleasant for them to hear;) That, he would have the Church established according to law, by the Proposals. They replied, it was none of their work to do it; that it was enough for them to waive the point, and they hoped enough for his Majesty, since he had waived the Government itself in Scotland. His Majesty said that he hoped that God had forgiven him that sin, and repeated often, You cannot do without me: you will fall to ruin if I do not sustain you.

1 What does Berkeley's account tell you about the attitude to these negotiations of:

a) Cromwell
b) the King?

2 What were the King's specific reasons for not treating the negotiations seriously?

3 Are there any reasons to suspect that Berkeley's recollections might not be accurate?

4 What are the main value and limitations of anyone's memoirs as a historical source?

The army and the Levellers

Early in August 1647, the New Model Army marched on and occupied London. On 26 July a mass of demonstrators, apparently encouraged by Holles and the Political Presbyterians, had entered the House of Commons, forcing MPs to vote in favour of both restoring Presbyterian control of the City militia and inviting Charles I to come to London. The army occupied London to prevent this Presbyterian 'counter-revolution'. Yet, despite this, the army's negotiations with the King continued. However, the longer the army occupied the capital, the more it became apparent that there were now greater rifts than ever before between the senior army officers and the agitators. These became very clear to see at the famous Putney Debates in the Army Council in October–November 1647.

Bear in mind the following questions as you study Sources 6.14–6.17:

• Why did the divisions within the army grow?
• What was the role of civilian Levellers in bringing them about?
• What *new* demands were now being made?

● **SOURCE 6.14**

A view of events from the cells of the Tower of London, September 1647. Sir Lewis Dyve was a Royalist prisoner in the Tower in 1647 and shared a cell with the Leveller leader, John Lilburne. Both were given a remarkable amount of freedom to communicate with friends outside the prison. In the autumn of 1647, Dyve wrote to the King with some important news.

cashiered: *dismissed from service*

[To Charles I, 29 September 1647]
There are six regiments that have CASHIERED their old agitators as unfaithful to the trust reposed in them by the soldiers, and have chosen new men in their places, who had solemn meeting yesterday in this town with divers well-affected brethren of the city.

[To Charles I, 5 October 1647]
In my last the 29 September I gave notice unto your Majesty of those new agitators that met here in town, since which time for the most part some of them have every day constantly met together and I am told by Mr Lilburne that they are resolved to do their utmost for the suppressing of Cromwell's faction.

1 Is Dyve a good source for developments within the army at this time?

2 Who does Dyve mean by 'divers well-affected brethren of the city'?

3 How close does Dyve think the connections were between the Levellers and the new agitators?

4 What do Dyve's letters suggest might have been the impact of the new agitators on the army?

113

July 1647–January 1648: why did the New Model Army's negotiations with the King fail?

● **SOURCE 6.15**

The Case of the Army Truly Stated,
October 1647. Although it was
signed by five of the new army
agents, it is not certain who wrote
this document. It is likely that the
new agents, Edward Sexby and the
Leveller John Wildman, probably had
the biggest hand in writing it. It was
presented to Fairfax by two of the
agents on 18 October (the title page
has 15 October but the correct date
is given at the end of the pamphlet).
The title page is shown on page 114.

---

arbitrary committees: *the
County Committees established
by Parliament during the Civil
War*

ignominy: *dishonour*

tithes: *payments made for the
upkeep of parish churches,
amounting to one-tenth of
incomes. By this period most
were, in fact, paid to secular
landowners.*

Whereas the grievances, dissatisfactions, and desires of the army, both as commoners and soldiers, hath been many months since represented to this Parliament; and the army hath waited with much patience to see their common grievances redressed ... In respect of the army, there hath been hitherto no public vindication thereof, about their first petition, answerable to the IGNOMINY, by declaring them enemies to the state & disturbers of the peace: No public clearing nor repairing of the credit of the officers, sent for about that petition as delinquents: No provision for apprentices, widows, orphans, or maimed soldiers, answerable to our reasonable addresses propounded in their behalf: No such indemnity, as provided security for the quiet, ease, or safety of the soldiers, disbanded or to be disbanded. No security for our arrears, or provision for present pay to enable the army to subsist without burdening the distressed country. And in respect to the rights and freedoms of ourselves and the people, that we declared we would insist upon, we conceive there is no kind or degree of satisfaction given; there is no determinate period of time set when Parliament shall certainly end: The House is in no measure purged, either from person unduly elected, or from delinquents ... None of the public burdens or oppressions by ARBITRARY COMMITTEES, injustice of the law, TITHES, monopolies and restraint of free trade, burdensome oaths, inequalities of assessments, excise, and otherwise are removed or lightened, the rights of the people in their parliaments concerning the nature and extent of that power, are not cleared and declared. So that we apprehend our own & the people's case, little (if in any measure) better, since the army last hazarded themselves for their own and the people's rights and freedoms. Nay, to the grief of our hearts, we must declare, that we conceive the people and the army's case much impaired, since the first rendezvous at Newmarket, when that Solemn Engagement was entered into ...

The love and affection of the people to the army, which is the army's greatest strength, is decayed, cooled, and near lost; it's already the common voice of the people, what good hath our new saviours done for us? What grievances have they procured to be redressed? Wherein is our condition bettered? Or how are we more free than before ...? Not only so, but the army is rendered as an heavy burden to the people, in regard more pay is exacted daily from them, and the people find no good procured by them, that's answerable or equivalent to the charge, so that now the people begin to cry louder for disbanding the army than they did formerly for keeping us in arms, because they see no benefit accruing. They say they are likely to be oppressed and enslaved both by king and parliament, as they were before the army engaged professedly to see their freedoms cleared and secured.

[Among the specific demands then made is the following.]

Whereas parliaments rightly constituted are the foundation of the hopes of right and freedom to the people, and whereas the people have been prevented of parliaments, though many positive laws have been made for a constant succession of parliaments, that therefore it be positively and resolvedly insisted upon, that a law paramount be made, enacting it to be unalterable by parliaments that the people shall of course meet without any warrants or writs once in every two years upon an appointed day in their respective counties, for the electing of their representatives in parliament, & that all the freeborn at the age of 21 years and upwards be the electors, excepting those that have or shall deprive themselves of their freedom, either for some years or wholly by delinquency, and that the parliament so elected and called may have a certain period of time set, wherein they shall of course determine, and that before the same period they may not be adjourned and dissolved by the king or any other except themselves.

Whereas all power is originally and essentially in the whole body of the people of this nation, and whereas their free choice or consent of the representatives is the only original or foundation of all just government; and the reason and end of the choice of all just governors whatsoever is their apprehension of safety and good by them, that it be insisted positively: That the supreme power of the people's representatives or Commons assembled in Parliament, be forthwith declared.

THE CASE OF THE ARMIE Truly stated, together with the mischiefes and dangers that are imminent, and some suitable remedies,

Humbly proposed by the Agents of five Regiments of Horse, to their respective Regiments, and the whole Army.

As it was presented by Mr. *Edmond Bear*, and Mr. *William Russell*, October 15. 1647. unto his Excellency, Sir *Thomas Fairfax*.

Enclosed in a Letter from the said Agents : Also his Excellencies Honourable Answer thereunto.

Deut. 20. 8. *What man is there that is fearefull and faint hearted? let him go and returne unto his House, least his brethrens heart faint as well as his heart.*
Judg. 7. 7. *And the Lord said unto Gideon, by the three hundred men that lapped, will I save you, and deliver the Midianites into thine hand, and let all the other people go, every man unto his place.*

LONDON Printed in the Yeare, 1647.

---

1 Were the authors justified in claiming that most of the army's demands had not been addressed?

2 Whom did the authors principally blame for the situation they describe?

3 Why did they think that the army had lost much popular support?

4 In what ways do the political demands in *The Case of the Army Truly Stated* differ from those made in the Heads of the Proposals?

On 27 October 1647, Robert Everard, one of the new agents (from Cromwell's regiment), brought a second document, *The Agreement of the People*, to the army's headquarters at Putney from the new agents and their Leveller allies. Like *The Case of the Army Truly Stated*, it was probably drafted by a group of people, agents and other soldiers, as well as Levellers. William Walwyn may have played a prominent part. The first three points called for:

• a redistribution of seats according to population
• the dissolution of the present Parliament
• future Parliaments to meet biennially.

● **SOURCE 6.16**

The Agreement of the People, October 1647. This is the fourth part.

---

impressing: conscription

Representatives of this nation: *Parliaments*

That the power of this and all future REPRESENTATIVES OF THIS NATION is inferior only to theirs who choose them, and doth extend, without the consent or concurrence of any other person or persons, to the enacting, altering, and repealing of laws, to the erecting and abolishing of officers and courts, to the appointing, removing, and calling to account magistrates and officers of all degrees, to the making of war and peace, to the treating with foreign states and, generally, to whatsoever is not expressly or impliedly reserved by the represented to themselves:

Which are as followeth:

1 That matters of religion and the ways of God's worship are not at all entrusted by us to any human power, because therein we cannot remit or exceed as title of what our consciences dictate to be the mind of God without wilful sin: nevertheless the public way of instructing the nation (so it be not compulsive) is referred to their discretion.

2 That the matter of IMPRESSING and constraining any of us to serve in the wars is against our freedom; and therefore we do not allow it in our representatives; the rather, because money (the sinews of war) being always at their disposal, they can never want numbers of men apt enough to engage in any just cause.

3 That after the dissolution of this present parliament, no person be at any time questioned for anything said or done in reference to the late public differences, otherwise than in the execution of the judgement of the present representatives or the House of Commons.

4 That in all laws made or to be made every person may be bound alike, and that no tenure, estate, charter, degree, birth, or place do confer any exemption from the ordinary course of legal proceedings.

5 That as the laws ought to be equal, so they must be good, and not evidently destructive of the people.

These things we do declare to be our native rights, and therefore are agreed and resolved to maintain them with our utmost possibilities against all opposition whatsoever; being compelled thereunto not only by the example of our ancestors, whose blood was often spent in vain for the recovery of their freedoms … but also by our own woeful experience, who, having long expected and dearly earned the establishment of these certain rules of government, are yet made to depend for the settlement of our peace and freedom upon him that intended our bondage and brought a cruel war upon us.

---

1 Where do the authors of the Agreement think that the powers of Parliament ('Representatives of this nation') come from?

2 What do they think those powers should be?

3 In what ways do they think that the powers of Parliament should be restricted?

4 What recent events might have led them to demand these restrictions on Parliament's powers?

5 What attitude is displayed towards the King in this document?

6 How would the following have reacted to *The Agreement of the People*:

   a) the King
   b) Parliament
   c) the country gentry
   d) the army generals?

The General Council of the Army met on 28 October to discuss the Agreement of the People. Thus began a few days of remarkable debates, the Putney Debates, which were recorded by William Clarke, an assistant of John Rushworth, Secretary to Fairfax and the Army Council. These debates reveal that differences between the agitators and their Leveller allies and the senior army officers (whom the Levellers began to refer to sarcastically as 'the grandees') were now very great. There is space here for only one extract, the confrontation between Ireton and the Army Leveller Colonel Thomas Rainsborough, together with the contribution of another army officer, Colonel Nathaniel Rich, on 29 October.

Rainsborough:

For really I think that the poorest he that is in England hath a life to live as the greatest he; and therefore truly, sir, I think it's clear, that every man that is to live under a government ought first by his own consent to put himself under that government; and I do think that the poorest he in England is not at all bound in a strict sense to that government that he hath not had a voice to put himself under.

Ireton:

I think that no person hath a right to an interest or share in the disposing or determining of the affairs of the kingdom, and in choosing those that shall determine what laws we shall be ruled by here … that hath not a permanent, fixed interest in this kingdom; and those persons together are properly the represented of this kingdom; and consequently are to make up the representatives of this kingdom, who taken together do comprehend whatsoever is of real or permanent interest in this kingdom.

Rich:

I confess there is weight in that objection that the Commissary General [Ireton] last insisted upon; for you have four to one in this kingdom that have no permanent interest. Some men have ten, some twenty servants, some more some less. If the master and servant shall be equal electors, then clearly those that have no interest in the kingdom will make it their interest to choose those that have no interest. It may happen that the majority may by law, not in confusion, destroy property; there may be a law enacted that there shall be an equality of goods and estate.

---

1 Summarise the main points made in each of these speeches.

2 Was Rainsborough proposing that *everyone* should have the vote?

3 What do you think was the most important reason why Ireton did not want the vote to be given to people without property?

4 Does this source suggest that there were serious divisions in the army by October/November 1647?

5 How would the following have reacted to the Putney Debates:

   a) the King
   b) Parliament
   c) the country gentry?

The Vote of No Addresses: the end of negotiations with the King?

As the divisions within the army grew, Fairfax, Cromwell and the senior officers ended the Putney Debates and on 15 November reimposed normal military discipline at an army rendezvous at Ware, in Hertfordshire, and elsewhere. What helped them do this was the King's escape from army custody on 11 November and his flight to the Isle of Wight, from where in the next few weeks he rejected more peace proposals from Parliament, known as the Four Bills.

The Four Bills would have forced Charles to agree that:

• Parliament should control the militia for 20 years
• all declarations issued by him against Parliament in the past were void
• all peerages granted by him since May 1642 were void
• Parliament was free to adjourn whenever it wanted and to any place it chose.

What horrified all Charles I's opponents, both within and outside the army, moderates as well as radicals, was that he also made a treaty with the Scots. In the Engagement of December

1647, Charles secretly agreed to establish a Scottish Presbyterian Church in England within three years in return for armed support from the Scots. This enabled the radical allies of the army leaders to get Parliament to pass the Vote of No Addresses, which prohibited any further addresses or applications to the King.

Source 6.18 consists of two brief extracts from the debate on the Vote of No Addresses.

● **SOURCE 6.18**

The debate on the Vote of No Addresses, January 1648. There was no record of parliamentary debates in the seventeenth century. Historians have to rely on other sources, of which private diaries of MPs are the most valuable. This source is an extract from the diary of a Kent MP, John Boys, which he wrote in a small notebook, covering the period from 7 September 1647 to 16 May 1648. John Maynard, the MP for Totnes in Devon, put the case for the Vote of No Addresses, to which Oliver Cromwell responded.

husbandmen: *small farmers*

Maynard:

In things of great change and fundamental, consider consequences etc. If the argument (some have gone upon) hold, that there was another government before that of Kings etc., so HUSBANDMEN was before gentlemen, and they before Lords etc. and so we must come to the Levellers' doctrine.

Cromwell:

We still hold to our interest, and that of the kingdom; true we declared our intentions for monarchy, and they still are, unless necessity enforce an alteration. It's granted the King hath broken his trust, yet you are fearful to declare you will make no further addresses.

---

1 What is Maynard's main objection to the radical demand for no further negotiations with the King? Compare his objection to the speeches made by Ireton and Rich at Putney in Source 6.17.

2 Why do you think that Cromwell says that the King has 'broken his trust'?

3 Decide which of the two theories, A or B, set out on page 111, you prefer as an explanation of why the Heads of the Proposals failed. You may, if you like, offer an alternative conclusion of your own, but you should explain why you prefer it.

Section C # January 1648–January 1649: why did the Second Civil War lead to the King's execution?

The search for a full explanation for Charles I's execution cannot end with the Vote of No Addresses in January 1648. Much of what happened in the months after it seemed to make inevitable not the execution of the King, but a settlement between King and Parliament.

● **Principal events marking the growing demand for a settlement with the King**

revoked: *repealed, cancelled*

March:	The beginning of a revolt against the New Model Army in South Wales
May:	The beginning of revolts in Kent and Essex
July:	The Scots invade England
August:	The Vote of No Addresses REVOKED in Parliament
September:	The beginning of new Parliamentary negotiations with the King at Newport on the Isle of Wight

The New Model Army spent much of the spring and summer of 1648 putting down the rebellions in South Wales and southern England and defeating the Scottish army in Lancashire. Then, after quashing the opposition, the New Model Army again, in December 1648, occupied London and, with the support of a handful of civilian radicals, expelled its enemies from Parliament (Pride's Purge, 6 December 1648). The purged Parliament (the Rump Parliament) then established a high court of justice, which tried and found the King guilty of treason against the people. He was executed on 30 January 1649.

Two major historical questions arise from these events:

- Why, despite yet more evidence of Charles I's untrustworthiness, did many in Parliament and the country press strongly for a settlement with the King throughout much of 1648?
- Why did a minority not only remain committed to the policy of never again negotiating with Charles I, but decide to get rid of him altogether?

Keep these questions in mind as you read the sources in Section C. They will form the basis of the task you are given at the end of the section.

The Second Civil War: the demand for a settlement with the King

Sources 6.19 and 6.20 have been chosen to illustrate the reasons why in the twelve months leading to Charles I's execution the Vote of No Addresses was overturned, the number of the King's opponents dwindled and opposition to the New Model Army grew.

● **SOURCE 6.19**

The Canterbury Christmas Day riots, December 1647. In the middle of his diary (see Source 6.18) John Boys copied the letter from the Parliamentary County Committee of Kent to the Speaker of the Commons, dated 21 January 1648, from which this extract is taken. It describes an incident which has a good claim to mark the start of the Second Civil War.

cried up: *praised*

premeditated: *planned beforehand*

... It appears unto us, that although the first hint of this insurrection seems to be taken from that darling of rude and licentious persons, called Christmas, which was made the ground or pretence of the first day's tumult upon the day so named, yet the scene was quickly changed, their next appearance upon the Monday following being with divers hundreds in a martial posture crying down the parliament and excise, and accordingly using outrages against those, whom by a continued opposite term to the King's party, they call Roundheads, assaulting them in the streets and in their houses, by day and night, spoiling their goods, beating some, wounding others, to the great danger of their lives ... chasing the mayor and well affected magistrates and ministers out of the city. All of which stirs, that they were not merely accidental but had a PREMEDITATED rise, we are induced to believe, both from sundry dangerous speeches proved unto us to be uttered beforehand, some plainly expressing, others somewhat darkly implying, threats against the parliament, and a course to be taken with Roundheads about Christmas and the like ... The first beginning being upon Christmas Day, by hurling of several footballs not that the season or the weather gave any invitation to it ... And as the unusual pastime upon that day, so the persons thereby and thereunto congregated gives us cause to judge it a contrived design, whose footballs drawing together on a sudden great numbers of rude persons not only of the city but of country fellows, strangers from the parts adjacent, whereby they speedily grew into a tumult, which having gotten strength their next appearance upon the Monday following became more formidable and warlike, the King CRIED UP, the parliament and excise cried down, and themselves being masters of the city, divers of the gentry began to show themselves amongst them, animating and encouraging them in the King's cause, with words and rewards and promises of assistance.

● **SOURCE 6.20**

The Declaration of the County of Dorset, 15 June 1648

We surviving inhabitants of the much despised and distressed county of Dorset having, like the rest of the kingdom, long groaned under the oppressive tyranny of those who we reputed for our redeemers ... We thought fit to declare to the world what we mean to do for ourselves and the kingdom.

1 We demand the speedy reintroduction of our imprisoned king to sit personally in the House of Peers: that the supreme court of the kingdom may no longer be called master without a head.

2 That the government of the Church may first be settled by the advice of a new assembly of Protestant divines, INDIFFERENTLY chosen by the clergy of each county or DIOCESE ...

3 That the common birthright of us all, the laws, may be restored to their former purity, ... without ... arbitrary power, or unequal ordinances and practices between them and their committees.

119

January 1648–January 1649: why did the Second Civil War lead to the King's execution?

Clubmen: *organised bands of people who armed themselves to try to isolate their villages from the war. They were found mainly in south-west England and South Wales in 1645*

compositions: *fines*

diocese: *a district governed by a bishop*

emissaries: *agents*

indifferently: *impartially*

sequestrators: *those who had confiscated Royalist estates in the Civil War*

4 That our liberties (purchased of our ancestors' blood) may be redeemed from former infringements, and preserved from henceforth inviolable; and that our ancient liberties may not lie at the mercy of those that have none, nor enlarged and repealed by votes and re-votes of those that have taken too much liberty to destroy the subjects.

5 That we may have a speedy and just account of all our moneys and estates cheated or wrested from us by loans, contributions, taxes, fines, excise or plunder; and that the estates of committees, SEQUESTRATORS, and all state officers (being lately purchased or raised out of the ruin of honest and loyal subjects) may be re-sequestered, and be made liable to give us and the kingdom's satisfaction.

6 That our knights and burgesses [i.e. their MPs] be recalled, as having broken their trust reposed by us in them; and that we may have free power and liberty to make new choice of such patriots as we can trust.

7 That we may no longer subjugate our necks to the boundless lusts and unlimited power of beggarly and broken committees, consisting generally of the tail of the gentry, men of ruinous fortune and despicable estates, whose insatiate desires prompt them to continual projects of … stripping us, and that we be not awed by their EMISSARIES, generally the most shirking and cunning beggars that can be picked out of the county.

8 That, instead we may be governed in military affairs and civil by men of visible estates and of unquestioned repute – well beloved by us …

10 That all of us sequestered, imprisoned, plundered or fined, or anyway abused or stripped of our estates for allegiance or loyal adherence to his Majesty, be restored to our estates without any more COMPOSITIONS and leave to take any legal course for due reparation. Petitions being useless we make absolute demands and have heretofore on less encouragement engaged our lives, liberties and estates, on the same grounds under the slighted and unprosperous notion of CLUBMEN. Notwithstanding our sufferings then, our ends are still the same and we doubt not our endeavours will be more successful.

---

1 What does Source 6.19 reveal about the attitude of the Kent County Committee to Christmas? What is the explanation for their attitude? (Material in Chapter 4 will also help you answer this question.)

2 What does the Committee's letter indicate were the reasons for the riot?

3 Summarise the main demands of the Dorset petitioners in Source 6.20.

4 What were the attitudes of the petitioners to:

a) the County Committee
b) the army?

5 From the evidence in Sources 6.19 and 6.20, what do you think were the main reasons why support for the King grew in 1648?

The Second Civil War and regicide

Sources 6.21–6.24 provide evidence of the reasons why a minority within and outside the army not only remained committed to the decision never again to negotiate with the King, but became convinced that he must die.

● **SOURCE 6.21**

The army prayer meeting at Windsor, April 1648. In response to revolts in many parts of the country against the army, the army officers called a prayer meeting at Windsor. This account was written eleven years later by William Allen, who had been an agitator and was probably at Windsor at that time on special duties. The prayer meeting lasted for three days, 28–30 April 1648.

And in this path the Lord led us not only to see our sin, but also our duty; and this so unanimously sat with weight upon each heart that none was able to speak a word to each other for bitter weeping, partly in the sense and shame of our INIQUITIES of unbelief, base fear of men, and CARNAL CONSULTATIONS (as the fruit thereof), with our wisdoms, and not with the Word of the Lord, which only is a way of wisdom, strength and safety, and all besides its way of snares; and yet we were also helped with fear and trembling to rejoice in the Lord … He did direct our steps, and presently we were led and helped to a clear agreement amongst ourselves, not any dissenting, that it was our duty of our day, with the forces we had, to go out and fight against those potent enemies, which that year in all places appeared against us, with a humble confidence in the name of the Lord only, that we should destroy them; also enabling us then,

<table>
<tr><td>

carnal consultations: *worldly negotiations (i.e. with the King)*

iniquities: *wickedness*

</td></tr>
</table>

after seriously seeking his face, to come to a very clear and joint resolution, on many grounds at large then debated amongst us, that it was our duty, if ever the Lord brought us back again in peace, to call Charles Stuart, that man of blood, to an account for that blood he had shed, and mischiefs he had done to his utmost against the Lord's cause and people in these poor nations.

> 1 What was the attitude of the army officers towards the King in April 1648 according to this source?
>
> 2 Do you think that they had already decided to put him on trial and execute him in April 1648?

Edmund Ludlow's memoirs, though they were drastically edited and changed in the 1690s, are a principal source for the history of this period. Ludlow was MP for Wiltshire and one of the few civilian Political Independents to continue his opposition to the King after the summer of 1648. He was later a judge at the King's trial and he signed the King's death warrant. Here he describes a visit he made from London to the army's headquarters at the siege of Colchester, when the Parliamentary negotiations with the King at Newport seemed to be making good progress. The New Model Army's siege at Colchester, defended by the Kent and Essex rebels, lasted from 14 June to 18 August 1648. When the town surrendered, two of the Royalist leaders, Sir Charles Lucas and Sir George Lisle, were court-martialled on the orders of Fairfax and Ireton and executed by a firing squad outside the walls of Colchester Castle. These executions were acts of severity unusual after battles on English (though not Irish) soil in the Civil Wars of the 1640s.

● **SOURCE 6.22**

An account of Edmund Ludlow's visit to Colchester from his memoirs

The treaty with the king being pressed with more heat than ever, and a design visibly appearing to render all our victories useless thereby; by the advice of some friends I went down to the army, which lay at that time before Colchester; where attending upon the General Sir Thomas Fairfax to acquaint him with the state of affairs at London, I told him, that a design was driving on to betray the cause in which so much of the people's blood had been shed; that the king being under a restraint, would not account himself obliged by any thing he should promise under such circumstances; assuring him, that most of those who pushed on the treaty [at Newport on the Isle of Wight] with the greatest vehemency, intended not that he should be bound by the performance of it, but designed principally to use his authority and favour in order to destroy the army; who, as they had assumed the power, ought to make the best use of it, and to prevent the ruin of themselves and the nation.

> 1 Ludlow was a Member of Parliament. What was his attitude towards Parliament's negotiations with the King?
>
> 2 What did Ludlow think were the real motives of the MPs who supported negotiations with Charles I?
>
> 3 Does the fact that the source is taken from Ludlow's memoirs affect its value as historical evidence?

Within a few weeks of the end of the siege of Colchester, Ireton had made up his mind to press for the King's trial. With the support of the Levellers and a barrage of petitions from the army, Ireton persuaded the Council of Officers, on 15 November, to accept a document he had drafted, the Remonstrance of the Army, that alleged that the King was 'guilty of the highest treason against law amongst men and … guilty of all the innocent blood spilt thereby', and should be brought to trial.

The conversion to regicide of the other key figure in the King's execution, Ireton's father-in-law, Oliver Cromwell, was a more prolonged process. For much of 1648 he was away from the main army headquarters in the south of England. In July, he was fighting the South Wales rebels; in August, he (and Lambert) defeated the Scots in Lancashire, and after that he was engaged in ending the last rebel resistance in Yorkshire. It was not until 6 December, after Pride's Purge had begun, that he returned to London and not until 26 December that he committed himself clearly to the King's trial.

Yet he did eventually break with his civilian Political Independent allies, who continued to support the Newport negotiations. When and why did Cromwell decide to take the course of revolution? The following are some key sources on Cromwell in what he later called 'that memorable year' of 1648. Source 6.23 contains extracts from three of Cromwell's letters and a report of a speech he made in 1648.

● **SOURCE 6.23**

28 June 1648. To Fairfax from Pembroke in South Wales during his campaign against the rebellion there led by Colonel John Poyer, Major-General Rowland Laugharne and Colonel Rhys Powell, all of whom had fought for Parliament in the first Civil War.

capitally: *alleging guilt of a crime punishable by death*

11 July 1648. To the Speaker of the Commons from Pembroke, after the defeat of the rebels, explaining why he had not given pardons to the three rebel leaders. They were later sent to London and forced to draw lots to decide which one of them should be executed. Poyer lost and a few months later was shot in the Piazza in Covent Garden.

25 November 1648. From Yorkshire to his friend Colonel Robert Hammond, governor of the Isle of Wight and the King's jailer

A contemporary report of Cromwell's speech in the Commons, 26 December 1648

I rejoice much to hear of the blessing of God upon your Excellency's endeavours. I pray God to teach this nation and those that are over us, and your Excellency and all that are under you, what the mind of God may be in all this, and what our duty is. Surely it is not that the poor godly people of this kingdom should still be made the object of wrath and anger, nor that our God would have our necks under the yoke of bondage; for these things that have lately come to pass have been the wonderful works of God; breaking the rod of the oppressor, as in the days of Midian not with garments much rolled in blood, but by the terror of the Lord; who will yet save His People and confound His enemies, as in that day. The lord multiply His spirit unto you, and bless you, and keep your heart upright; and then, though you be not conformable to the men of this world, nor to their wisdom, yet you shall be precious in the eyes of God, and he will be to you a sun and a shield.

The persons excepted are such as have formerly served you in a very good cause, but ... I did rather make election of them than of those who had always been for the king, judging their iniquity double, because they have sinned against so many evidences of Divine Presence going along with and prospering a righteous cause, in the management of which they had a share.

And to conclude. We in this northern army were in a waiting posture, desiring to see what the Lord would lead us to. And a declaration is put out, at which many are shaken; although we could perhaps have wished the stay of it till after the treaty, yet seeing it is come out, we trust to rejoice in the will of the lord, waiting his further pleasure.

When it was first moved in the House of Commons to proceed CAPITALLY against the king, Cromwell stood up and told them, that if any man moved this upon design, he should think him the greatest traitor in the world, but since providence and necessity had cast them upon it, he should pray God to bless their counsels, though he were not provided on the sudden to give them counsel.

By the time Cromwell made this speech the army had occupied London. On the day after a majority in the House of Commons had voted, on 5 December 1648, to continue negotiations with the King, Colonel Pride and a troop of soldiers forcibly prevented about 100 MPs from entering the parliamentary chamber. Some secret last-minute efforts may have been made to reach a settlement with the King (one proposal may have been that his younger son, James, should be appointed as Regent). When these failed, the purged Parliament (known as the Rump Parliament), urged on by Henry Ireton and Oliver Cromwell, began to make preparations to bring the King to trial.

● **SOURCE 6.24**

The charges against the King, January 1649

That the said Charles Stuart, being admitted King of England, and therein trusted with a limited power to govern by and according to the laws of the land, and not otherwise; and by his trust, oath and office, being obliged to use the power committed to him for the good and benefit of the people, and for the preservation of their rights and liberties; yet, nevertheless, out of a wicked design to erect and uphold in himself an unlimited and tyrannical power to rule according to his will, and to overthrow the rights and liberties of the people ... he, the said Charles Stuart, for accomplishment of such his designs, and for the protecting of himself and his adherents in his and their wicked practices, to the same ends hath traitorously and maliciously levied war against the present Parliament ... All which wicked designs, wars, and evil practices of him, the said Charles Stuart, have been, and are carried on for the advancement and upholding of a personal interest, of will, power, and pretended prerogative to himself and his family, against the public interest, common right, liberty, justice, and peace of the people of this nation, by and from whom he was entrusted as aforesaid.

By all of which it appeareth that the said Charles Stuart hath been, and is the occasioner, author, and continuer of the said unnatural, cruel and bloody wars; and therein guilty of all the treasons, murders, rapines, burnings, spills, desolations, damages and mischiefs to this nation, acted and committed in the said wars, or occasioned thereby.

1 With reference to Cromwell's letters in Source 6.23:

a) What does the letter of 28 June 1648 tell you about Cromwell's attitude to God?
b) In the letter of 11 July 1648, why was he particularly angry at the rebels of 1648? Compare his attitude with that of the soldiers in Source 6.21.
c) The 'declaration' referred to in Cromwell's letter to Hammond is Ireton's Remonstrance of the Army, 15 November 1648. What was Cromwell's attitude to it?

2 Summarise the main charges against the King in Source 6.24.

● **SOURCE 6.25**

A painting of Charles I's trial

123

January 1648–January 1649: why did the Second Civil War lead to the King's execution?

The King's defence at his trial

On 1 January 1649 the House of Commons passed an ordinance for bringing the King to trial on the charge of treason set out in Source 6.24. When the House of Lords rejected it, the House of Commons passed it a second time on 3 January, together with an ordinance establishing a High Court of Justice of 135 commissioners. On 5 January they established themselves as a law-making body without King or Lords and on 6 January the Act for the trial of Charles Stuart became law. Attendance at meetings of the commissioners was very thin. Even Fairfax failed to attend after the first meeting. But arrangements for the trial were made. John Bradshaw was appointed to be Lord President of the High Court of Justice and John Cook to present the charges against the King. On 19 January Charles was brought from Windsor to Westminster. His trial began on the following day in Westminster Hall (see Source 6.25) and continued on 22 and 23 January. Between 24 and 26 January the court met without the King, to hear witnesses, in the Painted Chamber. It convened with the King for the final session on 27 January, when the guilty verdict was announced.

● **SOURCE 6.26**

Extracts from the trial of Charles I, 20 January 1649

Charles I:

I am your King. I have a trust committed to me by God, by old and lawful descent. I will not betray to answer to a new unlawful authority ... I stand more for the liberty of my people than any here that sitteth to be my judge.

Bradshaw:

You, instead of answering, interrogate this court, which doth not become you in this condition.

Charles I:

Well, let me tell you, to say you have legal authority will satisfy no reasonable man.

22 January 1649

Bradshaw:

The court expects that you apply yourself to the charge not to lose any more time, but to give a positive answer thereto.

Charles I:

It is not my case alone, it is the freedom and liberty of the people of England. And, do you pretend what you will, I must justly stand for their liberties. For if power, without law, may make law, may alter the fundamental laws of the kingdom – I do not know what subject he is in England can be assured of his life or anything he can call his own. My reasons why in conscience of that duty I owe to God first, and my people afterwards for their lives, liberties and estates, I conceive I cannot answer at this time till I be satisfied of the legality of it.

Bradshaw:

Sir I must interrupt you ... it seems you are about the entering into arguments and disputes concerning the authority of the court ... You may not do it!

Charles I:

Sir, by your favour ... I do know law and reason though I am no lawyer professed. I know as much law as any gentleman in England, and therefore, Sir (by your favour), I do plead for the liberties of the people of England more than any of you do.

● **SOURCE 6.27**

His Majestie's Reasons against the Pretended Jurisdiction of the High Court of Justice. This is part of a pamphlet printed illegally on 5 February 1649. It sets out the reasons that the King had hoped to put to the High Court of Justice on 22 January 1649, but was not allowed to do so.

There is no proceedings just against any man what is warranted either by God's laws or the municipal laws of the country where he lives. Now I am most confident this day's proceedings cannot be warranted by God's law, for on the contrary the authority of obedience unto kings is clearly warranted and strictly commanded both in the Old and New Testaments ... Then for the law of the land, I am no less confident that no learned lawyer will affirm that an impeachment can lie against the king, they all going in his name ... Besides, the law upon which you ground your proceedings must be either old or new: if old, show it; if new, tell what authority warranted by the fundamental laws of this land hath made it, and when. But how the House of Commons can erect a court of judicature, which was never one itself ... I leave to God and the world to judge ... Besides all this, the peace of the kingdom is not the least in my thoughts, and what hope of settlement is there so long as power reigns without rule or law, changing the whole frame of that government under which this kingdom hath flourished for many hundred years?

● SOURCE 6.28

A copy of the King's death warrant

● SOURCE 6.29

An extract from Charles' speech on the scaffold, 30 January 1649

I shall begin first with my innocence. In truth I think it not very needful for me to insist long upon this, for all the world knows that I never did begin a war with the two Houses of Parliament. And I call God to witness, to whom I must shortly make an account, that I never did intend to encroach upon their privileges. They began upon me; it is the militia they began upon. They confessed that the militia was mine, but they thought it fit for to have it from me. And, to be short, if anybody will look at the dates of the commissions, of their commissions and mine, and likewise to the declarations, [they] will see clearly that they began these unhappy troubles, not I … You must give God his due by regulating rightly his Church (according to the Scripture) which is now out of order … A national synod freely called, freely debating among themselves, must settle this, when every opinion is freely and clearly heard.

I	On what grounds did the King challenge the legality of the High Court of Justice?
2	What other arguments did Charles I put in his defence?

● SOURCE 6.30

A print showing the execution of Charles I

What can you tell from Source 6.30 about:

    a) the execution of Charles I
    b) the attitude of the artist towards the execution
    c) the international significance of the execution?

● Summary Task

1 A debate: Should the King die?

    Choose two groups of two people. One group's task is to persuade the rest of the class (acting as the jury) that the King must die. The other group is the team of defence lawyers who have to try to persuade the jury that the King should live.

    The procedure for the debate should be as follows:

    Each group should speak, in turn, for a maximum of ten minutes to present their cases.

    Then each group should be given a maximum of five minutes to respond to points made by the opposing group or to introduce any new points which support their cases.

    There should then be an opportunity for the class–jury to ask questions of both the prosecution and defence teams.

    End by voting (preferably by a secret ballot) on the King's fate.

    (The outcome of your trial will probably be uncertain. At the real trial in January 1649 this was not the case. A guilty verdict was inevitable. This is one of the rare occasions in history when the use of the word 'inevitable' is justified.)

2 Write an essay of between 1,500 and 2,000 words answering one of the following questions.

    a) Why did all attempts to reach a settlement with Charles I after the end of the First Civil War fail?

    b) Most people in 1648–9 wanted Charles I to be restored as King. Why then was he executed in January 1649?

3 Examine the groups involved in the search for a settlement such as :

The King	Parliament divided between Political Presbyterians and Political Independents	The Scots	The New Model Army • the Grandees • the rank and file	Radical Groups like the Levellers

-   What different kind of settlement did each of these groups want?
-   Why did their failure to find a settlement lead to the Second Civil War?
-   How did the Second Civil War change the situation?

● Further reading

Begin by reading the relevant sections in general books such as Barry Coward, *The Stuart Age: England 1603–1714* (Longman, 1994) and A. G. R. Smith, *The Emergence of a Nation State: The Commonwealth of England 1529–1660* (Longman, 1984) or, in the Longman Seminar Studies book, M. Bennett, *The English Civil War* (1995).

    More detailed information can be found in Derek Hirst, *Authority and Conflict: England 1603–58* (Edward Arnold, 1985) and in David Underdown, *Pride's Purge: the Politics of the Puritan Revolution* (OUP, 1971), Chapters 4–6.

    The best book on the New Model Army is I. Gentles, *The New Model Army* (Blackwell, 1991). There is a good summary of his views in his article 'The Impact of the New Model Army' in John Morrill (ed.), *The Impact of the Civil War* (Collins and Brown, 1991).

    For growing support for a settlement with Charles I in this period see V. Pearl, 'London's "Counter-revolution"' in G. E. Aylmer (ed.), *The Interregnum: the Quest for Settlement* (Macmillan, 1973) and John Morrill, *The Revolt of the Provinces* (Longman, 1980), pp. 123–5.

chapter 7

How revolutionary were the ideas of the radical groups in England after the Civil War?

1643
August: John Milton publishes *The Doctrine and Discipline of Divorce.*

1644
November: John Milton publishes *Areopagitica.*

1645
July 7: The Leveller leaders jointly publish *A Remonstrance of Many Thousand Citizens.*

1647
October 15: *The Case of the Army Truly Stated* is presented to General Fairfax by the agitators of the New Model Army cavalry regiments; shortly afterwards it is redrafted and re-titled *The Agreement of the People.*
October 28–November 11: Putney Debates take place, at which the General Council of the Army discusses *The Agreement of the People.*
November 15: Fairfax and Cromwell suppress Leveller resistance in the army at Corkbush Field near Ware; one of the Leveller supporters, Richard Arnold, is shot after a court martial.

1648
September 11: The Leveller Large Petition is published.
December 6: Pride's Purge takes place.

1649
January: Gerrard Winstanley publishes *The New Law of Righteousness.*
January 30: Charles I is executed.
February 26: Lilburne publishes the first part of *England's New Chains Discovered.*
April 1: Winstanley and his Digger supporters establish their collective farm at St George's Hill, Surrey.
May 14: Cromwell defeats mutinying Leveller soldiers at Burford in Oxfordshire; three of the ringleaders are executed in Burford churchyard.
August: The Diggers move their farm to Cobham in Surrey.

1650
February: John Milton publishes *The Tenure of Kings and Magistrates.*
April: The Digger farm at Cobham is suppressed.

1652
February: Gerrard Winstanley publishes *The Law of Freedom in a Platform.*

Introduction

One of the important features which mark out revolutionary periods from more tranquil times is the intellectual ferment that usually accompanies them. This occurs largely because some of the men and women who live through revolutions have a strong sense that, having swept away the traditional structures that have surrounded them for many years, perhaps even for centuries, they have a unique opportunity to go back to first principles and re-establish politics, religion and society on an entirely fresh basis. This was certainly true of the 20 years of the English Revolution. Most of the traditional institutions of the Church and State were temporarily destroyed and large numbers of men and women took part in a vigorous and prolonged debate about how to re-organise their contemporary world for the better. In the course of this debate, some individuals and groups put forward extremely radical solutions to what they saw as the ills of their day; among the controversial ideas that found supporters were manhood suffrage, communism, vegetarianism, POLYGAMY, liberal divorce and free love. After the breakdown of press censorship in the early stages of the Civil War, it was relatively easy to produce cheap printed pamphlets and to distribute them over wide areas; as a consequence much of this intellectual discussion was conducted on the printed page and was available to a wide readership. Historians are fortunate that, thanks to the efforts of collectors such as the London bookseller George Thomason, many thousands of these printed documents are still available for consultation.

This chapter looks at some of the published material relating to four of the radical groups that emerged during the English Revolution:

- Section A The Levellers
- Section B The True Levellers or Diggers
- Section C The Ranters
- Section D The Fifth Monarchists.

Section E contains a selection of the work of the famous poet John Milton, who was also deeply involved in the contemporary discussions and whose views were notoriously radical and unorthodox. Another very important radical religious group from the 1650s, the Quakers or Society of Friends, will be considered later in Chapter 12.

In this chapter you will need to consider a number of key questions. From the sources, which describe the ideas of different groups, you will have to come to your own view about how revolutionary the ideas of the radical groups were in post-Civil War England.

There is a great deal of additional material that has been published on the groups that are featured in this chapter. Where possible you should supplement each section with further reading. There are suggestions at the end of this chapter.

There are several key questions to consider when investigating the question 'How revolutionary were the ideas of the radical groups in England after the Civil War?':

- Why did the radical groups emerge at this time?
- How revolutionary were they?
- How were they able to gather support?
- Why did they fail?

Bear these questions in mind as you investigate each of the radical groups.

polygamy: *the practice of one man having several wives*

Section A The Levellers

The Levellers were a radical group of political activists who emerged in London during the Civil War years. This group centred on three principal individuals: Richard Overton, John Lilburne and William Walwyn. All of these men began publishing political and religious pamphlets independently, but by the latter stages of the war they all knew each other and were working together to achieve their ends. Examples of their views about government are given in Sources 7.1–7.3.

● **SOURCE 7.1**

From the Leveller pamphlet *A Remonstrance of Many Thousand Citizens*, 1646

We are well assured, yet cannot forget, that the cause of our choosing you to be Parliament-men, was to deliver us from all kind of bondage and to preserve the commonwealth in peace and happiness, For effecting whereof, we possessed you with the same power that was in ourselves, to have done the same; for we might justly have done it ourselves without you, if we had thought it convenient, choosing you as persons whom we thought fitly qualified and faithful for avoiding some inconveniences.

revocable: *able to be cancelled*

usurpation: *wrongful seizure of power*

But ye are to remember, this was only of us but a power of trust, which is ever REVOCABLE and cannot be otherwise, and to be employed to no other end than our own well being. Nor did we choose you to continue our trusts longer than the known established constitution of this common-wealth will justly permit, and that could be but for one year at the most … We are your principals and you our agents; it is a truth which you cannot but acknowledge. For if you or any other shall assume or exercise any power that is not derived from our trust and choice thereunto, that power is no less than USURPATION and an oppression, from which we expect to be freed, in whomsoever we find it; it being altogether inconsistent with the nature of just freedom, which ye also very well understand …

● **SOURCE 7.2**

Title page of *A Remonstrance of Many Thousand Citizens*

A
REMONSTRANCE
OF
Many Thousand Citizens, and other Free-born
PEOPLE OF ENGLAND,
To their owne House of
COMMONS.

Occasioned through the Illegall and Barbarous Imprisonment of that Famous and Worthy Sufferer for his Countries Freedoms, Lievtenant Col.

JOHN LILBURNE.

Wherein their just Demands in behalfe of themselves and the whole Kingdome, concerning their Publike Safety, Peace and Freedome, is Express'd; calling those their Commissioners in Parliament to an Account, how they (since the beginning of their Session, to this present) have discharged their Duties to the Universality of the People, their Soveraigne LORD, from whom their Power and Strength is derived, and by whom (ad bene placitum,) it is continued.

July 7th   Printed in the Yeer, 1646.

● **SOURCE 7.3**

This portrait of John Lilburne, engraved by George Glove, appeared in the *Remonstrance*.

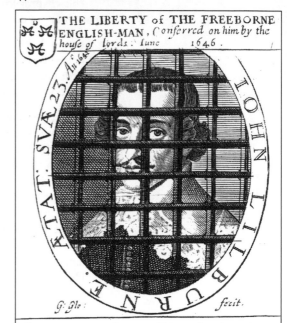

THE LIBERTY of THE FREEBORNE ENGLISH-MAN, *Conferred on him by the house of lords. Iune 1646.*

Gaze not upon this shaddow that is vaine,
But rather raise thy thoughts a higher straine,
To GOD (I meane) who set this young-man free,
And in like straits can oke deliuer thee.
Yea though the lords have him in bonds againe,
LORD of lords will his just cause maintaine.

● **SOURCE 7.4**

From the postscript to John Lilburne's pamphlet *The Free-man's Freedom Vindicated,* 1646

appropriate: *take*

donation: *gift or grant*

… all and every particular and individual man and woman … are … by nature all equal and alike in power, dignity, authority and majesty, none of them having by nature any authority, dominion or magisterial power one over or above another; neither have they, nor can they exercise any, but merely by institution or DONATION, that is to say by mutual agreement or consent, given, derived or assumed by mutual consent and agreement, for the good benefit and comfort each of other, and not for mischief, hurt, or damage of any; it being unnatural, irrational … wicked and unjust for any man or men whatsoever to part with so much of their power as shall enable any of their Parliament-men, commissioners, trustees, deputies … or servants to destroy and undo them therewith. And unnatural, irrational, sinful, wicked, unjust, devilish and tyrannical, it is for any man whatsoever, spiritual or temporal, clergyman or layman, to APPROPRIATE and assume unto himself a power, authority and jurisdiction, to rule, govern or reign over any sort of men in the world without their free consent …

● **SOURCE 7.5**

A page from William Walwyn's pamphlet *England's Lamentable Slaverie*, 1645

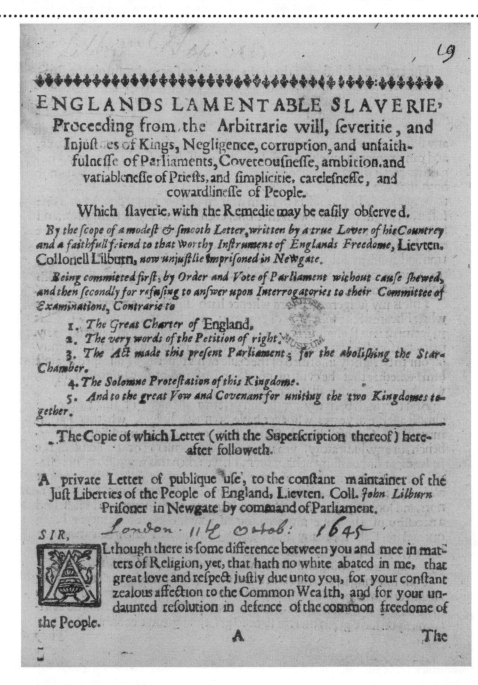

● **SOURCE 7.6**

From William Walwyn's pamphlet *England's Lamentable Slaverie*, 1645

episcopacy: *rule of the Church through bishops*

extirpation: *wiping out*

This parliament was preserved and established by the love and affections of the people because they found themselves in great bondage … both spiritual and temporal; out of both which the parliament proposed to deliver them in all their endeavours …

And for the first, it was a great thing, the EXTIRPATION of EPISCOPACY, but that merely is not the main matter the people expected which indeed is, that none be compelled against conscience in the worship of God, nor any molested for conscience's sake, the oppression for conscience having been the greatest oppression that ever lay upon religious people, and therefore except that be removed, the people have some case by removal of the bishops, but rather will be in greater bondage if more and worse spiritual taskmasters be set over us …

And what became of that common and threadbare doctrine that kings were accountable only to God, what good effects did it produce? No, they are but corrupt and dangerous flatterers that maintain any such fond opinions concerning either kings or parliaments.

What prejudice is it to any in any authority, meaning well, to be accountable ... Doth any man entrust and not look for justice and good dealing from him he trusts ...

1 What, according to these Leveller writers, is the source of the power of governments?

2 What do they believe to be the purpose of governments?

3 How do their ideas challenge the widely accepted theory of the divine right of kings?

4 What religious principle was fundamental to the Levellers?

5 Can you detect any differences between these three writers?

By 1646 these men and their followers had established a simple party structure in London, and over the next few years they campaigned hard to spread their ideas, by petitioning, CANVASSING and demonstrating. In September 1648, they sent a petition to the House of Commons, whose members were still trying to reach a settlement with the King, calling upon it instead to end those negotiations and to take a number of radical measures.

canvassing: *seeking support*

● **SOURCE 7.7**

From the Leveller Petition to the House of Commons, September 1648

The truth is ... we have long expected things of another nature from you, and such as we are confident would have given satisfaction to all serious people of all parties:

1 That you would have made good the Supreme [Authority] of the people in this honourable House from all pretence of negative voices, either in King or Lords.

2 That you would have made laws for election of REPRESENTATIVES yearly ...

4 That you would have exempted matters of religion and gospel from the compulsive or restrictive power of any authority upon earth, and reserved to the Supreme Authority an uncompulsive power only of appointing a way for the public [worship], whereby abundance of misery, persecution and heart-burning would for ever be avoided.

5 That you would have DISCLAIMED IN yourself and all future representatives a power of pressing and forcing any sort of men to serve in wars ...

9 That you would have abbreviated the proceedings in law, mitigated and made certain the charges thereof in all particulars.

10 That you would have freed all trade and merchandising from all MONOPOLISING AND ENGROSSING, by companies or otherwise.

11 That you would have abolished excise, and all kinds of taxes except subsidies, the old and only just way of England ...

13 That you would have considered the many thousands that were ruined by perpetual imprisonment for debt, and provided to their enlargement.

14 That you would have ordered some effectual course to keep people from begging and beggary in so fruitful a nation as through God's blessing this is ...

16 That you would have removed the tedious burden of TITHES, satisfying all IMPROPRIATORS and providing a more equal way of maintenance for the public ministers ...

18 That you would have bound yourselves and all future parliaments from abolishing PROPRIETY, levelling men's estates or making all things common.

19 That you would have declared what the duty or business of the kingly office is, and what not, and ascertained the revenue, past increase or DIMINUTION, that so there might never be more quarrels about the same ...

23 That you would not have followed the example of former tyrannous and superstitious parliaments, in making orders, ordinances or laws, or in appointing punishments concerning opinions or things supernatural, styling some BLASPHEMIES, others HERESIES, when as you know yourselves easily mistaken, and that divine truths need no human helps to support them, such proceedings having been generally invented to divide the people amongst themselves and to affright men from that liberty of discourse by which corruptions and tyranny would soon be discovered.

24 That you would have declared what the business of the [House of] Lords is, and ascertained

blasphemies: *comments or actions attacking religion*

derogating: *detracting*

diminution: *reduction*

disclaimed in: *denied*

heresies: *beliefs contrary to orthodox religion*

impropriators: *lay people, who as a result of their ownership of former monastic land, received tithes*

lenity: *lenience*

monopolising and engrossing: *practices which restricted free competition*

propriety: *property*

representatives: *Members of Parliament*

tithes: *taxes (a tenth of the produce of each individual) paid to the clergy* their condition, not DEROGATING from the liberties of other men, that so there might be an end of striving about the same.

25 That you would have done justice upon the capital authors and promoters of the former or late wars, many of them being under your power, considering that mercy to the wicked is cruelty to the innocent, and that all your LENITY doth but make them the more insolent and presumptuous …

These and the like we have long hoped you would have minded, and have made such an establishment for the general peace and contentful satisfaction of all sorts of people, as should have been to the happiness of all future generations, and which we most earnestly desire you would set yourselves speedily to effect, whereby the almost dying honour of this most honourable House would again be revived, and the hearts of your petitioners and all other well affected people be afresh renewed unto you …

1 Which institution did the Levellers believe should have supreme power in the State?

2 Over which areas did they believe Parliament should not have power to legislate?

3 What were their main economic and social demands?

4 What evidence can you find that the Levellers did not believe in complete social and economic equality?

5 Why did they want to abolish tithes?

As we saw in Chapter 6, by 1647 the Leveller leaders had come to realise that their best chance of achieving their political goals lay in winning over the New Model Army to their programme (see pages 114–15 on *The Agreement of the People*, the Levellers, most famous publication). During the summer of 1647, some of them helped in the drawing up of the documents that put the grievances of the ordinary soldiers to the officers. In the autumn several civilian Levellers were present at the debates in Putney at which the army council discussed its political aims. Some of the contributions to the debate at Putney were made by the two civilian Levellers who were present: a London tradesman, Maximilian Petty, and a lawyer, John Wildman.

● **SOURCE 7.8**

An extract from the Putney Debates, October–November 1647

132

How revolutionary were the ideas of the radical groups in England after the Civil War?

● **SOURCE 7.9**

From the Putney Debates (see also Source 6.17 on page 116)

40 shillings freehold: *freehold land worth 40 shillings (£2) a year or more*

representative of the nation: *Parliament*

Petty:

We judge that all inhabitants that have not lost their birthright should have an equal voice in elections …

Petty:

And for this changing of the REPRESENTATIVE OF THE NATION, of changing those that choose the representative, making of them more full, taking more into the number than formerly, I had verily thought we had all agreed in that more should have chosen – all that had desired a more equal representative than we now have. For now those only choose who have 40 SHILLINGS FREEHOLD. A man may have a lease for £100 a year … [but no vote] …

Wildman:

Our case is to be considered thus, that we have been under slavery. That's acknowledged by all. Our very laws were made by our conquerors … and I conceive there is no credit to be given to any of them; and the reason is because those that were our lords and made us their vassals … We are now engaged for our freedom. That's the end of parliaments: not to constitute what is already, [but to act] according to just rules of government. Every person in England hath as clear a right to elect his representatives as the greatest person. I conceive that's the undeniable maxim of government: that all government is in the free consent of the people. If [so] then upon that account there is no person that is under a just government, or hath justly his own, unless he by his own free consent be put under that government. This he cannot be unless he be consenting to it, and therefore according to this maxim, there is never a person in England [but should have a vote] …

Petty:

I conceive the reason why we would exclude apprentices or servants [from the vote], or those that take alms, is because they depend upon the will of other men and should be afraid to displease [them]. For servants and apprentices, they are included in their masters, and so for those that receive alms from door to door; but if there be any general way taken for those that are not bound, it would be well …

1 Who had been allowed to vote before the Civil War?

2 Whom would the Levellers have given the vote to, and whom would they have continued to exclude from voting?

3 Which large section of society, not specifically mentioned by either Petty or Wildman, would also not have been given the vote by the Levellers on the grounds that they too 'depend upon the will of other men'?

Throughout its short history, the Leveller movement had many women supporters, and on occasions they had taken part in predominantly female petitions and demonstrations. In the following petition to the House of Commons, in May 1649, some Leveller women responded to criticisms in Parliament of their involvement in politics and also complained about the imprisonment in the Tower of London of Lilburne, Overton, Walwyn and another prominent Leveller, Thomas Prince.

● **SOURCE 7.10**

From the Women's Petition, May 1649

sensible: *aware*

sottish: *foolish*

… since we are assured of our creation in the image of God, and of an interest in Christ equal unto men, as also of a proportionable share in the freedoms of this commonwealth, we cannot but wonder and grieve that we should appear so despicable in your eyes as to be thought unworthy to petition or represent our grievances to this honourable House. Have we not an equal interest with the men of this nation in those liberties and securities contained in the Petition of Right, and other of the good laws of the land? Are any of our lives, limbs, liberties, or goods to be taken from us more than from men, but by due process of the law and conviction of twelve sworn men of the neighbourhood? And can you imagine us to be so SOTTISH or stupid as not to perceive, or not to be wholly SENSIBLE when daily those strong defences of our peace and welfare are broken down and trod underfoot by force and arbitrary power? …

Would you have us keep at home in our houses, when men of such faithfulness and integrity as the four prisoners, our friends in the Tower, are fetched out of their beds and forced from their houses by soldiers, to the affrighting and undoing of themselves, their wives, children and families? Are not our husbands, ourselves, our children and families by the same rule as liable to the like unjust cruelties as they …

And therefore again we entreat you to review our last petition in behalf of our friends above mentioned, and not to slight the things therein contained because they are presented unto you by the weak hand of women, it being a usual thing with God by weak means to work mighty effects …

1 What does this source reveal about seventeenth-century attitudes towards women?

2 Despite the arguments presented here, Leveller women never asked for the vote for themselves and no male Leveller seems to have argued that they should have it. What reasons can you suggest to explain this?

In the immediate aftermath of the Putney Debates the Leveller attempt to win control of the army was prevented by the swift action of the leading officers, especially Cromwell and Fairfax, who quashed several Leveller mutinies and reimposed discipline by executing several of the ringleaders. A year later, however, following the Second Civil War and the decision by some sections of the army leadership that Charles should be put on trial, the army high command entered into negotiations with the Levellers, and a compromise Agreement of the People was drawn up. This more moderate document was supposed to form the basis of a new republican constitution which would be established after the removal of the King. Following the army coup of December 1648 and January 1649, however, the officers ignored it and replaced the old monarchical constitution with the unrepresentative Rump (see Chapter 8). The outraged Levellers immediately protested and once more tried to pull their rank-and-file supporters away from their allegiance to their officers. Their resistance was ended at Burford in Oxfordshire in May 1649. Following a short skirmish, Cromwell captured several hundred mutinying troops who were on their way to a Leveller rendezvous at Banbury. After holding them prisoner in Burford church for several days, he forced them to watch the execution of their leaders in the churchyard. After the failure of this second attempt to achieve power, support for the Levellers rapidly evaporated.

What reasons can you suggest to explain why the Levellers failed?

Section B The True Levellers or Diggers

Although the Digger movement was never of the same size or importance as the Levellers, its political philosophy was even more remarkable. Whereas the Levellers had gone out of their way to deny allegations that they wished to level society by abolishing private property, the Diggers, who called themselves the True Levellers, fully embraced a communistic solution to the inequalities of their society.

The movement was dominated by the personality of Gerrard Winstanley. A deeply religious man, Winstanley had grown up in Wigan in Lancashire and had taken up an apprenticeship in London before the Civil War. By 1642 he was trading in his own right in the capital but, soon after, he became bankrupt and travelled down to the Cobham area of Surrey, where he made a meagre living looking after livestock. In the spring of 1649, he and a group of friends began to squat on some common grazing land on St George's Hill, Weybridge, in Surrey, and to cultivate vegetables on the collective farm they set up there. Over the next few months they faced continual harassment from the local landowners, who eventually drove

Liberation theology: *a radical Christian movement which aims to promote justice and eradicate poverty and oppression*

pre-Marxist: *before the work of Karl Marx, the nineteenth-century political philosopher*

them away in early 1650. Several other Digger communes were established in other parts of the south-east of the country at about the same time, but they all met the same fate.

Historians have been interested in the Diggers not because of their contemporary political significance, but because of the extreme radicalism of their actions and ideas. Winstanley, the principal theorist of the group, explained their views in a series of pamphlets that reveal him to be not only a PRE-MARXIST communist but also an early advocate of what today we would label LIBERATION THEOLOGY and environmentalism.

● **SOURCE 7.11**

From Gerrard Winstanley's pamphlet *The True Levellers' Standard Advanced*, April 1649

enclosures: *large enclosed farms*

hereupon: *after this*

manifest: *shown*

propriety: *property*

straits: *difficulties*

In the beginning of time the great creator Reason made the earth to be a common treasury, to preserve beasts, birds, fishes and man, the lord that was to govern this creation; for man had domination given to him over beasts, birds, and fishes; but not one word was spoken in the beginning that one branch of mankind should rule over another. But ... HEREUPON the earth (which was made to be a common treasury of relief for all, both beasts and men) was hedged into ENCLOSURES by the teachers and rulers, and the others were made servants and slaves; and that earth, that is within this creation made a common storehouse for all, is bought and sold and kept in the hands of a few, whereby the great creator is mightily dishonoured, as if he were a respecter of persons, delighting in the comfortable livelihood of some, and rejoicing in the miserable poverty and STRAITS of others. From the beginning it was not so.

The work we are going about is this, to dig up George's Hill and the waste ground thereabouts, and to sow corn, and to eat our bread together by the sweat of our brows.

And the first reason is this. That we may work in righteousness and lay the foundation of making the earth a common treasury for all, both rich and poor, that everyone that is born in the land may be fed by the earth his mother that brought him forth, according to the reason that rules in the creation. Not enclosing any part into any particular hand, but all as one man working together and feeding together as sons of one father, members of one family; not one lording over another, but all looking upon each other as equals in the creation; so that our Maker may be glorified in the work of his own hands, and that everyone may see that he is no respecter of persons, but equally loves his whole creation ...

And that this civil PROPRIETY is the curse is MANIFEST thus: those that buy and sell land and are landlords, have got it either by oppression or murder or theft; and all landlords live in breach of the seventh and eighth Commandments, *Thou shalt not steal nor kill ...*

1 Summarise Winstanley's beliefs as expressed in this source.

2 What source of authority does Winstanley claim for his beliefs?

3 What is Winstanley's attitude to landlords and property owners?

● **SOURCE 7.12**

From Gerrard Winstanley's pamphlet *A New Year's Gift to the Parliament and Army*, 1650

covetousness: *greed*

portion: *inheritance*

raiment: *clothing*

take pattern: *copy*

... and all this falling out or quarrelling among mankind is about the earth, who shall, and who shall not enjoy it, when indeed it is the PORTION of every one and ought not to be striven for, nor bought, nor sold whereby some are hedged in and others hedged out. For better not to have had a body than to be debarred the fruits of the earth to feed and clothe it; and if every one did but quietly enjoy the earth for food and RAIMENT, there would be no wars, prisons nor gallows, and this action which men call theft, would be no sin, for universal love never made it a sin, but the power of COVETOUSNESS made that a sin and made laws to punish it ...

And what other lands do, England is not to TAKE PATTERN, for England (as well as other lands) has lain under the power of that Beast, kingly property. But now England is the first of nations that is upon the point of reforming ... for if ever the creation [is to] be restored, this is the way which lies in this twofold power:

First, community of mankind, which is comprised in the unity of spirit of love, which is called Christ in you or the law written in the heart, leading mankind into all truth and to be of one heart and one mind.

The second is community of the earth, for the quiet livelihood in food and raiment without using force, or restraining one another. These two communities, or rather one in two branches, is that true levelling which Christ will work at his more glorious appearance for Jesus Christ the saviour of all men is the greatest, first and truest Leveller that ever was spoke of in the world ...

For I tell you and your preachers, that scripture which says 'The poor shall inherit the earth' is really and materially to be fulfilled. For the earth is to be restored from the bondage of sword property, and is to become a common treasury in reality to all mankind ...

---

1   What are Winstanley's views on the causes of wars?

2   Why did he believe that at the time of writing there was a real opportunity in England to implement these ideas?

● **SOURCE 7.13**

From Gerrard Winstanley's pamphlet *Fire in the Bush*, 1650

Antichrist: *enemy of Christ*

apace: *quickly*

Therefore, woe, woe, woe, to the inhabitants of the earth when Christ rises in power and begins to come in glory with his saints. This discovery is coming on APACE.

Therefore you soldiers, and you great powers of the earth, you need not fear that the Levellers will conquer you by the sword; I do not mean the fighting Levellers, for they be your selves; but I mean Christ levelling who fights against you by the sword of love, patience and truth; for whosoever takes the iron sword to fight against you are your own sons that fight against you; For Christ came not to destroy but to save, but ANTICHRIST, whose power you are, came not to save but to destroy ...

● **SOURCE 7.14**

Rules for Winstanley's ideal state, from his pamphlet *The Law of Freedom in a Platform*, 1652

entice: *tempt*

substance: *subsistence*

Every family shall come into the fields with sufficient assistance at seed-time to plough, dig and plant, and at harvest time to reap the fruits of the earth and carry them into the storehouses as the overseers order the work and the number of workmen ...

If any refuse to learn a trade or refuse to work in seed-time or harvest time or refuse to be a waiter in storehouses, and yet will feed and clothe himself with other men's labours, the overseers shall first admonish him privately, and if he continue idle he shall be reproved openly before all the people by the overseers ...

The waiters in storehouses shall deliver the goods under their charge without receiving any money, as they shall receive in their goods without paying any money ...

If any man ENTICE another to buy and sell, and he who is enticed doth not yield, but make it known to the overseer, the enticer shall lose his freedom for twelve months ...

If any do buy and sell the earth or the fruits thereof ... they shall be both put to death as traitors to the peace of the commonwealth ...

The storehouses shall be every man's SUBSTANCE and not any one's ...

No man shall either give or take hire for his work, for this brings in kingly bondage ...

He who professes the service of a righteous God by preaching and prayer, and makes a trade to get possession of the earth, shall be put to death for a witch and a cheater ...

Every freeman shall have a freedom in the earth to plant or build or fetch from the storehouses any thing he wants, and shall enjoy the fruits of his labours without restraint from any: he shall not pay rent to any landlord ...

● **SOURCE 7.15**

Extracts from a song composed by the St George's Hill Diggers, the original tune of which is unknown

disdain: *dismiss*

The Digger Song

You noble Diggers all, stand up now, stand up now
You noble Diggers all, stand up now
The waste land to maintain, seeing Cavaliers by name
Your digging does DISDAIN, and persons all defame
Stand up now, stand up now

Your houses they pull down, stand up now, stand up now
Your houses they pull down, stand up now
Your houses they pull down, to fright poor men in town
But the gentry must come down, and the poor shall wear the crown
Stand up now, Diggers all

The gentry are all around, stand up now, stand up now
The gentry are all around, stand up now
The gentry are all around, on each side they are found
Their wisdom's so profound, to cheat us of our ground
Stand up now, stand up now

'Gainst lawyers and 'gainst priests, stand up now, stand up now
'Gainst lawyers and 'gainst priests, stand up now
For tyrants they are both, even flat against their oath
To grant us they are loath, free meat and drink and cloth
Stand up now, Diggers all

The Cavaliers are foes, stand up now, stand up now
The Cavaliers are foes, stand up now
The Cavaliers are foes, themselves they do disclose
By verse not in prose, to please the singing boys
Stand up now, Diggers all

To conquer them by love, come in now, come in now
To conquer them by love, come in now
To conquer them by love, as it does you behove
For he is king above, no power is like to love
Glory here, Diggers all

1 **What were the main differences between the political programmes of the Levellers and the Diggers?**

2 **How did Winstanley justify his communistic views?**

3 **What kind of people do you think would have been:**

   a) **attracted to the Diggers**
   b) **hostile to the Diggers?**

4 **Why do you think the Diggers failed?**

Section C The Ranters

> **libertines:** *immoral and irresponsible people*
>
> **pantheist:** *the idea that God is to be found in nature*

Like the Diggers, the Ranters were a very small group which emerged at the end of the 1640s. They too put forward ideas that were extremely unusual for their day and scandalised many of their contemporaries. In most other ways, however, the two movements were very different; Winstanley wrote a pamphlet denouncing the Ranters as LIBERTINES, and when several of them turned up at the Digger commune at St George's Hill they caused considerable disruption. For, whereas the Diggers believed in the communal cultivation of the land, the Ranters' ideas were grounded in 'antinomianism' – the belief that, as they had been predestined to heaven, they were no longer bound by the moral law and could indulge in activities such as swearing, excessive drinking and casual sex without sinning. Some Ranters also rejected the idea of a God who was separated from the created world, and instead put forward the PANTHEIST idea that the divine was to be found within nature.

The particular ideas that the Ranter Abiezer Coppe was forced to recant by Parliament in 1651 were: 'that there is no sin'; 'that there is no God'; 'that man or the mere creature is very God'; 'that God is in man, or in the creature only, and no where else'; 'that cursing and swearing is no sin'; 'that adultery, fornication and uncleanness is no sin'; and 'that community of wives is lawful'.

The next sources are extracts from several of the pamphlets written by Ranter writers.

● **SOURCE 7.16**

From Laurence Clarkson's pamphlet
A Single Eye All Light, No Darkness,
1650

apprehendeth: understand

esteemest: consider

… But to the matter in hand, Thou hast heard all acts that are, had their being and birth from God, yea acted by God, to be plain those acts by you called swearing, drunkenness, adultery and theft etc., these acts simply as acts were produced by the power of God, yea, perfected by the wisdom if God.

What, said I, a swearer, a drunkard, an adulterer, a thief, had these the power and wisdom of God, to swear, drink, whore and steal?… O blasphemy of the highest nature! What, make God the author of sin? so a sinful God! … there is no such act as drunkenness, adultery and theft in God; though by his power and wisdom thou executest this act and that act, yet that appearance by which thou APPREHENDETH and ESTEEMEST them to be acts of sin, that estimation was not in God, though from God …

No matter what scripture, saints or churches say, if that within thee do not condemn thee, thou shalt not be condemned …

I declare that whosoever doth attempt to act from flesh, in flesh, to flesh, hath, is and will commit adultery; but to bring this to a period, for my part, till I acted that so called sin, I could not predominate over sin; so that now whatsoever I act, is not in relationship to the title, to the flesh, but that eternity in me; so that with me, all creatures are but one creature, and this is my form, the representative of the whole creation: So that, see what I can, act what I will, all is but one most sweet and lovely. Therefore, my dear ones, consider that without act [there is] no life; without life, no perfection; and without perfection, no eternal peace and freedom indeed, in power, which is the everlasting Majesty, ruling, conquering and dancing all into its self, without end for ever.

● **SOURCE 7.17**

From an anonymous work, *A Justification of a Mad Crew,* 1650

plague: denounce

… but now in the last of these days am I made to stand upon my feet and to curse and damn the inhabitants of the world, until there be but one inhabitant, and till there be but a man left in all the earth who is, was, and shall be the glory of the Woman. I will now lie openly before the sun with many women, and yet with my own wife, and I will PLAGUE even bitterly they that lie with any save their own wives in the dark, in their thoughts and desires, in their words, I will make them gnaw their tongues, and gnash their teeth for pain, who pretend to be holy and not to touch a woman, and yet can and sometimes have lain with women in the dark; yea you that ever did it actually, but in thought and desire, you have committed adultery before me, and for it shall ye be damned. O you hypocrites, you can spend your selves to the full, as oft as your lusts carries you out, upon one woman called your wife, and there do as much as any whore-master in the world upon many women, and this is no sin, no pollution … what difference is there between your wife and another woman? O, you say you are married to your wife, and that is no evil: Why, what is marriage? is it any more but to gain the love and affections of a woman to be yours to serve you and to declare this openly? this is your marriage. Well then, if I the lord in a man gain the love, affections and desires of all women, and make them sweetly to serve me, and hav[ing] done so, lie with them all, and use them as oft as I please, and set not up an idol in my heart by having one woman only, damning and cursing and estranging myself from all other women, is not this the truest marriage …

1　How do the Ranters argue that there is no such thing as sin?

2　In what ways did these writers reject the fundamentals of orthodox Christianity?

3　Why do you think the Ranters provoked so much hostility?

A great deal of the information we have about the activities of the Ranters is derived from contemporary newsbook accounts of what went on at their meetings. Several of these are given below.

138

How revolutionary were the ideas of the radical groups in England after the Civil War?

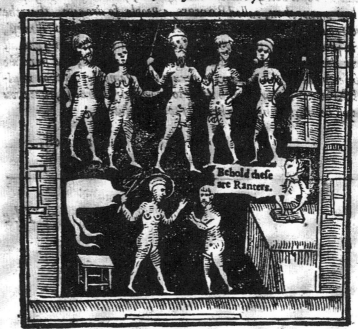

The Ranters Religion.

OR,

A faithfull and infallible Narrative of their damnable and
diabolical opinions, with their detestable lives & actions.

With a true discovery of some of their late prodigious
pranks, and unparalleld deportments; with a paper of
most blasphemous Verses found in one of their pockets,
against the Majesty of Almighty God, and the most sacred Scriptures, rendred *verbatim*.

Published by Authority.

Behold these
are Ranters.

London, Printed for *R. H.* 1650.

● **SOURCE 7.19**

From *The Ranters' Religion*, 1650

... They affirm that all women ought to be in common, and when they are assembled
altogether (this is a known truth) they first entertain one another, the men those of their
own sex, and the women their fellow females, with horrid oaths ... then they fall to boozing,
and drink deep healths ... to their brother God, and their brother Devil; then being well
heated with liquor, each brother takes his she other upon his knee, and the word (spoken in
derision of the sacred writ) being given, viz. *Increase and Multiply*, they fall to their LASCIVIOUS
embraces ...

They maintain that to have their women in common is their Christian liberty ... This they
frequently, and with much fervency affirm ...

One of these ROYSTERS sitting over his cups (with the rest of his companions) evacuating
wind backwards, used this blasphemous expression, *let everything that hath breath praise the Lord.*

Another of them taking a piece of boiled beef betwixt his hands, and tearing it in pieces,
gave part thereof to one of his companions, using these words (in derision of the blessed
sacrament), *the body and blood of Jesus Christ.*

A she Ranter said openly in the hearing of many (a friend of mine accidentally one of them)
that she should think herself a happy woman, and should esteem herself a SUPERLATIVE servant
of God's, if any man would accompany with her carnally in the open market place.

lascivious: *lustful*

roysters: *merrymakers*

superlative: *excellent*

O wretched people! O monstrous times! I pray God put it into the hearts of our vigilant senators … to go through with it and make these monsters of mankind examples to the whole world … such Devils clad in flesh are not fit to have subsistence amongst those who boast themselves Christians, but merit (as unsavoury salt) to be thrown out and to be trodden under foot of men.

● **SOURCE 7.20**

A page from *The Routing of the Ranters*, published in 1650

THE

ROVTING

OF THE

RANTERS

a full Relation of their uncivil carriages, and blasphemous words actions at their mad meetings, their several kind of musick, dances, and ryotings, and belief and opinions concerning heaven and hell. With their examinations taken before office of Peace, and a Letter or Summons sent to their sisters or fellow creatures in the of the Divel, requiring them to meet Belzebub, Lucifer, Pluto, and twenty more of infernall spirits at the time and place appointed. Also, a true description how they may be own in al companies and the names of the chief Ring-leaders of this new generation that ll all others in wickednesse. Novemb: 19 1650

● **SOURCE 7.21**

From *The Routing of the Ranters*, 1650

… Having given you a general description of them, I shall … come to speak of some of their particular meetings: the first that I have heard of to be frequented by this brutish people was about Shoemakers Alley [in London] … This time of meeting began about four of the clock in the afternoon and was continued by some until nine or ten of the clock the next day; which time was spent in drunkenness, uncleanness, blasphemous words, filthy songs, and mixed dances of men and women stark naked … their ringleader [Abiezer] Coppe … when he perceived that he should be called to answer for the wicked blasphemies he had uttered at sundry times, he took two of his she-disciples and went to the city of Coventry, where it was soon dispersed abroad that he commonly lay in bed with two women at a time: whereof he being soberly admonished by an officer of the army, he replied that it was his liberty and he might use it ...

> 1 Comment on the language and style of Sources 7.14 and 7.15.
>
> 2 Do you think that these sources provide reliable evidence about the Ranters?
>
> 3 What sort of effect were these sources designed to have on their readers? What effect do you think they actually had?

Ranters ideas circulated for several years following the execution of Charles I, but the authorities soon moved against the movement's leaders, who in most cases quickly recanted. The Ranters faded away as quickly as they had emerged.

Section D The Fifth Monarchists

The Fifth Monarchists, or Fifth Monarchy Men, also emerged in the early 1650s. They were dedicated to preparing the way for the Second Coming of Christ, which they, as millenarians (see page 17), believed was likely to occur very soon, probably before the end of the 1650s. Their name derived from one of the dreams of Daniel from the Old Testament, in which Daniel observed four earthly monarchies which were swept away upon the foundation of the fifth monarchy of King Jesus. The Fifth Monarchists believed the fourth monarchy was that of the Pope of Rome. They shared their millenarianism with a large number of their contemporaries from across the political spectrum. The extraordinary events that had occurred since 1642 had led many English men and women to conclude that they were living through the last days of the world. The Fifth Monarchists differed from these others, however, both in their commitment to the use of violence to prepare the way for Christ's return, and in their belief that the Second Coming must be preceded by radical measures to eliminate social inequality.

By the closing months of the Rump in 1653, the Fifth Monarchists had established power bases in parts of Wales, sections of the army and several London parishes. One of Cromwell's generals, Thomas Harrison, had also been converted to Fifth Monarchist ideas, and it was largely through his influence that Cromwell was persuaded to call together the members of Barebone's Parliament in 1653. This assembly contained a small but very powerful group of Fifth Monarchists; it was they who promoted some of the radical measures that alarmed Cromwell and the more conservative elements in the army and, eventually, led to the Parliament's closure in December 1653 (see Chapter 9). The Fifth Monarchists continued to plan for Christ's return and in 1661 they launched an abortive armed uprising in London against Charles II's restored government.

The next two sources are extracts from Fifth Monarchist writings.

● **SOURCE 7.22**

From John Rogers, *Sagrir, or Doomesday Drawing Nigh*, 1653, in which he, as a Fifth Monarchist, gives some advice to the members of Barebone's Parliament

Are you a Parliament man? mind your work then, and the Fifth Monarchy ... Your work is about the laws and tithes ... It is not enough to change some of these laws, and so to reform them (as is intended by most of you), according to the rule of the Fourth Monarchy, which must fall to pieces; O no! that will be to poor purpose and is not your work now, which is to provide for the Fifth [Monarchy] ... by bringing in the laws of God given by Moses for republic laws.

● **Source 7.23**

From William Medley's pamphlet *A Standard Set Up*, 1657. This outlined the Fifth Monarchists' political and social demands.

abrogated: *abolished*

endued: *invested*

legislative: *law-making*

Sanhedrin: *Council and Court of Justice in ancient Jerusalem*

tenure of lands: *tenancies without a formal legal basis*

... That all earthly governments, and worldly administrations may be broken and removed by the first administration of the kingdom of Christ, appointed unto him by the decree of the Father, and is the inheritance of the saints, as joint heirs with him ...

That the supreme absolute LEGISLATIVE power and authority to make laws for the governing of the nations, and the good and well being of mankind, is originally and essentially in the Lord Jesus Christ, by right ... who is the only absolute single person whom the Father hath loved, decreed, sworn to, anointed, and given all power unto in heaven and in earth ...

That a SANHEDRIN, or Supreme Council ... men of choicest light and spirit, ENDUED with judgement, righteousness, wisdom, knowledge, [and] understanding; able men, men of truth and of known integrity, fearing God ... be duly chosen and constituted upon and according to the principles of right and freedom ...

That such a Council, so constituted, shall be the representative for our Lord and King, of the whole body of the saints, whose day this is, and people in the nations ...

That in this blessed interest of our Lord Jesus, men, as they are men, shall be blessed, preserved, and protected in their peaceable enjoyment of their estates, liberties and privileges, under him ...

First as under the law of the commonwealth, they shall be freed from violence and oppression, and all tyrannical and Antichristian yokes upon the outward man: he shall break in pieces the oppressor. And:

That no man be committed or detained in prison without cause be legally expressed and known ...

That there be no impressing, or enforcing of men for soldiers ...

That there be no longer continuance of that wicked and unlawful oppression of excise, neither of customs upon the native inhabitants.

That there be no assessments of taxes levied upon and compelled from the people in times of peace, neither in time of war, but by their common consent and according to our law ...

That all oppressions and grievances in the TENURE OF LANDS ... be ABROGATED and clean removed.

That there be no place found for tithes, being judged as Antichristian, and altogether inconsistent with the gospel spirit ...

---

1   Use Sources 7.22 and 7.23 to summarise the demands of the Fifth Monarchists.

2   How similar are they to the demands of the Levellers, the Diggers and the Ranters?

3   Why did those in authority view the Fifth Monarchists as being particularly dangerous?

Section E **John Milton**

masques: *musical plays*

notary: *solicitor*

John Milton, one of England's most famous poets, was born in 1608 into the family of a London NOTARY. He showed great intellectual ability from an early age and was already, by the 1630s, making a name for himself as a poet and writer of MASQUES. He was also fiercely critical of the religious policies promoted by William Laud, and he welcomed the recall of Parliament in 1640 in the hope that it might move swiftly to bring about far-reaching religious reforms. When the Civil War broke out in 1642, Milton immediately began to produce political works justifying the Parliamentarian cause. He was not, however, a totally uncritical supporter, and when he heard that the Long Parliament MPs were considering bringing in legislation to regulate printing, he responded with the 1644 tract *Areopagitica*.

142

How revolutionary were the ideas of the radical groups in England after the Civil War?

AREOPAGITICA;

A

SPEECH

OF

Mr. JOHN MILTON

For the Liberty of VNLICENC'D
PRINTING,

To the PARLAMENT of ENGLAND.

Τὰλⲇ θεϱὸν δ᾽ ἐκεῖνο, εἴ τις θέλⲇ πόλⲇ
Χϱηϛὸν τι βάλⲇ μ᾽ εἰς μέσον φέϱειν, ἔχων.
Καὶ ταῦθ᾽ ὁ χϱῄζων, λαμπϱὸς ἐϛ᾽, ὁ μὴ θέλων,
Σιγᾷ, τί τύτων ἐϛιν ἰσαίτεϱον πόλⲇ;

Euripid, Hicetid.

This is true Liberty when free born men
Having to advise the public may speak free,
Which he who can, and will, deserv's high praise,
Who neither can nor will, may hold his peace;
What can be juster in a State then this?

Euripid. Hicetid.

LONDON,
Printed in the Yeare, 1644.

… What would ye do then? Should ye suppress all this flowering crop of knowledge and new light sprung up and yet springing daily in this city? Should ye set an OLIGARCHY of twenty ENGROSSERS over it to bring a famine upon our minds again when we shall know nothing but what is measured to us … Believe it, Lords and Commons, they who counsel ye to such a suppressing do as good as bid ye suppress yourselves: and I will soon show how. If it be desired to know, the immediate causes of all this free writing and free speaking, there cannot be

apprehensions: *understandings*

are more capacious: *have more potential*

enfranchised: *given a voice to*

engrossers: *monopolists*

oligarchy: *rule by a small group*

propagated: *nurtured*

valorous: *brave*

wits: *persons of great knowledge*

assigned a truer than your own mild and free and humane government. It is the liberty, Lords and Commons, which your own VALOROUS and happy counsels have purchased us, liberty which is the nurse of all great WITS; this is that which hath rarefied and enlightened our spirits like the influence of heaven, this is that which hath ENFRANCHISED, enlarged and lifted up our APPREHENSIONS degrees above themselves. Ye cannot make us now less capable, less knowing, less eagerly pursuing of the truth, unless ye first make yourselves, that made us so, less the lovers, less the founders of our true liberty. We can grow ignorant again, brutish, formal and slavish as ye found us; but you then must first become that which ye cannot be, oppressive, arbitrary and tyrannous, as they were from whom ye have freed us. That our hearts ARE MORE CAPACIOUS, our thoughts more erected to the search and expectation of greatest and exactest things, is the issue of your own virtue PROPAGATED in us; ye cannot suppress that unless ye reinforce an abrogated and merciless law, that fathers may dispatch at will their own children … Give me the liberty to know, to utter and to argue freely according to conscience, above all liberties …

1   Why does Milton believe freedom of thought and speech are so important?

2   Comment on the style of language and arguments he uses to win the support of the MPs.

Milton also thoroughly approved of the execution of Charles I and the declaration of the republic in 1649. He wrote a number of pamphlets to justify Charles I's execution.

● **SOURCE 7.26**

From another of John Milton's pamphlets, *The Tenure of Kings and Magistrates*, 1649

havoc: *devastate*

magnanimity: *generosity*

pismires: *ants*

potentate: *ruler*

precedent: *an earlier example*

transgressors: *wrongdoers*

… It follows lastly that, since the king or magistrate holds his authority of the people both originally and naturally for their good in the first place and not his own, then may the people as oft as they shall judge it for the best, either choose him or reject him, retain him or depose him though no tyrant, merely by the liberty and right of free born men to be governed as seems to them best … How much more justly then may they fling off tyranny or tyrants, who being once deposed can be no more than private men, as subject to the reach of justice … as any other TRANSGRESSORS …

Though perhaps until now no Protestant state or kingdom can be alleged to have openly put to death their king … it is not, neither ought to be, the glory of a Protestant state never to have put a king to death, it is the glory of a Protestant king never to have deserved death [before]. And if parliament and the military council do what they do without precedent, if it appear their duty, it argues the more wisdom, virtue and MAGNANIMITY that they know themselves able to be a PRECEDENT for others … to dare execute highest justice on them that shall by force of arms endeavour the oppressing and bereaving of religion and their liberty at home, that no unbridled POTENTATE or tyrant but to his sorrow for the future may presume such high and irresponsible licence over mankind to HAVOC and turn upside down whole kingdoms of men, as though they were no more in respect of his perverse will than a nation of PISMIRES.

1   What arguments does Milton use to justify the execution of Charles I?

2   In what ways do they differ from traditional views about the monarchy in the seventeenth century?

Milton was not, however, only a political radical. In 1643 he received much criticism for publicly suggesting that the regulations governing marriage should be relaxed to allow divorce. Milton was very conscious that many other European Protestant states had adopted more liberal divorce laws than England. His principal motivation, however, in opening up this debate was his wish to escape from the unwise marriage he himself had made in the early 1640s to a woman half his age, who he believed lacked the education and intelligence to relate to him.

● **SOURCE 7.27**

From John Milton's pamphlet *The Doctrine and Discipline of Divorce,* 1643

To remove therefore if it is possible this great and sad oppression which through the strictness of a literal interpreting hath invaded and disturbed the dearest and most peaceable estate of household society, to the over burdening, if not the overwhelming of many Christians better worth than to be so deserted of the churches' considerate care, this position shall be laid down, first proving, then answering what may be objected either from scripture or light of reason.

That indisposition, unfitness or contrariety of mind, arising from a cause in nature unchangeable, hindering and ever likely to hinder the main benefits of conjugal society, which are solace and peace, is a greater reason of divorce than natural frigidity, especially if there be no children and that there be mutual consent.

1 In what circumstances did Milton believe that divorce was justified?

2 How might those who did not wish the divorce laws to be liberalised have answered Milton's arguments?

Although Milton was worried by the move away from a republic to the Protectorate in 1653, he continued to support Oliver Cromwell until Cromwell's death in 1658. He acted as a secretary and translator for the Council of State and lost his eyesight as a result of his long hours of study and writing by candlelight. In 1660, as the Restoration approached, he attempted to persuade his countrymen not to recall the Stuarts, and after the return of Charles II he was lucky to avoid imprisonment or more serious punishment. He devoted the last years of his life to the writing of his famous epic poems, *Paradise Lost, Paradise Regained* and *Samson Agonistes*. Besides discussing the timeless question of man's relationship with God, these works also contain Milton's thoughts on the revolutionary events he had lived through, as he tried to understand why God had abandoned the Parliamentary cause and allowed the return of the monarchy.

● **SOURCE 7.28**

Some extracts from *Samson Agonistes*. Here Milton compares both himself and the defeated republican cause to the Old Testament warrior Samson, who was captured by the Philistines.

Milton, nonetheless, manages to end the poem on a note of optimism.

… Promise was that I
Should Israel from Philistian Yoke deliver
Ask for this great deliverer now and find him
Eyeless in Gaza at the mill with slaves
Himself in bonds under Philistian yoke

All is best, though we oft doubt
What the unsearchable dispose
Of highest wisdom brings about
And ever best found in the close
Oft he seems to hide his face
But unexpectedly returns
And to his faithful champion hath in place
Bore witness gloriously

● **Summary Task**

1 Construct a chart like the one below and use it to summarise the main ideas you have discovered about the radical people covered in this chapter.

Group/Individual	MAIN IDEAS				
	Government	**Society**	**Economy**	**Religion**	**Others**
Levellers					
Diggers					
Ranters					
Fifth Monarchists					
John Milton					

2   The ideas of which group or individual would you describe as the most revolutionary and why?

3   Is it possible to talk about a united revolutionary movement in the 1640s and 1650s?

4   On the basis of the sources you have studied in this chapter and your own wider research, why were such ideas able to emerge in England during this time?

5   Why did these groups achieve so little success?

6   You will be studying the Quakers, another important radical group, in Chapter 10 (Nayler's case, pages 182–3) and in Chapter 12 (pages 208–13). You should then add the Quakers to your chart.

(Remember that you will have to read widely and bring in evidence from other sources in order to provide a full answer, especially to questions 4 and 5.)

7   Divide the class into five groups. Each group should assume the role of one of the radical groups or of John Milton and produce a speech, written commentary or video presentation on Britain today containing their answers to the following questions:

*   What aspects of life today would they approve of?
*   What aspects of life would they disapprove of?
*   What changes would need to be made in British society for it to conform to their ideas?

● Further reading

One of the most interesting and accessible surveys of radical ideas is Christopher Hill, *The World Turned Upside Down* (Penguin, 1972), though as with all of Hill's work this study is written from a distinct left-wing perspective. More recent and rather more balanced introductions are given in F. D. Dow, *Radicalism in the English Revolution* (Blackwell, 1986), and Barry Reay and J. F. McGregor (eds.), *Radical Religion in the English Revolution* (OUP, 1984). For the Levellers, the best recent general study is G. E. Aylmer, *The Levellers in the English Revolution* (Thames and Hudson, 1975) and for a good introduction to Winstanley and the Diggers see Christopher Hill (ed.), *The Law of Freedom and Other Writings* (Penguin, 1973). The best study of the Fifth Monarchists is Bernard Capp, *The Fifth Monarchy Men* (Faber, 1972). The Ranters have been the subject of much historical controversy over the last few years. The traditional view of them as expressed in *The World Turned Upside Down* and A. L. Morton's *The World of the Ranters* (Lawrence and Wishart, 1970) was seriously challenged in 1986 by J. C. Davis, who argued in *Fear, Myth and History: The Ranters and the historians* (CUP, 1986) that the group had not really existed. He suggests they were an invention both of conservative contemporaries who wished to create a 'moral panic', and of a number of modern left-wing historians, such as Hill, whose own fascination with their ideas led them to exaggerate their importance greatly. For Milton's political significance, from the same left-wing perspective, see Christopher Hill, *Milton and the English Revolution* (Faber, 1979). For an accessible collection of Milton's political writings, see Douglas Bush (ed.), *The Portable Milton* (Penguin, 1976).

chapter 8

The Rump, 1649–53: revolutionaries who became corrupt?

1648
December 6–7:   Pride's Purge leaves only 154 MPs, the Rump, in Parliament.

1649
January 1:   The ordinance to create a High Court of Justice to try Charles I is passed by the Rump, but is rejected by the Lords.

January 4:   The Rump votes that it has the sole legislative authority.

January 6:   The ordinance which establishes the High Court of Justice to try Charles I is passed by the Rump.

January 20–7:   The trial of Charles I is held.

January 30:   Charles I is executed.

February 1:   100 MPs who had not voted in favour of continuing negotiations with Charles I on 5 December 1648 are readmitted into Parliament.

February 13:   A Council of State of 41 members, to be re-elected annually, is appointed by the Rump to perform executive government functions.

March 17:   The Act abolishing the monarchy is passed.

March 19:   The Act abolishing the House of Lords is passed.

March 28:   The Leveller leaders are arrested.

April 1:   The Rump begins the sale of Crown lands. The Rump issues debentures (rights to land) to soldiers as back-pay.

May 9:   The Act declaring England to be a Commonwealth is passed.

May 14–15:   The Leveller-led mutinies in the army are crushed at Burford; the Leveller movement ends.

August 15:   Cromwell arrives in Ireland with 30,000 men.

September: The Irish garrison is massacred at Drogheda. The Act relieving poor prisoners imprisoned for debt is passed.

September 20:   The Act imposing censorship on printed material is passed.

October: The Irish garrison at Wexford is massacred.

1650
January 2:   The Rump orders all adult males to take the Engagement – an oath of obedience to the Commonwealth.

April: The Act against non-observance of the Sabbath is passed.

May 10:   The Adultery Act is passed, imposing the death penalty for adultery.

May 26:   Cromwell returns from Ireland, leaving Ireton to complete the conquest.

June 6:   A government newspaper, the *Mercurius Politicus,* is launched.

June 26:   Cromwell is appointed commander of the New Model Army after Fairfax's resignation.

August: Cromwell invades Scotland.

August 9:   The Blasphemy Act is passed to restrain the extreme Puritan sects.

September 3:   The Scots are defeated at the Battle of Dunbar by Cromwell.

September 27:   The Act repealing the Elizabethan laws that enforced compulsory attendance at a parish church is passed.

October: The Rump discusses 'recruiter' elections (to fill vacant seats).

December: The Act declaring that all legal proceedings should be held in English is passed.

1651
April: The Act for the Propagation of the Gospel in Northern England and Wales is passed.

July 16:   The Act permitting sale of Royalist lands is passed.

August 1:	Charles II invades England at the head of a Scottish army.
September 3:	Cromwell defeats Charles II's army at the Battle of Worcester; Cromwell returns to London soon afterwards.
September 25:	A Committee is appointed to make recommendations for new elections.
October 9:	Navigation Acts are passed (stating that all imported goods must be carried in English ships or in ships from the goods' country of origin).
November 18:	The Rump declares that it will dissolve no later than 3 November 1654.
December:	The Hale Commission is appointed to propose legal reforms.

1652

April:	The Rump declares that tithes should continue.
May:	The Anglo-Dutch War breaks out.
August 13:	The Council of Officers petitions the Rump to arrange elections for a new Parliament.
August 17:	The Rump reappoints the committee to make recommendations for elections.
November 18:	The Act confiscating estates of over 600 Royalists is passed.
December:	The Hale Commission's recommendations are rejected.

1653

February 23:	The Rump begins debating a Bill for new elections.
April 1:	The Act for the Propagation of the Gospel is not renewed.
April 19:	A meeting takes place between Cromwell, army officers and 20 MPs to discuss a new government.
April 20:	The Rump is dissolved by Oliver Cromwell.

Introduction

On 5 December 1648, Parliament agreed to continue negotiations with Charles I by 129 votes to 83. The next morning, MPs found the entrance to the House of Commons blocked by Colonel Pride and a regiment of soldiers. 'Pride's Purge', as this event became known, forcibly prevented about 100 MPs from entering the Commons and another 260 withdrew voluntarily. The small, unrepresentative minority that remained, about one third of the MPs, were branded by their opponents with the unflattering name of the 'Rump'. Three weeks later the Rump MPs voted to give themselves supreme legislative powers and subsequently passed measures that put Charles I on trial, abolished the monarchy and House of Lords, declared the country to be a Commonwealth and established religious toleration. The Rump and the Council of State it set up were to rule England for the next three-and-a-half years.

The army, the Levellers, the Puritan sects and other radical groups had high expectations of the Rump in 1649. They hoped that the execution of the King would be followed by sweeping political and legal reforms, the abolition of tithes and an extensive programme of godly reform which would pave the way for the thousand-year rule of 'King Jesus' and the Saints on earth. Such hopes were to be bitterly disappointed. After the Rump's initial surge of revolutionary activity in early 1649, the Levellers were quickly crushed and during the next three years the new regime showed little interest in radical reform. The Rump's legal reforms looked half-hearted and its religious measures seemed to be more concerned with restricting religious toleration than promoting the cause of godly reform. The Rump MPs' failure to extend the franchise or hold new elections gained them the reputation of being interested only in keeping themselves in power.

Finally, in April 1653, after a period of increasing tension between the Rump MPs and the army, Oliver Cromwell entered the House accompanied by guards and dismissed the members. The closure of the Rump by direct military action was undoubtedly an illegal act; the terms of the Act of 10 May 1641 had stated that the Long Parliament, of which the Rump was a remnant, could not be dissolved except by its own consent. There were few protests, however, about the Rump's dissolution. Cromwell's subsequent remark that it was followed by 'not so much as the barking of a dog' is usually regarded as evidence of the apathy with which the closure of the Rump was viewed and, therefore, of its unpopularity and ineffectiveness as a regime.

The purpose of this chapter is to introduce you to the continuing historical debate about the Rump and help you to reach a valid assessment of the regime. It consists of a selection of contemporary sources and extracts from historians' accounts, arranged into four sections:

- Section A Studying the Rump's words and actions
- Section B Analysing motives and intentions
- Section C Studying attitudes and influences
- Section D Studying events: a case study of the dissolution of the Rump.

These sections will present you with different views to evaluate. If you are following an A Level course which requires you to study this topic in greater depth, you should supplement these sources with your own wider research.

Section A Studying the Rump's words and actions

In this section we will try to reach some preliminary conclusions about the Rump by studying what it *did* between 1649 and 1653 – and the kind of language it used in some of its main Acts. Study the table of events at the beginning of the chapter and the sources below.

● **SOURCE 8.1**

From the Act abolishing the monarchy, 17 March 1649

Where it is and hath been found by experience, that the office of a King in this nation … is unnecessary, burdensome and dangerous to the Liberty, safety and public interest of the people; be it therefore enacted and ordained by this present Parliament … that the office of a King in this nation shall not henceforth reside in or be exercised by any one single person.

● **SOURCE 8.2**

Extract from the Act abolishing the House of Lords, 19 March 1649

From henceforth the House of Lords in Parliament shall be and is thereby wholly abolished and taken away … Nevertheless it is hereby declared, that neither such Lords as have demeaned themselves with honour, courage and fidelity to the Commonwealth … shall be excluded from the public counsels of the nation, but shall be admitted thereunto, and have their free vote in Parliament, if they shall be thereunto elected.

● **SOURCE 8.3**

The Act declaring England to be a Commonwealth, 19 May 1649

Be it declared and enacted by this present Parliament … that the people, of England … are and shall be … a Commonwealth and Free State, and [be] governed … by the representatives of the people in Parliament and by such as they shall appoint … without any King or House of Lords.

● **SOURCE 8.4**

The Great Seal of England, 1651

1 Study the table of events on pages 146–7.

   a) Make a list of the Rump's actions which you consider to be revolutionary.
   b) Make another list of the Rump's actions which you think are conservative.
   c) Do your lists appear to support the view that the Rump was a revolutionary regime at first but became increasingly conservative as time passed?
   d) Most recent historians think that 1651 was a dividing line in the history of the Rump. Does your study of the table of events support this conclusion?
   e) The table of events is a record of the Rump's *actions*. Is this sufficient evidence for you to make a full evaluation of the Rump's government of England from 1649 to 1653?

2 Study Sources 8.1–8.4.

   a) What difference can you detect between the language used to abolish the monarchy in Source 8.1 and the language used about the House of Lords in Source 8.2? What significance, if any, do you place upon this difference?
   b) Why, in Source 8.3, do you think that the Rump did not use the term 'republic'?
   c) Does the language used in these sources support the view that the Rump MPs were revolutionaries?

Section B Analysing motives and intentions

A study of a regime's words and actions, however thorough, cannot produce a complete assessment of it. Historians also need to analyse the motives and intentions which led it to act in the way that it did. In this section we will examine some contemporary assessments of the motives and intentions of the Rump MPs.

● **SOURCE 8.5**

The view of Clement Walker. Walker was a member of the Long Parliament but was purged and briefly imprisoned in 1648.

This fag end, this veritable Rump of a Parliament with corrupt maggots in it … It were endless to name the father and the son, brother and brother that fills this house; they come in couples more than unclean beasts to the Ark.

● **SOURCE 8.6**

An opinion expressed by Oliver Cromwell in 1652, taken from the memoirs of Bulstrode Whitelocke, a Rump MP, who is referring to a private conversation he had with Oliver Cromwell in November 1652.

Really their pride, and ambition, and self-seeking, ingrossing all places of honour and profit to themselves and their friends, and their daily breaking forth into new and violent … factions, their delay of business and designs to perpetuate themselves and to continue the power in their own hands … and the scandalous lives of some of the chief of them … do give too much ground for people to open their mouths against them … So that unless there be some authority and power so full and so high as to restrain and keep things in better order … it will be impossible to prevent our ruin.

● **SOURCE 8.7**

An account of Oliver Cromwell's speech to the Rump when he dissolved it on 20 April 1653, from the memoirs of Edmund Ludlow. Ludlow was a Rump MP and a member of the Council of State and was on service with the army in Ireland in 1651–5.

Cromwell loaded the Parliament with the vilest reproaches, charging them not to have a heart to do anything for the public good, to have espoused the corrupt interest of the Presbytery and the lawyers, who were the supporters of tyranny and oppression, accusing them of an intention to perpetuate themselves in power … and thereupon told them that the Lord had done with them, and had chosen other instruments for the carrying on his work that were more worthy.

1 What, according to these sources, were the main motives and intentions of the Rump MPs?

2 How satisfactory do you find each of these sources to be as evidence of the Rump's motives and intentions?

3 To what extent can these accusations be supported by the evidence you studied in Section A?

4 What conclusions about the Rump, if any, can you make on the basis of these sources?

Section C Studying attitudes and influences

In Section B you studied three contemporary assessments of the Rump, but you should have noticed that they all came from opponents of the regime. Clement Walker and Oliver Cromwell both had their own reasons for presenting hostile accounts of the Rump. Traditionally, however, most historians have tended to reach similar conclusions about the Rump. The following extract is typical of the poor reputation the Rump has had amongst many historians.

● **SOURCE 8.8**

From George Yule, *The Independents in the English Civil War* (1958)

oligarchy: *government by a small, unelected group*

The Rump was an OLIGARCHY with no positive policy except that of self-interest.

In order to understand the actions of groups and individuals more fully than is possible merely from their actions and the hostile comments of contemporaries, historians also need to examine the factors which worked upon them: the long-term influences which shaped their attitudes and the shorter-term influences which created the conditions in which their actions were taken. In this section we will examine the work of two recent historians which, by placing the actions and motives of the Rump MPs in a wider context, has served to challenge traditional views of the Rump.

● **SOURCE 8.9**

David Underdown's analysis of the Rump MPs in *Pride's Purge: Politics During the Puritan Revolution* (1971). David Underdown carried out detailed research into the backgrounds and voting behaviour of all the members of the Long Parliament at the beginning of 1648, including the MPs who were removed by Pride's Purge and the MPs who continued to sit in the Rump.

fait accompli: *something that has already happened*

Inns of Court: *training colleges for lawyers in London*

recruiter: *someone elected to Parliament after the Civil War to take the place of a Royalist MP*

secluded: *expelled*

The 471 MPs (excluding vacancies, absentees etc.) can be divided into five groups: the active revolutionaries who openly committed themselves to the revolution while it was in progress during December and January [1649]; the conformists who avoided formal commitment at that time, but accepted the FAIT ACCOMPLI in February, when they could no longer be incriminated in the execution of the King; the abstainers, who were not actually secluded, but showed their opposition by staying away from Parliament at least until the spring of 1649; the victims of the Purge who were secluded; and the hard core of the Army's enemies, who suffered imprisonment as well as seclusion …

We have then 471 MPs divided into the following categories:

Revolutionaries	71	15%
Conformists	83	18%
Abstainers	86	18%
SECLUDED	186	40%
Imprisoned	45	9%

The typical Revolutionary was a married man in his mid-forties. He had probably inherited an estate, but was quite possibly a younger son. He had gone to one of the INNS OF COURT … and was less likely to have attended university. He may possibly have come from the North of England. He had no previous parliamentary experience, entered the Long Parliament in a by-election after August 1645, and attached himself to the radical wing of the Independents. In religion he probably, but not necessarily, turned to Independency. Of country gentry status, he came from rather an insecure family, and was probably not a rich man, having a pre-war income of less than £500 a year; if richer, he may have been in serious debt.

The typical Secluded was a married man in his mid-forties, and had probably inherited an estate, although he might possibly be the heir to one with a father still living. He had gone to Oxford or an Inn of Court … He came either from the south-east or the south-west. Another RECRUITER without previous experience in parliament, he may have been under suspicion of having flirted with the Royalists, and if he adopted a political stance in the Long Parliament it was as a Presbyterian. His religious views were outwardly Presbyterian, though secretly he may have preferred moderate episcopacy. Of greater gentry status, stable family, and a large income (over £1,000 a year) … he was in fact a very solid and representative country gentleman.

● SOURCE 8.10

Barry Coward's reasons for the Rump's conservatism from *The Stuart Age, England 1603–1714* (2nd ed., 1994)

Before the autumn of 1651 the Rump had sound reasons to explain its failure to act quickly and effectively to remedy the grievances of the soldiers and saints. The new regime was launched during what was arguably the worst economic crisis of the seventeenth century. Nor was the security situation conducive to a period of social experimentation. The most immediate danger came from Ireland which had been in revolt since 1641 ... Not only was this a serious military threat to the new regime; it also added to the Rump's already large financial problems. Despite an assessment of £90,000 per month from March 1649, the Rump was never free of crushing financial demands.

Hardly had the Irish expedition been organised and financed than the infant English republic was faced with another major crisis in Scotland. [The author then describes Cromwell's invasion of Scotland in 1650 and Charles II's invasion of England which ended in defeat at the Battle of Worcester in September 1651.] Before Worcester the Rump was faced by the prospect of invasion and with almost universal international hostility provoked by the execution of Charles I. The pursuit of international respectability and adequate defence were consequently given a higher priority than the creation of a UTOPIA. But it is fairly certain that this alone does not adequately explain the Rump's reactionary record. By 1650 the immediate economic crisis was over, and after Worcester there was no longer the excuse of imminent royalist or foreign invasion. Recent studies of the Rump have emphasised the unrevolutionary nature of its members ... there were few MPs in the Rump ... who held revolutionary opinions.

The antipathy between the Rump and the army was possibly the major factor in the Commonwealth's dismal failure to produce far-reaching reform. As a result, religious Independents, as well as Presbyterians, opposed any extension of toleration. Similarly, not only lawyers resisted changes in the law. So too did many Rumpers ... for whom moderate legal reform came to be associated with army rule and extremism. The Rump was not a revolutionary regime ... The Rump was a victim of the republican dilemma; it was too conservative for the army and the sects, but not conservative enough to heal the breach which Pride's Purge and the King's execution had opened up.

Utopia: *a perfect society*

1   To which of Underdown's five categories (Source 8.9) did the MPs of the Rump belong?

2   According to Underdown's findings, were there any significant differences between the 'Revolutionary' and 'Secluded' MPs?

3   Do Underdown's findings support the view that the Rump MPs were revolutionaries in 1648–9?

4   What reasons does Coward (Source 8.10) give to explain the Rump's failure to carry out radical reforms? In what ways does his account differ from the explanations you read in Section B?

5   What does Coward consider to be the main cause of the Rump's conservatism?

6   In what ways does Coward make use of Underdown's findings (Source 8.9)?

7   To what extent has your study of Sources 8.9 and 8.10 led you to revise your conclusions about the Rump?

Section D   Studying events: a study of the dissolution of the Rump, April 1653

It should go without saying that any historical assessment should be based upon a detailed study of what happened. The nature of historical evidence, however, often means that our knowledge of events is not clear cut. The immediate circumstances which led to the dissolution of the Rump on 20 April 1653 are a case in point. The precise contents of the Bill for new elections which the Rump MPs were preparing to pass, which clearly so outraged Cromwell, are not known because the Bill has not survived. As the extracts below illustrate, this has led to sharply divergent explanations of the Rump's closure. Source 8.11 is a traditional explanation; Source 8.12, when it was first published in 1974, was a surprising new interpretation. Which one you think is the most convincing explanation will carry enormous implications for your overall assessment of the regime.

● **SOURCE 8.11**

Roger Lockyer's traditional explanation of the Rump's dissolution from *Tudor and Stuart Britain* (1985)

Now that peace had been restored to England [1651] Cromwell assumed that the members of the Rump would vote for the dissolution of Parliament, and make way for a new and more representative body to decide on a settlement of Church and state. But the Rumpers saw no reason to abdicate their authority. New elections might open the way to a Royalist revival … Cromwell's anger was directed at what seemed to him to be efficiency without realism, government without morality. He could not believe that a great war had been fought and an ancient monarchy overthrown simply to give power to a handful of men who had come to stand for nothing but themselves. When, in April 1653, he heard that the Rump was planning to increase its numbers through by-elections instead of risking a general appeal to public opinion, he strode off to the House, calling on his guards to follow him. Once inside he listened to the debate for a while, his anger mounting until he could sit no longer … Cromwell called his troops into the house and told them to clear it.

● **SOURCE 8.12**

Blair Worden's analysis of the dissolution of the Rump, from *The Rump Parliament, 1648–53* (1974)

… the bill provided for completely fresh elections; and it follows from this that the generally accepted view of the Rump as a regime selfishly determined to perpetuate its power must be abandoned. The conflict of 20 April 1653 was not between a Parliament determined to perpetuate its power and an army resolved to hold elections, but between a Parliament which had resolved to hold elections and an army determined to prevent it from doing so. At some point before the dissolution … the roles of Parliament and the army were reversed.

The Rump had never regarded itself as anything other than an interim government, and it had always acted on the assumption that it would eventually make way for a newly elected Parliament. Before Worcester this attitude had the support of the army officers. After Worcester, the attitude was hardened by the army's hostility to the Rump. In January 1653 it at last became clear that the Rump would be obliged to dissolve before the army were disbanded. Faced with this realisation the House … [took] the decision to proceed with a new representative. That they were prepared to do so is a reminder of their continuing lack of commitment to the form of government which had emerged after the execution of the King. There is no doubt that the bill would have led to the election of men who had not sat since December 1648 and men of similar views. What the Rump was planning on 20 April was not the perpetuation of its authority; it was revenge for Pride's Purge.

1 How do these accounts differ over the contents of the Bill which the Rump was discussing in April 1653?

2 What different implications do these two explanations of the Bill's contents have for:

   a) your understanding of the Rump
   b) your understanding of Cromwell?

3 In the light of the evidence you have studied in this chapter, which explanation do you find the more convincing and why?

● **Summary Task**

On the basis of the sources you have studied in this chapter and, if appropriate, your wider research, which of these interpretations do you think offers the most convincing historical assessment of the Rump?

Interpretation A
The Rump was a revolutionary regime at first but then became a corrupt, self-interested oligarchy. The Rump MPs carried out revolutionary acts in 1649 in order to seize power but then became increasingly conservative in order to retain it.

Interpretation B
The Rump MPs were conservative from the start. They were only reluctant revolutionaries in 1649 and, thereafter, their true conservative instincts increasingly came to the fore.

● **Further reading**

Useful, concise and accessible chapters on the Rump are contained in Michael Lynch, *The Interregnum, 1649–1660* (Hodder and Stoughton, 1994), Toby Barnard, *The English Republic, 1649–1660* (Longman, 1982) and A. Woolrych, *England without a King* (Methuen, 1983). The most thorough recent study of the Rump is still Blair Worden, *The Rump Parliament, 1648–1653* (CUP, 1974). For Underdown's analysis of the Rump MPs see his *Pride's Purge: Politics in the English Revolution* (Clarendon Press, 1971) from which Cambridge University Press have produced a computer database called 'Pride's Purge'. A useful collection of documents is contained in Chapter 5 of *Politics, Religion and Society in Revolutionary England, 1640–1660* by Howard Tomlinson and David Gregg (Macmillan, 1989).

chapter

9

Were the members of Barebone's Parliament 'a pack of weak, senseless fellows'?

1653

April 20:	Cromwell forcibly dissolves the Rump Parliament.
July 4:	Barebone's Parliament meets for the first time; the opening speech is made by Cromwell.
December 12:	Barebone's Parliament dissolves itself and hands back power to Cromwell.
December 13:	John Lambert presents the Instrument of Government to Cromwell.
December 16:	The Protectorate is proclaimed.

Introduction

With the closure of the Rump of the Long Parliament in April 1653, the English State lost the last remnant of the traditional constitution. All the long-established institutions of government – King, Lords and Commons – had been destroyed by the New Model Army, which now controlled the country purely through force of arms. The pressing concern for Cromwell and his colleagues was to find a new civilian constitution for the country which would be acceptable to the army. During the early summer they decided to entrust this task to a select group of individuals whom they knew to be strongly committed to their cause. About 140 men were invited by Cromwell and the Council of State to sit in a new constitutional assembly which met for the first time in early July. This body has been known by various names; while the most accurate of these titles is 'the Nominated Assembly', it was known at the time both as 'the Little Parliament' and as 'Barebone's Parliament', after one of its members, a London merchant, Praise-God Barebone.

Barebone's Parliament met for six months in the second half of 1653. It approached the work of reform with great commitment and enthusiasm and, encouraged by a small group of Fifth Monarchists amongst its members, it soon displayed a clear radical stance. Among the proposals it discussed were the relief of those in debt and poor prisoners, sweeping legal reform, the abolition of tithes and the reduction of taxes. It also displayed its anticlericalism by abolishing church weddings and reconstituting marriage as a purely secular undertaking, a measure which is discussed more fully in Chapter 11, pages 194–5. These activities angered its moderate members and more importantly soon alienated it from Cromwell and the more socially conservative army leaders. They came to see its reform initiatives as the beginning of a general attack on property rights. In mid-December the more moderate members were persuaded by one of the army commanders, John Lambert, to hand back power to Cromwell. Several days later Lambert presented Cromwell with the Instrument of Government which set up the Protectorate and installed Cromwell as Lord Protector.

● SOURCE 9.1

An engraving of Barebone's
Parliament, from a leaflet published
in August 1653

● SOURCE 9.1

An engraving of Barebone's
Parliament, from a leaflet published
in August 1653

The nature and composition of Barebone's Parliament

The members of Barebone's Parliament were widely viewed by their opponents as a group of religious fanatics who were markedly inferior to those who usually sat in Parliaments, in terms of both their social background and their ability and experience. Source 9.2 below provides some examples of this dismissive comment.

● SOURCE 9.2

In the weeks that preceded the meeting of Barebone's Parliament, a Royalist informant in England made the following comments about the members of this assembly in the reports he sent to Edward Hyde, who was with the exiled King's court in Paris.

anabaptistical: *believing in adult baptism*
attorneys: *lawyers*
mechanics: *artisans*
pettifogger: *inferior and often corrupt lawyer*
stocking-mongers: *sellers of socks or stockings*

13th May: I have seen a private list of them and find that many of them are no better than ATTORNEYS, tanners, wheelwrights, and the meanest sort of MECHANICS.

3rd June: the generality of them are the most unknown in the commonwealth, PETTIFOGGERS, inn-keepers, mill-wrights, STOCKING-MONGERS and such a rabble as never had hopes to be of a Grand Jury.

17th June: The new parliament consists chiefly of the most obscure persons in the nation, generally ANABAPTISTICAL and men of blood. Cromwell was moved to nominate his son, Henry, for one, but refused, saying that he had not yet given the world sufficient testimony of his close walking with the Lord.

● **SOURCE 9.3**

The comments of the Venetian ambassador in London, who sent these two reports to his masters in Italy

covertly: *secretly*

ignoramuses: *ignorant people*

29th June 1653: The vast personal energies of Cromwell and the council ... are daily active over the new form of government. He has already nominated 120 persons who with five each for Scotland and Ireland will constitute the body of the new representative. In his choice of members few persons of quality are included and those are his warm adherents ... The rest are all low people who invariably agree to his orders.

25th December 1653: I have to announce the dissolution of the second parliament on Monday last. The majority of this body consisted of Anabaptists, of whom there are a great many in London ... From the very first and always with the support of Harrison, the major-general of the cavalry, they did their utmost, though COVERTLY, to benefit their own party by discrediting all others and especially the presbyterians. To this end they launched a number of acts betraying their real object. After disgusting the people in general and General Cromwell in particular, the parliament, consisting mostly of IGNORAMUSES in governance, was bent on abolishing what from their antiquity give lustre to England, viz. the universities and colleges of Oxford and Cambridge, where every sort of knowledge and literature may be said to be cultivated with success. It had also determined to abolish tithes and to dispense with public preachers in order to render their own sect more powerful.

---

1 What criticisms are made in these extracts of:
   a) the members of Barebone's Parliament;
   b) their actions?

2 From where do you think these writers get their information?

3 Do you think that one of these accounts is likely to be more reliable than the other?

4 For what reasons do you think these writers were so hostile to Barebone's Parliament?

The verdicts of two contemporary historians, James Heath and Edward Hyde, Earl of Clarendon, were equally condemning.

● **SOURCE 9.4**

In *Flagellum*, his damning biography of Cromwell published just after the Restoration, Heath wrote these comments on the members of Barebone's Parliament.

convention: *meeting*

partisans: *strong supporters*

This Council of State did next give birth to that monster of the Little Parliament which, like an abortive cub, was cast by Cromwell and fondly and vainly licked by Harrison, both who had most different ends on this CONVENTION, in the one a temporal, in the other a spiritual pride and covetousness (though not altogether purified from the deceits of the world) worked in this mysterious knack of a new and unheard of legislative authority, who, by name of men of integrity and fidelity to the cause of God were by bare summons from Oliver called to the settlement of the state, that was to be stirrups or foot-steps to the throne whereon Cromwell should tread, they being abject and mean people ... of the most destructive principles to all community and society, either as men or Christians ... They were persons for the most part of such mean ... extractions that, so far they were from being taken notice of by their shires, each of whom but two or three represented, that they were scarce known in the very towns where they were born or afterwards inhabited, till the excise, the committees for sequestration and the war in their respective counties made them infamously known. The rest were of his PARTISANS in the parliament and the High Court of Justice.

● **SOURCE 9.5**

From Edward Hyde, Earl of Clarendon, *History of the Rebellion*, written in the 1660s

He [Cromwell] resolved therefore to choose them [the Barebone's members] himself, that he might with the more justice unmake them when he should think fit; and with the advice of his council of state, he made choice of a number of men, consisting of above one hundred and forty persons, who should meet as a parliament to settle the government of the nation. It can hardly be believed that so wild a notion should fall into any man's imagination, that such a people should be fit to contribute towards any settlement, or that from their actions any thing could result that might advance his particular design. Yet, upon the view and consideration of the persons made choice of, many did conclude, 'that he had made his own scheme entirely to himself; and though he communicated it with no man, concluded it the most natural way to ripen and produce the effects it did afterwards, to the end he proposed to himself'.

There were amongst them some few of the quality and degree of gentlemen, and who had estates ... But much the major part of them consisted of inferior persons, of no quality or name, ARTIFICERS of the meanest trades, known only by their gifts in praying and preaching; which are now practised by all degrees of men, but scholars, throughout the kingdom. In which number, that there may be a better judgement made of the rest, it will not be amiss to name one, from whom the parliament itself was afterwards DENOMINATED, who was Praise-God (that was his Christian name) Barebone, a leather-seller in Fleet-street, from whom (he being an eminent speaker in it) it was afterwards called Praise-God Barebone's Parliament. In a word, they were a pack of weak, senseless fellows, fit only to bring the name and reputation of parliaments lower than it was yet.

artificers: *craftsmen*

denominated: *named*

---

1 How does Heath suggest that Cromwell and Harrison were not in full agreement about the purpose of Barebone's Parliament?

2 On what basis do Heath and Clarendon dismiss the members of Barebone's Parliament as being incapable of governing?

3 What motive do Heath and Clarendon suggest Cromwell may have had in calling the sort of men he did to sit in Barebone's Parliament?

4 In what ways could each of these accounts have been influenced by hindsight?

Few at the time came to the defence of Barebone's Parliament, but one who did go into print only a few days after the end of the assembly in an attempt to vindicate its proceedings was one of the actual members, Samuel Highland, a lay preacher from Southwark.

● **SOURCE 9.6**

From Samuel Highland, *An Exact Relation of the Proceedings and Transactions of the Late Parliament,* 1653

Canaan: *the Holy Land*

hearsay: *rumour, gossip*

ministry: *clergy*

passes for current: *is widely believed*

per ann.: *per year*

Had not great blasphemy, reproach and scorn been offered everywhere unto the holy name of God, his truth, his ways, his servants, by evil men to the great grief of many fearing God, the following relation and discourse had never seen the light; the particular persons loaded with great reproach and scandal could in regard of themselves have been contented to have borne all patiently with silence and left the clearing of their innocency to the most righteous God. It is no new thing in the world for good men to be reproached for well doing and to have no other reward for endeavouring to do their country service and labouring to take off their heavy oppressions and grievances than to be counted evil doers. What is generally reported is as easily believed and taken for truth, though it be never so false, great lightness and vanity attending persons as is too evident. That one part of the House would have destroyed all the MINISTRY, the good as well as the bad PASSES FOR CURRENT, when as they were only against that old, corrupt, unequal, burdensome, and debate-making way of their maintenance by tithes. In which way besides other things many a good soul hath only £20 or £30 per ann. to keep him and his alive, and others of less desert have £300 or £400 PER ANN. or more, they thinking some more equal and less burdensome way might be found out and provided … Reader, if thou thinkest that thou art come into CANAAN, the land of rest, and that there is attainable unto the full end aimed at and intended by Almighty God in answer to all those mighty works and wonders (near unto miracles) that he hath wrought in these lands, if thou thinkest there is already the harvest of all that treasure spent and blood spilt in the late wars, then rejoice and be glad; but if thou judgeth God intended greater and more high things than yet thou hath seen in the way of removing wickedness and oppression and the advance of justice and righteousness, then believe and wait and pray, so adviseth he that is a well wisher to the interests of the Lord Christ, the welfare of the saints and the prosperity of the commonwealth of England … is it not much when as godly sober men in discharge of their duty and trust for the glory of God and the good of their country should leave their habitations, relations and enjoyments, spend their time and means to serve their country and be so rewarded with scandal and false reports and to have judgement of high condemnation passed on them upon HEARSAY, without the least show of proof …

---

1 In what ways does Highland disagree with Heath and Clarendon?

2 How does Highland defend his colleagues in the assembly against the sort of attacks outlined in Sources 9.2–9.5?

3 How would you try to decide which of these differing assessments of Barebone's Parliament is the more accurate?

The best way that historians can decide which of these contrasting assessments of the members of Barebone's Parliament is the more accurate is by carrying out detailed research into the backgrounds and attitudes of each member of the assembly. Some years ago this work was carried out by the historian Austin Woolrych. He presented his findings in a long appendix at the end of his book, *Commonwealth and Protectorate*, published in 1982. A simplified version of it appears below.

● **SOURCE 9.7**

Key to the abbreviations
O = Oxford University
C = Cambridge University
G = GRAY'S INN
MT = MIDDLE TEMPLE
L = LINCOLN'S INN
IT = INNER TEMPLE
GG = greater gentry and aristocracy
CG = county gentry
LG = lesser gentry
M = merchant
P = professional
Rad = radical
Mod = moderate
5M = Fifth Monarchist
Sh = Member of the Short Parliament
JP = Justice of the Peace

Gray's Inn, Middle Temple, Lincoln's Inn and Inner Temple: colleges in London which provided training for lawyers

Name	Age in 1653	Education	Social status	Religion	Parliamentary experience	JP before 1653?
J. Anlaby	c. 40	G	LG	Rad	47–53/59	yes
T. Baker	47		LG	Rad 5M?		yes
G. Baldwin			LG	Mod		yes
P. Barebone	57?		M	Rad		no
H. Barrington		C	M	Rad		yes
H. Barton			M	Mod		no
N. Barton			LG	Mod	54	yes
J. Bawden			M	Rad		yes
G. Bellot	29	O	LG	Rad?		yes
G. Bennett			M	Mod	54/56/59	yes
R. Bennett	43	O, MT	LG	Rad	51–3/54/59	yes
J. Bingham	43	O, MT	CG	Mod	45–53/54/56/59	yes
H. Birkenhead	53	O	LG	Rad?		yes
R. Blake	54	O	P	Mod	40(Sh)/45–53/54/56	no
T. Blount	48	O, G	LG	Rad		yes
W. Botterell			M	Rad		no
B. Bowtell			LG	Mod?		yes
F. Brewster	53	C	LG	Mod		yes
J. Brewster	49		LG	Mod		no
A. Brodie	36		CG	Mod		no
T. Brooke	40		CG	Mod	54	yes
A. Broughton	50	IT	P	Rad	59	no
J. Browne	45?		LG	Rad 5M		no
W. Brownlow	57	O, IT	GG	Mod		yes
W. Burton			M	Mod?		no
J. Caley			M	Rad 5M		yes
J. Carew	31	O, IT	GG	Rad 5M	47–53	yes
R. Castle	49	C	CG	Mod	54/56	yes
E. Cater	c. 39	C, IT	CG	Rad?		yes
J. Chetwood	54	O, IT	LG	Rad		yes
J. Clarke		G?	M	Mod	54/56/59	no
J. Clarke	43	C?	LG	Mod	54/56/59	yes
E. Cludd			LG	Mod	56	yes
R. Coates			P	Rad		yes
A. Cooper	32	O, L	GG	Mod	54, 56, 59, 60	yes
H. Courtney	51?		LG	Rad 5M		yes
J. Crofts			LG	Rad	56	no
H. Cromwell	25		LG	Mod		no
W. Cullen			M	Mod	54	no
R. Cunliffe	49		LG	Mod		no
R. Cust	31	C, IT	CG	Rad?	79/80/81	yes
H. Danvers	c. 31	O	LG	Rad 5M		yes
H. Dawson			M	Mod		yes
T. Dickenson			M	Mod	54/56/59	yes
W. Draper	43	O	LG	Rad?		yes
R. Duckenfield	34	G	CG	Mod		yes
S. Dunch	61	O, G	CG	Mod	21	yes
R. Dunkon	57		M	Rad?		no
J. Erisey	37	L	LG	Mod		yes
C. Erle	29	O, MT	LG	Rad?		yes
G. Eure			CG	Mod	54/56	no
T. Eyre	37		LG	Rad		no
R. Fenwick			LG	Mod	54/56	yes
G. Fleetwood	30		CG	Mod	45–53/54	yes
T. French	c. 52	G	M	Rad		yes
T. Frere	63	G	LG	Mod	54	yes
E. Gill	43		LG	Mod	54/56	yes
J. Goddard	37	O, C	P	Mod		no
V. Goddard			LG	Mod		no

Name	Age					
V. Gookin	c. 34		CG	Mod	54/56/59	yes
N. Greene			LG	Rad?		yes
H. Henley	c. 46		CG	Mod	54/59/60/79/ 80/81/90	yes
J. Herring			LG	Rad		yes
J. Hewson			M	Mod	54/56	no
S. Highland			LG	Rad	54/56	yes
J. Hildesley	57		LG	Mod	54/56/59/60	yes
D. Hollister			M	Rad		no
R. Holmes			LG	Rad		yes
J. Hope	39		GG	Rad		no
E. Horseman	37		LG	Mod	54/59	yes
C. Howard	24		GG	Mod	54/56/60	yes
D. Hutchinson			M	Mod		no
J. Ireton	38		M	Rad		no
A. Jaffray	39		P	Rad		no
J. James	43		CG	Rad 5M		yes
R. Jermy	c. 50	C, MT	CG	Rad?		yes
P. Jones	35		CG	Mod	50–3/54/56	yes
W. Kenrick	39		LG	Rad	59	yes
H. King			M	Mod		yes
R. King	c. 54	C	GG	Mod	54/56	no
F. Langdon	47		LG	Rad 5M		yes
J. Langley	41		M	Mod		yes
F. Lascelles	c. 42	G	LG	Mod	45–53/54/56/60	yes
H. Lawrence	53	C, G	CG	Mod	46–8/54/56	no
W. Lockhart	32		GG	Mod	54/56	no
R. Lucy	34	O, G	CG	Mod	54/56/59/60/61	yes
R. Major	49	O	LG	Mod	54	yes
B. Mansell	30		CG	Rad?	60/79/80/81 89/90/95/98	yes
L. Marsh	33		LG	Rad		yes
C. Martyn			LG	Mod	47–53/59/60	yes
J. Matthews	c. 35	L	M	Mod	54/56/59	yes
G. Monck	45		LG	Mod	60	no
E. Montagu	28		GG	Mod	45–8/54/56/60	yes
S. Moyer	c. 44		M	Rad		yes
W. Neast	30	O, MT	LG	Mod	56	yes
R. Norton	38	O, G	GG	Mod	45–53/54/56/59/60/ 61/79/80/81/89/90	yes
J. Odingsells	49	C, G	LG	Mod		yes
H. Ogle	53		LG	Mod	54	yes
S. Pheasant	36	C, G	LG	Mod	54	yes
J. Phillips	59	O	CG	Mod	54/56/59/ 60/61	yes
G. Pickering	42	C, G	GG	Mod	40–53/54/56	yes
E. Plumstead	c. 40	C	LG	Rad		no
J. Pratt			LG	Mod		yes
R. Price			LG	Rad 5M		no
J. Pyne	c. 57	O, MT	CG	Rad	25/26/28/40(Sh)/40–53	yes
W. Reeve			M	Rad		no
W. Roberts	48	C, G	GG	Mod	54/56	yes
W. Rogers			M	Rad	56/59	yes
A. Rous	c. 50	MT	CG	Mod	54/56	yes
F. Rous	74	O, MT	GG	Mod	26/28/40(Sh) 40–53	yes
J. Sadler	38	C, L	P	Mod	59	no
J. St Nicholas	49	C	LG	Mod		yes
T. St Nicholas	51	C, IT	P	Rad	56/59	yes
R. Salwey	38	IT	M	Rad	45–53	no
T. Saunders			LG	Mod	54/56	yes
J. Sawrey			LG	Rad?		no
P. Sidney	34	O, G	GG	Mod	40(Sh)/40–53	yes
E. Smith	c. 23	L	CG	Mod		no
W. Spence	32	C, L	LG	Rad	59	yes
A. Squibb			LG	Rad 5M		yes
A. Stapley	63	C?, G	CG	Rad	24/25/26/40(Sh)/ 40–53/54	yes
J. Stone	c. 47	C?, G?	M	Mod	54/56/59	no
W. Strickland	55	C, G	CG	Mod	46–53/ 54/56/61	yes
N. Studley	c. 49	G	LG	Rad?		yes
R. Sweet			M	Rad		no
J. Swinton	c. 32		GG	Rad	54/56	no

W. Sydenham	38		LG	Mod	45–53/54/56	yes
N. Taylor	c. 33	C, G	P	Rad		yes
D. Templer	26	C	LG	Mod	56	yes
W. Thompson			LG	Mod		yes
R. Tichborne			M	Mod		yes
H. Walcott		C, G	LG	Mod	56	yes
S. Warner			LG	Mod		no
W. West	c. 34	G	LG	Rad	59/60	no
J. Williams			LG	Rad 5M		yes
A. Wingfield	c. 42	L	P	Mod		yes
R. Wolmer			LG	Mod		no
C. Wolseley	23		GG	Mod	54/56/60	no
T. Wood			LG	Mod		no

● SummaryTask

Work in groups. Share out the questions below among the groups. You could enter the information into a spreadsheet program such as Microsoft Excel or Claris Works to present your findings in the form of graphs or pie charts.

1 What percentage of the members of Barebone's Parliament:

   a) were gentry, greater gentry or county gentry?
   b) were known to have attended university or the Inns of Court?
   c) had parliamentary experience before 1653?
   d) had parliamentary experience after 1653?
   e) had parliamentary experience outside the period 1640–60?
   f) sat in no other Parliament?
   g) had administrative experience as Justices of the Peace before Barebone's Parliament met?
   h) were moderate in religion?
   i) were religious radicals?
   j) were Fifth Monarchists?

2 What was the average age of the members whose ages are known?

3 What was the most common social status of the members?

For discussion

4 Each group should report its findings to the rest of the class.
   In the light of your findings, do you think the comments of Heath and Clarendon in Sources 9.4 and 9.5 about the backgrounds and abilities of the members of Barebone's Parliament are justified?

● SOURCE 9.8

These are the conclusions that Woolrych himself drew from the data.

Barebone's Parliament differed unquestionably in its social composition from a normal House of Commons, and for nearly half the members this was their sole appearance at Westminster. Nevertheless the great majority of them were drawn from the top 5 per cent of the population, and the traditional governing class was strongly represented. Contrary to popular report, the number of tradesmen was small, and of lay preachers still smaller. The range of experience on which the assembly could draw, especially in local administration, was not contemptible. Neither social inferiority nor ignorance of the tasks of government was a sufficient … reason why it should fail, given the limited duration and interim nature of the authority to which Cromwell summoned it.

5 On the basis of your study of Source 9.7, do you agree with Woolrych's conclusions?

6 Why do you think there have been such different assessments of Barebone's Parliament?

● Further reading

The most detailed modern study of Barebone's Parliament is A. Woolrych, *Commonwealth to Protectorate* (Clarendon Press, 1982). A summary of Woolrych's views can be found in A. Woolrych, 'Oliver Cromwell and the Rule of the Saints', in R. H. Parry (ed.), *The English Civil War and After* (Macmillan, 1970), pp. 59–77. For a sympathetic evaluation of the work of Barebone's Parliament see Christopher Hill, *God's Englishman* (Penguin, 1972), pp. 132–40.

Oliver Cromwell and the English Republic, 1649–58

chapter 10

1649
January: The King is tried and executed.

February: The principal Leveller leaders are arrested.

March: The Rump Parliament passes Acts abolishing the monarchy and the House of Lords.

May: Parliament passes an Act that declares that England is now a republic (the Commonwealth). Fairfax and Cromwell put down army mutinies at Burford (Oxfordshire) and elsewhere.

August: Cromwell sets off with the New Model Army to put down a rebellion in Ireland.

September–October: The New Model Army takes Drogheda and Wexford and its soldiers massacre civilians as well as soldiers.

1650
June: Cromwell returns from Ireland to a hero's welcome and is appointed to lead the army against opposition to the Republic from the Scots, who are now allied to Charles II.

September: Cromwell wins a victory over the Scots at Dunbar.

1651
September: Cromwell defeats the Royalists led by Charles II at Worcester. Charles flees to the continent.

1652
May: War with the Dutch Republic is declared.

1653
April: Cromwell dissolves the Rump Parliament by force.

July: Barebone's Parliament begins its sessions.

December: After Barebone's Parliament ends, Cromwell accepts a new constitution, devised by John Lambert, and is installed as Lord Protector of Britain.

1654
Before September: Cromwell and the Protectorate Council pass ordinances: establishing a commission in London, called 'triers', to approve the appointment of Church ministers; establishing local commissions (ejectors) to expel ministers deemed to be unfit to hold office and to unite England and Scotland.

August: War with the Dutch is ended by the Treaty of Westminster.

September: The First Protectorate Parliament meets.

December: A combined naval–military expedition (the Western Design) departs to attack Spanish colonies in the Caribbean.

1655
January: Cromwell dissolves the First Protectorate Parliament after only five months, following its attack on the army and its attempts to restrict religious freedom.

March: A Royalist rebellion in Wiltshire (Penruddock's Rebellion) is suppressed.

April: The Western Design army suffers a major defeat at San Domingo in the Caribbean.

May: The Western Design army captures Jamaica.

August: Eleven Major-Generals are appointed to govern the localities.

October: The Major-Generals are given revised instructions; after an Anglo-French treaty war is declared against Spain.

1656

September: The Second Protectorate Parliament meets.

October: James Nayler, a Quaker, is arrested and charged by Parliament with 'horrid blasphemy'. He is subsequently convicted and punished.

1657

January: Cromwell agrees to dismantle the system of Major-Generals.

March: Cromwell is presented with proposals for a new constitution (the Humble Petition and Advice) that include the offer of the crown.

May: Cromwell accepts all parts of the new constitution except the crown.

June: Cromwell is installed again as Protector under the new constitution. The first session of the Second Protectorate Parliament ends.

1658

January: The second session of the Second Protectorate Parliament starts.

February: Cromwell angrily dissolves Parliament after civilian republicans try to get army support in their attacks on the new constitution.

September: Cromwell dies and is succeeded as Protector by his eldest son, Richard.

Introduction

One of the central concerns of historians is to evaluate the role played by individuals in historical events. Were individuals in the past pawns in the historical process, helpless in the face of powerful forces beyond their control? Or were they able to make decisions or take actions that decisively influenced the course of events? In Chapter 2 of this book it has been seen that historians have given quite different degrees of 'blame' to one individual, Charles I, for what happened in the early 1640s. Oliver Cromwell, however, is such a dominating historical personality that there is widespread agreement that he had a major role in determining the course of the English Revolution, at least after 1649. Before 1649, it is possible (and some historians have fallen into this trap) to exaggerate his importance in the history of the Civil War and immediately afterwards; after 1649, it is difficult to exaggerate his role in the history of the Republic.

What *exactly* this role was, however, is as controversial as many other aspects of Cromwell's career. This chapter reproduces sources with the overall aim of helping you to make up your own mind about his role.

Here is a hypothesis for you to consider as you read this chapter; your main task at the end of the chapter will be to decide whether or not you agree with it. The hypothesis is a straightforward one. It is that central to Cromwell's role in the 1650s were his religious aspirations. All other aims were to Cromwell, in the last resort, of lesser importance and, if pursuing them threatened his religious ideals, he was always willing to get rid of them.

Not everyone by any means would agree with that hypothesis and so it allows room for ample discussion.

To underline the controversial nature of the study of Oliver Cromwell, this chapter begins in Section A with some sources that illustrate the extent to which, even during (or shortly after) his lifetime, Cromwell's contemporaries disagreed violently about him.

Section B contains sources about Cromwell's aims. Did he have principled aims or was he merely seeking to secure and increase his own power? Was he sincere in what he said he stood for, or was he an unprincipled hypocrite, a tyrant?

Section C then looks at sources from the four major phases of the Republic between 1649 and Cromwell's death in 1658, focusing on major historical problems about Cromwell and his role:

- The Commonwealth 1649–53: why did Cromwell forcibly expel the Rump Parliament which had ruled the country since the establishment of the Republic?
- The establishment of the Protectorate and the First Protectorate Parliament, 1653–5: why did Cromwell agree to become Lord Protector and accept a new constitution, the Instrument of Government, and why was the first Parliament of the constitution a disastrous failure?

- Cromwell's 'personal rule' and the Major-Generals, 1655–6: why did Cromwell embark on a period of authoritarian rule?
- Cromwell and the Second Protectorate Parliament, 1656–8: why did Cromwell refuse the offer to become King Oliver?

Section A Contemporary views of Cromwell

The official views of Cromwell are best reflected in visual images.

● **SOURCE 10.1**

Coins from the 1650s

Commonwealth shilling, 1652
The inscriptions read:
a) The Commonwealth of England
b) God with us

a   **b**

Oliver Cromwell half-crown, 1656
The inscriptions read:
a) Oliver, by the grace of God, Protector of the Republic of England, Scotland and Ireland, etc.
b) Peace is sought by War

a   **b**

● **SOURCE 10.2**

The Great Seal of England which was used to seal all major government documents.
The inscriptions read:
a) The Great Seal of England 1651
b) The Third Yeare of Freedome by God's Blessing Restored

a

b

● **SOURCE 10.3**

Many official pamphlets contained images of Cromwell. This portrait, depicting him as a heroic military leader, is the title page of one such pamphlet: *A Perfect Table of One Hundred Forty and Five Victories Obtained by the Lord Lieutenant of Ireland*, published in 1650.

A Perfect Table of one hundred forty and Five Victories obtained by the Lord Lieutenant of *Ireland*, and the Parliaments Forces under his Command, since his Excellency was made Governour Generall by the Parliament of *England*; From VVednesday August 1. 1649. to March the last, 1650. VVith a briefe Chronicle of the chiefe matters of the Irish VVarres, from that time to this present.

THE Right Honorable and Undaunted Warrior OLIVER CROMWELL Lt Governour of IRELAND

LONDON, Printed by Robert Ibbitson, and are to be sold by William Ley at Pauls Chain, 1650.

---

1 What aspects of Cromwell were these images probably meant to point out to people at the time?

2 Can you think of similar uses of pictures and other visual images by governments at other times?

Sources 10.4–10.7 contain some hostile views of Cromwell.

● Source 10.4

This cartoon is a crude example of Royalist propaganda and the origins of the hatred of Cromwell it represents are fairly obvious.

● Source 10.5

From *The Hunting of the Foxes*, a pamphlet written by a Leveller radical shortly after the King's execution in 1649

You shall scarce speak to Cromwell about any thing, but he will lay his hand on his heart, elevate his eyes, and call God to record, he will weep, howl and repent, even while he doth smite you under the first rib.

● Source 10.6

This engraving was printed by Clement Walker in his *The History of Independency: The Second Part*, 1649. Walker was a Presbyterian MP who was excluded from Parliament by Colonel Pride in December 1648.

● **SOURCE 10.7**

From a pamphlet by a civilian republican, Slingsby Bethel, *The World's Mistake in Oliver Cromwell*, 1668

habeas corpus: *from the Latin for 'have the body'. It refers to the legal right of a prisoner to be brought before a court to have his or her case heard.*

To prove … that Oliver's time was full of oppressions and injustice, I shall but instance in a few of many particulars, and begin with John Lilburne … John in 1649 was by order of the then Parliament tried for his life … but the jury not finding him guilty, he was immediately, according to law, generously set at liberty … [But] Cromwell … contrary to law … kept him in prison, until he was so far spent in a consumption, that he only turned him out to die. [Second]ly Mr Cony's case [see page 178] is so notorious, that it needs little more than naming. He was a prisoner at Cromwell's suit, and being brought to the King's Bench bar by a HABEAS CORPUS, had his counsel taken from the bar, and sent to the Tower for no other reason, than the pleading of their client's cause; an act of violence, that I believe the whole story of England doth not parallel. [Bethel lists other similar cases of Cromwell's alleged disregard for the law.]

Sources 10.5–10.7 were produced by people who had at one time or another, like Cromwell, opposed Charles I. After looking at each example:

a) Suggest reasons why those responsible for them might have loathed Cromwell so much.
b) Put into your own words the principal criticisms that are being made of Cromwell.

Section B **What were Cromwell's aims?**

Unlike Sources 10.1–10.7, most of the sources in the rest of this chapter are from Cromwell's mouth and pen. They are, therefore, equally open to the charge of being subjective and self-justificatory, and they should be read with that possible limitation in mind. Yet it would be unwise to follow his hostile contemporaries and dismiss *everything* that Cromwell said and wrote as insincere hypocrisy. Historians of Cromwell (like those who study any historical figure) have got to come to their own judgements about whether and when they can accept at face value what he said and wrote.

The sources in Section B relate to Cromwell's attitude to:

• the constitution
• the social order and reform
• religion.

Cromwell and the constitution

Sources 10.8–10.10 refer to Cromwell's attitude to Parliaments.

● **SOURCE 10.8**

A letter from Cromwell (and Fairfax) to the sheriff and gentry of Cornwall, 8 September 1645

Be sensible of the interest of Religion, and of the rights and liberties of yourselves and the rest of the people of England, of which the power and authority of Parliaments hath been in former ages and is ever like to be (under God) the best conservatory and support.

● **SOURCE 10.9**

From Cromwell's speech at the Putney Debates, 28 October 1647

They may have some jealousies and apprehensions that we are wedded and glued to forms of government; so that whatsoever we may pretend, it is in vain for you to speak to us … You will find that we are far from being so particularly engaged to anything … that we should not concur with you that the foundation and supremacy is in the people, radically in them, and to be set down by them in their representations.

● **SOURCE 10.10**

Cromwell's speech to the First Protectorate Parliament, 4 September 1654

One thing more this government hath done. It hath been instrumental to call a free Parliament, which, blessed be God, we see here this day. I say a free Parliament; and that it may continue so, I hope is in the heart and spirit of every good man in England … It is that which, as I have desired all my life, I shall desire to keep it so above my life.

1   In what ways might Cromwell have shaped his views on Parliaments on these three occasions in order to gain support from those who listened to or read them?

2   What episodes in Cromwell's career could be used to cast doubts on the sincerity of his attachment to Parliament's place in the constitution?

3   Look at the three written constitutions Cromwell supported during his career (The Heads of the Proposals, page 111, The Instrument of Government, page 177 and The Humble Petition and Advice, page 183). What light do they throw on the sincerity of Cromwell's views expressed here?

The question of why Cromwell refused to become king in 1657 will be dealt with later. Sources 10.11 and 10.12 touch on Cromwell's attitude to the monarchy in *general*.

● **SOURCE 10.11**

From Bulstrode Whitelocke's account of a discussion by army officers and civilian politicians about the constitution at the London house of William Lenthall, the Speaker of the Rump Parliament, December 1651

his brother: *James Duke of York, later James II*

the King's eldest son: *Charles II*

Lord Chief Justice Oliver St John [a Political Independent ally of Cromwell in the 1640s who had taken no part in the execution of the King, but who accepted office in the Commonwealth]:
It will be found that the Government of this Nation, without something of Monarchical power, will be very difficult to be so settled as not to shake the foundation of our Laws, and the liberties of the People …

Whitelocke:
There may be a day given for the KING'S ELDEST SON, or for the Duke of York HIS BROTHER, to come to the Parliament. And upon such terms as shall be thought fit, and agreeable both to our Civil and Spiritual liberties, a Settlement may be made with them.

Cromwell:
That will be a business of more than ordinary difficulty! But really I think, if it may be done with safety, and preservation of our Rights, both as Englishmen and as Christians, that a Settlement with somewhat of Monarchical power in it would be very effectual.

● **SOURCE 10.12**

Cromwell's speech to a parliamentary committee, 13 April 1657

constable: *local official responsible for maintaining law and order*

I am a man standing in the place I am in, which place I undertook not so much out of hope of doing any good, as out of a desire to prevent mischief and evil, which I did see was imminent upon the nation. I saw we were running headlong into confusion and disorder, and would necessarily run into blood … I profess I had not that apprehension when I undertook this place, that I could do much good; but I did think I might prevent imminent evil … And in that, as far as I can, I am ready to serve not as a King, but as a CONSTABLE. For truly I have as before God thought it often, that I could not tell what my business was, nor what I was in the place I stood, save by comparing it with a good constable to keep the peace of the parish.

1   How reliable do you think Source 10.11 is as an indication of Cromwell's real attitude to monarchy?

2   Although Cromwell played a leading role in the execution of the King in 1649 and refused the offer to become king in 1657, what other evidence, apart from Source 10.11, suggests that Cromwell was not opposed to monarchy in principle?

3   What do you think Cromwell meant in Source 10.12 by comparing his role to that of a 'good constable' of a parish rather than that of a king?

Cromwell and the social order and social reform

● **SOURCE 10.13**

From Cromwell's letter to two members of the Parliamentary County Committee of Suffolk during the Civil War, 29 August 1643

I beseech you be careful what captains of horse you choose, what men be mounted; a few honest men are better than numbers … If you choose godly, honest men to be captains of horse, honest men will follow them … I had rather have a plain russet-coated captain that knows what he fights for, and loves what he knows, than that which you call a gentleman and is nothing else. I honour a gentleman that is so indeed.

● **SOURCE 10.14**

From Cromwell's speech to the First Protectorate Parliament, 4 September 1654, looking back to the dangers that he believed the nation had faced from Levellers in the recent past

magistracy: government

What was the face that was upon our affairs as to the interest of the nation? to the authority of the nation? to the MAGISTRACY? to the ranks and orders of men, whereby England had been known for hundreds of years? A nobleman, a gentleman, a yeoman? That is a good interest of the nation and a great one. The magistracy of the nation, was it not almost trampled under foot, under despite and contempt by men of Levelling principles? I beseech you, for the orders of men and ranks of men, did not that Levelling principle tend to the reducing all to an equality? Did it think to do so, or did it practise towards it for propriety and interest? What was the design, but to make the tenant as liberal a fortune as the landlord?

● **SOURCE 10.15**

From the same speech, 4 September 1654

The great end of your meeting … [is] healing and settling. And the remembering transactions too particularly, perhaps instead of healing, at least in the hearts of many of you, may set the wound fresh a bleeding. I must profess this to you, whatever thoughts pass upon me, that if this day, that if this meeting, prove not healing, what shall we do?

1 Are the views expressed in Source 10.13 compatible with the support Cromwell gave to the existing social order in Source 10.14?

2 How justified were Cromwell's fears of the Levellers in Source 10.14? (Refer back to Chapter 7.)

3 What do you think Cromwell meant by 'healing and settling' in Source 10.15? What light does it throw on Cromwell's social attitudes?

The next two sources are examples of Cromwell's demands for social reform.

● **SOURCE 10.16**

From Cromwell's letter to William Lenthall, Speaker of the Rump Parliament, on 4 September 1650, the day after his remarkable victory over the Scots at Dunbar in Scotland. Cromwell demands that Parliament undertake a reform programme.

We that serve you beg of you not to own us, but God alone; we pray you own His people more and more, for they are the chariots and horsemen of Israel. Disown yourselves, but own your authority, and improve it to curb the proud and insolent, such as would disturb the tranquillity of England, though under what specious pretences soever; relieve the oppressed, hear the groans of poor prisoners in England; be pleased to reform the abuses of all professions; and if there be any one that makes many poor to make a few rich, that suits not a Commonwealth.

● **SOURCE 10.17**

From Cromwell's speech to the First Protectorate Parliament, 4 September 1654

The government … hath had some things in desire and it hath done some things actually. It hath desired to reform the laws … and for that end it hath called together persons … [of] as great integrity as are in these nations, to consider how the laws might be made plain and short, and less chargeable to the people, how to lessen expense for the good of the nation … There hath been care taken to put the administration of the laws into the hands of just men, men of most known integrity and ability. The Chancery hath been reformed … And as to the things depending there, which made the burden of the work of the honourable persons intrusted in those services beyond their ability, it hath referred many of them to those places where Englishmen love to have their rights tried, the Courts of Law at Westminster.

1 Explain to another member of your class Cromwell's demands for social reform.

2 Why do you think that Cromwell pushed hard for reform after the military victories? (See Sources 10.16 and 10.17.)

3 Do the sources reproduced so far justify the belief that Cromwell did not want to change the existing political and social structure but wanted to ensure that it operated more fairly?

Cromwell and religion

Sources 10.18–10.26 illustrate four aspects of Cromwell's religious attitude: his belief in providence, in religious toleration, in moral reform (what he called 'a reformation of manners') and that England's condition in the 1650s had strong similarities with that of the Old Testament Israelites.

Sources 10.18–10.19 are two of many examples where Cromwell said that God had helped him on (as well as off) the battlefield.

● **SOURCE 10.18**

From Cromwell's letter to his brother-in-law, Colonel Valentine Walton, 5 July 1644, informing him of the death of the Colonel's son at the Battle of Marston Moor, three days earlier. In it Cromwell refers to the death of his own son from smallpox earlier in the year.

Truly England and the Church of God hath had a great favour from the Lord, in this great victory given unto us … It had all the evidences of an absolute victory obtained by the Lord's blessing upon the godly party principally. We never charged but we routed the enemy … God made them as stubble to our swords, we charged their regiments of foot with our horse, routed all we charged … Give glory, all the glory to God. Sir, God hath taken away your eldest son by a cannon-shot … Sir, you know my trials this way: but the Lord supported me with this, that the Lord took him into the happiness we all pant and live for. There is your precious child full of glory, to know [neither] sin nor sorrow any more … He was a precious young man, fit for God. You have cause to bless the Lord. He is a glorious saint in Heaven, wherein you ought exceedingly to rejoice. Let this drink up your sorrow; seeing these are not feigned words to comfort you, but the thing is so real and undoubted a truth. You may do all things by the strength of Christ. Seek that, and you shall easily bear your trial. Let this public mercy to the Church of God make you … forget your private sorrow. The Lord be your strength.

● **SOURCE 10.19**

From Cromwell's letter to the Speaker of the Commons, July 1645, reporting the New Model Army's victory at Langport (Long Sutton)

Thus you see what the Lord hath wrought us. Can any creature ascribe anything to itself? Now can we give all the glory to God, and desire all may do so, for it is all due to Him! Thus you have Long Sutton mercy added to Naseby mercy. And to see this, is it not to see the face of God?

---

1 Do you share the Levellers' view (see Source 10.5) that Cromwell's belief in providence was insincere?

2 Have you found evidence in other chapters of this book that belief in providence was common among godly Protestants in this period?

● **SOURCE 10.20**

From Cromwell's letter to the Speaker of the Commons, June 1645, reporting the New Model Army's victory at Naseby. When the Commons published this letter in print it omitted this extract.

Honest men served you in this action. He that ventures his life for the liberty of his country, I wish he trust God for the liberty of his conscience, and for the liberty he fights for.

● **SOURCE 10.21**

From the Instrument of Government, 1653

licentiousness: *practices (often sexual) that disregard generally accepted codes of behaviour*

public profession: *the religion officially followed by the government*

Clause 35. That the Christian religion, as contained in the Scriptures, be held forth and recommended as the PUBLIC PROFESSION of these nations …

Clause 36. That to the Public Profession held forth none shall be compelled by penalties or otherwise; but that endeavours be used to win them by sound doctrine and the example of a good conversation.

Clause 37. That such as profess faith in God by Jesus Christ (though differing in judgement from the doctrine, worship or discipline publicly held forth) shall not be restrained from, but shall be protected in, the profession of the Faith, and exercise of their religion; so as they abuse not this liberty to the civil injury of others, and to the actual disturbance of the public peace on their parts. Provided this liberty be not extended to popery nor Prelacy, nor to such as, under the professions of Christ, hold forth and practise LICENTIOUSNESS.

Clause 38. That all laws, statutes, and ordinances … to the contrary of the aforesaid liberty, shall be esteemed as null and void.

● **SOURCE 10.22**

From Cromwell's speech to the Second Protectorate Parliament, 17 September 1656

I will tell you the truth, that that which hath been our practice since the last Parliament, hath been to let all this nation see that whatever [their] pretensions be to religion, if quiet, peaceable, they may enjoy conscience and liberty to themselves, so long as they do not make religion a pretence for arms and blood. Truly we have suffered them, and that cheerfully, so to enjoy their own liberties ... If men will profess – be those under Baptism, be those of the Independent judgement simply, and of the Presbyterian judgement – in the name of God encourage them, countenance them, while they do plainly hold forth to be thankful to God, and to make use of the liberty given them to enjoy their own consciences ... This is the peculiar interest all this while contended for. That men that believe in Jesus Christ – that is the form that gives the being to true religion, faith in Christ, and walking in a profession answerable to that faith – men that believe in the remission of sins through the blood of Christ and free justification by the blood of Christ, and live upon the grace of God, that those men, that are certain they are so, are members of Jesus Christ and are to him as the apple of his eye. Whoever hath this faith, let his form be what it will, if he be walking peaceably, without the prejudicing the others under another form, it is a debt due to God and Christ and he will require it, if he may not enjoy this liberty. If a man of one form will be trampling upon the heels of another form, if an Independent, for example, will despise him under Baptism, and will revile him, and reproach, and provoke him, I will not suffer it in him.

---

1   Why do you think the Commons did not print Source 10.20?

2   In what ways do Sources 10.21–10.22 suggest that there were limits to Cromwell's 'toleration'? What other evidence have you seen that might also lead you to that conclusion?

3   Contrast Cromwell's commitment to 'liberty of conscience' with the ecclesiastical policies of Charles I.

4   Do these sources support the view that Cromwell looked back, trying to maintain a united Protestant national Church?

Like many other godly Protestants in this period, Cromwell sought 'a reformation of manners'. What this meant is illustrated in Sources 10.23–10.24.

● **SOURCE 10.23**

An ordinance for ejecting scandalous, ignorant and insufficient ministers and schoolmasters, 28 August 1654

---
wakes: *merry-making at fairs, etc., held to celebrate the dedication of churches*

[This established local commissions (ejectors) with powers to inspect Church ministers and schoolteachers and to 'eject' those who were guilty of] ignorance, insufficiency, scandal in their lives and conversations, or negligence ... or guilty of profane cursing or swearing, perjury ... or maintain ... popish opinions ... or be guilty of adultery, fornication, drunkenness, common haunting of taverns or alehouses, frequent quarrelling or fighting, frequent playing at cards or dice, profaning of the Sabbath day; such as have ... used the Common Prayer Book ... such as do ... scoff at or revile the strict profession or professors of religion or godliness, or do encourage and countenance ... any Whitsun-ales, WAKES, morris dances, maypoles, stage plays, or such like licentious practices.

● **SOURCE 10.24**

From Cromwell's speech to the First Protectorate Parliament, 4 September 1654

Many honest people, whose hearts are sincere [have been deceived by] the mistaken notion of the Fifth Monarchy. A thing pretending more spirituality than anything else. A notion I hope we will all honour, wait, and hope for, that Jesus Christ will have a time to set up his reign in our hearts, by subduing those corruptions and lusts, and evils that are there, which reign now more in the world than I hope in due time they shall do. And when more fullness of the Spirit is poured forth to subdue iniquity and bring in everlasting righteousness, then will the approach of that glory be.

Also, like many of his contemporaries, Cromwell was very familiar with the Bible. It coloured his language and he drew many of his phrases from it (e.g. 'apple of his eye' in Source 10.22). One particular biblical story had a powerful influence on him (and on others): the dramatic story in the Old Testament of the escape of the Israelites from Egyptian bondage, their long period of exile in the wilderness, and then (once they had regained God's blessing after purging themselves of sin) their victory over their enemies in battles such as that at Jericho, which enabled them to inherit the Promised Land of Jerusalem, Canaan, which they renamed Israel. In Sources 10.25–10.26, which are from Cromwell's keynote speeches at the start of the two Protectorate Parliaments, he uses that story to explain why a 'reformation of manners' was one of the main aims (perhaps *the* main aim?) of his life.

● **SOURCE 10.25**

From Cromwell's speech to the First Protectorate Parliament, 4 September 1654

Truly, I thought it my duty to let you know, that though God hath thus dealt with you, yet these are but entrances and doors of hope, wherein through the blessing of God you may enter into rest and peace. But you are not entered. You were told today [in a sermon at the start of the session] of a people brought out of Egypt towards the land of Canaan, but, through unbelief, murmuring, repining, and other temptations and sins, wherewith God was provoked, they were fain to come back again, and linger in the wilderness, before they came to a place of rest. We are thus far through the mercy of God. We have cause to take notice of it, that we are not brought into misery; but, as I said before, a door is open, and his presence go along with the management of affairs at this meeting, you will be enabled to put the top-stone to this work, and make the nation happy.

● **SOURCE 10.26**

From Cromwell's speech to Parliament, 17 September 1656

[England does not need] a captain to lead us back into Egypt, if there be such a place – I mean metaphorically and allegorically so – that is to say, returning to all those things that we think we have been fighting against and destroying of all that good … we have attained unto … Therefore I say … it is a thing I am confident, that the liberty … of this nation depends upon reformation, to make it a shame to see men to be bold in sin and profaneness, and God will bless you. You will be a blessing to the nation … Truly these things do respect the souls of men, and the spirits, which are the men. The mind is the man. If that be kept pure, a man signifies somewhat; if not I would fain to see what difference there is betwixt him and a beast.

1 In Source 10.25, what reason does Cromwell give to explain why the people brought out of Egypt (the Israelites) were forced to linger in the wilderness?

2 What lessons does Cromwell draw for England's future development from this biblical story? Why does he say in Source 10.26 that England's 'liberty … depends upon reformation'?

Conclusion

Source 10.27 is one of the rare cases in which Cromwell summarises his practical and religious beliefs. Like Source 10.28 it suggests that Cromwell divided his aims into two 'concernments' or 'interests'.

● **SOURCE 10.27**

From Cromwell's speech to Parliament, 12 September 1654

There are some things … that are fundamental … about which I shall deal plainly with you … The government by a single person and a Parliament is a fundamental … In every government there must be somewhat fundamental, somewhat like a Magna Charter, that should be standing and unalterable … That Parliaments should not make themselves perpetual is a fundamental. Of what assurance is a law to prevent so great an evil, if it lie in one or the same legislator to unlaw it again? Is the like to be lasting? It will be like a rope of sand; it will give no security, for the same men unbuild what they have built.

Is not liberty of conscience a fundamental? So long as there is liberty of conscience for the supreme magistrate, to exercise his conscience in erecting what form of church-government he is satisfied he should set up, why should he not give it to others? Liberty of conscience is a natural right; and he that would have it ought to give it … And I may say it to you … all the money of this nation would not have tempted men to fight, upon such an account as they have engaged, if they had not had hopes of liberty, better than they had from Episcopacy, or than would have been afforded them from a Scottish Presbytery; or an English either, if it had made such steps or been as sharp and rigid as it threatened when it was first set up. This I say is a fundamental.

● **Source 10.28**

From Cromwell's speech to a parliamentary committee, 3 April 1657, commenting on the Humble Petition and Advice

You have been zealous of the two greatest concernments that God has in the world. The one is that of religion and the preservation of the professors thereof, to give them all due and just liberty … The other thing cared for is the civil liberties and interests of the nation, which, although it be, and indeed ought to be subordinate to a more peculiar interest of God, yet it is the next best God hath given men in this world … If anyone whatsoever think that the interest of God's people and the civil interest are inconsistent, I wish my soul may not enter into his or their secret.

Section C Cromwell and his role

Cromwell believed that it was possible to reconcile his aims of achieving a satisfactory constitutional settlement and a godly reformation. Whether he was right to be so optimistic is a question you should bear in mind as you follow in this section the history of his attempts to achieve both broad aims between 1649 and 1658. During that period Cromwell's career (like the history of the country) falls into four periods.

Cromwell and the Commonwealth, 1649–53

As has been seen in Chapter 8, the English Republic that replaced the monarchy in 1649 was often known at the time as 'the Commonwealth'. That is also the name that historians have used to describe the government of the Republic between 1649 and the establishment of the Protectorate in 1653. Between 1649 and 1651 Cromwell's main role was as defender of the infant Republic against attacks on it from both within and outside England.

● **Source 10.29**

From Cromwell's speech to army officers, 23 March 1649

I think there is more cause of danger from disunion amongst ourselves than by any thing from our enemies; and I do not know anything greater than that; and I believe, and I may speak with confidence, till we admire God and give Him glory for what he has done. For all the rest of the world, ministers and profane persons, all rob God of all the glory, and reckon it to be a thing of chance that has befallen them. Now, if we do not depart from God, and disunite by that departure, and fall into disunion amongst ourselves, I am confident, we doing our duty and waiting upon the Lord, we shall find He will be as a wall of brass round about us till we have finished that work that He had for us to do … In the next place we are to consider Ireland. All the Papists and the King's party … are in a very strong combination against you … If we do not endeavour to make good our interest there, and that timely, we shall not only have … our interest rooted out there, but they will in a very short time be able to land forces in England, and to put us to trouble here. I confess I have had these thoughts with myself, that perhaps may be carnal and foolish, I had rather be overrun with a Cavalierish interest than a Scotch interest; I had rather be overrun with a Scotch interest, than an Irish interest; and I think of all this is most dangerous. If they shall be able to carry on their work, they will make this the most miserable people in the earth, for all the world knows their barbarism … Now that should awaken all Englishmen, who perhaps are willing enough he [the King] should have come in upon an accommodation, but not that he must come from Ireland or Scotland.

● **Source 10.30**

John Lilburne was under arrest for publishing *England's New Chains Discovered*, which attacked the new regime. He was interrogated by the Council of State on 28 March 1649. This is his account of what he said he heard Cromwell say as he listened at the door after he was taken from the room.

'I tell you sir,' Cromwell declared, thumping the table, 'you have no other way to deal with these men but to break them or they will break you; yea, and bring all the guilt of the blood and treasure spent and shed in this kingdom upon your heads and shoulders, and frustrate and make void all that work that, with so many years' industry, toil, and pains, you have done, and so render you to all rational men as the most contemptibilest generation of silly, low-spirited men in the earth, to be broken and routed by such a despicable, contemptible generation of men as they are, and therefore, sir, I tell you again, you are necessitated to break them.'

1 What do these two sources suggest were Cromwell's principal aims immediately after the establishment of the Republic?

2 Who does he think were the main enemies of the Republic at this time and why?

3 What does Cromwell mean by the last sentence of Source 10.29: 'Now that should awaken … Scotland'?

Cromwell's ruthless military campaign in Ireland in 1649–50 has become legendary and the hostility it aroused in Ireland has not yet disappeared. Sources 10.31–10.34 are drawn from that episode.

Cromwell in Ireland

When his army captured Drogheda and Wexford in 1649, Cromwell ordered his troops 'not to spare any that were in arms'. Many people in these towns were killed. These are exceptional cases; in neither England nor Scotland did Cromwell allow his soldiers to commit such acts of brutality. As you read Sources 10.31–10.34, you should look for explanations for why Cromwell not only acted with extreme ferocity against all opponents of his army in Ireland, but also spoke so viciously about the Irish.

● **SOURCE 10.31**

From Cromwell's letter to the Speaker of the Rump Parliament, September 1649, reporting on the massacre at Drogheda

imbrued: *stained*

I am persuaded that this is a righteous judgement of God upon these barbarous wretches, who have IMBRUED their hands in so much innocent blood; and that it will tend to prevent the effusion of blood for the future, which are the satisfactory grounds to such actions, which otherwise cannot but work remorse and regret … It was set upon some of our hearts, that a great thing should be done, not by power or might, but by the Spirit of God. And is it not so clear? … And therefore it is good that God alone have all the glory.

● **SOURCE 10.32**

From Cromwell's letter to the Speaker of the Rump Parliament, 14 October 1649, reporting on the massacre at Wexford

We intending better to this place than so great a ruin, hoping the town might be of more use to you and your army, yet God would not have it so; but, by an unexpected providence, in His righteous justice, brought a just judgement upon them, causing them to become a prey to the soldier, who in their piracies had made preys of so many families, and made with their bloods to answer the cruelties which they had exercised upon the lives of divers poor Protestants.

● **SOURCE 10.33**

From Cromwell's letter to the Governor of Ross, 19 October 1649, replying to his request that, when the town surrendered, the inhabitants should be allowed liberty of conscience

For that which you mention concerning liberty of conscience, I meddle not with any man's conscience. But if by liberty of conscience you mean a liberty to exercise the mass, I judge it best to use plain dealing, and to let you know, where the Parliament of England have power, that will not be allowed of.

● **SOURCE 10.34**

Cromwell's declaration to the Irish Catholic clergy, January 1650

traffic: *trade*

You, unprovoked, put the English to the most unheard-of and most barbarous massacre (without respect of age or sex) that ever the sun beheld. And at a time when Ireland was in perfect peace, and when, through the example of the English industry, through commerce and TRAFFIC, that which was in the natives' hands was better to them than if all Ireland had been in their possession, and not an Englishman in it. And yet, I say, was this unheard-of villainy perpetrated by your instigation, who boast of peace-making and union against this common enemy. What think you by this time, is not my assertion true? Is God, will God be, with you? I am confident He will not! … You are a part of Antichrist, whose kingdom the Scripture so expressly speaks should be laid in blood; yea in the blood of the Saints. You have shed great store of it already, and ere it be long, you must all of you have blood to drink; even the dregs of the cup of the fury and the wrath of God, which will be poured out unto you! … For those who … persist and continue in arms, they must expect what the Providence of God (in that which is falsely called the chance of war) will cast upon them.

1   What are the main points of Cromwell's justification for the massacres committed by his troops at Drogheda and Wexford in Sources 10.31–10.32?

2   What is the 'barbarous massacre' Cromwell refers to in Source 10.34?

3   In the light of their content, language and intended audience, what conclusions can you draw about Cromwell from Sources 10.33 and 10.34?

Cromwell and the Scots

In Source 10.29 Cromwell said he preferred 'a Scotch interest' to 'an Irish interest'. The letters and declarations he issued to the Scots on his military expedition to Scotland in 1650–1 give some clues that help to explain both this and why his campaigns in Scotland were not marked by the kinds of atrocities he committed in Ireland.

● **Source 10.35**

From a declaration from the New Model Army to the Scots from Newcastle, July 1650

As for the Presbyterian, or any other form of church-government, they are not by the Covenant to be imposed by force; yet we do and are ready to embrace so much as doth, or shall be made appear to us to be according to the Word of God. Are we to be dealt with as enemies, because we come not to your way? Is all religion wrapped up in that or any one form? Doth that name, or thing, give the difference between those that are members of Christ and those that are not? We think not so. We say, faith working by love is the true character of a Christian; and, God is our witness, in whomsoever we see any thing of Christ to be, there we reckon our duty to love, waiting for a more plentiful effusion of the spirit of God to make all those Christians, who, by the malice of the world are diversified ... to be of one heart and one mind, worshipping God with one consent.

● **Source 10.36**

From Cromwell's letter to the General Assembly of the Kirk of Scotland, 3 August 1650

Is it ... infallibly agreeable to the Word of God, all that you say? I beseech, in the bowels of Christ, think it possible you may be mistaken.

1   Why did Cromwell find Scottish Presbyterianism much more acceptable than Irish Catholicism?

2   What was Cromwell hoping to achieve by making these appeals to the Scots in Sources 10.35–10.36?

Cromwell and the dissolution of the Rump, 1653

Cromwell's demands for reform became more insistent as the military threat to the Republic receded after his victories in Ireland, Scotland and finally over the Scots and Charles II at Worcester on 3 September 1651. The next three sources help to explain why he became increasingly dissatisfied with the Rump Parliament, which he dissolved with the use of armed force on 20 April 1653.

● **Source 10.37**

From Cromwell's conversation with Edmund Ludlow, June 1650

He [Cromwell] professed to desire nothing more than that the government of the nation might be settled in a free and equal Commonwealth ... adding to this, that it was his intention to contribute the utmost of his endeavours to make a thorough reformation of the Clergy and Law; but, said he ... we cannot mention the reformation of the law, but they presently cry out, we design to destroy property: whereas the law, as it is now constituted, serves only to maintain the lawyers, and to encourage the rich to oppress the poor … saying farther that Ireland was as a clean paper in that particular, and capable of being governed by such laws as should be found agreeable to justice; which may be so impartially administered, as to be a good precedent even to England itself.

● **Source 10.38**

From Bulstrode Whitelocke's account of a conversation he had with Cromwell in London in November 1652

Cromwell: As for the Members of Parliament, the army begins to have a strange distaste against them, and I wish there were not too much cause for it; and really their pride, and ambition, and self-seeking … their delays of business, and designs to perpetuate themselves … these things, my Lord, do give too much ground for people to open their mouths against them, and to dislike them.

[After Whitelocke expressed the hopes that Cromwell would continue to keep the army under control and that the Rump would become decisive, Cromwell continued]

My Lord, there is little hopes of a good settlement to be made by them, really there is not; but a great deal of fear, that they will destroy again what the Lord hath done graciously for them and us; we all forget God and God will forget us, and give us up to confusion … Some course must be thought on to curb and restrain them, or we shall be ruined by them.

● **Source 10.39**

From Cromwell's speech to Barebone's Parliament, 4 July 1653

Upon our [himself and his fellow army officers'] return [from the battle at Worcester], we came … to use all fair and lawful means we could, to have had the nation to reap the fruit of all that blood and treasure that had been expended in this cause … [Under army pressure MPs] began to take the Act for the New Representative to heart … but finding plainly that the intendment of it was … to perpetuate themselves … we came to this first conclusion … that … necessity would have taught us patience; but that … we should become traitors to God and man. And when God had laid this to our hearts, and we found that the interest of the people was grown cheap … this did add more consideration to us that there was a duty incumbent upon us [i.e. to take action to dissolve the Rump].

● **Source 10.40**

From eye witness accounts of Cromwell's dissolution of the Rump Parliament, 20 April 1653

[Algernon Sidney describes the start of what happened] The Parliament sitting as usual, and being on debate upon the Bill with the amendments, which it was thought would have been passed that day, the Lord General Cromwell came into the House, clad in plain black clothes, with grey worsted stockings, and sat down as he used to in an ordinary place. After a while he rose up, put off his hat, and spake; at the first and for a good while, he spake to the commendation of the Parliament … but afterwards he changed his style …

[Bulstrode Whitelocke's account takes up the story] In a furious manner [Cromwell] bid the Speaker leave his Chair, told the House, that they had sat long enough … that some of them were Whore-masters, looking then towards Henry Marten and Sir Peter Wentworth. That others of them Drunkards, and some corrupt and unjust Men and scandalous to the PROFESSION OF THE GOSPEL, and that it was not fit they should sit as a Parliament any longer, and desired them to go away …

[Edmund Ludlow's account adds] Cromwell then said, referring to the Speaker's mace, 'What shall we do with this bauble? Here take it away.'

profession of the Gospel: what is written in the Bible

1 Compare Source 10.37 with Sources 10.17 and 10.20. Why did military victory intensify Cromwell's yearning for reform?

2 According to these sources, and material in Chapter 8, why did Cromwell dissolve the Rump?

● **Source 10.41**

A contemporary Dutch print of Cromwell's dissolution of the Rump Parliament

In what ways does the artist in Source 10.41 reveal his attitude towards the dissolution of the Rump?

Cromwell and the establishment of the Protectorate and the First Protectorate Parliament, 1653–5

The Nominated Assembly, 1653

After dissolving the Rump, Cromwell and the army officers choose 138 men 'of approved fidelity and honest' reputation to take the place of a normal elected Parliament.

They rapidly gained the nickname of Barebone's Parliament (see Chapter 9, page 154).

● **Source 10.42**

From Cromwell's speech at the opening of Barebone's Parliament, 4 July 1653

[After a very long history lesson on what had happened since 1640, 'that series of providences', and a justification for the expulsion of the Rump Parliament, Cromwell turned to his hopes for this assembly.] Truly God hath called you to this work by, I think, as wonderful providences as ever passed upon the sons of men in so short a time … I confess I never looked to see such a day as this – it may be nor you neither – when Jesus Christ shall be so owned as he is this day and in this world … I say you are called with a high call … this way may be the door to usher in things that God hath promised and prophesied of … Truly seeing these things are so, that you are at the edge of the promises and prophecies … you should be sensible of your duty … And as I have said elsewhere, if I were to choose the meanest officer in the Army or Commonwealth, I would choose a godly man that hath principles … and I would all our Magistrates were so chosen … Truly I am sorry that I have troubled you, in such a place of heat as this is, so long.

1 Why was Cromwell so enthusiastic about what Barebone's Parliament might achieve? (Use the sources in Section A of this chapter to help you with your answer.)

2 On what other occasion had Cromwell said that he preferred 'a godly man that hath principles'?

● **SOURCE 10.43**

From Cromwell's letter to
Lieutenant-General Fleetwood, 22
August 1653

Dear Charles ... Truly I never more needed all helps from my Christian friends than now! Fain would I have my service accepted of the saints (if the Lord will), but it is not so. Being of different judgements, and of each sort most seeking to propagate their own, that spirit of kindness that is to them all, is hardly accepted of any.

● **SOURCE 10.44**

From Cromwell's speech to a
parliamentary committee, 21 April
1657

[Cromwell looks back to Barebone's Parliament.] Truly I will now come and tell you a story of my own weakness and folly, and yet it was done in my simplicity ... It was thought then that men of judgement that had fought in the wars and were all of a piece upon that account, why surely these men will hit it, and these men will do to that purpose whatsoever can be desired! ... And such a company of men were chosen and did proceed into action. And truly this was the naked truth, that the issue was not answerable to the simplicity and honesty of the design ... [The result was that] sober men of that meeting ... came and returned my power as far as they could ... into my hands, professing and believing that the issue of the meeting would have been the subversion of the laws and of all the liberties of this nation, the destruction of the Ministry of this nation, in a word the confusion of all things.

> 1 What were the origins of Cromwell's complaint to Fleetwood in Source 10.43?
>
> 2 What had caused Cromwell's enthusiasm for Barebone's Parliament as seen in Source 10.42 to be replaced by the damning verdict on it in Sources 10.43 and 10.44?

The establishment of the Protectorate, December 1653

On the day after some members of Barebone's Parliament handed power back to Cromwell (12 December 1653), he received from a fellow army officer, John Lambert, a draft document which became the constitution of the Protectorate: the Instrument of Government.

> ● **The major provisions of the Instrument of Government, 1653**
>
> 1 The executive power was to be held by a Lord Protector, advised by a Council of State, both elected by Parliament.
> 2 The Protector and Council could issue ordinances when Parliament was not in session which had to be approved by Parliament later.
> 3 Single-chamber Parliaments were to meet for at least five months every three years, representing England, Ireland and Scotland.
> 4 All Christian religious views were tolerated *except* Catholicism, those which allowed Church government only by bishops, and those which encouraged people to break the peace or offend conventional morality.

The First Protectorate Parliament, 1654–5

The first Parliament under the Instrument of Government met on 4 September 1654. Parts of Cromwell's speeches to it on 4 and 12 September have already been reproduced. Cromwell's relations with Parliaments in the 1650s were to be as troubled as Charles I's with his Parliaments had been in the 1620s. So disillusioned was Cromwell with the First Protectorate Parliament that he angrily dissolved it as soon as he was legally entitled to, on 22 January 1655. Why this was so is the question you should now bear in mind.

Despite the fact that many Commonwealthsmen (supporters of the Rump, republican MPs) withdrew on 12 September 1654, refusing to sign 'the Recognition' acknowledging the legitimacy of government by Protector and Parliament, criticism of the Protector in Parliament continued.

That the providences of God are like a two-edged sword, which may be used both ways; and God in his providence, doth often permit of that which he doth not approve; and a thief make as good a title to every purse by the highways.

That if titles be measured by the sword, the Grand Turk may make a better title than any Christian Princes.

> 1   What were the major criticisms of the Protectorate and the Instrument of Government that Goddard recorded in Source 10.45?
>
> 2   Why were the Commonwealthsmen particularly hostile to the Protector?

The next source raises another reason why relations between Protector and Parliament were so troubled.

● **Source 10.46**

From Cromwell's speech dissolving the First Protectorate Parliament, 22 January 1655

If you had … made such good and wholesome provision … for the settling of such matters in religion as would have upheld and given countenance to a Godly ministry, and yet would have given a just liberty to Godly men of different judgements, though men of the same faith with them that you call the orthodox ministry in England, as is well known the Independents are, and many under the form of baptism [the Baptists], who are sound in faith, only may perhaps be different in judgement in some lesser matters, yet are true Christians … you might have … settled peace and quietness amongst all professing Godliness … Are these things done? Or anything towards them? Is there not yet upon the spirits of men a strange itch? Nothing will satisfy them, unless they can put their fingers upon their brethren's consciences, to pinch them there … What greater hypocrisy than for those who were oppressed by bishops to become the greatest oppressors themselves so soon after their yoke was removed?

> Why do you think MPs in this Parliament (like those in the Long Parliament in the 1640s and in the Rump Parliament) would have disagreed with Cromwell's willingness to tolerate Independents and Baptists? (You will find information from elsewhere in this book, e.g. Source 6.3, helpful in answering this question.)

Cromwell, 'the personal rule' and the Major-Generals

The establishment of the Major-Generals, 1655

From January 1655 until September 1656 Cromwell ruled in what has often been seen as a very authoritarian manner without calling Parliaments. His 'iron-fisted' actions in this period included his imprisonment of Cony's lawyers, mentioned by Bethel in Source 10.7.

> ● **The case of George Cony, 1654–5**
>
> In November 1654 George Cony, a London merchant, was imprisoned for refusing to pay both customs duties on silk he had imported and a fine imposed on him for preventing customs officials from seizing his property. When the case came before the Court of Upper Bench (the new name for the ancient Court of King's Bench) in early 1655, Cony's lawyers argued that the Protector had no right to collect customs duties that had not been approved by Parliament. Cromwell and the Council responded by throwing Cony's lawyers in prison, only releasing them after they had withdrawn their case.

The most famous example of Cromwell's authoritarian actions is the rule of the Major-Generals.

As you will see from the time chart at the start of this chapter, in the late summer of 1655 Cromwell divided England and Wales into eleven regions, each of which was to be governed by a Major-General. The rule of the Major-Generals lasted only about a year and was formally abandoned early in 1657. One of their main functions was to organise new local militias that were to be funded by a new tax (nicknamed the 'decimation tax') to be paid by all those who had fought for the King in the Civil War. But, as you will see from Sources 10.47 and 10.48 (and also Source 11.1), Cromwell hoped that the Major-Generals would achieve much more than safeguarding the regime from its enemies.

● **FIGURE 10.1**

Map of Major-Generals' rule and Royalist risings, 1655

● **SOURCE 10.47**

From Cromwell's speech to the Lord Mayor and Corporation of the City of London, 5 March 1657

The sole end of this way of procedure [the Major-Generals] was the security of the peace of the nation, the suppressing of vice and encouragement of virtue, the very end of magistracy.

● SOURCE 10.48

From Cromwell's speech to the Second Protectorate Parliament, 17 September 1656

When we found that the Cavaliers would not be quiet … truly when this insurrection [Penruddock's Rising, March 1655] was … there was a little thing invented, which was the erecting of the Major-Generals, to have a little inspection upon the people, thus divided, thus discontented, thus dissatisfied in divers interests by the Popish party … Truly, if ever I think anything were honest, this was, as anything that ever I knew … And truly if any man be angry at it, I am plain and shall use a homely expression, let him turn the buckle of his girdle behind him. If this were to be done again, I would do it! How the Major-Generals have behaved themselves in that work! … They are men as to their persons of known integrity and fidelity, and men that have freely adventured their blood and lives for that good cause … And truly England doth yet receive one day more of lengthening out its tranquillity by that occasion and action … It hath been more effectual towards the discountenancing of vice and settling religion, than anything done these fifty years. I will abide it, notwithstanding the envy and slander of foolish men, but I say that hath been a justifiable design. I confess I speak that to you with a little vehemency … If you make laws of good government, that men may know how to obey and do, for government; you may make laws that have frailty and weakness, aye, and good laws that may be observed. But if nothing should be done but what is according to law, the throat of a nation may be cut, till we send for some to make a law.

---

1 Explain what Cromwell meant by the two goals he set the Major-Generals. (It will help you to do this if you refer to the official instructions given to the Major-Generals in Chapter 11, Source 11.19.)

2 Why did Cromwell decide to appoint eleven Major-Generals in 1655 to supervise government in Wales and the English localities?

3 Why do you think the Major-Generals were so unpopular with MPs?

The Vaudois Massacre, 1655

Early in May 1655, news reached London of a massacre of 200–300 Protestants, known as the Vaudois, who lived in the isolated Alpine valleys in Piedmont in northern Italy, by the troops of their Roman Catholic overlord, the Duke of Savoy. Sources 10.49–10.51 refer to that event.

● SOURCE 10.49

From John Milton's poem *On the Late Massacre in Piedmont*

Babylonian woe: *this refers to the captivity of the Jews by Nebuchadnezzar in Babylon in the sixth century* BC.

Avenge, O Lord, thy slaughter'd saints, whose bones
Lie scatter'd on the Alpine mountains cold;
Ev'n them who kept Thy truth so pure of old,
When all our fathers worshipp'd stocks and stones,
Forget not; in Thy Book, record their groans
Who were Thy sheep, and in their ancient fold
Slain by the bloody Piedmontese, that roll'd
Mother with infant down the rocks, and they
To Heav'n. Their martyr'd blood and ashes sow
O'er all th' Italian fields, where still doth sway
The triple Tyrant; that from these may grow
A Hundredfold, who, having learn'd Thy way
Early may fly the BABYLONIAN WOE.

● SOURCE 10.50

From a summary of a letter from a pastor and divinity reader at Geneva to another godly minister, 6 June 1655, filed in the state papers of Cromwell's secretary of state, giving news of the Vaudois massacre

Besides the cruelty you have heard formerly, I have been lately informed by those that saw it, that those massacrers have ripped the bellies of women in child, and took the infants upon the point of their halberds [combined spears and battle-axes]; and that they have nailed divers persons upon the branches of trees, and so made them cruelly die. They have carried away a great number of children, whom they have sacrificed to the idol. They do torment the prisoners in a strange manner, to force them to change their religion; and if they refuse it, they put them to death in the prison, where they have strangled many, or make them languish and linger starving them, and giving them but four ounces of bread and a little water.

SOURCE 10.51

From an undated letter from
Charles Fleetwood and other
officers in Ireland to Cromwell

We thought it our duty to inform Your Highness, how deeply sensible we are of the sad
condition of the servants of the Lord in Piedmont … upon the informations, that have
hitherto come to us. Sad tidings are these … Who knoweth whether the Lord hath not
intrusted and exalted you, for such a time as this? We do not the least distrust of your
tenderness towards them, sense of their sufferings, readiness to manifest both, as the
providence of the Lord shall call; but desire to strengthen your hand in that good work of God,
and continue your prayers at the throne of grace for them … Let the blood of Ireland be fresh
in your view and their treachery cry aloud in your ears, that the frequent solicitation,
wherewith you are encompassed, may not slack your hand … That the Lord may direct you,
and make you a polished shaft in his quiver, to wound to the heart cruel and proud oppressors,
is the prayer of

Your Highness's humble servants.

I   Why did the Vaudois massacre have such an impact in England? Explain, in particular, the reference
in Source 10.51 to 'the blood of Ireland' (refer back to page 48).

2   Why do you think that this event might have contributed to Cromwell's urgency in pushing
through a programme of moral reform by authoritarian means?

The Western Design, 1654–5

Just as Cromwell and the Council were considering the orders to be given to the Major-
Generals, news came in of another overseas disaster, the failure of the Western Design, a
combined English naval–military expedition to attack Spanish possessions in the Caribbean. In
April it suffered a humiliating defeat at San Domingo, Hispaniola. It took weeks for the news
to reach London, but when it did Cromwell shut himself in a room for a day and, later, the
commanders of the expedition were thrown in the Tower. Read the following sources, asking
yourself why the failure of the Western Design had such a traumatic impact on Cromwell.

SOURCE 10.52

Notes on a debate in the Council of
State, 20 July 1654, about whether
or not to embark on the Western
Design

superfluity: *sufficient*

Cromwell:
We consider this attempt, because we think God has not brought us hither where we are but to
consider the work that we may do in the world as well as at home, and to stay from attempting
until you have SUPERFLUITY is to put it off for ever, our expenses being such as in all probability
never admit that. Now Providence seems to lead us hither, having 160 ships swimming
[Cromwell is referring to the ships that were unemployed after the end of the Dutch War].

SOURCE 10.53

From Cromwell's letters to two
officers in the Caribbean after the
failure of the Western Design,
October 1655

To Major-General Richard Fortescue in Jamaica:
Sir, You will herewith receive Instructions for the better carrying-on of your business, which is
not of small account here, although our discouragements have been many; for which we desire
to humble ourselves before the Lord, who hath very sorely chastened us … As we have cause
to be humbled for the reproof God gave us at St. Domingo, upon the account of our own sins
as well as others', so, truly, upon the report brought hither to us of the extreme avarice, pride,
and confidence, disorders and debauchedness, profaneness and wickedness, commonly
practised in that Army, we … desire … that a very special regard may be had … as that all
manner of vice may be thoroughly discountenanced, and severely punished; and that such a
frame of government may be exercised that virtue and godliness may receive due
encouragement.

To Vice-Admiral William Goodson in Jamaica:
It is not to be denied but the Lord hath greatly humbled us in that sad loss sustained at
Hispaniola; no doubt but we have provoked the Lord, and it is good for us to know so, and to
be abased for the same … Let the reproach and shame that hath been for our sins, and through
(also may we say) the misguidance of some, work up your hearts to a confidence in the Lord …
And though He hath torn us, yet He will heal us.

1   Why was Cromwell so devastated (as is seen in Source 10.53) at the failure of the expedition? Read Sources 10.18 and 10.19 again. This will help you answer this question.

2   What was the lesson that Cromwell drew from the disaster?

Cromwell, the Second Protectorate Parliament and the offer of the Crown, 1656–8

The opening of the Second Protectorate Parliament, 1656

In the late summer of 1656 Cromwell was forced to recall Parliament to provide the money to pay for the war with Spain. Like the first Parliament, the Second Protectorate Parliament ended in conflict. It began fairly harmoniously, however, no doubt because about 100 Commonwealthsmen had been excluded from sitting. What helped also was the fact that most MPs probably shared the sentiments expressed in Cromwell's opening speech.

● **SOURCE 10.54**

From Cromwell's speech to the Second Protectorate Parliament, 17 September 1656

Spaniolised: *supporters of Catholic Spain*

Truly, your great enemy is the Spaniard … He is a natural enemy … As your danger is from the common enemy abroad, who is the head of the Papal interest, the head of that anti-Christian interest, that is so described in Scripture … upon this account you have the quarrel with the Spaniard. And truly he hath an interest in your bowels, he hath so. The Papists in England they have been accounted, ever since I was born, SPANIOLISED … They will not … admit it to be unworthy, un-Christian, un-English-like. Therefore I say it doth serve to let you see your danger.

Nayler's case, 1656

Cromwell's relations with Parliament soon deteriorated, however, because of the case of James Nayler, a Quaker who had re-enacted Christ's entry into Jerusalem in Bristol. For this 'crime' Nayler was arrested by magistrates in the West Country and brought to Parliament for trial.

● **SOURCE 10.55**

A report of the parliamentary debates on James Nayler's case, December 1656, from the parliamentary diary of Thomas Burton

mosaic law: *the law of Moses*

intestine: *internal*

The articles against him [Nayler] read, and summed thus – That he assumed the gesture, words, names and attributes of our Saviour Christ.

Major-General Philip Skippon:
I do not marvel at this silence. Every man is astonished to hear this report. I am glad it is come hither; I hope it will mind you to look about you now … It has always been my opinion, that the growth of these things is more dangerous than the most INTESTINE of foreign enemies. I have often been troubled in my thoughts to think of this toleration; I think I may call it so. Their growth and increase [i.e. of the Quakers] is too notorious, both in England and Ireland; their principles strike at both ministry and magistracy … This offence is so high a blasphemy, that it ought not to be passed.

Major-General William Boteler:
The punishment ought to be adequate to the offence. By the MOSAIC LAW, blasphemers were to be stoned to death.

[6 December 1656]
Skippon:
I heard the supreme magistrate [Cromwell] say, It was never his intention to indulge these things; yet we see the issue of this liberty of conscience … If this be liberty, God deliver me from such liberty.

[8 December 1656]
Henry Lawrence, Lord President of the Council of State:
If you hang every man that says, 'Christ is in you the hope of glory', you will hang a good many.

Dr Thomas Clarges:
In my opinion James Nayler is guilty of horrid blasphemy … I shall speak no more; but let us all stop our ears, and stone him.

On 16 December 1656 a proposal to bring in a Bill to punish Nayler by death was defeated by 96 to 82 votes; instead it was resolved that Nayler should be put in the pillory at Westminster and the City and whipped by the common hangman between the two places. In the City his tongue was to be bored with a hot iron and his forehead branded with the letter B (for blasphemer). He was then to be taken to Bristol and paraded through the city riding bare-back backwards on a horse, before being publicly whipped. He was then to be imprisoned for an indefinite time in the Bridewell, London, on a regime of hard labour.

These punishments were carried out in January 1657.

Why was Nayler so detested by many MPs that arguments like those put by Lawrence went unheeded? (Refer to Chapter 12 when answering this.)

Cromwell's reactions are reflected in the next two sources.

● SOURCE 10.56

From Cromwell's letter to the Speaker of the Commons, 25 December 1656

Having taken notice of a judgement lately given by yourselves against James Nayler; although We detest and abhor the giving or occasioning the least countenance to persons of such opinions and practices, or who are under the guilt of such crimes as are commonly imputed to the said person, yet We … not knowing how far such proceedings (wholly without us) may proceed in the consequence of it, do desire that the House will let Us know the grounds and reasons whereupon they have proceeded.

● SOURCE 10.57

From Cromwell's speech to army officers, 27 February 1657

It is time to come to a settlement, and lay aside arbitrary proceedings so unacceptable to the nation. And by the proceedings of this Parliament you see they stand in need of a check or balancing power, [Meaning the House of Lords, or a house so constituted] for the case of James Nayler might happen to be your case. By their judicial power they fall upon life and member, and doth the Instrument [of Government] in being enable me to control it?

1   What light does Source 10.56 throw on Cromwell's belief in religious liberty?

2   Why did the Nayler Case convince Cromwell that the Instrument of Government must be abandoned?

The Humble Petition and Advice, and the offer of the Crown

In March 1657 Parliament presented Cromwell with a proposed new constitution, the Humble Petition and Advice. (It was at this time that the hostility to the Major-Generals led to Cromwell's decision to abandon them.)

● The main ways in which the Humble Petition and Advice differed from the Instrument of Government

1   It proposed that Cromwell be King not Lord Protector.

2   He was to be advised by a Privy Council not a Council of State.

3   Parliaments were to meet regularly as before but were now to consist of two chambers, including 'the Other House' of 40–70 men appointed by Cromwell and approved by the Commons. Purges of the lower house were to be banned.

4   The only difference in its religious provisions was the addition of penalties for blasphemy.

Cromwell's reaction to the Humble Petition and Advice is reflected in the next sources.

● **SOURCE 10.58**

From Cromwell's speech to a parliamentary committee on the Humble Petition and Advice, 21 April 1657

I think you have provided for the liberty of the people of God and of the nation; and I say, he sings sweetly that sings a song of reconciliation betwixt these two interests, and it is a pitiful fancy, and wild and ignorant, to think they are inconsistent. They may consist, and … I think in this government [constitution] you have made them to consist.

● **SOURCE 10.59**

From Cromwell's speech to a parliamentary committee, 13 April 1657

Jericho: the first Canaanite city taken and destroyed by the Israelites before their eventual capture of Jerusalem. (For the significance of this to Cromwell, see Sources 10.25–10.26.)

I have had a great deal of experience of providence … Truly the providence of God has laid the title [of king] aside providentially … And God has seemed providentially not only to strike at the family [the Stuarts] but at the name … He hath not only dealt with the persons and the family, but he hath blasted the title … And you know … I can see no conclusion but this … I would not seek to set up that which providence hath destroyed and laid in the dust, and I would not build JERICHO again … It is that which hath an awe upon my spirit.

● **SOURCE 10.60**

From Edmund Ludlow's account of Cromwell's refusal of the title of king. Ludlow believed that Cromwell had decided to accept the title and had called MPs to meet him to tell them so. He thought that the following episode caused Cromwell to change his mind.

Meeting with Col. Desborough in the great walk of the park, and acquainting him with his resolution [to accept the Crown], the Colonel made answer, that he then gave the cause and Cromwell's family also for lost; adding that although he was resolved never to act against him, yet he would not act for him after that time. So after some other discourse upon the same subject, Desborough went home, and there found Col. Pride … and having imparted to him the design of Cromwell to accept the crown, Pride answered, 'he shall not'. 'Why,' said the Colonel, 'how wilt thou hinder it?' To which Pride replied, 'Get me a petition drawn, and I will prevent it.'

> To what extent was Cromwell justified in asserting that the Humble Petition and Advice had reconciled his two main 'interests'?

● **SOURCE 10.61**

From Christopher Hill's pamphlet *Oliver Cromwell* (1984)

A first attempt was made in 1657 to restore the parliamentary constitution as it would have existed after 1642 if Charles I had been prepared honestly to accept it. The Humble Petition and Advice subordinated Council and armed forces to Parliament; taxation was to be reduced to a stated maximum. Which precluded a large Army … Something as like the old House of Lords as possible was to be revived; Oliver was offered the crown. This was too much for the generals. They blackmailed Oliver by threatening military revolt if he accepted the crown.

● **SOURCE 10.62**

From Peter Gaunt, *Oliver Cromwell* (1996), pp. 196–9

Cromwell does not come across as a man who stood in fear of army mutiny … Another factor may have played a part in Cromwell's eventual refusal of the crown … he may have been uncomfortably aware that it would be seen as another sign of personal advancement … He may have feared that, in accepting the crown, he would be falling into the mire of personal advancement and that, far from doing God's work, he would lose the Lord's favour.

> 1 Use the information in Sources 10.58–10.62 (together with information from your further reading) to make two lists of reasons that might have made Cromwell want/not want to become king. What do you think was the decisive factor which finally persuaded Cromwell to turn down the chance to become King Oliver I?
>
> 2 Write an essay to answer this question: Why did Cromwell refuse the offer of the Crown?

The closure of the Second Protectorate Parliament, 1658

Cromwell accepted all the other parts of the new constitution and was reinaugurated as Protector in a lavish, regal-looking ceremony in June 1657. This did not improve his relations with Parliament. When it reassembled for a second session early in 1658, Cromwell dissolved it. He came under severe attack not only from the Commonwealthsmen, who were now allowed to sit, but also from elements in the army, no doubt angry at the fact that Cromwell had accepted a more civilian-looking constitution. His dissolution speech contains a note of weariness as well as of anger.

● SOURCE 10.63

From Cromwell's speech dissolving the Second Protectorate Parliament, 4 February 1658

No man, but a man mistaken … could think that I, that hath a burden upon my back for the space of fifteen or sixteen years … would seek such a place as I bear. I can say in the presence of God … that I would have been glad … to have been living under a woodside to have kept a flock of sheep, rather than to have undertaken such a place as this was … I did look that you, that did offer it unto me, should have made it good … Upon such terms really I took it, and I am failed in these terms.

Cromwell only lived for a few more months. He died on 3 September 1658, the anniversary of two of his most sensational military victories at Dunbar (1650) and Worcester (1651). His last months of life were filled with personal tragedies (his health deteriorated badly and his favourite daughter, Elizabeth, died of cancer in August) and his political troubles remained. Did this mean that he died a broken man, worn out by the heavy burdens he carried as Protector? This is another of the many fascinating questions about Cromwell to which it is impossible to give a 'correct' answer. The answer to it depends very much on your approach to the important question that is at the heart of the following task: how sincere were Cromwell's hopes of bringing about a godly reformation in Britain?

● **Summary Task**

1 **For class debate**
   Ever since Cromwell's own day, people have disagreed heatedly about whether Cromwell was a hypocrite or a man motivated by religious principles. There is plenty of scope for a classroom debate. Begin with two students putting the case for Cromwell as:

   a) a self-seeking, ambitious, unprincipled politician
   b) a man with deeply held principles.

2 Write an essay to answer the following question: Religious aspirations were far more important to Cromwell than any other aims during his military and political career. To what extent do you agree with this statement?

● **Further reading**

There are three good introductory books to the 1650s: T. Barnard, *The English Republic* (Longman Seminar Series, 1982); A. Woolrych, *England Without a King* (Lancaster Pamphlets, 1983) and Ronald Hutton, *The British Republic 1649–60* (Macmillan, 1990). I. Roots, *The Great Rebellion 1640–60* (Batsford, 1966 and reprinted many times) is more detailed.

Much has been written on Cromwell. The most readable biographies are by Antonia Fraser, *Cromwell Our Chief of Men* (Weidenfeld and Nicolson, 1973) and Christopher Hill, *God's Englishman* (Penguin, 1970).

The following four books reflect recent historical research on Cromwell and the Protectorate: Barry Coward, *Oliver Cromwell* (Longman Profiles in Power, 1991); D. Smith, *Oliver Cromwell: Politics and Religion in the English Revolution 1640–58* (CUP, 1991); John Morrill (ed.), *Oliver Cromwell and the English Revolution* (Longman, 1990); Peter Gaunt, *Oliver Cromwell* (Blackwell, 1996).

Why did the Puritans want to change the behaviour of the English people and why did their attempt fail?

1642
February: The Long Parliament announces the first of the monthly days of public fasting and humiliation.
September: The Long Parliament closes London theatres.

1644
April: The Long Parliament passes legislation aimed at the better observance of Sundays and the outlawing of the celebration of May Day.

1645
January: The Presbyterian Directory for Public Worship is published.

1647
June: The Long Parliament passes legislation outlawing the celebration of the major Christian festivals, including Christmas, Easter and Whitsun, and institutes a non-religious holiday on the second Tuesday of every month.

1649
February: The last of the monthly days of fasting and humiliation is announced.

1650
April: The Rump Parliament passes legislation aimed at the better observance of Sundays.
May: The Rump Parliament passes legislation making adultery punishable by death and fornication by three months' imprisonment.
June: The Rump Parliament passes legislation to punish anyone caught swearing.

1653
August: Barebone's Parliament passes legislation banning weddings in church.

1655
October: Cromwell instructs his Major-Generals to encourage and promote godliness in the English counties.

1657
June: The Second Protectorate Parliament passes legislation aimed at the better observance of Sundays.
April: The Second Protectorate Parliament reinstates church weddings.
June: The Second Protectorate Parliament passes legislation banning betting and music in taverns and alehouses.

● Who were the Puritans?

As you have seen in Chapter 1, Puritans were religious reformers who emerged in England shortly after the formation of the Church of England in 1559. They wished to see the Church founded by Elizabeth I reformed in a number of important ways. Puritans believed that the Bible was the only source of religious truth and they led their lives in strict obedience to its teachings. They were not prepared to accept any religious practice which was not approved by the Bible. They were very keen on the preaching of the Word of God and wanted to attend sermons as often as they could. In particular, they believed that Sunday should be given over entirely to religious worship. They objected to many of the religious services laid down in the Elizabethan Book of Common Prayer on the grounds that they were too close to the ceremonies of the Roman Catholic Church, and they preferred plain and undecorated church interiors. Believing that human nature was essentially corrupt and that individuals could very easily become sinners, they were very anxious to control their own behaviour, and wherever they gained any political influence they attempted to enforce their strict moral code upon other people, denouncing and prohibiting all dancing, excessive drinking, unruly sports and sexual immorality. Before 1640 they had become very influential in a number of English towns, especially Dorchester, Banbury and Colchester. As a result of Parliament's victory in the Civil War, they gained control of the whole country and set about imposing their beliefs upon the English people.

Introduction

One of the most important characteristics of the period 1646–60 was that it was a period of Puritan rule. Oliver Cromwell and his closest colleagues in government were all strong supporters of the programme of religious reform which the Puritans had campaigned for since the Elizabethan religious settlement of 1559. Nothing was more important to them than furthering the cause of 'true religion'. Between 1646 and 1660 they spared no pains in an attempt to eradicate the traditional culture of the English people and replace it with their own very different godly culture. This attempted 'cultural revolution' was directed in particular at three aspects of social life, each of which will be considered separately below:

- Section A The traditional festive calendar
- Section B Baptism, marriage and burial: how were they changed?
- Section C How did the Puritans try to improve moral behaviour?

Finally, in Section D, we will examine the reaction of the people to these changes and consider why this attempted revolution failed.

Section A The traditional festive calendar

In the century before the Civil War, Puritans had consistently attacked the traditional celebrations that marked the main festivals of the Christian year, such as Christmas and Easter. Following their victory against Charles I, England's new Puritan rulers in Parliament lost no time, passing in June 1647 an ordinance that was supposed to sweep away these centuries-old festivities.

188

Why did the Puritans want to change the behaviour of the English people and why did their attempt fail?

● **Source 11.1**

The illustration from the title page of a pamphlet supporting the celebration of Christmas, first published in 1652

● **Source 11.2**

An ordinance for Abolishing Festivals, June 1647

approbation: *approval*

Forasmuch as the Feasts of the Nativity of Christ, Easter and Whitsuntide, and other Festivals commonly called Holy-Days have been heretofore superstitiously used and observed, be it ordained by the Lords and Commons in Parliament assembled that the said feast of the Nativity of Christ, Easter and Whitsuntide and all other festival days, commonly called Holy-days be no longer observed as festivals or holy-days within the kingdom of England and dominion of Wales … And to the end that there may be a convenient time allotted to scholars, apprentices and other servants for their recreation, be it ordained by the authority aforesaid that all scholars, apprentices and other servants shall, with the leave and APPROBATION of their masters respectively first had and obtained, have such convenient reasonable recreation and relaxation from their constant and ordinary labours on every second Tuesday in the month throughout the year, as formerly they used to have on such aforesaid festivals commonly called Holy-days. And that masters of all scholars, apprentices and servants shall grant unto them respectively such time for their recreations on the aforesaid second Tuesdays in every month as they may conveniently spare from their extraordinary and necessary services and occasions …

The reasons why Puritans wished to abolish the important feast of Christmas were outlined in a number of pamphlets which appeared after the end of the Civil War.

● **Source 11.3**

In his *Certain Queries Touching the Rise and Observation of Christmas,* published in 1648, Joseph Hemming, a Puritan minister from Staffordshire, presented the case against Christmas in a series of questions addressed to those who favoured its celebration.

apostolical practice: *the practice of the earliest followers of Christ (the Apostles)*

Lord's Day: *Sunday*

vocations: *jobs*

warranted: *authorised*

Whether such religious customs that are binding to all the churches of Jesus Christ ought not to have sure footing upon the Word of God or APOSTOLICAL PRACTICE.

Whether you can substantially prove that Christ was born on 25th December and what your proofs are.

Whether celebration of that day … can be clearly WARRANTED by you from Scripture and what your Scriptures are.

Whether you can clear it by sound consequence from the New Testament …

Whether in the case it can be evidenced by none of these … it be not a mere human invention …

Whether the saints are bound to rejoice in the birth of Christ on that day men superstitiously call Christmas more than at other times. And whether the LORD'S DAY be not [the] day appointed for them to rejoice on.

Whether Christmas day ought in any respect to be esteemed above another of the weekdays. And whether people may not without offence to God follow their lawful VOCATIONS on that day.

Whether (since most men and women in England do blindly and superstitiously believe Christ was born on that day) preaching on it doth not nourish and strengthen them in that belief.

Whether this feast had not its rise and growth from Christians' conformity to the mad feast Saturnalia (kept in December to Saturn the Father of Roman Gods) in which there was a sheaf offered to Ceres, Goddess of Corn … And whether those Christians by name to cloak it did not afterwards call it Yule … And whether it be not yet by some … called Yule and the mad plays or sports (wherewith 'tis celebrated like those Saturnalia) Yule games …

Whether conformity to, and retention of heathenish customs be commendable in Christians, suitable or agreeable with gospel principles …

Whether in case you return no answer to these queries, I have not ground sufficient to conclude you utterly unable to give any rational account of your practice …

● **SOURCE 11.4**

Two years later, in 1650, Thomas Mocket, the Puritan rector of Gilston in Hertfordshire, put forward similar arguments in his *Christmas, the Christians' Grand Feast.*

in room of: *in place of*

interludes, masques, mummeries: *light dramatic entertainments*

Saturn's idolatrous riotous feast: *the Roman feast of Saturnalia*

solemnised: *celebrated*

… we must know also that heathenish idolatrous holy days were turned into Christian as Christ's nativity was appointed to be kept and hath long been generally observed on the very time and day when SATURN'S IDOLATROUS RIOTOUS FEAST was SOLEMNISED and IN ROOM OF and imitation thereof and therefore that time was anciently called Yule as the heathens called it and mad, riotous, profane plays and sports [were held] in Christmas time [and] Yule games and Christmas carols sung in praise of Christ as the heathens did the hymn in honour of the idol Ceres … [and] all the heathenish customs and pagan rites and ceremonies that the idolatrous heathens used, as riotous drinking, health drinking, gluttony, luxury, wantonness, dancing, dicing, stage plays, INTERLUDES, MASQUES, MUMMERIES, with all other pagan sports and practices [were brought] into the Church of God.

1 For what reasons did Puritans object to the celebration of Christmas?

2 What can we learn about the religious beliefs of Puritans from these extracts?

● **SOURCE 11.5**

To replace the old religious calendar, Parliament introduced several new holidays. The ordinance of June 1647, which abolished the old feasts, established a new holiday for scholars, apprentices and servants on the second Tuesday of every month. Several weeks later, Parliament passed another ordinance to regulate this holiday.

bailiffs: *officers*

detriment: *disadvantage*

headboroughs: *minor local officials*

… And lest such days of Recreation might be abused to the dishonour of God, scandal to religion and DETRIMENT both of masters and servants … be it likewise provided and ordained that if any such apprentice or other servant shall riotously spend or abuse such days of Recreation, either to his own hurt or the damage of his master, and being therefore lawfully convicted and found guilty before any one Justice of the Peace, it shall and may be lawful for such master at his pleasure to detain and withhold such apprentices or other servants from their recreation on such allowed days …

And it is lastly ordained that all mayors, sheriffs, BAILIFFS, constables, HEADBOROUGHS and all other officers and ministers are hereby authorised to make or cause to be made diligent searches for such apprentices or other servants in taverns, alehouses and gaming houses, and such apprentices or other servants as shall be found in any such place after eight of the clock in the evening, or being drunk or otherwise disorderly, or shall there remain after eight of the clock in the evening on such days of Recreation, [the officers] shall bring or cause to be brought such apprentices or other servants before any Justice of the Peace in the county, city or Town …, or before the said Chamberlain of London … who shall cause the statutes to be executed upon them that are in such cases provided for the punishment of offenders.

Another entirely new Puritan holiday was the regular public fast-day, or day of 'fasting and humiliation', that, throughout the period from 1642 to 1649, was held on the last Wednesday of every month. English Puritans had been committed to the practice of communal public fasting for many years, and success in the Civil War had now given them the chance to impose it on the whole nation. Although the regular monthly day was abandoned shortly after Charles I's execution, additional, occasional fast-days continued to be called throughout the 1650s.

● SOURCE 11.6

In 1645, detailed directions for the observing of these days were included in the Directory for Public Worship, the document which outlined the prayers and services of the new Presbyterian English Church which Parliament intended to establish throughout the country.

admonish: *warn*

importunity: *persistence*

lascivious: *lustful*

premeditation: *thought*

Days of Fasting and Humiliation

A religious fast requires total abstinence not only from all food … but also from all worldly labours, discourses and thoughts … and from all bodily delights … rich apparel, ornaments and such like during the fast; and much more from whatever is in the nature or use scandalous and offensive, as garish attire, LASCIVIOUS habits and gestures and other vanities of either sex …

Before the public meeting, each family and person apart are privately to use all religious care to prepare their hearts to such a solemn work; and so be early at the congregation.

So large a portion of the day as conveniently may be is to be spent in public reading and preaching of the Word with singing of psalms fit to quicken affections suitable to such a duty, but especially in prayer … In all these the ministers who are the mouths of the people unto God ought so to speak from their hearts upon serious and thorough PREMEDITATION of them, that both themselves and the people may be much affected and even melted thereby, especially with sorrow for sins, that it may indeed be a day of deep humiliation and afflicting the soul …

Before the close of public duties the minister is in his own and the people's names to engage his and their hearts to be the Lord's, with professed purpose and resolution to reform whatever is amiss among them, and more particularly such sins as they have been more remarkably guilty of, and to draw nearer unto God and to walk more closely and faithfully with him …

He is also to ADMONISH the people with all IMPORTUNITY that the work of the day doth not end with the public duties of it, but they are so to improve the remainder of the day and of their whole life in re-inforcing upon themselves and their families in private all those godly affections and resolutions which they professed in public.

● SOURCE 11.7

A variant of these days of fasting and humiliation was the public days of thanksgiving which were called from time to time, usually after some notable Parliamentary success.

carnal: *of the body, worldly*

dismission: *dismissal*

exhortation: *encouragement*

repast: *food*

testifications: *declarations*

Days of Public Thanksgiving

The day being come [and] the congregation (after private preparation) being assembled, the minister is to begin with a word of EXHORTATION to stir up the people to the duty for which they are met and with a short prayer for God's assistance and blessing … according to the particular occasion of their meeting.

Let him then make some pithy narration of the deliverance obtained or mercy received or of whatsoever hath occasioned that assembly of the congregation, that all may better understand it, or be minded of it and more affected with it.

And because the singing of psalms is … most proper … for the expressing of joy and thanksgiving, let some pertinent psalm or psalms be sung for that purpose before or after the reading of some portion of the Word suitable to the present business.

Then let the minister who is to preach proceed to further exhortation and prayer before his sermon with special reference to the present work, after which let him preach upon some text of scripture pertinent to the occasion.

The sermon ended … let him dismiss the congregation with a blessing that they may have some convenient time for REPAST and refreshing.

But the minister (before their DISMISSION) is solemnly to admonish them to beware of all excess and riot, tending to gluttony or drunkenness … and to take care that their rejoicing be not CARNAL but spiritual, which may make God's praise to be glorious and themselves humble and sober, and that both the feeding and rejoicing may render them more cheerful and enlarged further to celebrate his praises in the midst of the congregation when they return unto it in the remaining part of the day.

When the congregation shall be again assembled, the like course in praying, reading, preaching, singing of psalms and offering up of more praise and thanksgiving that is before directed for the morning is to be renewed and continued … And the people are to be exhorted at the end of the latter meeting to spend the residue of the day in holy duties and TESTIFICATIONS of Christian love and charity one towards another and of rejoicing more in the Lord.

Unlike the second Tuesday and last Wednesday of the month, the regular Sunday break from work was not a new addition to the calendar, but the way it was observed after the Puritan take-over was very different than in the pre-war period.

● **SOURCE 11.8**

Instructions for the observance of the Sunday break were also included in the Directory for Public Worship.

catechising: *instructing by means of question and answer*

impediments: *obstacles*

piety: *holiness*

requisite: *necessary*

sanctification: *keeping holy*

The Lord's Day ought to be so remembered beforehand, as that all worldly business of our ordinary callings may be so ordered, and as timely and seasonably laid aside as they may not be IMPEDIMENTS to the due sanctifying of the day when it comes.

The whole day is to be celebrated as holy to the Lord, both in public and private, as being the Christian sabbath. To which end it is REQUISITE that there be a holy cessation or resting all the day from all unnecessary labours, and an abstaining not only from all sports and pastimes, but also from all worldly words and thoughts.

That the diet on the day be so ordered as that neither servants be unnecessarily detained from public worship, nor any other person hindered from the SANCTIFICATION of that day.

That there be private preparation of every person and family by prayer, for themselves, and for God's assistance of the minister, and for a blessing upon his ministry, and by such other holy exercises as may further dispose them to a more comfortable communion with God in his public ordinance.

That all the people meet so timely for public worship that the whole congregation may be present at the beginning, and with one heart solemnly join together in all parts of the public worship; and not depart till after the blessing.

That what time is vacant between or after the solemn meetings of the congregation in public, be spent in reading, meditation, repetition of sermons (especially by calling their families to an account of what they have heard) and CATECHISING of them, holy conferences, prayers for a blessing upon the public ordinance, singing of psalms, visiting the sick, relieving the poor, and such like duties of PIETY and charity and mercy accounting the sabbath a delight.

● **SOURCE 11.9**

In 1650 the Rump Parliament decided to pass legislation to tighten up on the way in which Sundays and fast-days were observed.

drover: *someone who drives herds of animals to market*

tippling: *drinking*

victualling-house: *shop selling food*

No traveller, waggoner, butcher, DROVER … shall travel or come into his or their inn or lodging after twelve of the clock on any Saturday night, nor shall any person travel from his house, inn or other place till after one o'clock on Monday morning without good or urgent cause …

And it is further enacted and declared that every person and persons which upon the said Lord's Day, days of humiliation and thanksgiving shall be in any tavern, inn, alehouse, tobacco-house or shop, or VICTUALLING-HOUSE … and every person or persons which upon the said days shall be dancing, profanely singing, drinking or TIPPLING in any tavern, inn, alehouse, victualling house or tobacco-house or shop, or shall harbour or entertain any person or persons so offending; or which shall grind or cause to be ground in any mill, any corn or grain upon any the said days … every such offender shall forfeit and pay the sum of 10 shillings for every offence …

1 What sort of holiday activities were the Puritans who drew up these regulations trying to stop?

2 How were the new Puritan holidays meant to be spent?

3 What was the purpose of the monthly days of fasting and humiliation?

4 What activities were specifically banned on Sundays and fast-days?

5 How were the population expected to spend Sundays?

6 What further questions would you want to ask about the legislation contained in these sources?

Section B Baptism, marriage and burial: how were they changed?

English Puritans had long objected to many of the features of the 1559 Book of Common Prayer, which contained the procedures of all the most important ceremonies of the Church established by Elizabeth I. They particularly resented those Prayer-Book services which marked important stages in the life cycle, in particular baptism, marriage and burial. When they came to power in the 1640s they set about removing them and introducing their own simplified services to mark these important events.

> The traditional Book of Common Prayer ceremonies and their replacements in the Directory for Public Worship, 1645, are given below. Read them and identify the main differences between them.

Baptism

● SOURCE 11.10

From the Book of Common Prayer

The people are to be ADMONISHED that it is most convenient that baptism should not be administered but upon Sundays and holy days …

And note that there shall be for every male child to be baptised two godfathers and one godmother and for every female child one godfather and two godmothers.

When there are children to be baptised the parents shall give knowledge thereof over night or in the morning before morning prayer to the CURATE. And then the godfathers and godmothers and the people with the child must be ready at the FONT … and the priest coming to the font … shall take the child in his hands and shall say to the godfathers and godmothers, 'Name this child'. And then naming it after them (if they shall certify him that the child may well endure it) he shall dip it in the water discreetly and warily, saying, 'N, I baptise thee in the name of the Father, and of the Son, and of the Holy Ghost, Amen' …

Then the priest shall say, 'We receive this child into the congregation of Christ's flock and do sign him with the sign of the cross in token hereafter he shall not be ashamed to confess the faith of Christ crucified.'

> **admonished:** *instructed*
>
> **curate:** *assistant priest*
>
> **font:** *large receptacle usually at the back of the church which holds the water used for baptism*

● SOURCE 11.11

From the Directory for Public Worship

Baptism as it is not unnecessarily to be delayed so it is not to be administered in any case by any private person but by a minister of Christ … Nor is it to be administered in private places or privately, but in the place of public worship and in the face of the congregation where the people may most conveniently see and hear and not in places where fonts in the time of Popery were unfitly and superstitiously placed.

The child to be baptised, after giving notice to the minister the day before, is to be presented by the father …

Before the baptism the minister is to use some words of instruction touching the institution, nature, use and ends of this SACRAMENT …

Then the minister is to demand the name of the child, which being told him, he is to say, 'I baptise thee in the name of the Father, Son and Holy Ghost'.

After he pronounceth the words, he is to baptise the child with water which for manner of doing it is not only lawful but sufficient and most expedient to be by pouring or sprinkling water on the face of the child without adding any other ceremony.

> **sacrament:** *religious ceremony*

Marriage

● SOURCE 11.12

From the Book of Common Prayer

First the BANNS of all that are to be married together must be published in the church three several Sundays or holy days in the time of divine service.

At the time appointed for the solemnisation of MATRIMONY, the persons to be married shall come into the body of the church with their friends and neighbours, and then standing together, the man on the right hand and the woman on the left, the priest shall say,

'Dearly beloved, we are gathered here in the sight of God and in the face of this congregation to join together this man and this woman in holy matrimony …

● SOURCE 11.13

From the Directory for Public Worship

… After solemn charging of the persons to be married before the great God who searcheth all hearts, and to whom they must give a strict account at the last day, that if either of them know any cause, by precontract or otherwise, why they may not lawfully proceed to marriage, that they now discover it; the minister (if no impediment be acknowledged) shall cause first the man to take the woman by the right hand saying these words:

'I, N, do take thee N to be my married wife and I do, in the presence of God and before this congregation, promise and COVENANT to be a loving and faithful husband unto thee, until God shall separate us by death.'

[Then the priest asks if anyone knows any impediment to the marriage.]

If no impediment be alleged then shall the curate say to the man,

'N, wilt thou have this woman to thy wedded wife, to live together after God's ordinance in the holy estate of matrimony. Wilt thou love her, comfort her, honour and keep her in sickness and in health, and forsaking all other keep thee only unto her, so long as ye both shall live?'

The man shall answer 'I will'.

Then the priest shall say to the woman,

'N, wilt thou have this man to thy wedded husband to live together after God's ordinance in the holy estate of matrimony. Wilt thou obey him and serve him, love, honour and keep him in sickness and in health, and forsaking all other keep thee only unto him so long as ye both shall live?'

The woman shall answer 'I will'.

[Then the man holding the woman's right hand says,]

'I, N, take thee, N, to my wedded wife, to have and to hold from this day forward, for better for worse, for richer for poorer, in sickness and in health, to love and to cherish till death us do part' …

[Then the woman holding the man's right hand says,]

'I, N, take thee, N, to my wedded husband, to have and to hold from this day forward, for better for worse, for richer for poorer, in sickness and in health, to love, cherish and to obey, till death us do part' …

Then shall they again loose their hands and the man shall give unto the woman a ring, laying the same upon the Book … And the priest taking the ring shall deliver it to the man to put on the fourth finger of the woman's left hand. And the man holding the ring there and taught by the priest shall say,

'With this ring I thee wed, with my body I thee worship and with all my worldly goods I thee endow' …

[Then the couple kneel for prayers.]

Then the woman shall take the man by his right hand and say these words:

'I, N, do take thee N to be my married husband, and I do, in the presence of God and before this congregation, promise and covenant to be a loving, faithful and obedient wife unto thee, until God shall separate us by death.'

Then, without any further ceremony, the minister shall in the face of the congregation pronounce them to be husband and wife according to God's ordinance; and so conclude the action with a prayer …

---

banns: *notice of an intended marriage*

matrimony: *marriage*

---

covenant: *agree*

Burial

● SOURCE 11.14

From the Book of Common Prayer

The priests and clerks meeting the corpse at the entrance to the churchyard and going before it either into the church or towards the grave shall say or sing,

'I am the resurrection and the life (sayeth the Lord), he that believeth in me, though he were dead, he shall live, and whosoever liveth and believeth in me shall never die.'

[Then several psalms are read, followed by reading from the New Testament of the Bible.]

When they come to the grave, while the corpse is made ready to be laid in the earth, the priest shall say, or the priest and clerks shall sing,

'Man that is born of woman hath but a short time to live and is full of misery. He cometh up and is cut down like a

● SOURCE 11.15

From the Directory for Public Worship

When any person departeth this life, let the dead body upon the day of Burial be decently attended from the house to the place appointed for public burial and there immediately INTERRED without any ceremony.

And because the customs of kneeling down and praying by, or towards the dead corpse, and other such usages in the place where it lies before it be carried to burial are superstitious: and for that praying, reading and singing both in going to and at the grave have been grossly abused, are no way beneficial to the dead, and have proved many ways hurtful to the living, therefore let all such things be laid aside.

flower, he fleeth as it were a shadow and never continueth in one stay. In the midst of life we are in death, of whom may we seek for SUCCOUR but of thee, O Lord …'

Then while the earth shall be cast upon the body by some standing by the priest shall say,

'Forasmuch as it hath pleased Almighty God of his great mercy to take unto himself the soul of our dear brother here departed, we therefore commit his body to the ground, earth to earth, ashes to ashes, dust to dust, in sure and certain hope of the resurrection to eternal life'.

Then shall be said or sung,

'I heard a voice from heaven, saying unto me, Write, From henceforth blessed are the dead which die in the Lord, even so sayeth the Spirit, for they rest from their labours'.

HOWBEIT we judge it very convenient that the Christian friends who accompany the dead body to the place appointed for public burial do apply themselves to meditations and conferences suitable to the occasion: and that the minister, as upon other occasions so at this time, if he be present, may put them in remembrance of their   duty …

---

succour: *comfort*

---

howbeit: *nevertheless*
interred: *buried in the ground*

● SOURCE 11.16

Even the Directory's marriage reforms were later considered inadequate. In 1653 the fiercely anti-clerical members of Barebone's Parliament decided to break the link between marriage and the Church by declaring marriage to be a purely secular undertaking. In August 1653 they passed 'An Act touching Marriages and the Registering thereof'.

---

places of abode: *homes*
Register: *registrar*
thenceforth: *after that time*

Be it enacted by authority of this present Parliament that whosoever shall agree to be married within the Commonwealth of England after the nine and twentieth day of September … shall … deliver in writing … unto the REGISTER … for the respective parish where each party to be married liveth, the names, surnames, additions and PLACES OF ABODE of the parties to be married, and of their parents, guardians or overseers; all which the said Register shall publish … three several Lords-days then next following at the close of the morning exercise in the public meeting-place commonly called the church or chapel; or (if the parties so to be married shall desire it) in the market-place next to the said church or chapel on three market days …

And it is further enacted that all such persons so intending to be married shall come before some Justice of the Peace within and of the same county, city or town corporation where publication shall be made as aforesaid; and shall bring a certificate of the said publication and shall make sufficient proof of the consent of their parents or guardians, if either of the said parties shall be under the age of one and twenty years: And the said Justice shall examine by witnesses upon oath … concerning the truth of the certificate … And (if there appear no reasonable cause to the contrary) the Marriage shall proceed in this manner.

The man to be married, taking the woman to be married by the hand shall plainly and distinctly pronounce these words:

'I, AB, do here in the presence of God the searcher of all hearts take thee, CD, for my wedded wife; and do also, in the presence of God and before these witnesses, promise to be unto thee a loving and faithful husband.'

And then the woman, taking the man by the hand, shall plainly and distinctly pronounce these words:

'I, CD, do here in the presence of God the searcher of all hearts take thee, AB, for my wedded husband; and do also in the presence of God and before these witnesses, promise to be unto thee a loving, faithful and obedient wife.'

And it is further enacted that the man and woman having … expressed their consent unto marriage in the manner and by the words aforesaid … the said Justice of the Peace may and shall declare the said man and woman to be from THENCEFORTH husband and wife; and from and after such consent so expressed and such declaration made, the same … shall be good and effectual in law. And no other marriage whatsoever within the Commonwealth of England after the 29th September 1653 shall be held or accounted a marriage according to the laws of England …

1 How did the civil marriage ceremony differ from the services in both the Book of Common Prayer and the Directory for Public Worship?

2 As a class discuss the features of Anglican and Presbyterian beliefs and how they differed.

3 Using your own version of this table make a summary of your findings from your discussion and from the sources in this chapter.

	Anglican Book of Common Prayer	Presbyterian Directory of Public Worship, 1645	Barebone's Parliament 1653
Baptism			▉▉▉▉▉▉
Marriage			
Burial			▉▉▉▉▉▉

Section C How did the Puritans try to improve moral behaviour?

The vital importance of maintaining high standards of personal and public morality had been a constant theme of Puritan preaching and writing before the Civil War. Puritans had frequently denounced what they saw as widespread sexual promiscuity and excessive indulgence in drinking, gaming, dancing and swearing. After 1646, therefore, the Puritans attempted to bring about changes in the moral behaviour of the population.

● **SOURCE 11.17**

Two important initiatives, in the form of Acts against swearing and adultery, were introduced by the Rump Parliament in May and June 1650. From the Act against Swearing

esquires: *substantial*

For the better preventing and suppressing of the detestable sins of profane swearing and cursing, be it enacted by this present Parliament ... that if any person or persons shall hereafter offend by profane swearing or cursing ... that then every such offender shall for every time so offending forfeit and pay to the use of the poor of that parish where the same is or shall be committed, for the first offence according to the degree and quality of such person and persons so offending in manner and form following ...

[Peers: 30 shillings (£1.50); knights and baronets: 20 shillings (£1); ESQUIRES: 10 shillings (50p); gentlemen: 6s 8d (34p); others: 3s 4d (17p). Fines were to be doubled for second offences and persistent swearers were to be bound over for their good behaviour. Those who failed to pay their fines could be placed in the stocks, and children under the age of twelve could be whipped.]

● **SOURCE 11.18**

From the Adultery Act, June 1650

For suppressing of the abominable and crying sins of incest, adultery and fornication, wherewith the land is much defiled and Almighty God highly displeased, be it enacted by the authority of this present Parliament ... that in case any married woman shall from and after the four and twentieth day of June [1650] be carnally known by any man (other than her

felony: *a serious criminal offence*

ravishment: *rape*

husband) (except in case of RAVISHMENT) and of such offence or offences shall be convicted as aforesaid by confession or otherwise, every such offence and offences shall be and is hereby adjudged FELONY, and every person, as well the man as the woman, offending shall suffer death as in case of Felony …

Provided that this shall not extend to any man who at the time of such offence committed is not knowing that such woman with whom such offence is committed is married.

And be it further enacted by the authority aforesaid that if any man shall from and after the four and twentieth day of June aforesaid have carnal knowledge of the body of any virgin, unmarried woman or widow, every man so offending and confessing the same or being thereof convicted by verdict upon indictment or presentment, as also every such woman so offending … shall for every such offence be committed to the common gaol … there to continue for the space of three months …

---

1 According to Sources 11.17 and 11.18 how were the following offences to be punished:

a) swearing
b) adultery?

2 In what way could the Adultery Act be said to discriminate against women?

The campaign for moral reform was sustained throughout the early 1650s. In 1655, Cromwell sent the Major-Generals into Wales and the English provinces, and made the task of improving the people's behaviour one of the top priorities for these new local governors.

● **SOURCE 11.19**

An extract from the instructions given to the Major-Generals by Cromwell and the Council of State in October 1655

abated: *lessened*

houses of evil fame: *brothels*

profaneness: *disrespect for religion*

They are to have a strict eye … that no horse-races, cock-fighting, bear-baitings, stage plays, or any other unlawful assemblies be permitted within their counties, forasmuch as treason and rebellion is usually hatched and contrived against the State upon such occasions, and much evil and wickedness committed …

They shall in their constant carriage and conversation encourage and promote godliness and virtue, and discourage and discountenance all PROFANENESS and ungodliness; and shall endeavour with the other justices of the peace, and other ministers and officers who are entrusted with the care of those things, that the laws against drunkenness, blaspheming and the taking of the name of God in vain, by swearing and cursing, plays and interludes, and profaning the Lord's Day, and such like wickedness and abominations, be put into effectual execution …

That no house standing alone and out of town be permitted to sell ale, beer or wine, or to give entertainment, but that such licences be called in and suppressed …

And for the effecting more particularly a reformation in the cities of London and Westminster, that all gaming houses and HOUSES OF EVIL FAME be industriously sought out and suppressed …

That all alehouses, taverns and victualling houses towards the outskirts of the said cities, or either of them, be suppressed, except such as are necessary and convenient to travellers; and that the number of alehouses in all other parts of the town be ABATED, and none continued but such as can lodge strangers and are of good repute.

● **SOURCE 11.20**

Parliamentary Act abolishing the celebration of Christmas, 1652

Friday *the Four and twentieth day of* December, 1652.

Resolved by the Parliament,

THat the Markets be kept to Morrow, being the Five and twentieth day of *December*; And that the Lord Major, and Sheriffs of *London* and *Middlesex*, and the Iustices of Peace for the City of *Westminster* and Liberties thereof, do take care, That all such persons as shall open their Shops on that day, be protected from VVrong or Violence, and the Offenders punished.

Resolved by the Parliament,

That no Observation shall be had of the Five and twentieth day of *December,* commonly called *Christmas-Day*; nor any Solemnity used or exercised in Churches upon that Day in respect thereof.

Ordered by the Parliament,

That the Lord Major of the City of *London*, and Sheriffs of *London* and *Middlesex,* and the Iustices of Peace of *Middlesex* respectively, be Authorized and Required to see this Order duly observed within the late Lines of Communication, and weekly Bills of Mortality.

Hen: Scobell, Cleric. Parliamenti.

London, Printed by *John Field,* Printer to the Parliament of *England.* 1652.

---

1 What specific measures were the Major-Generals required to take to suppress immorality?

2 Why did Cromwell's government object to rural sports such as horse races and cockfights?

3 Does godly reform appear to be the only motive behind these measures?

4 How important was it for Cromwell to ensure internal security?

198

Why did the Puritans want to change the behaviour of the English people and why did their attempt fail?

Section D How successful was Puritan reform?

The Puritan reform measures described above – the attack on the seasonal festivals that had traditionally marked the turning year, the transformation of the rites associated with important stages in the life cycle and the measures designed to raise standards of moral behaviour – represented nothing less than a Puritan attempt to bring about a 'cultural revolution'. The Puritans tried to turn their backs on tradition and the past in much the same way as did the Red Guards who led the Cultural Revolution in Chairman Mao's China in the 1960s. We will now study some sources which illustrate how the nation reacted and consider how successful the reforms were.

This source material from contemporary newsbooks and parliamentary records is on the subject of the celebration of Christmas in the late 1640s and 1650s.

● SOURCE 11.21

From *The Kingdom's Weekly Post*, 29 December 1647–5 January 1648

In some places in the country so eager were they of a sermon that day by such as they approved of that the church doors were kept with swords and other weapons defensive and offensive whilst the minister was in the pulpit …

● SOURCE 11.22

A message from the Council of State to the Rump Parliament, 27 December 1650

avowing: *supporting*

contemptuous: *disrespectful*

malignancy: *Royalism*

… [There was] a very wilful and strict observation of the day commonly called Christmas Day throughout the cities of London and Westminster, by a general keeping of their shops shut up and that there were CONTEMPTUOUS speeches used by some in favour thereof. Which the council, conceiving to be upon the old grounds of superstition and MALIGNANCY and intending to the AVOWING of the same and contempt of the present laws and government, have thought fit that parliament be moved to take the same into consideration …

● SOURCE 11.23

From *The Flying Eagle*, 25 December 1652–1 January 1653

Bacchus: *Greek god of wine*

phoenix: *a mythical bird*

tap houses: *drinking houses*

… it was as rare a thing to see a shop open as to see a PHOENIX or a bird of Paradise. [St] Paul's the mother church and all her daughters languishing without the old and usual mirth of bells, bellows and bag-pipes, taverns and TAP HOUSES having all the custom, BACCHUS bearing the bell amongst the people as if neither custom nor excise were any burden to them, nor the monthly assessment … For Christmas's sake the parliament's orders are condemned, tumults raised, the Ten Commandments broken. Yea the thief will steal and rob his own father against Christmas though it cost him dear, and the poor will pawn all to the clothes of their back to provide Christmas pies for their bellies and the broth of abominable things in their vessels, though they starve or pine for it all the year after.

● SOURCE 11.24

Proceedings in Parliament, 25 December 1656, from the diary of Thomas Burton

Col Matthews:
The house is thin; much I believe occasioned by the observation of this day. I have a short bill to prevent the superstition for the future. I desire it to be read.

Mr Robinson:
I could get no rest all night for the preparation of this foolish day's solemnity. This renders us, in the eyes of the people to be profane. We are, I doubt, returning to Popery.

Sir William Strickland:
It is a very fit time to offer the bill, this day, to bear testimony against it, since people observe it with more solemnity than they do the Lord's Day. I desire it may be read.

Major-General Kelsey and Major Morgan:
If this had been ten days since, it might have been in good time; but let not this business jostle out great and eminent business, you having a twelve-month's time to provide this law. It is too late now to make a law against it.

Major-General Packer, Major Audley and Sir Gilbert Pickering:
If ever a bill was well timed this bill is. You see how the people keep up these superstitious

observations to your face; stricter, in many places, than they do the Lord's Day. One may pass from the Tower to Westminster and not a shop open, nor a creature stirring. It is a fit time now. They desired it might be read.

Mr Godfrey:
If this bill had not been moved to be read, I should not have pressed it; but seeing you have admitted it to a debate, and at this time, I hope we shall all witness against it; otherwise it will be said abroad that these superstitious days have favourites in this House.

● SOURCE 11.25

A newsletter sent from London to the army in Scotland, 28 December 1657

auditors: *congregation*

canonical votary: *religious follower*

Common Prayer: *Book of Common Prayer*

gaming ordinaries: *gambling houses*

sequestered: *ejected*

Christmas Day was never more exactly observed by this city than the last, very few or no shops at all being opened therein. Several disaffected congregations met this day in public and had the COMMON PRAYER read unto them by SEQUESTERED ministers. After sermons were ended [they] were secured by the soldiers (who were then dispersed in and near the city to prevent mischief) till the names of all of the AUDITORS were taken in writing and then dismissed. Several people were likewise the night before apprehended at the GAMING ORDINARIES by the soldiers and brought down prisoner to the garrison of James … At one church by Garlick Hill I hear they had got some old choristers and new taught singing boys and, after the common prayer at length … ended, a young CANONICAL VOTARY went up into the pulpit and made an oration or sermon … and all the people bowed and cringed as if there had been mass …

1 What traditional ways of celebrating Christmas were still being observed in the late 1640s and 1650s according to these sources?

2 What kind of people appear to have been involved in these celebrations?

3 Do these sources prove that most of the population opposed the banning of Christmas?

The following sources provide evidence about the reaction of the population to the Puritan fast-days and Sundays.

● SOURCE 11.26

An order of the Somerset Assize Court, August 1646

assizes: *session of the assize court which dealt with serious crime*

contempt: *failure to follow orders*

… whereas this court is informed that the last Wednesday in every month which is appointed a day of solemn fasting and humiliation over the whole kingdom is not observed and kept as it ought to be by divers persons and in many places within this county; and also that the Lord's Day, likewise appointed to be kept holy, is profaned by many lewd people and not kept and observed in many places as it ought to be. It is therefore ordered by this court that if any person or persons hereafter shall not observe and keep the said fast day or shall profane the said Lord's Day, that then the next Justice of the Peace upon complaint to him made shall bind over the said person or persons so offending to the next ASSIZES to answer his CONTEMPT. And all constables and other officers are hereby required to take especial care to see this order performed, as they will answer to the contrary and from whom this court will expect a good account of the performance thereof.

1 What particular Puritan reforms were being ignored in Somerset according to this source?

2 How widespread were these practices?

3 Who was given responsibility for enforcing the law?

4 What would the consequences be of their failing to take action?

5 What are the advantages and disadvantages of this source as evidence of the behaviour of the English people?

● **SOURCE 11.27**

Extracts from the diary of Ralph Josselin, Puritan minister of Earls Colne in Essex

hearing: *attending church*

insensible: *uncaring*

laid down: *abandoned*

nigh: *nearly*

western successes: *military victories of the New Model Army in the West Country*

25 September 1644: Was a day of public humiliation: it would make a man bleed to see how regardless people are of the same, nothing moves them …

26 November 1645: The day of the P[ublic] Fast, preached twice … the [fast] days are common and neglected and yet sins and judgements continue, and now no sense of either, Lord whither will this evil tend; oh that mercy might humble us and prepare us for good …

16 April 1646: Kept a P[ublic] day of thanks for our WESTERN SUCCESSES and over Sir Jacob Astley, wherein the Lord was good to me, and also in breaking up a match of wrestling in the town, whereat were gathered NIGH 500 people.

19 May 1646: P[ublic] day of thanks. The Lord good to me; few of the parish HEARING.

22 September 1646: A Public Thanksgiving, wherein the lord was merciful to me, in some measure enabling me for the same, a very thin congregation, oh how backward are people to wait upon God in his ordinances …

28 October 1646: This day the P[ublic] Fast: sadly neglected by people, and my heart very much out of frame to such duties, custom makes us INSENSIBLE.

9 May 1647 [Sunday]: … [the] congregation grows very thin, oh Lord do not give my flock over to looseness and error, people seldom frequent hearing the word, little care of his worship.

26 September 1647: People, especially the poor of both sexes and men are exceeding careless of the sabbath, profaneness is ready to overrun us.

24 November 1647: P[ublic] Fast, generally neglected, for my part I shall endeavour to keep it, and preach, though other ministers and my own people should lay it down.

30 March 1648: My uncle Ralph Josselin was with me early on the fast day morning … the Lord was good and merciful unto me in enabling me to expound and preach: there was the thinnest audience that ever I had …

30 August 1648 P[ublic] F[ast]; a wet night and wettish day, as if God would have called men to his worship: but there was no regard of the same …

25 October 1648: This day was P[ublic] Fast, a cold day, and we like it in our affections.

31 January 1649: this day was a fast, a very cold day, I suppose they will now be LAID DOWN, people do so exceedingly neglect the same.

---

1 What do the entries in the diary reveal about the attitude of Josselin's parishioners to fast-days and Sundays?

2 What evidence do they give about the reasons for the abandoning of the monthly day in 1649?

3 How reliable is Josselin's testimony?

The following sources are concerned with the reaction of the population to the introduction of civil marriage by Barebone's Parliament in August 1653 (see Source 11.16). The first group are taken from some of the newsbooks for September 1653.

● **SOURCE 11.28**

From the *Mercurius Democritus*, 14–21 September 1653

Democritus: *a Greek philosopher* (c. 460–c. 370 BC)

Nodnol: *London*

portions: *dowries*

The distressed maids of the city of NODNOL are very much dejected for husbands and will all be married out of hand, to which intent some of them have been lately with DEMOCRITUS desiring him to print them a Bill of about 500 young lasses that are maidservants with their several places of dwelling and what qualities they are of, whether seamstresses, knitters, bone-lace makers, body stitchers, glovers, cook-maids, chamber maids or the like, with their several PORTIONS, because their tender consciences will not permit them to be married after the new way … no less than 550 and odd of citizens and others were married the last week within the city … and more and more go daily to it.

● **SOURCE 11.29**

From *The Weekly Intelligencer*, 20–27 September 1653

blind alley: *cul de sac*

hard by: *near*

Sure the sign is now in Gemini; there were yesterday nine and twenty marriages in one church and five and twenty in another. There is a poor BLIND ALLEY HARD BY me … not above eight houses in all, and in four of them the parties are agreed and above two hours ago are gone to the parson to be married.

● **SOURCE 11.30**

From *Mercurius Democritus*, 21–28 September 1653

Nodnolshire: *London*

occomy: *coarse flax rope*

The young lasses are now all become so mad of marrying that all the lads in NODNOLSHIRE will not be half a sufficient number to find them husbands … The goldsmiths are so heavily put to it for gold to make wedding rings fast enough, that some they make hollow and others they gild over OCCOMY with gold, they being so mad of them that they sell them off at any price.

● **SOURCE 11.31**

From *Mercurius Democritus*, 28 September–5 October 1653

exchange seamstresses: *the women who sewed clothes at the Exchange in London*

… The EXCHANGE SEAMSTRESSES by reason of the late multiplicity of marriages being not able to provide smocks fast enough for newly married brides … many of them that married in haste do now repent by leisure and lie by the sides of their beloved spouses more like senseless blocks than active husbands.

1   What sort of publications are these extracts taken from and what sort of readership would they have had?

2   What do they tell us about the popular response to the Civil Marriage Act?

3   How reliable do you think their evidence is?

Below are some historians' estimates of the numbers of marriages contracted in England during the 1650s.

● **SOURCE 11.32**

The estimated number of marriages contracted in England during the 1650s in the month of September	
1650:	1534
1651:	2739
1652:	2917
1653:	9884
1654:	4282
1655:	4859
1656:	4087
1657:	4089
1658:	3736
1659:	3169

The estimated number of marriages contracted in England in each month of 1653	
January:	1727
February:	4127
March:	1535
April:	3734
May:	2807
June:	2844
July:	1918
August:	1401
September:	9884
October:	714
November:	1913
December:	2240

What do these figures reveal about the success of Puritan attempts to enforce civil marriage?

● **Source 11.33**

One woman who wrote about her personal reaction to civil marriage was Anne Murray. She married Sir James Halket in March 1656 and described the process in her memoirs.

closet: *small private room*

parchment: *type of paper made from animal skin*

sack: *wine*

Upon Saturday the first of March 1656, Sir James and I went to Charlton and took with us Mr Gaile, who was chaplain to the countess of Devonshire, who preached (as he sometimes used to do) at the church the next day; and after supper he married us in my brother Newton's CLOSET, none knowing of it in the family or being present but my brother and sister and Mr Neale. Though [to] conform to the order of those that were in power, who allowed of no marriage lawful but such as were married by one of their Justices of the Peace, that they might object nothing against our marriage, after evening sermon my sister pretending to go [to] see Justice Elkonheed, who was not well, living at Woolwich, took Sir James and me with her in the coach and my brother and Mr Neale went another way afoot and met us there; and the Justice performed what was usual for him at that time, which was only holding the Directory [for Public Worship] in his hand, asked Sir James if he intended to marry me. He answered, 'Yes'; and asked if I intended to marry him, I said 'Yes'. 'Then', says he, 'I pronounce you man and wife.' So calling for a glass of SACK, he drank and wished much happiness to us, and we left him, having given his clerk money, who gave in PARCHMENT the day and witnesses and attested by the Justice that he had married us. But if it had not been done more solemnly … by a minister I should not have believed it lawfully done.

1   What was Anne Murray's attitude to the new form of marriage ceremony?

2   How did she and her prospective husband show their support for religious marriage?

3   How carefully were the regulations in the civil marriage Act observed on this occasion?

4   In what ways does this source reflect the accuracy of the figures in Source 11.32?

● **Source 11.34**

Contemporary woodcut of the interior of an alehouse

● **SOURCE 11.35**

The entries for November 1655 in the diary of Robert Beake, who was mayor of Coventry from 1655 to 1656. He was a particularly committed Puritan and very anxious to enforce the new moral and cultural standards upon the townspeople of Coventry.

carnal knowledge: sex

distrained: fined

distress: forfeiting of goods

house of correction: workhouse

ostler: stableman

outing of: ejection

tapster: barman

transgressing: breaking the regulations

12 November: Upon complaint of Mr Bedford, his son, Rogers, Martin, Hoult, Ash, etc., were summoned to answer their being at an alehouse (being Ward's house) at 10 o'clock and there staying though three times ordered to depart by Mr Bedford. Upon refusal to pay 3s 4d [17p] a piece (the two former only appearing) a warrant was granted for DISTRESS.

14 November: Corversley and Goode, servants to Goody Hite upon confession that they had CARNAL KNOWLEDGE of each other, were sent the one to the gaol, the other to the HOUSE OF CORRECTION.

15–16 November: I sat at [the] Crown [Inn] and made order for the OUTING OF Walford, minister of Wishaw, for scandal in life.

18 November: A man for travelling from Allesley, being the Lord's Day, was set in the stocks.

19 November: Three Quakers for travelling on the Lord's Day were set in a cage; Memorandum: it grieved me that this poor deluded people should undergo punishment of such a nature.

A man Travelling from Ryton [on Dunsmore] to Exhall to be a godfather was DISTRAINED and paid 10s [50p].

21 November: Goodman Yardley was convicted for grinding on the Lord's Day; and also Goody Newland, Turley and Parker for selling ale without licence.

Henry Walsmeley and Frances Rotten confessed that they had carnal knowledge of each other for which the one was sent to the gaol, the other to the house of correction.

A warrant against Remington of Stoke for shutting in the churchwardens when they came to search it (being an alehouse) on the Lord's Day.

A warrant against Goodman Prior and one Clare of Wyken for tippling in one Hind's house at Stoke on the Lord's Day.

22 November: Goody Newland committed to the house of correction for a month for selling ale without licence.

23 November: Warrant issued to Stychell and Stoke to summon alehouse keepers to appear before me to give an account of disorders and selling ale without licence.

A warrant to distrain Goodman Hill for selling ale.

26 November: A warrant against Prior in Muchpark Street ward for TRANSGRESSING against the Lord's Day directed to the constables of the ward

27 November: A warrant to carry Goody Pywell to the house of correction for living idly, etc.

A warrant to distrain John Lawrance for being drunk and swearing two oaths.

30 November: A warrant against Goody Keeling of Stoke for selling ale without licence.

A warrant against the OSTLER at the Red Lion for tippling at new Sunday.

Goody English of Stoke promises by this fortnight to give over the selling of ale and the constable is to give notice of it.

Goody Remington of Stoke to be bound to be of good behaviour for abusing churchwardens and to appear the 7 December.

A warrant to the constables of [Walsgrave on] Sowe, Exhall, Foleshill and Wyken to summon in alehouse keepers by 7 December.

Goodman Ange hath promised not to sell ale and the constables to look to it.

A warrant to John Carver, constable, to distress the TAPSTER at the Bull for tippling.

Another against Wm Cooke for tippling and [sent] to John Carver.

Another directed against Richard Clare of Wyken for travelling on the Lord's Day, 18 November.

1   List the main offences referred to in this extract.

2   How does this extract show that the attempt to change behaviour was taken seriously by Puritans?

3   How does it show that it was not proving very successful?

4   How valuable is this source as evidence of the failure of the Puritan campaign?

Further evidence about the failure of the Puritan attempt at moral reformation was delivered by one of Cromwell's godly Major-Generals, Hezekiah Haynes, in the summer of 1656.

● **SOURCE 11.36**

From a letter written by Hezekiah Haynes to Oliver Cromwell on 15 August 1656, about the election campaign for the Second Protectorate Parliament

Such is the prevalency of that spirit which opposeth itself to the work of God upon the wheel that the spirits of those that are otherwise minded have been much perplexed and discouraged from almost appearing at the election, seeing no visible way of balancing that interest … The only God be counsel and strength unto your highness whilst you are conflicting with so many difficulties in the present work [that] I am persuaded God hath called you and pointed your heart for, and give you at length to reap some harvest of your hopes for encouragement in that which yet remains for you to do.

● **SOURCE 11.37**

A few days later, after Hezekiah had heard of the result of the election in Norfolk, he wrote again to Cromwell's secretary, John Thurloe.

ascertain: *find out*

gratified: *pleased*

malignants: *Royalists*

ministry: *clergy*

profane: *anti-religious*

There was as clear a combination as never was known before to bring in persons of apparent contrary principles to the government, and but few of them such as continued to own that parliament interest, by which choice the PROFANE MALIGNANTS of the disaffected party and scandalous MINISTRY are only GRATIFIED. I cannot yet ASCERTAIN what choice the other counties have made: I hope something different from these … It is a difficult time: the all wise God direct you and all those at [the] stern safely and resolutely to steer the ship of this commonwealth in this troublesome and stormy season, directing you for his glory and the preservation of that interest that fears God in the nation …

● **Summary Task**

1 In what ways do these letters suggest that the Puritan campaign for moral change in Norfolk had not been successful?

2 Write short essays answering the following questions:

  a) In what ways did the Puritans try to change the behaviour of the English people?
  b) How successful was the Puritan attempt to change the behaviour of the English people and why?

3 What traditional customs of the Anglican Church did the Puritans object to and why?

● **Further reading**

For more detail see Christopher Durston, 'Puritan Rule and the Failure of Cultural Revolution' in Christopher Durston and Jacqueline Eales (eds.), *The Culture of English Puritanism* (Macmillan, 1996). Other useful information is given in John Morrill, *Revolution and Restoration* (Collins and Brown, 1992). The best recent study of popular culture in early modern England is Ronald Hutton, *The Rise and Fall of Merry England: The Ritual Year 1400–1700* (OUP, 1994).

chapter

12 Why was the monarchy restored in 1660?

1658
September: Richard Cromwell is inaugurated as Protector.

1659
January: The Third Protectorate Parliament meets.
April: Meetings of the General Council of Officers demand that the army's wage arrears are paid. When these demands are opposed by Protector and Parliament, the army mobilises in and around London, forcing the Protector to dissolve Parliament. When the army decides to recall the Rump Parliament (dissolved by his father in 1653), Richard resigns as Protector.
May: The Rump Parliament begins to rule the country. It appoints Charles Fleetwood as commander-in-chief of the army.
August: The army easily puts down George Booth's Royalist rebellion in Cheshire.
October: After conflict between army officers and the Rump Parliament over its condemnation of army demands for godly reform, the Rump orders the army to be placed under civilian control. The army responds by forcibly dissolving the Rump and by establishing an army Committee of Safety to govern the country.
October – December: The Committee of Safety faces immense problems as army unity disintegrates. Soldiers in the Portsmouth garrison and the Irish army declare for the Rump. So too does the commander-in-chief of the English army in Scotland, General George Monck.
December 26: The Rump Parliament begins to rule the country again.
December 1659– January 1660: The restored Rump Parliament expels officers who opposed it (including Charles Fleetwood, John Desborough and John Lambert) from the army.

1660
January: Monck marches southwards from Scotland.
February: Monck arrives in London as petitions flood in in favour of a 'free Parliament' and the readmission to Parliament of the MPs excluded by Pride's Purge in 1648. Monck agrees to allow the readmission of MPs excluded in 1648.
March: The Rump passes an Act for new elections and declares itself dissolved.
April: After new elections a new Parliament (called the Convention Parliament) meets.
May: The King's Declaration of Breda is read in the Convention Parliament.
May 5: Parliament declares in favour of government by King, Lords and Commons. Charles II returns from exile to London.

Introduction

When Richard Cromwell replaced his father as Protector in September 1658 his position seemed very secure. Loyal addresses of support flooded in from all parts of the country and there are few grounds for doubting their sincerity. Even George Monck, who at the end of 1659 was to play a vital part in bringing about the Restoration, placed his support firmly behind the Republic for much of 1658–9. As you will see from Source 12.12 below, he wrote to the new Protector advising him how to *strengthen* the Republic. Even more conclusive evidence of the unexpectedness of the Restoration is the fact that a planned series of Royalist rebellions in England in the summer of 1659 were a dismal failure. Only one of them, led by Sir George Booth in Cheshire (see below, Source 12.10), actually got off the ground; it received little support and was easily crushed by the New Model Army. In the autumn of 1659 letters to and from the court of the exiled Charles II indicate that everyone around the King was pessimistic about the chances of a restoration of the Stuart monarchy.

All this makes the question that you will be asked to answer at the end of the chapter a very interesting one: why, only a few months after the ignominious failure of Booth's rebellion, was the monarchy restored in May 1660 amidst scenes of popular rejoicing, and restored with no conditions other than the promises Charles II had given in the Declaration of Breda (see Source 12.14 below)?

Were people frightened by the collapse of government in 1659?

One possible explanation for the shift in public opinion towards acceptance of the return of the King is the failure of the regimes after Oliver Cromwell's death to establish stable government. Perhaps the threat of anarchy and chaos seemed very great to people at the time.

It is clear that no regime after Oliver Cromwell's death managed to survive in power for very long. This can be seen from the table of events between September 1658 and December 1659 at the beginning of this chapter.

These changes of regime in the few months between Oliver Cromwell's death in September 1658 and the end of 1659 (the Protectorate, the Rump, military government and the Rump again) must have seemed bewildering at the time. Events seemed to confirm fears that law and order, as well as government, were collapsing.

Source 12.1, taken from Thomas Rugg's diurnal (the seventeenth-century equivalent of a collection of newspaper cuttings) describes the major riots that occurred in London in December 1659. Elsewhere, too, there were demonstrations by riotous soldiers declaring for the Rump, and in some cases bandits appeared, taking advantage of the lack of control by the government. All this took place against the background of renewed economic depression after the generally prosperous 1650s.

● **SOURCE 12.1**

From Thomas Rugg's account of riots in London

November 1659: Now in the City of London the apprentices and other of the discontented persons were much displeased with the army, that at that time had so many garrisons in the City, and that the soldiers were so thick in the City that gentlemen did care but [not] to go into the City to buy their commodities; and the apprentices finding that their shops were but very empty of customers, they did press on for the answer of their petition that they had before presented and had only promised for. They found that the Lord Mayor were very loath to act any thing that might displease the soldiers; but these young men did very much affront the soldiers as they went up and down the streets, and the soldiers were a laughing stock. These so often affronts to the soldiers the Committee of Safety took it very ill that their soldiers and commands were little set by.

5 December 1659: The apprentices and other discontented young men did, as well as [they] could, gather themselves together, for that overnight they had contrived a rising in the morning, if possible; for they were now quite weary of the soldiery, which they knew well enough. In the morning the apprentices began to appear in a disorderly manner, but with a football, thinking that there would appear a party in arms for them; for they knew where to have arms, but still they wanted a head to lead them on, [and had] but here and there a pocket pistol. Now the Committee of Safety, having intelligence that in London they had a great mind to be rid of the soldiery, they ordered that some regiments of HORSE AND FOOT should forthwith march into the City, which accordingly they did, of horse and foot three thousands. But in their march they met with great oppositions … there was [sic] many affronts offered and a great many of uncivil actions offered to them in their march into the City, but especially to Colonel Hewson's regiment of foot; they were more abused than any other. He was a cobbler by trade, but a very STOUT man, and a very good commander of foot; but in regard of his former employment and [what] the apprentices once got into their mouths, they very well employed their mouths. He had but one eye, but they called him blind cobbler, blind Hewson, and did throw old shoes and old slippers and turnip tops, BRICK BATS and stones and tiles at him and his

brick bats: *half bricks used as weapons*

horse and foot: *cavalry and infantry*

stout:: *brave*

207

Were people frightened by the collapse of government in 1659?

soldiers. He marched through the City to the Royal Exchange, where he stood a little space. Then he marched to Guildhall, where he met with many affronts on the way, so that among the rude multitude there were some did fire a pistol at the soldiers and some that threw great stones at the soldiers, that did very much kindle wrath, that at last they fired in earnest, and four or five of the apprentices and others, whereof one was a cobbler, were killed and others wounded, and some likewise of the army very dangerously wounded … Then the Lord Mayor appeared in this tumultuous multitude and made a short speech, and desired them that they would desist from that headstrong actions acted by them … and at the last by his much entreating, they left and resorted home, although not well pleased in their minds.

Some interpreted what was happening as the total collapse of the social order. As in the period immediately after the execution of Charles I (see Chapter 7), some began to believe that the established world was about to be turned upside down.

Source 12.2

Alice Thornton, the wife of a substantial Yorkshire landed gentleman, wrote her autobiography towards the end of her life in 1707. This is her recollection of her feelings and what happened to her in 1659–60.

1659: About this time we were all in a great confusion in this kingdom, none knowing how the government of the land would fall, some desiring the continuation of Oliver Cromwell's race to stand, others desired the return of the blessed king, and to establish their arbitrary power again, others intended through the weakness of Richard, son of Oliver, who then ruled as Protector, to advance the interest of Lambert in public authority, which was a man highly for Independency, and so would have utterly destroyed both Church and State, in lopping of all who had affection and dependency on either, rooting out the very face of a clergyman or gentleman or the civiler sort of commonalty. In this distraction each man looked upon [each] other strangely, none knowing whom to trust, or how to be secured from the rage, rapine and destruction of the soldiery, in whose sole power was both the civil and ecclesiastical sword since the year 1648. And we had all suffered so deeply under those oppressions, that even the contrary party to the king did heartily wish an alteration from these pressures. Insomuch that most sober, wise people of this nation began to have a good opinion of the ancient government of this realm, under which they had lived so many peaceable years … Thus did it please the Divine Wisdom so to order it, in great and miraculous mercy, that when we had felt the evils of our sad divisions, and our growing higher towards utter destruction in their continuance in them, He thereby taught the nation wisdom, and did incline their hearts to turn to the old station, under the notion of a free parliament … Yet till that time was come, great and heavy was our fears and burdens, groaning under that tyranny, both Church and State, having our dear sovereign, King Charles the 2nd banished, and not enjoying those rights … from his three kingdoms, which was unjustly detained by usurpation, which caused us daily to pour out our complaints to God, with incessant cries and tears for His Church and anointed to be restored again, which might be the re-establishment of the gospel of peace amongst us, and the true religion in these flourishing kingdoms.

In the middle of the political crisis, on 17 April 1660, Mrs Thornton had her sixth child, a boy. Two weeks later, however, he died, as she recorded in her autobiography.

It so please God to shorten this joy, lest I should be too transported. [The new baby] having had three hours' sleep, his face when he awoke was full of red round spots like the smallpox, being of the compass of a halfpenny, and all wealed white over and being in a slumber in my arms on my knee he would sweetly lift up his eyes to heaven and smile, as if the old saying was true in this sweet infant, that he saw angels in heaven. [Shortly afterwards the baby died.] After the Lord had taken my child from me, I had some weakness upon my body by reason of the return of the milk; but in much mercy I was restored to a pretty degree of strength … In this time we had that grand blessing to the whole nation given to us in the restoration of our dread sovereign Lord King Charles, when we each moment feared ruin and destruction.

Source 12.3

From the papers of the Duke of Newcastle, 1660. He had been one of the King's principal army commanders in the early years of the first Civil War. After his defeat at the battle of Marston Moor in 1644 he went into exile and his estates were confiscated by Parliament.

The Bible in English under every weaver's and chambermaid's arms hath done us much hurt. That which made it one way is the universities. Abounds with too many scholars. Therefore, if every college had but half the number, they would be better fed and as well taught. But that which hath done us most hurt is the abundance of grammar schools and inns of court. The Treasurer Burghley [Elizabeth I's minister] said there was [sic] too many grammar schools, because it made the plough and the cart to be neglected, which was to feed us and defend us, for there are few that can read that will put their hands to the plough or the cart, and armies are made of the common soldiers, and there are very few that can read that will carry a musket. And there are so many schools now as most read, so indeed there should be, but such a proportion as to serve the church and moderately the law and the merchants, and the rest for the labour, for else they run out to idle and unnecessary people that becomes a factious burthen to the Commonwealth. For when most was unlettered, it was a much better world both for peace and war.

1 What were the causes of the clashes between apprentices and soldiers in London in November and December 1659, as described in Source 12.1?

2 How justified was Mrs Thornton in Source 12.2 in using language like:

   a) 'rage, rapine and destruction' to describe the actions of soldiers
   b) a country 'groaning under tyranny, both Church and State' to describe England during the Republic?

3 What reasons did Mrs Thornton and the Duke of Newcastle have in common for wanting the restoration of the monarchy?

Were people frightened of the Quakers?

One special feature of the history of England in 1659–60 deserves particular emphasis. Fear of Quakers among 'respectable' people, which had been apparent throughout the 1650s (see the Nayler case in 1656 in Chapter 10), now reached a state approaching nationwide hysteria. Why this was so and how it contributed to bringing about the Restoration are important questions you should consider. Firstly, however, you need to know something about the origins and early history of the Quakers.

● Quakers in the 1650s

Quakerism developed after the end of the first Civil War, at a time when many militant Protestants (including Oliver Cromwell) had become disillusioned with religious Presbyterianism. They demanded the right of each congregation to choose its own form of worship, independent of the national Church. Hence they became known as religious Independents. Some, however, reacted even more drastically against the idea that there should be only one national Church. These included the early Quakers, men and women who, from the later 1640s onwards, began to claim that Church government and ordained ministers were irrelevant to the worship of God. They even claimed that the Scriptures were relatively insignificant. 'Every man', wrote one of the early Quakers, George Fox, in his journal, 'was enlightened by the divine light of Christ.' He and other Quakers preached that salvation was open to all and that it was the duty of everyone to follow what their consciences told them to. They often called this their 'inner light' and said that this, not what Church ministers or anyone else said, was the true voice of God. In this respect, their beliefs were very similar to those of the Ranters (see Chapter 7).

In the early days, the Quakers found most support in the north of England, but, as a result of a preaching campaign by enthusiastic travelling preachers such as Fox and Nayler, Quakerism rapidly spread to all parts of Britain. One of the Quakers' enemies, the Presbyterian William Prynne, believed that the Old Testament prophecy had come true, that 'out of the north an evil shall break forth upon all the inhabitants of the land'. As early as 1650, there may have been about 50,000 Quakers, largely drawn from the middling and poorer groups in society.

One of the most important points to understand about the early Quakers in the 1650s is that they were very different from modern Quakers. Until the late seventeenth century

Quakers were militant activists. They campaigned against tithes. They refused to swear oaths or even to take off their hats in the presence of social 'superiors'. They insisted on following what their 'inner light' told them to do, even when this had alarming consequences. Quakers, for example, often protested vehemently in churches when they disagreed with the views being expressed by Church ministers. Some tore off their clothes and worshipped God in the nude. Unlike the pacifism of later Quakers, some were willing to fight. Quakers flocked to join the militias formed to defend the Republic in the aftermath of Booth's rising. For many Quakers, 1659 was a time of exciting expectation.

SOURCE 12.4

Dorothy White lived in Weymouth in Dorset. This is an extract from her short pamphlet *A Diligent Search*, 1659.

Upon the 25th day of the second month 1659 as I was passing along the street, I heard a cry in me. Again on the 26th day of the same month the same cry was in me; again on the 27th day the same cry was in me. And as I was waiting upon the Lord in silence, the word of the Lord came unto me, saying *write, and again I say write* … O you bloodthirsty rulers of England, you rule by the powers of darkness. You have joined with the strengths of Hell to ensnare the innocent … Although many are saying, there are a people risen up that go about to turn the world upside down, if we let them go on. But I tell you it is not the people, but it is the power of God, for He is come to turn the world upside down. That that which hath ruled over may be brought down under and that which hath been of low degree may be raised by the power of God, to rule and have the dominion, for God is coming to throw down the kingdom of Antichrist that hath had the dominion.

Against that background, look at the following sources, which reflect how 'respectable' society reacted to the Quakers.

SOURCE 12.5

Complaints against Quakers, from *Depositions from the Castle of York Relating to Offences Committed in the Northern Counties in the Seventeenth Century*

[Jane Holmes, an itinerant Quaker preacher, arrived in Malton in Yorkshire in the summer of 1652 and started attacking the local minister and holding her own services in private houses and fields. According to the clergyman she 'endeavoured by delusion to draw his people away from him and told the people that he was a blind guide, a thief and a robber'. Several townspeople later testified about the damaging effects of her activities. These included Thomas Dowsley, who reported that]
… his wife doth usually resort to Roger Hebden's house [to see Holmes] and doth not come home never at night until twelve o'clock and some nights not at all. And his son Thomas doth deny his true obedience unto him and denies that he is any more to him than any other man. The said Jane is a wandering person and an instrument of drawing his wife and son from him and she is the cause of tumults and assemblies at unseasonable times of the night, and as it is credibly reported she hath had three bastards.

[Another local inhabitant, Major Baildon, stated that]
… the said Jane hath by delusion drawn the affection of his wife from him so he cannot keep her at home for this Jane, but she doth delude and draw her away, and he hath wanted her many days and one night and often she hath come into his house at unseasonable times at night, and she saieth that she ought to owe him not more than another man. He went to Roger Hebden's house and found the said Jane and his wife among a hundred people and desired his wife to go home and she said she would not go. And some of that party threw him violently down the stairs and put him in danger of his life and struck him on the breast.

THE QVAKERS DREAM: 14

OR,
The Devil's Pilgrimage in England:
BEING

An infallible Relation of their several Meetings,

Shreekings, Shakings, Quakings, Roarings, Yellings, Howlings, Trem-
blings in the Bodies, and Pangs in the Bellies: With a Narrative of
their several Arguments, Tenets, Principles, and strange D ctrin: The
strange and wonderful Satanical Apparitions, and the appearing of the
Devil unto them in the likeness of a black Boar, a Dog with flaming eyes,
and a black man without a head, causing the Dogs to bark, the Swine
to cry, and the Cattel to run, to the great admiration of all that shall
read the same.

London, Printed for *G. Horton*, and are to be sold at the Royal
Exchange in Cornhil, 1655. *Aprill. 26.*

SOURCE 12.7

The title page of an anti-Quaker pamphlet, *The Four-Legg'd Quaker*, 1659

THE FOUR-LEGG'D QUAKER,

To the Tune of the DOG and Elder's MAID,

Or, the LADY'S FALL.

The Four-Legg'd Quaker alleged that a Quaker called Green had been guilty of bestiality with a horse in a field near Colchester in Essex. This was a story that produced many other scurrilous pamphlets, including Source 12.8.

SOURCE 12.8

From *A Relation of a Quaker That to the Shame of his Profession Attempted to Bugger a Mare near Colchester*, May 1659. This single-page broadsheet contained a poem of which these are the first two verses. William Woodcock, like George Fox and James Nayler, was a noted Quaker preacher.

All in the land of Essex
Near Colchester the zealous
On the side of a bank
Was played such a prank
As would make a stone-horse jealous.

Help Woodcock, Fox and Nayler
For Brother Green's a stallion.
Now, alas, what hope
Of converting the Pope
When a Quaker turns Italian.

● **SOURCE 12.9**

Notes on a debate in the Third Protectorate Parliament on a Quaker petition, 16 April 1659. The petition began, 'Friends, who are called a Parliament of these nations'. Its signatories offered to go to prison if their fellow Quakers who were already in prison were released.

Colonel Grosvenor:
I took notice of a great number of people called Quakers, in the Hall yesterday and today. I wish you would take some course with the Petition that had laid a long time before you; and that they be dispersed.

Mr Annesley:
They are a fanatic crew. I would have their Petition referred to a committee, to put it off your hands.

Mr Fowell:
I move to whip them home as vagrants.

Mr Danby:
I move that a law be provided to suppress that railing against the ministers. He instanced what Mr Bulkeley and Dr Reynolds had overheard some of them say: 'the priests and lawyers are bloody men, give them blood to drink'.

Sir Walter Earle:
I except against the title 'friends', and 'the Parliament so called' in the Petition …

Mr Swinfen:
Order them, every one of them, to go to their calling, and apply themselves to the law, which is their protection …

Major-General Kelsey:
No reasoning by scripture will convince them … They call miscalling the ministers speaking the truth. The justices of the peace do well to imprison them. Disturbers of the peace, they deserve it. They will not conform to the law …

Colonel West:
I cannot justify them in their affronts to the ministers …

Mr Lechmere:
You are not, as a Christian magistracy, bound to bend your laws to every pretender's conscience. I am against referring it [the petition] to a committee. Who dare attend it … I dare not. They refuse to answer upon oath … Their language is as little justifiable as the [blank in the manuscript] of Rome. For their railings against the ministers see their books. The question will be, whether you will dispense with that CAST OF THE HAT …

Mr Steward:
They complain not of anything done contrary to law, but according to law. Though they seem but a small number, yet lesser beginnings have grown to great heights. In their books I find a denunciation of judgement. They will easily believe they are the persons appointed by God to execute this judgement. They are not of that simplicity as is moved, but wolves under sheep's clothing.

Mr Stephens:
… The Jesuits have too great a stroke amongst them.

[At the conclusion of the debate it was ordered that the petitioners return to their homes and 'submit themselves to the laws of the nation, and the magistrates they live under'.]

cast of the hat: *the Quaker practice of refusing to take off their hats in the presence of magistrates*

1   What common reasons can you find in Sources 12.5–12.9 that explain why many people loathed Quakers? Illustrate your answer using examples from these sources.

2   How justified were contemporary fears of the Quakers? Were they in fact as great a threat to the social order as many people feared?

3   Why do you think groups such as the Ranters and the Quakers gained such an enthusiastic following during this period?

Now read Sources 12.10 and 12.11.

● **SOURCE 12.10**

Sir George Booth's letter of 2 August, showing the reasons for his Royalist rebellion in Cheshire in August 1659

Though the indifferency that lies upon other men's spirits might flat ours; yet we cannot think, but if it were represented to them, how the present power doth oblige us to put out our right eyes when they require us to acknowledge them as a Parliament, and lay upon us such heavy and grievous burthens, and such deceitful ones as a year's tax in three months, besides many other impositions for excise etc. and by raising among us a militia, they cut off our right hand by subjecting us under the meanest and fanatic spirits of the nation, under pretence of protection, their spirits would be warmed into the same zeal that ours are kindled with.

Now consider what it is we ask, and consider whether it be not the same thing we have asserted with our lives and fortunes, a free parliament.

And what a slavery it is to our understanding, that these men that now call themselves a Parliament, should declare it an act of illegality and violence in the late aspiring General Cromwell, to dissolve their body in 1653 and not to make it the like in the garbling the whole body of the parliament from 400 to 40 in 1648. What is this but to act what they condemn in others? Why do they associate themselves to the present army ... and keep out their numerous fellow-members: if committing violence upon a Parliament be so notorious a crime? ... What is this but under another shape to act the condemned acts of usurpation and tyranny in their old general? ...

And what will be the issue of all this? A mean and SCHISMATICAL PARTY must depress the nobility ...

Let the nation freely choose their representatives, and they as freely sit without awe, or force of soldiery, and what ever, in such an assembly, is determined; shall be by us freely and cheerfully submitted to.

> **schismatical party:** *a group intent on bringing about division (schism) within the Church and society*

● **SOURCE 12.11**

An Act for the Uniformity of Public Prayers and Administration of Sacraments and Other Rites and Ceremonies, 1662

Whereas in the first year of the late Queen Elizabeth there was one uniform Order of Common Service and Prayer and of the administration of Sacraments, rites and ceremonies in the Church of England (agreeable to the Word of God and usage of the Primitive Church) ... set forth in one book, entitled 'The Book of Common Prayer' ... very comfortable to all good people desirous to live in Christian conversation and most profitable to the estates of this realm ... and yet, this notwithstanding, a great number of people in divers parts of this realm, following their own sensuality and living without knowledge and due fear of God, do wilfully and schismatically abstain and refuse to come to their parish churches ... and whereas by the great and scandalous neglect of ministers in using the said order or liturgy so set forth and enjoined as aforesaid great mischiefs and inconveniences during the times of the late unhappy troubles have arisen and grown, and many people have been led into factions and schisms, to the great decay and scandal of the reformed religion of the Church of England, and to the hazard of many souls ... [To prevent these things the Act ordered that all church services should use a revised Book of Common Prayer, that all Church ministers who did not by 24 August 1662 swear an oath acknowledging the legitimacy of the Book should be expelled from their livings, and that everyone holding an office in the Church and all schoolteachers should take the following oath:] I, AB, do declare that it is not lawful upon any pretence whatsoever to take arms against the king, and that I do abhor that traitorous position of taking arms by his authority against his person or against those that are commissioned by him, and that I will conform to the liturgy of the Church of England as it is now by law established.

> **sectaries:** *member of religious sects, which are seen as schismatical and heretical*

Barry Reay in *The Quakers and the English Revolution* (page 81) argues that 'in 1659, as part of a more general fear of SECTARIES, hostility towards Quakerism persuaded many to look to the monarchy as the only salvation from social and religious anarchy'.

To what extent do Sources 12.10 and 12.11 confirm this view?

How important was the role of General Monck between December 1659 and March 1660 in bringing about the Restoration?

It is easier to explain what happened between December 1659 and March 1660 than it is to answer this question.

In December 1659 George Monck, the commander of the English army in Scotland, announced his support of the Rump Parliament. However, early in January 1660 he and his army crossed the Anglo-Scottish border and marched southwards, reaching London in February. As evidence of the widespread unpopularity of the Rump became apparent, he ordered the readmission to Parliament of those MPs excluded by Colonel Pride in December 1648. This made inevitable the Rump's decision to order elections for a new Parliament and to declare itself dissolved.

What were Monck's motives during this exciting time? Here historians face a major problem: at the time Monck never explained what his intentions were. Later he was happy to claim that he intended to bring about the restoration of the monarchy, especially since it brought him rich rewards, including his creation as Duke of Albemarle. But he never declared for the return of Charles II until after the elections to the new Parliament in April 1660. Source 12.12 was written by Monck long before then and indicates what he wanted from the Protectorate.

● SOURCE 12.12

A private letter from Monck to Richard Cromwell on his accession, September 1658

magistracy: *government (by courts and Parliament)*

union accommodation: *finding common ground among people with different views*

Remonstrance of what I desire you to communicate to his highness.

Since by the providence of God his highness is settled in the supreme MAGISTRACY of these nations, it will be necessary for his firmer establishment, that he endeavours to engage to him those of power and interest amongst the people; for which he has a better opportunity than his father, having not the same obligations to many disquieted spirits.

The greatest part of the people are not the best part. But of those, that are the best, the most considerable are such as have a great regard to discipline in the church of God; for want whereof we have almost lost religion amongst us, which is crumbled into dust by seperatism [sic] and divisions, and we are become the scorn of our enemies, and the grief of our friends.

[He goes on to advise the calling of a Parliament and an assembly of divines] to agree upon some way of UNION ACCOMMODATION, that we may have union in all things necessary, and clarity in all; which will put a stop to that progress of blasphemy and profaneness, that I fear is too frequent in many places by the great extent of toleration.

In what ways might events after he wrote that letter have persuaded Monck that no other regime but the monarchy could provide what he wanted?

The next source is from the most famous diarist of the day, Samuel Pepys.

● SOURCE 12.13

From Samuel Pepys's diary

7 February 1660: This day Mr Crew told me that my Lord St. John [a prominent Political Independent of the 1640s who had not supported the execution of the King and who had been only a lukewarm supporter of the Protectorate] is for a free Parliament, and that he is very great with Monke – who hath now the absolute command and power to do anything that he hath a mind to do. Mr Moore told me of a picture hung up at the Exchange, of a great pair of buttocks shitting of a turd into Lawson's mouth, [John Lawson was a naval commander who had declared for the Rump a few months earlier] and over it was writ 'The thanks of the House'. Boys do now cry 'Kiss my Parliament' instead of 'Kiss my arse', so great and general a contempt is the Rump come to among all men, good and bad.

11 February 1660: I saw many people give the soldiers drink and money, and all along in the streets cried, 'God bless them' and extraordinary good words … In Cheapside there was a great many bonfires, and Bow Bells and all the bells in the churches as we went home were a-ringing. Hence we went homewards, it being about 10 a-clock. But the common joy that was everywhere to be seen! The number of bonfires, there being fourteen between St. Dunstan's and the Temple-bar. And at Strand bridge I could at one view tell 31 fires. In King Street, seven or eight; and all along burning and roasting and drinking, for rumps – there being rumps tied upon sticks and carried up and down. The butchers at the maypole in the Strand rang a peal with their knifes when they were going to sacrifice their rump. On Ludgate hill there was one turning of the spit, that had a rump tied upon it, and another basting of it. Indeed it was past imagination, both the greatness and the suddenness of it. At one end of the street, you would think there was a whole lane of fire, and so hot that we were fain to keep still on the further side merely for heat. We came to the Chequer at Charing Cross ... Thence home ... and my wife and I ... went out again to show her the fires; and after walking as far the Exchange, we returned and to bed.

Might the events described by Pepys have influenced what Monck decided to do once he reached London?

How persuasive was the King's Declaration of Breda?

Were people in 1659–60, besides being pushed by events in the country towards acceptance of the Restoration, also pulled by the attractive promises made by the King in the Declaration of Breda, issued from the exiled royal court?

● SOURCE 12.14

The Declaration of Breda, 4 April 1660, drafted by Edward Hyde and approved by Charles II. It was issued from Breda in Holland, to coincide with parliamentary elections which were taking place in England.

Charles, by the Grace of God, king ... to all our loving subjects, of what degree or quality [what]soever, greeting. If the general distraction and confusion which is spread over the whole kingdom doth not awaken all men to a desire and longing that those wounds which have so many years together been kept bleeding may be bound up, all we can say will be to no purpose. However, after this long silence we have thought it our duty to declare how much we desire to contribute thereunto, and that, as we can never give over the hope in good time to obtain the possession of that right which God and Nature hath made our due, so we do make it our daily suit to the Divine Providence that he will, in compassion to us and our subjects, after so long misery and sufferings, remit and put us into a quiet and peaceable possession of that our right, with as little blood and damage to our people as possible. Nor do we desire more to enjoy what is ours, than that all our subjects may enjoy what by law is theirs, by a full and entire administration of justice throughout the land, and by extending our mercy where it is wanted and deserved.

And to the end that the fear of punishment may not engage any, conscious to themselves of what is passed, to a perseverance in guilt for the future, by opposing the quiet and happiness of their country in the restoration both of king, peers and people to their just, ancient and fundamental rights, we do by these presents declare, that we do grant a free and general pardon, which we are ready upon demand to pass under our Great Seal of England, to all our subjects, of what degree or quality soever, who within 40 days after the publishing hereof shall lay hold upon this our grace and favour, and shall by any public act declare their doing so, and that they return to the loyalty and obedience of good subjects (excepting only such persons as shall hereafter be excepted by parliament). Those only excepted, let all our loving subjects, how faulty soever, rely upon the word of a king, solemnly given by this present Declaration, that no crime whatsoever committed against us or our royal father before the publication of this shall ever rise in judgement or be brought in question against any of them, to the least endamagement of them either in their lives, liberties, or estates, or (as far forth lies in our power) so much as to the prejudice of their reputations by any reproach or term of distinction from the rest of our best subjects, we desiring and ordaining that henceforward all notes of discord, separation and difference of parties be utterly abolished among all our subjects, whom we invite and conjure to a perfect union among themselves, under our protection, for the resettlement of our just rights and theirs in a free parliament, by which, upon the word of a king, we will be advised.

And because the passion and uncharitableness of our times have produced several opinions in religion, by which men are engaged in parties and animosities against each other, which, when they shall hereafter unite in a freedom of conversation, will be composed and better understood, we do declare a liberty to tender consciences, and that no man shall be disquieted or called in question for differences of opinion in matters of religion which do not disturb the peace of the kingdom; and that we shall be ready to consent to such an act of parliament as, upon mature deliberation, shall be offered to us, for the full granting that indulgence.

And because, in the continued distractions of so many years and so many and great revolutions, many grants and purchases of estates have been made, to and by many officers, soldiers and others, who are now possessed of the same, and who may be liable to actions at law upon several titles, we are likewise willing that all such differences, and all things relating to such grants, sales and purchases, shall be determined in parliament, which can best provide for the just satisfaction of all men who are concerned.

And we do further declare, that we will be ready to consent to any act or acts of parliament to the purposes aforesaid, and for the full satisfaction of all arrears due to the officers and soldiers of the army under the command of the General Monk, and that they shall be received into our service upon as good pay and conditions as they now enjoy.

Given under our Sign Manual and privy Signet, at our Court at Breda, this 4th day of April, 1660, in the twelfth year of our reign.

---

1 Charles spent most of the 1650s in France. Why do you think he travelled to Holland to issue this declaration?

2 Explain the elements in the Declaration of Breda which you think might have appealed in April 1660 to:

a) Parliamentarian MPs, soldiers, Puritans and new landowners
b) those who had been attracted by many of the things that the Republic had stood for and who were therefore fearful of the restoration of the monarchy.

3 In what ways does the Declaration of Breda project an image of Charles as a moderate, constitutional monarch?

4 How do you think the Declaration of Breda was likely to affect the elections for a new Parliament in England?

How popular was the Restoration?
The return of Charles II, May 1660

Within a week of the first meeting of the new Parliament in April 1660 (the Convention Parliament), after hearing news of the Declaration of Breda, MPs passed a resolution in favour of government by King, Lords and Commons. A few weeks later Charles II returned to England and on 29 May (his 30th birthday) he rode into London amidst scenes of popular rejoicing.

Before you begin to work out your own explanation of why the monarchy was restored, it is worth considering whether the Restoration was in fact as popular as it seems to have been.

The following extracts from the diaries of Samuel Pepys and John Evelyn and the diurnal of Thomas Rugg are certainly typical of other accounts of rejoicing at what was happening. Source 12.18, too, reflects the violent hatred of Cromwell and others felt in the Convention Parliament in 1660.

● **SOURCE 12.15**

From Samuel Pepys's diary. He was secretary to Edward Montague, a commander of the navy, who was sent to bring Charles II to England in May 1660. Pepys went with him. In these extracts Pepys combines his description of great public events with an eye for mundane detail.

23 May 1660: The King, with the two Dukes, the Queen of Bohemia, Princess Royal, and Prince of Orange, came on board; where I in their coming in kissed the King's, Queen and princesses' hands, having done the other before. Infinite shooting off of the guns, and that in disorder on purpose, which was better than if it had been done otherwise. All day nothing but Lords and persons of Honour on board, that we were exceeding full. Dined in a great deal of state, the Royal company by themselves in the coach, which was a blessed sight to see … After dinner, the King and Duke … altered the names of some of the ships, viz. the *Naseby* into *Charles* – the *Richard, James*; the *Speaker, Majesty* – the *Dunbar* (which was not in company

with us) the *Henry – Winsby, Happy Return – Wakefield, Richmond – Lamport* [i.e. Langport], the *Henrietta – Cheriton,* the *Speedwell – Bradford,* the *Success.* That done, the Queen, Princess Royal, and the Prince of Orange took leave of the King, and the Duke of York went on board the *London,* and the Duke of Gloucester the *Swiftsure* – which done, we weighed anchor, and with a fresh gale and most happy weather we set sail for England – all the afternoon the King walking here and there, up and down (quite contrary to what I thought him to have been), very active and stirring. Upon the quarter-deck, he fell in discourse of his escape from Worcester. Where it made me ready to weep to hear the stories that he told of his difficulties that he had passed through.

25 May 1660: About noon ... he [the King] would go in my Lord's barge with the two Dukes; our captain steered, and my Lord went along ... with him. I went, and Mr Mansell and one of the King's footmen, with a dog that the king loved (which shit in the boat, which made us all laugh and me think that a King and all that belong to him are but just as others are) went in a boat by ourselves; and so got on shore when the King did, who was received by General Monke with all imaginable love and respect at his entrance upon land at Dover. Infinite the crowd of people and the gallantry of the horsemen, citizens, and noblemen of all sorts ... The mayor of the town came and gave him his white staff, the badge of his place, which the king did give him again. The mayor also presented him from the town a very rich Bible, which he took and said it was the thing that he loved above all things in the world ... and so into a stately coach there set for him; and so straight away through the town toward Canterbury without making any stay at Dover.

● **SOURCE 12.16**

From the diary of John Evelyn. Evelyn had been a consistent Royalist sympathiser throughout the 1640s and 1650s. Note, though, the belief in Providence which he shared with Cromwell and others.

Babylonish: *see Source 10.49 for John Milton's reference to this*

myriads: *a great number*

29 May 1660: This day his Majesty Charles II came to London after a sad and long exile and calamitous suffering, both of the King and Church, being 17 years. This was also his birthday, and with a triumph of above 20,000 horse and foot, brandishing their swords and shouting with inexpressible joy; the ways strewed with flowers, the bells ringing, the streets hung with tapestry, fountains running with wine; the mayor, aldermen, and all the companies in their liveries, chains of gold, and banners; lords and nobles clad in silver, gold, and velvet; the windows and balconies, well set with ladies; trumpets, music and MYRIADS of people flocking, even so far as from Rochester, so as they were seven hours in passing the City, ... I stood in the Strand and beheld it, and blessed God. And all this was done without one drop of blood shed, and by that very army which rebelled against him; but it was the Lord's doing, for such a restoration was never mentioned in any history ancient or modern, since the return of the Jews from the BABYLONISH captivity; nor so joyful a day and so bright ever seen in this nation, this happening when to expect or effect it was past all human policy.

● **SOURCE 12.17**

From The Diurnal of Thomas Rugg, 1659–61

The latter end of April and the beginning of this month [May 1661] was spent in several places, days and nights, for joy of his Majesty's coronation. Many letters was [sic] sent to London from their friends in the country, but in regard there were so many I omit to write them down, only one or two heads of their joy.

The town of Bruton in Somersetshire for joy of the coronation, their bells all day and night ringing, their stage pageants, songs, town music, playing nothing but The King Enjoys His Own Again, their musketeers and pikes with great order and repeated volleys, plenty of drink and at noon a sermon preached out of 1 Kings, I.39. So Zadoc the priest took an horn of oil out of the tabernacle and anointed Solomon, and they blew the trumpet and all the people said: God save King Solomon.

And in Cambridge: On the coronation day the town was strewed with green herbs, the windows hanged with tapestry, pictures and garlands, with much plate and jewels, his Majesty's picture exposed to view, richly adorned, the chapel encompassed on the outside with maids hand in hand. The two county troops and captain rose in arms and gave many volleys upon the market hill, where in the morning was hanged on a gibbet the effigy of Oliver Cromwell, carved very like him. It was designed by Lames Alders, the promoter of that condemned spectacle, to have the effigy, gibbet and all burnt at night; but one of the troopers about noon fired it before the designed time, all except the head, which was afterwards fastened on the top of the gallows and so stood all day till night, when it was burnt with the gibbet, the conduit in time running with wine.

● **SOURCE 12.18**

An order of the Lords and Commons, 1660

Ordered by the Lords and Commons assembled in Parliament, that the carcasses of Oliver Cromwell, Henry Ireton, John Bradshaw, Thomas Pride, whether buried at Westminster Abbey or elsewhere, be with all expedition taken up, and drawn upon a hurdle to Tyburn, and there hanged up in their coffins for some time, and after that buried under the said gallows.

● **FIGURE 12.1**

A photograph of Oliver Cromwell's skull. The skull is kept at Sidney Sussex College, Cambridge

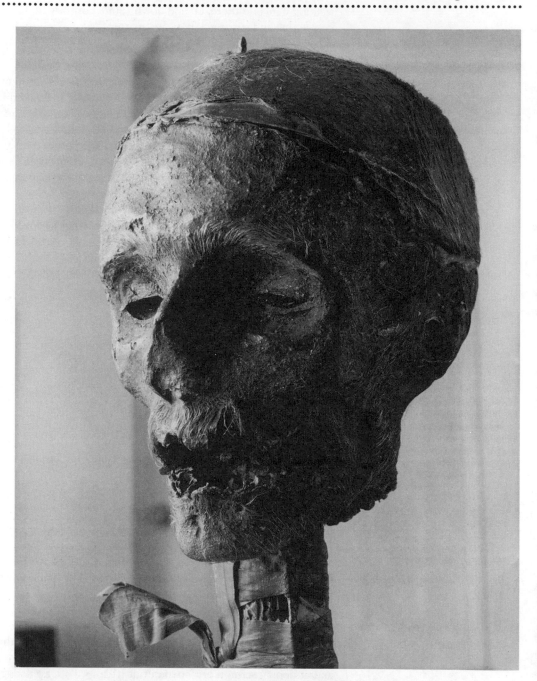

1   In what ways is it possible to determine the political views of the authors of Sources 12.15, 12.16 and 12.17?

2   Are there grounds for not taking Evelyn's account of the scenes on Charles II's return at face value?

3   Is it possible that the celebrations noted by Rugg in Bruton and Cambridge on Charles II's coronation were officially organised ones and not spontaneous popular demonstrations? Can you think of examples of similar official celebrations in more recent times that were not necessarily matched by universal popular support?

Whether everyone rejoiced at the King's return and shared in the hatred shown in Parliament for Cromwell is not known. Evidence of popular opposition to the Restoration in the early 1660s is much more hard to come by than the kind of material in Sources 12.15–12.18. Yet not everyone welcomed the return of the monarchy, as can be seen in Sources 12.19 and 12.20.

● **SOURCE 12.19**

Extracts from the court records from Middlesex and Surrey, c. 1660

[A London lady] 'A pox on all kings. I do not give a turd for never a King in England.'
[A Wapping man] said he 'would gladly spend five shillings to celebrate the execution of the king' and would not mind being the executioner himself.
[A Londoner in 1662] 'hoped ere long to trample in the King's and bishops' blood'.

What might lead you not to accept these extracts from court proceedings as good evidence of popular opposition to the Restoration?

John Milton (1609–74) is most famous for his great poetry, including the three epics, *Paradise Lost*, *Paradise Regained* and *Samson Agonistes*. But he also used his pen in the service of the English Republic. In 1649 he was appointed Latin Secretary to the government and he wrote a stream of pamphlets and books defending the Republic and justifying the execution of the King (including *The Tenure of Kings and Magistrates*). Despite both his increasing blindness in the early 1650s and his doubts about the legitimacy of the establishment of the Protectorate in 1653, he continued his official duties, writing diplomatic letters as well as propaganda material for the republican government. (See also Chapter 7, pages 141–4.)

● **SOURCE 12.20**

From John Milton, *The Readie and Easie Way to Establish a Free Commonwealth*. In writing this plea for the continuation of the Republic and attack on the return of the monarchy in the last weeks of February 1660, Milton put his life in peril, since this was a time when the Restoration was likely to happen soon. The tract was published at the end of February or the beginning of March 1660. In it Milton supported not only the continued rule of the Rump Parliament but the devolution of power to local authorities controlled by the nobility and gentry.

assertours: *old-fashioned spelling of assertor, a champion or advocate*

The Parliament of England assisted by a great number of the people who appeared and stuck to them faithfullest in the defence of religion and their civil liberties, judging kingship by long experience a government burdensome, expensive, useless and dangerous, justly and magnanimously abolished it, turning regal-bondage into a free Commonwealth ... After our liberty thus successfully fought for, gained and many years possessed, except in those unhappy interruptions, which God hath removed, and wonderfully now the third time brought together our old Patriots, the first ASSERTOURS of our religious and civil rights, now that nothing remains, but in all reason the certain hopes of a speedy and immediate settlement to this nation for ever in a firm and free Commonwealth, to fall back, or rather to creep back so poorly as it seems the multitude would, to their once abjured generate corruption suddenly spread among us, fitted and prepared for new slavery, but will render us a scorn and derision to all our neighbours ... If we return to kingship, and soon repent, as undoubtedly we shall, when we begin to find the old encroachments coming on by little and little upon our consciences, which must necessarily proceed from king and bishop united inseparably in one interest, we may be forced to fight all over again all that we have fought, and spend over again all that we have spent, but are never like to attain thus far as we are now advanced, to the recovery of our freedom, never likely to have it in possession, as we now have it ... if by our ungrateful backsliding we make these fruitless to our selves, all his gracious condescensions and answers to our once importuning prayers against the tyranny which we then groaned under to become now of no effect, by ... running headlong again with full stream wilfully and obstinately into the same bondage: making vain and viler than dirt the blood of so many thousand faithful and valiant Englishmen, who left us in this liberty, bought with their lives ...

Having thus far shown with what ease we may now obtain a free Commonwealth and by it with as much ease all the freedom, peace, justice, plenty that we can desire, on the otherside, the difficulties, troubles, uncertainties nay rather impossibilities to enjoy these things constantly under a monarch, I will now proceed to show more particularly wherein our freedom and flourishing condition, will be more ample and secure to us under a free Commonwealth than under a kingship.

The whole freedom of man consists either in spiritual or civil liberty. As for spiritual, who can be at rest, who can enjoy any thing in this world with contentment, who hath not liberty to serve God and to save his own soul, according to the best light which God hath planted in him to that purpose, by the reading of his revealed will and the guidance of his holy spirit? That this is best pleasing to God, and that the whole Protestant Church allows no supreme judge or rule in matters of religion, but the scriptures, and these to be interpreted by the scriptures themselves, which necessarily infers liberty of conscience, hath been heretofore proved ... He who cannot be content with this liberty to himself, but feels violently to impose what he will to be the only religion, upon other men's consciences, let him know, bears a mind not only unchristian and irreligious, but inhuman also and barbarous ... If there was no meddling with Church matters in State counsels ... much peace and tranquillity would follow; as the United Netherlands have found by experience ... since they have left off persecuting, they have lived in much more concord and prosperity ...

The other part of our freedom consists in the civil rights and advancement of every person according to his merit: the enjoyment of those never more certain, and the access to these never more open, than in a free Commonwealth. And both in my opinion may be best and soonest obtained, if every county in the land were made a little commonwealth, and their chief town a city, if it be not called already; where the nobility and chief gentry may build, houses or palaces, befitting their quality, may bear part in the government, make their own judicial laws, and execute them by their own elected judicatures, without appeal, in all things of civil government between man and man. So they shall have justice in their own hands, and none to blame but themselves, if it be not well administered ...

If ... [we shall] put our necks again under kingship, as made use of by the Jews to return back to Egypt ... our condition is not sound but rotten both in religion and all civil prudence ... What I have spoken is the language of the good old cause.

1   Who or what does Milton call 'the first Assertours of our religious and civil rights, who are brought together for 'the third time'?

2   In what ways does Milton's plea for what he calls 'the good old cause' (a phrase often used in the late 1650s):

a) echo Oliver Cromwell's hopes and aims as seen in Chapter 10
b) differ from Cromwell's aspirations?

3   How would a supporter of the Restoration have replied to Milton's arguments?

4   Do you think that there is much doubt that the majority of people in the country supported the return of Charles II in 1660?

● Summary Task

1   Write an essay on this question: Why was the monarchy restored in 1660?
Before starting this essay, divide the class into three groups. Group One should discuss the relative importance of *long-term* and *short-term* factors. Group Two should consider the *push* and *pull* factors. Group Three should discuss *necessary* and *contingent* factors.

2   As a class, consider not only the answer to the question but also the relative usefulness of the three different ways of approaching the question.

● Further reading

See the last section of Ronald Hutton, *The British Republic* (Macmillan, 1990). More detailed books and articles are: Barry Reay, 'The Quakers, 1659, and the Restoration of the Monarchy', *History*, vol. 63, (1978) and his *The Quakers and the English Revolution* (CUP 1985); A. Woolrych, 'The Good Old Cause and the Fall of the Protectorate', *Historical Journal*, vol. 13 (1957) and 'Last Quests for Settlement 1657–60' in G. E. Aylmer (ed.), *The Interregnum: the Quest for Settlement* (1973). The most detailed account of the period is Ronald Hutton, *The Restoration: a Political and Religious History 1658–67* (OUP, 1985).

What were the consequences of the English Revolution?

Introduction

This is the last big question that faces anyone studying the English Revolution. It has not been the subject of as much or as heated controversy as the question which began Chapter 2: 'What were the causes of the English Revolution?' Yet it has been much written about and the answers to it have changed considerably over the years. Moreover, even in the present day there is no 'correct' answer that all historians are agreed upon, any more than there is a generally accepted explanation of why the English Revolution began in 1640–1.

Let us examine three broad theories that have been suggested to answer the question, 'What were the consequences of the English Revolution?' Each is supported by extracts from the writings of historians. Read them carefully and then at the end of the chapter decide which (if any) of these theories you prefer as an answer to this question.

Theory A

The English Revolution was an important turning point in the history of the country, bringing about major, positive changes that helped to transform medieval England into modern Britain.

This interpretation, that the period 1640–60 marked a major turning point in the history of Britain, was one that was very fashionable when I (Barry Coward) first began to study this period as an undergraduate and then as a university teacher in the 1960s. Its major proponent is Christopher Hill, who has a good claim to be the most exciting historian of seventeenth-century England in this century. These are extracts from one of his textbooks, in which he argues that the English Revolution transformed Britain in many fundamental ways. With someone who believes, as Hill does, that the English Revolution was brought about by powerful and deep-rooted historical processes, it is not surprising to find him arguing that its effects were equally clear-cut, decisive and permanent.

In this first extract Hill argues that the English Revolution brought about major changes in the economy and society.

● **SOURCE 13.1**

From Christopher Hill, *Reformation to Industrial Revolution: a Social and Economic History of Britain, 1530–1780* (1967)

In agrarian relations the Middle Ages were brought to an end in 1646 by the abolition of FEUDAL TENURES and the COURT OF WARDS. When in April 1660 the Convention Parliament agreed to the return of Charles II, the next business it turned to was confirmation of their abolition.

The importance of this was … [that] land was freed from the arbitrary death duties and spoliation of wardship, and so long-term planning and investment of capital in estate management were made possible … Most obstacles to enclosure were removed: the agricultural boom of the late seventeenth and eighteenth centuries redounded to the benefit of big landowners and capitalist farmers, not of peasant proprietors …

Court of Wards: *the royal court that supervised the monarch's feudal right of wardship. This was the right of the monarch, when land was inherited by a minor (i.e. someone who was not yet legally an adult), to administer the estates and arrange the marriage of the minor (see Chapter 1, page 13).*

feudal tenures: *these were the conditions under which landowners held their land from the monarch. By the seventeenth century land was no longer held in return for military service, but landowners still owed some legal obligations to monarchs in return for owning land. The main one was wardship.*

Contemporaries attributed to the revolutionary decades a number of agricultural improvements … Many of the improvements of the later seventeenth and eighteenth centuries were proclaimed in Blyth's *English Improver* (1649) and the vastly increased literature on agriculture which began to appear in the forties. Already the crop yields of the Low Countries and England were well ahead of the rest of Europe. As historians push the Industrial Revolution forward to the later eighteenth century, they pull the agricultural revolution back into the seventeenth century.

In the next extract Hill argues that the mid-seventeenth century was also the point at which the government of the country began to change in a modern direction: monarchs lost the predominant position they had traditionally held and the balance of power in the constitution shifted towards Parliaments.

● **SOURCE 13.2**

From Christopher Hill, *Reformation to Industrial Revolution*

The sixteen forties and 'fifties marked the end of medieval and Tudor England … This revolution in government was much more important than that of a century earlier: the old state was not restored in 1660, only its trappings. The Prerogative Courts did not return, and so the sovereignty of Parliament and common law remained. The Privy Council henceforth had no effective control over local government. Taxation and therefore ultimately policy were controlled by Parliament. The government of the country for many years by the House of Commons and its committees was an experience that could never be forgotten: so were the execution of Charles I, the abolition of bishops and the House of Lords, [and] the existence of an English republic whose foreign and imperial policies were as impressively successful as those of the Stuart monarchy had been inglorious.

In this last extract Hill widens the case for a mid-seventeenth-century turning point even further.

● **SOURCE 13.3**

From Christopher Hill, *Reformation to Industrial Revolution*

It is difficult to exaggerate the social significance of the religious and intellectual revolution of the sixteen forties and 'fifties. The year 1641 was no less a turning point for the church than for the state. In that year the High Commission was abolished, and with it the government's control over the parishes. Bishops and church courts ceased to function, church lands were sold. Ecclesiastical censorship ceased to exist, as did ecclesiastical control over education … For many years after 1640 there was effective religious toleration. Sects hitherto illegal, whose members were drawn mainly from the lower classes, now met and discussed in public, and their views were printed. We should be careful not to read backwards into this period sectarian divisions which crystallised later. Most Englishmen, including most parsons, were content to remain members of the English church, whether that church was Episcopalian, Presbyterian or more broadly Protestant. For a brief period Episcopalians, Presbyterians, Congregationalists and Baptists worked side by side in a national church … The attempt after 1660 to reimpose a narrow Anglican uniformity failed, and henceforth it could never again be pretended that all Englishmen belonged to a single church. Whether or not religious toleration was legalised, the existence of organised religious bodies outside the state church was a fact of which account had to be taken. The long-term liberating effect of the competition of rival religious views, as against the monopoly which the established church had enjoyed until 1641, is impossible to calculate …

fillip: *a stimulus, a sharp push forward*

Scientific ideas received a FILLIP during the revolution, thanks to the greater freedom of publication and discussion, to the introduction of scientists to Oxford by the Parliamentary Commissioners, and to the formation in London and Oxford of the groups which after the Restoration took the initiative in founding the Royal Society. Again and again in his writings John Aubrey, FRS [Fellow of the Royal Society], refers to superstitions which prevailed before the civil war and had disappeared by the end of Charles II's reign … Nature came to be thought of as a machine that could be understood, controlled and improved upon by knowledge.

Theory B

The English Revolution was not a major turning point in the transition from medieval England to modern Britain. On the contrary, the major consequences of the English Revolution were negative ones, as people reacted against the violence and radicalism of what had happened between 1640 and 1660.

This interpretation (as you will see from the dates when the writings of the historians who support it were published) was popular at roughly the same time as the phase of revisionism that marked the 'causes of the English Revolution' debate (see Chapter 2). Revisionist writings on the later period were not as numerous in the later 1970s and 1980s or as controversial in tone as those on early seventeenth-century history. But they represented as great a change in historians' approaches to the history of Restoration England.

The first extract is from Lawrence Stone. In this extract, rather surprisingly for someone who had a few years earlier written a book (see Chapter 2) which supported the case that the English Revolution was caused, in part, by long-term social and economic developments, he argues that its social and economic impact was slight.

● **SOURCE 13.4**

From Lawrence Stone's article 'The Results of the English Revolution', in J. G. A. Pocock (ed.), *Three British Revolutions* (1980)

laissez-faire: *is French for 'leave to do'. The phrase is used to describe the idea that governments should not interfere but should leave individuals, industrialists, merchants, etc., to get on with their economic affairs themselves.*

The effect of the Revolution on economic and demographic trends is … obscure. Those who … see the upheaval as the first bourgeois revolution, argue that it opened the way for LAISSEZ-FAIRE capitalism and middle-class influence in government. In fact, however, there is little evidence to suggest that it did more than accelerate and consolidate trends that were already apparent long before the Revolution began. Only one of the graphs of basic trends shows any signs of decisive change during the two decades of the Revolution. Rapid demographic growth came to an end in 1630 and did not pick up again much before 1740 … The 130-year price revolution certainly reached its climax in about 1650, to be followed by another 120 years of rough stability or even decline, but it is impossible to attribute this change to the processes of revolution. There is no logical explanation for such a connection, and in fact the change occurred all over Europe at varying times in the middle third of the seventeenth century, and so was not an exclusively English phenomenon at all.

Agricultural productivity rose uninterruptedly throughout the period from 1520 to 1740, partly through the expansion of land under cultivation, and partly as a result of technical improvements that increased yields per acre … Many of these innovations were copied from Holland, and this process was at most only accelerated during the Revolution. The civil wars of the 1640s caused considerable devastation and loss of crops and cattle, but tithes and rents had recovered by the mid-1650s. The setback was only temporary, and was confined to areas that had been fought over. So far as the long-term history of agriculture is concerned, the Interregnum might never have taken place …

The effect of the mid-century Revolution on science and technology has been intensely debated for the last twenty-five years, but the results are still inconclusive … Ideas [for scientific reform] and their advocates were patronised by some parliamentary leaders, and two groups of talented experimental scientists gathered in Oxford and London in the 1640s and 1650s. They formed the nucleus of the post-Restoration Royal Society … But there is nothing to show that the patronage and support given to these men and their ideas by the Long Parliament and the Protectorate were any greater than that given to them by Charles II, the Court aristocracy and the higher clergy in the 1660s. Both were far more receptive to … scientific ideas than the Court of Charles I … but this shift was common to all seventeenth-century European culture and might well have taken place without the stimulus of the Revolution.

A normal aspect of a revolution is the dispossession of an old elite and its replacement by a new one. Half-hearted efforts were made in this direction by the confiscation of the land of leading royalist exiles, the heavy fining of thousands of others for the right to regain their property, and the imposition of a 10 per cent tax on ex-royalists in 1656. It was hoped that these measures would financially cripple the leading royalist families. Confiscated lands of ex-royalists, the Church, and the Crown were sold on easy terms or granted as a reward to the leading supporters of the revolutionary regime.

The net effects of these half-hearted attempts to create a new landed elite were virtually nil. In 1660 all the old Crown and Church properties were restored to their original owners, and it has now been proved that the great bulk of the few royalist estates that were confiscated and put up for sale by the Commonwealth was bought back by their former owners, through DUMMY AGENTS … There is no evidence to show either that a new class of landowners emerged as a result of the Revolution, or that the former squires and gentry suffered more than some temporary financial discomfort. There was almost no turn-over of landed elites as a result of the twenty-year Revolution …

Nor was this all. The experience of the late 1640s and early 1650s, when the counties were ruled by committees drawn mainly from the ranks of the humbler lesser gentry, induced the wealthy squires to close ranks in 1660 and to consolidate their monopoly of local power and status … Social revolution, insofar as it occurred, merely resulted in social reaction.

> **dummy agent:** *someone secretly acting on behalf of the former landowner*

In the next extract John Miller argues that those of the monarchy's powers that were restored in 1660 are more important than those that it lost.

● SOURCE 13.5

From John Miller's article 'The Later Stuart Monarchy', in J. R. Jones (ed.), *The Restored Monarchy* (1979)

Most historians, in writing about the restored monarchy, stress its weaknesses rather than its strengths, with some plausibility. The Crown's COERCIVE POWERS had been reduced by the abolition in 1641 of Star Chamber, the Council of the North and the High Commission. They were not revived at the Restoration. Similarly, the legislation of 1641 which declared illegal many of Charles's unpopular fiscal devices was preserved intact and was supplemented by an Act abolishing feudal tenures and the Court of Wards. As a result, with a few minor exceptions, the King could now raise money only by means explicitly approved by Parliament. Moreover, although Parliament reverted to the traditional doctrine that the King should 'LIVE OF HIS OWN', it showed itself reluctant to enlarge his ordinary revenue too far, preferring to vote temporary extraordinary grants to meet his immediate needs. There were several possible reasons for this reluctance to grant Charles II too large a permanent revenue. As representatives of the taxpayer, MPs were never eager to vote money without a very good reason. They realised, too, that Charles was much more likely to meet Parliament regularly if he were kept short of money … Finally, an impoverished monarch would be unable to afford a substantial army and Englishmen had had enough of military rule. This last anxiety also underlay Parliament's refusal in the early 1660s to reform the militia and thus make it a more effective force.

These restrictions on the monarchy, important as they were, were perhaps less significant than the restrictions that were *not* imposed. Had they wished, the Convention of 1660 and the CAVALIER PARLIAMENT elected in 1661 could have refrained from giving Charles II an adequate permanent revenue and used their financial power to reduce Charles to a figurehead. Instead they seemed to go out of their way to build up the power of the Crown. Not only did they vote an ordinary revenue which was intended to be sufficient to cover the normal costs of administration but they abandoned Parliament's two main constitutional demands of 1641–8: a share in the King's choice of ministers and in the control of the armed forces. At the Restoration the King's exclusive right to control the militia was explicitly reaffirmed while his right to choose his advisers was tacitly acknowledged. Thus all the basic royal prerogatives remained intact. Apart from controlling appointments and the armed forces the King was responsible for the conduct of foreign policy and the provision of justice and, in general, he was expected to see to the day-to-day administration of the country.

The restoration of monarchical authority was quite deliberate … The monarchy's effective powers were restored … because the Convention and Cavalier Parliament wanted Charles II to be an effective ruler.

> **Cavalier Parliament:** *the name by which the Parliament elected in 1661 is known*
>
> **coercive powers:** *ability to use force*
>
> **live of his own:** *is the phrase used at that time to refer to the expectation that monarchs should normally (i.e. in peacetime) run the country using the money they received from their own resources, i.e. royal estates, feudal revenues and customs dues. Only in extraordinary circumstances (i.e. mainly in wartime) were monarchs expected to raise money by Parliamentary taxation.*

In the next extract, Ian Green argues that the horror at the radicalism of the English Revolution which drove the propertied classes to want to restore a strong monarchy also triggered the restoration of a very intolerant Church. For Green, Restoration England was certainly not a time when religious passions began to cool!

● **SOURCE 13.6**

From Ian Green, *The Re-establishment of the Church of England 1660–3* (1978)

Clarendon Code: *a series of Acts of Parliament passed in the early 1660s. Amongst other things, these Acts restricted the right to worship of non-Anglicans and made it illegal for them to hold public offices.*

comprehension: *a national Church that included a broad range of Protestant opinion*

royal indulgence: *religious toleration granted by the King*

There remain too many examples of persecuting intent for us to doubt that the Cavalier House of Commons as a whole was 'very zealous for the Church'. Indeed, such was their sense of urgency that they pushed aside the king's own views and his other, more pressing business in their campaign to impose Anglican worship on all his subjects. In the preambles to the acts which constitute the 'CLARENDON CODE' we can see the driving forces behind their campaign: their hatred of what Puritanism had done in the past, their fear of what it could still do in the future, and their reliance on the episcopal Church of England as a bulwark against the 'poisonous principles of schism and rebellion' … The gentry … attacked those forces which challenged the ecclesiastical hierarchy and the existing order of society …

The more one examines the Restoration church settlement, the more difficult it is to escape the conclusion that the most important single influence upon its shape was the zeal of the gentry for the episcopal Church of England, both in the counties and at Westminster. It was this more than anything else which forced Charles to abandon first the idea of COMPREHENSION and then the possibility of a ROYAL INDULGENCE. It was probably this factor too which undermined the morale of the Puritan clergy, so that in August 1662 well over a thousand ministers … left their livings quietly and resignedly.

Theory C

The English Revolution was not a major turning point in the history of the country; it had no clear-cut consequences one way or the other. What had happened in the 1640s and 1650s ensured that the country would never be the same again, but the consequences of the English Revolution were diverse and contradictory. As a result very little (apart from the restoration of a monarchical constitution) was settled at the Restoration.

This is a theory that I supported in an article I wrote in 1986.

● **SOURCE 13.7**

From Barry Coward's article 'Was There an English Revolution in the Middle of the Seventeenth Century?' in C. Jones, M. Newitt and S. Roberts (eds.), *Politics and People in Revolutionary England* (1986)

Valuable as these new approaches to the consequences of the English Revolution are [referring to revisionist interpretations like those in Sources 13.4–13.6], it is possible to take them too far. Just as the causes and course of the English Revolution cannot be fully explained without taking account of diverse, contrasting strands in the history of England before 1660, so there needs to be a recognition that the consequences of the Revolution were not totally negative but were many and ambivalent. In some respects the English Revolution did speed up, rather than hold back, economic, social and intellectual changes. For example, knowledge among English farmers and landlords of advanced agricultural techniques and new crops used by farmers in the Low Countries became much more widespread as a result of the enforced continental travels of royalist émigrés like Sir Richard Weston, who wrote *A Discourse on Husbandry in Brabant and Flanders* in the 1640s, and, more importantly, by the publication of agricultural treatises which, like printed books and pamphlets of all kinds, underwent a publication boom during the English Revolution. Moreover, the conditions of lax censorship during much of the Revolution which made this possible and the consequent intellectual ferment of the period provided a congenial intellectual climate in which to pursue scientific research. John Aubrey exaggerated when he said that 'the searching into Natural Knowledge began but since or about the death of King Charles the first', but his comment is a reminder that the effects of the English Revolution were not simply reactionary.

However, it is in religious and political history that there is perhaps the greatest danger of historians failing to recognise that the English Revolution had diverse, contrasting effects. The more one reads about the religious and political history of Restoration England, the more one is able to detect a positive, as well as a negative, reaction to what had happened before 1660. It is a less obvious response because it was often expressed quietly, unlike strident, militant Anglicanism. It is to be seen, not in public parliamentary speeches, but in private diaries, and

Whigs and **Tories:** *these were the names given to the first political parties which slowly emerged in England after 1660. They can first be clearly seen in the later 1670s, when the Whigs tried to secure the exclusion from the succession to the throne of the Roman Catholic James, Duke of York.*

They were opposed by the Tories. After 1689 Whig–Tory political rivalries became very fierce on a range of issues. The main one was the attitude taken to Protestant Dissenters (i.e. those who were not allowed to become members of the Church of England). Whigs were much more willing than Tories to tolerate Protestant Dissenters.

above all in the activities (or rather the inactivities) and the beliefs of some Anglican gentlemen, divines and academics. The more work that is done on the local history of Restoration England, the more it becomes apparent that historians have been blinded by those who have written about Protestant Dissent after 1660 in terms of 'the period of the Great Persecution'. While the Clarendon Code was enacted and put into effect in the early 1660s against some Dissenters, notably Quakers and Baptists, it is clear that if one takes a longer perspective the Code was enforced in a far from systematic and extensive manner. Why were not all Anglican J.P.s infected by the vindictive mood of militant Anglicanism? When more work on Restoration England has been done it may be found that they were more sympathetic to the long post-Reformation tradition of a comprehensive church, broken by Charles I and Laud in the 1620s and 1630s and revived by Cromwell in the 1650s, than they were to the narrow church erected in the 1660s … Like many others, they reacted against 'the enthusiasm' of the Quakers, Ranters and others, but, unlike High Church divines, they reacted not negatively by urging repression of Dissent but positively by stressing the importance in religion of rational arguments rather than faith and revelation. Moreover, they turned away from the intolerance of the High Church Tory party to advocate a widening of toleration, a position which became associated in the party politics of later Stuart England with the WHIGS.

Both features of later Stuart politics – the more tolerant attitudes of the Whigs as well as the bigotry of the TORIES – were rooted in the English Revolution. In the present state of knowledge of Restoration England this division and its connections with the English Revolution are more apparent in the Westminster political scene … Nevertheless, there are a few indications that in the localities, as well as at Westminster, the struggle between factions over the question of toleration of Protestant dissenters was a central feature of political life that persisted in a major 'church–chapel' divide in English society.

In this and in many other ways the consequences of the English Revolution were diverse. It set in motion contradictory trends: negative forces of reaction and suppression alongside more positive responses to what had happened. As a result the legacy of the English Revolution was neither what seventeenth-century admirers of the Good Old Cause wanted, nor was it a complete restoration of the state of affairs before the Revolution … Ivan Roots [in his textbook *The Great Rebellion*] neatly expressed the same substantive point when he wrote that 'the Great Rebellion had permanent consequences. Like some many-lived Cheshire cat it left a persistent grin behind'.

The final extract is from an article that explains recent historians' approaches to the history of Restoration England.

● **SOURCE 13.8**

From Tim Harris's article 'Introduction: Revising the Restoration', T. Harris *et al.* (eds.), *The Politics of Religion in Restoration England* (1991)

The traditional picture [of Restoration England] … needs to be challenged in a number of respects. To begin with, the year 1660 should not be seen as marking too much of a watershed … If we look at the struggles which emerged in the 1670s and 1680s we find there were more continuities than is usually recognised. In the first place, there was a significant continuity of personnel. Many of those who led or shaped the opposition to the restored monarchy in the 1670s and 1680s had gained their formative political experience during the struggles of the 1640s and 1650s … The continuity of personnel that existed also provided for a continuity of issues from the period before 1660 …

A central factor in providing cohesion to the first Whig movement was a common concern about the security of religion. In the first place, of course, there was a concern about the growth of popery … The issue of popery was not primarily a concern about possible arbitrary rule under a Catholic successor (that is, a concern about the constitutional threat, which lay mainly in the future) but rather a concern about the religious dangers created by the reign and policies of Charles II (that is, the threat was in the present, and very much a religious one) … The issue of popery was not a new one that emerged from the 1670s … the crisis of popery of 1678–83 was little more than a re-run of the similar crisis of 1637–42.

[He goes on to argue that behind the political tensions of the 1670s and 1680s lay differences between Protestants that had existed before 1660.] These fundamental tensions within English protestantism remained and were perpetuated after the Restoration. While there was probably a fairly widespread consensus on the need to bring back monarchy in 1660, there was certainly no consensus in religious terms, where anglicans, presbyterians and separatists all expected different things from the restored regime … The old religious tensions survived and, reinforced by persecution, fed into the political tensions which became particularly acute in the 1670s and 1680s … These tensions centred … on attitudes towards dissent (sympathy or hostility) …

The association of the Whig platform with the cause of dissent was much closer than had usually been recognised … Their [the Tories'] basic strategy was to identify all Whigs as nonconformists and republicans, whose real aim was to destroy the established church and monarchy and bring England once more into a puritan commonwealth … The concern of the Tories was as much to protect the interests of the church as anything else … The partisan conflicts of the exclusion era were so intense precisely because they did not represent new areas of dispute of concern only to the central government elite, but because what was happening at Westminster was but an intensification of conflicts which had been fought out in a variety of local settings for some years going back to the Restoration and even before.

● Summary Task

1   Use the material in this chapter to answer the question, 'What were the consequences of the English Revolution?' Organise your answer under the following headings:

- Political and constitutional
- Religious
- Social and economic
- Other.

In your conclusion you should explain which of the three theories presented in this chapter you find most convincing.

2   Write an essay answering this question: Does what happened in England between 1640 and 1660 deserve to be called 'The English Revolution'?
    Before doing this you could do two exercises that will help you to work out your own answer to this question. One should be done individually; the other could be done as a class discussion.

An individual task
Take two pieces of paper. Head one of them: 'What was changed as a result of the events of the 1640s and 1650s?'. Head the other: 'What was not changed by the events of the 1640s and 1650s?'. Divide each paper into four columns with the following headings: Society and economy; Religion; Government and politics; Culture and ideas.
    Using the material in this chapter and any other information you have gained from other sources, write down points under the relevant headings.

A group exercise
A class discussion: What do we mean by 'revolution'?
    Everyone should write a short paragraph, defining what is meant by 'a revolution'.
    One or two should be read out as the beginning of a discussion aimed at reaching an agreed definition of 'revolution'.

Class discussion
The following features are often found in periods of revolutionary activity, as in the French, Russian and Chinese Revolutions which you may have studied in Years 10–11 in your GCSE course.
    Discuss in class which of these features did and did not occur in England in 1640 and 1660.

Features	Yes	No
Intellectual ferment		
Questioning of old ideas		
Violence		
Change in social structure		
Change in political institutions		
Destruction of the old ruling class		
The emergence of a new class in power		
Breakdown of censorship		

Features	Yes	No
Major cultural change		
The ending of religious monopoly		
Major economic change		
The lasting transformation of life in the country		

3 When you have completed the group discussion, write a short essay explaining whether you think the events in England between 1640 and 1660 should be remembered as:

- a revolution
- a rebellion rather than a revolution
- a failed revolution.

Sources

Chapter 1

Source 1.1 Montacute House in Somerset. The Clifton-Maybank frontispiece dates from late sixteenth/early seventeenth century

Source 1.2 Beggars being punished, from Holinshed's *Chronicle*, 1577

Source 1.3 The Apotheosis of James I by Peter Paul Rubens,1635. One of a series of paintings commissioned by Charles I for the Royal Banqueting House, Whitehall

Chapter 2

Source 2.1–2.5 Lawrence Stone, *The Causes of the English Revolution* (Routledge, 1972)

Source 2.6 Conrad Russell, 'Parliamentary history in perspective, 1604–29', *History*, vol. 61 (1976)

Source 2.7 Nicholas Tyacke, 'Puritanism, Arminianism and counter-revolution' in Conrad Russell (ed.) , *The Origins of the English Civil War* (Macmillan,1973)

Source 2.8 Jenny Wormald, 'James VI and I; two kings or one?', *History*, vol. 68 (1983)

Source 2.9 Kevin Sharpe, 'The Personal Rule of Charles I' in H. Tomlinson (ed.), *Before the English Civil War* (St Martin's Press, 1983)

Source 2.10 Alan Everitt, 'The county community' in E. W. Ives (ed.), *The English Revolution* (1968)

Source 2.11 Conrad Russell, *Parliaments and English Politics, 1621–29* (OUP, 1979)

Source 2.12 'The Personal Rule of Charles I' (as above)

Source 2.13 'Puritanism, Arminianism and counter-revolution' (as above)

Source 2.14 John Morrill, 'The religious context of the English Civil War', *Transactions of the Royal Historical Society*, 5th series, vol. 34 (1984), reprinted in John Morrill (ed.), *The Nature of the English Revolution* (Longman, 1993)

Source 2.15 Conrad Russell, 'The British Problem and the English Civil War', *History*, vol. 72 (1987)

Source 2.16 Derek Hirst, *Authority and Conflict: England 1603–58* (Edward Arnold, 1985)

Source 2.17 Anne Hughes, *The Causes of the English Civil War* (Macmillan, 1991)

Source 2.18 Johann Sommerville, 'Ideology, Property and the Constitution' in Richard Cust and Anne Hughes (eds.), *Conflict in Early Stuart England: Studies in Religion and Politics, 1603–42* (Longman,1989)

Source 2.19 Richard Cust, *The Forced Loan and English Politics, 1626–28* (OUP, 1987)

Source 2.20 Richard Cust and Anne Hughes, 'Introduction: after revisionism' in Cust and Hughes, *Conflict in Early Stuart England: Studies in Religion and Politics, 1603–42* (Longman, 1989)

Source 2.21 John Rushworth (ed.), *Historical Collections*, vol. 1(1680)

Chapter 3

Source 3.1–3.4 J. P. Kenyon (ed.), *The Stuart Constitution* (CUP, 1986)

Source 3.5 A contemporary view of Strafford's execution at Towerhill, May 1641

Source 3.6 A Dutch engraving of Strafford's execution

Source 3.7 British Museum

Source 3.8 A Protestant artist's view of the Massacre of Portadown Bridge in 1641, Ashmolean Museum

Source 3.9 A Protestant account of the Catholic Rebellion of 1641, British Library, Thomason Tracts, E.180.15

Source 3.10 *The Stuart Constitution* (as above)

Source 3.11 Sir P. Warwick, *Memoirs of the Reign of King Charles I* (1701)

Source 3.12 S. R. Gardiner (ed.), *Constitutional Documents of the Puritan Revolution* (Clarendon Press, 1906)

Source 3.13 J. Bruce (ed.), *Verney Papers: Notes on Proceedings in the Long Parliament by Sir Ralph Verney Knt*, Camden Society Publs, vol. 31 (1845)

Source 3.14 John Rushworth (ed.), *Historical Collections*, vol. 4 (1680)

Source 3.15 *The Stuart Constitution* (as above)

Sorce 3.16 *The Attempted Arrest of the Five Members*, a nineteenth-century painting

Source 3.17 Edward Hyde from *History of the Rebellion* (1702–4) in G. Huehns (ed.), *Selections from Clarendon* (OUP, 1978)

Source 3.18 W. H. Coate (ed.), *The Journal of Sir Simonds D'Ewes* (Yale University Press, 1970)

Source 3.19–3.22 *Constitutional Documents of the Puritan Revolution* (as above)

Source 3.23 B. Schofield (ed.), *The Knyvett Letters 1620–1644*, Norfolk Records Society publs, vol. 20 (1949)

Source 3.24–3.25 British Library, Thomason Tracts

Source 3.26–3.27 *The Stuart Constitution* (as above)

Source 3.28 C. H. Wilkinson (ed.), *The Poems of Richard Lovelace* (Clarendon Press, 1930)

Source 3.29 Sir Edmund Verney painted by the Flemish artist Anthony Van Dyck. The original hangs in Claydon House, Buckinghamshire

Source 3.30 *Selections from Clarendon* (as above)

Source 3.31 *Calendar of State Papers Domestic 1641–3*

Source 3.32 T. Taylor Lewis (ed.), *The Letters of Lady Brilliana Harley*, Camden Society Publs, vol. 58 (1854)

Source 3.33 W. Dunn Macray (ed.), *History of the Rebellion*, vol. 2 (Clarendon Press, 1888)

Source 3.34 John Morrill (ed.), *The Revolt of the Provinces* (Longman, 1976)

Source 3.35 *Selections from Clarendon* (as above)

Chapter 4

Source 4.1 British Library, Thomason Tracts, E.126.13

Source 4.2–4.3 Charles Carlton, *Going to the Wars* (Routledge, 1992)

Source 4.4 British Library, Thomason Tracts, E.100.8

Source 4.5 British Library, Thomason Tracts, E.455.16

Source 4.6–4.7 *Going to the Wars* (as above)

Source 4.8 R. E. Sherwood, *Civil Strife in the Midlands* (Phillimore, 1974)

Source 4.9 *Going to the Wars* (as above)

Source 4.10–4.11 John Morrill (ed.), *The Revolt of the Provinces* (Longman, 1976)

Source 4.12 R. Howell, *Newcastle upon Tyne and the Puritan Revolution* (Clarendon Press, 1967)

Source 4.13 J. P. Kenyon (ed.), *The Stuart Constitution* (CUP, 1986)

Source 4.14 F. Bamford (ed.), *A Royalist's Notebook* (Constable, 1936)

Source 4.15 *The Stuart Constitution* (as above)

Source 4.16–4.17 *The Revolt of the Provinces* (as above)

Source 4.18 *The Stuart Constitution* (as above)

Source 4.19 *The Revolt of the Provinces* (as above)

Source 4.20 Alan Everitt, *The Community of Kent and the Great Rebellion* (Leicester University Press, 1966)

Source 4.21 British Library, Thomason Tracts, E.85.6

Source 4.22 British Library, Thomason Tracts, E.70.5

Source 4.23–4.24 Historical Manuscripts Commission, 11th Report, Appendix VII

Source 4.25 Historical Manuscripts Commission, *Portland Manuscripts*, vol. I

Source 4.26 Bodleian Library, *Tanner Manuscripts*, vol. 60, part 2

Source 4.27 Warwickshire Records Office, *Feilding Family Manuscripts*, CR 2107, C1, letter 17

Source 4.28 Warwickshire Records Office, *Feilding Family Manuscripts*, CR 2107, C1 letter 24

Source 4.29 Warwickshire Records Office, *Feilding Family Manuscripts*, CR 2107, C1, letter 28

Source 4.30–4.32 F. P. and M. M. Verney, *Memoirs of the Verney Family during the Seventeenth Century*, vol. I (Barnes and Noble, 1970)

Source 4.33 T. Taylor Lewis (ed.), *The Letters of Lady Brilliana Harley*, Camden Society Publs, vol. 58 (1853)

Source 4.34 British Museum, Additional Manuscripts, 28,003, f. 17

Source 4.35 John Loftis (ed.), *The Memoirs of Anne, Lady Halkett and Anne, Lady Fanshawe* (Clarendon Press, 1979)

Chapter 5

Source 5.1 Christopher Hill, *The Century of Revolution* (Nelson, 1961)

Source 5.2 Charles Wilson, 'Economics and Politics in the Seventeenth Century', *Historical Journal V*, No. 1 (1962)

Source 5.3 Sir Charles Firth, *Cromwell's Army* (Methuen, 1902)

Source 5.4 Mark Kishlansky, *The Rise of the New Model Army* (CUP, 1979)

Source 5.5 Ronald Hutton, *The Royalist War Effort, 1642–1646* (Longman, 1982)

Source 5.6 John Morrill, 'The Stuarts', in K. Morgan (ed.), *The Oxford History of Britain* (OUP, 1984)

Source 5.7 Angela Anderson, *The Civil Wars, 1640–49* (Hodder and Stoughton, 1995)

Source 5.8 Barry Williams, *Elusive Settlement* (Nelson, 1984)

Chapter 6

Source 6.1 J. Bruce (ed.), *Charles I in 1646. Letters of King Charles the First to Queen Henrietta Maria*, Camden Society Publs, old series, vol. LXIII (1856)

Source 6.2 S. R. Gardiner (ed.), Constitutional Documents of the Puritan Revolution (Clarendon Press, 1906)

Source 6.3 Thomas Edwards, *Gangraena* (1646) reprinted by the Rota of the University of Exeter (1977)

Source 6.4 C.H. Firth (ed.), *The Clarke Papers*, Camden Society Publs, new series, vol. I (1899)

Source 6.5–6.7 A.S.P. Woodhouse, *Puritanism and Liberty* (Dent, 1974)

Source 6.8 John Rushworth, *Historical Collections*, vol. 6 (1680)

Source 6.9–6.10 *The Clarke Papers* (as above)

Source 6.11 *Publications of the Thoresby Society*, vol. XI (1904)

Source 6.12 *The Clarke Papers* (as above)

Source 6.13 'The Memoirs of Sir John Berkeley in F. Maseres (ed.), *Select Tracts Relating to the Civil War in England* (1815)

Source 6.14 H. G. Tibbutt (ed.), *The Tower of London Letterbook of Sir Lewis Dyve 1646–7*, Bedfordshire Historical Record Society, vol. XXXVIII (1958)

Source 6.15 D. M. Wolfe, *Leveller Manifestoes of the Puritan Revolution* (Nelson, 1944)

Source 6.16 *Constitutional Documents of the Puritan Revolution* (as above)

Source 6.17 *The Clarke Papers* (as above)

Source 6.18 David Underdown (ed.), *The Parliamentary Diary of John Boys*, Bulletin of the Institute of Historical Research (1966)

Source 6.19 *The Parliamentary Diary of John Boys* (as above)

Source 6.20 John Morrill (ed.), *The Revolt of the Provinces* (Longman, 1976)

Source 6.21 J. P. Kenyon (ed.), *The Stuart Constitution* (CUP, 1986)

Source 6.22 Edmund Ludlow, *Memoirs of Edmund Ludlow*, vol. I (Clarendon Press, 1894)

Source 6.23 W. C. Abbott (ed.), *The Writings and Speeches of Oliver Cromwell*, vol. I (Harvard University Press, 1937–44)

Source 6.24 *Constitutional Documents of the Puritan Revolution* (as above)

Source 6.25 *The Trial of Charles I*, Nelson, *Report of the trial* (1684)

Source 6.26 quoted in Pauline Gregg, *King Charles I* (Dent,1981)

Source 6.27 *The Stuart Constitution* (as above)

Source 6.28 The death warrant of Charles I, 29 January 1649

Source 6.29 *The Stuart Constitution* (as above)

Source 6.30 *The execution of Charles I*, Sutherland Collection, Ashmolean Museum

Chapter 7

Source 7.1 Anne Hughes (ed.), *Seventeenth-Century England: A Changing Culture* (Open University, 1980)

Source 7.2 Title page of *A Remonstrance of Many Thousand Citizens*, 1646

Source 7.3 John Lilburne's portrait, engraved by George Glover. The original is in the Thomason Collection in the British Museum , E.343.(11)

Source 7.4 A. S. P. Woodhouse, *Puritanism and Liberty* (Dent, 1974)

Source 7.5 A page from William Walwyn's pamphlet, *England's Lamentable Slaverie*, 1645

Source 7.6 J. R. McMichael and B. Taft (eds.), *The Writings of William Walwyn* (University of Georgia Press, 1989)

Source 7.7 J. P. Kenyon (ed.), *The Stuart Constitution* (CUP, 1986)

Source 7.8 An extract from the Putney Debates, October-November 1647; Bodleian Library

Source 7.9 *The Stuart Constitution* (as above)

Source 7.10 *Puritanism and Liberty* (as above)

Source 7.11–7.15 G. H. Sabine (ed.), *The Works of Gerrard Winstanley* (Russell and Russell, 1965)

Source 7.16 N. Smith (ed.), *A Collection of Ranter Writings from the Seventeenth Century* (Junction Books, 1983)

Source 7.17 J. C. Davis, *Fear, Myth and History: The Ranters and the historians* (CUP, 1986)

Source 7.18 The frontispiece of an anti-Ranter pamphlet, *The Ranters Religion*, published in 1650

Source 7.19 *Fear, Myth and History: The Ranters and the historians* (as above)

Source 7.20 A page from *The Routing of the Ranters*, 1650

Source 7.21 *Fear, Myth and History: The Ranters and the historians* (as above)

Source 7.22 A. Woolrych, *Commonwealth to Protectorate* (Clarendon Press, 1982)

Source 7.23 *Seventeenth-Century England: A Changing Culture* (as above)

Source 7.24 The title page of the first edition of John Milton's *Areopagitica* (1644) Bodleian Library Arch G.e.44(10)

Source 7.25–7.27 D. Wolfe (ed.), *The Complete Prose Works of John Milton*, vol. 22 (Yale University Press, 1953–82)

Source 7.28 J. Milton, *Samson Agonistes* (1671)

Chapter 8

Source 8.1 The Act abolishing the monarchy, 17 March 1649

Source 8.2 The Act abolishing the House of Lords, 19 March 1649

Source 8.3 The Act declaring England to be a Commonwealth, 19 May 1649

Source 8.4 The Great Seal of England, 1651, the British Library

Source 8.5 Clement Walker, *Complete History of Independency* (1661)

Source 8.6 Bulstrode Whitlock, *Memorials of the English Affairs*, vol. III (1682)

Source 8.7 Edmund Ludlow, *The Memoirs of Edmund Ludlow*, vol. 1 (Clarendon Press, 1894)

Source 8.8 George Yule, *The Independents in the English Civil War* (CUP, 1958)

Source 8.9 David Underdown, *Pride's Purge: Politics in the English Revolution* (Clarendon Press, 1971)

Source 8.10 Barry Coward, *The Stuart Age : England 1603–1714* (2nd ed., Longman, 1994)

Source 8.11 Roger Lockyer, *Tudor and Stuart Britain* (Longman, 1985)

Source 8.12 Blair Worden, *The Rump Parliament, 1648–53* (CUP, 1974)

Chapter 9

Source 9.1 A engraving showing a meeting of Barebone's Parliament, published in a leaflet in 1653

Source 9.2 W. Dunn Macray, *Calendar of Clarendon State Papers*, vol. 2 (Clarendon Press, 1888)

Source 9.3 *Calendar of State Papers Venetian, 1653–4*

Source 9.4 James Heath, *Flagellum* (London, 1663)

Source 9.5 Edward Hyde from *History of the Rebellion* (1702–4) in G. Huehns (ed.), *Selections from Clarendon* (OUP, 1978)

Source 9.6 British Library, Thomason Tracts, E.729.6

Source 9.7 A. Woolrych, *Commonwealth to Protectorate* (Clarendon Press, 1982)

Source 9.8 *Commonwealth to Protectorate* (as above)

Chapter 10

Source 10.1 Commonwealth shilling, 1652, and Oliver Cromwell half-crown, 1656, the Tower Mint, London; in the British Museum

Source 10.2 The Great Seal of England, 1651, the British Library. Side b shows the House of Commons in session

Source 10.3 Cromwell as a heroic military leader; the title page of *A Perfect Table of One Hundred Forty and Five Victories Obtained by the Lord Lieutenant of Ireland* (London, 1650)

Source 10.4 Royalist propaganda showing Cromwell as the Devil, 1649. See John Morrill (ed.), *Impact of the English Civil War* (Collins and Brown, 1991)

Source 10.5 A Leveller pamphlet, *The Hunting of the Foxes*, 1649

Source 10.6 Engraving, *The Royall Oake of Brittayne* by Clement Walker; in the British Library

Source 10.7 Slingsby Bethel, *The World's Mistake in Oliver Cromwell* (1668) reprinted by the Rota at the University of Exeter (1972)

Source 10.8 W. C. Abbott (ed.), *The Writings and Speeches of Oliver Cromwell*, vol. 1 (Harvard University Press, 1937–44)

Source 10.9 *The Writings and Speeches of Oliver Cromwell*, vol. 1 (as above)

Source 10.10 I. Roots (ed.), *The Speeches of Oliver Cromwell* (Dent, 1989)

Source 10.11 *The Writings and Speeches of Oliver Cromwell*, vol. 2 (as above)

Source 10.12 *The Speeches of Oliver Cromwell* (as above)

Source 10.13 *The Writings and Speeches of Oliver Cromwell*, vol. 1 (as above)

Source 10.14–10.15 *The Speeches of Oliver Cromwell* (as above)

Source 10.16 *The Writings and Speeches of Oliver Cromwell*, vol. 2 (as above)

Source 10.17 *The Speeches of Oliver Cromwell* (as above)

Source 10.18–10.20 *The Writings and Speeches of Oliver Cromwell*, vol. 1 (as above)

Source 10.21 J. P. Kenyon (ed.), *The Stuart Constitution* (CUP, 1986)

Source 10.22 *The Speeches of Oliver Cromwell* (as above)

Source 10.23 *The Stuart Constitution* (as above)

Source 10.24–10.28 *The Speeches of Oliver Cromwell* (as above)

Source 10.29–10.37 *The Writings and Speeches of Oliver Cromwell*, vol. 2 (as above)

Source 10.38–10.39 *The Speeches of Oliver Cromwell* (as above)

Source 10.40 *The Writings and Speeches of Oliver Cromwell*, vol. 2 (as above)

Source 10.41 An imaginative Dutch print of Cromwell's dissolution of the Rump Parliament in April 1653

Source 10.42 The *Speeches of Oliver Cromwell* (as above)

Source 10.43 *The Writings and Speeches of Oliver Cromwell*, vol. 3 (as above)

Source 10.44 *The Speeches of Oliver Cromwell* (as above)

Source 10.45 J.T. Rutt (ed.), *The Parliamentary Diary of Thomas Burton*, vol. 1 (London,1826

Source 10.46 *The Speeches of Oliver Cromwell* (as above)

Source 10.47 *The Writings and Speeches of Oliver Cromwell*, vol. 4 (as above)

Source 10.48 *The Speeches of Oliver Cromwell* (as above)

Source 10.49 John Milton, *On the Late Massacre in Piedmont* (1655)

Source 10.50 T. Birch (ed.), *A Collection of the State Papers of John Thurloe Esq*, vol. 3 (London,1742)

Source 10.51 *Thurloe State papers* (as above)

Source 10.52–10.53 *The Writings and Speeches of Oliver Cromwell*, vol. 3 (as above)

Source 10.54 *The Speeches of Oliver Cromwell* (as above)

Source 10.55 *The Parliamentary Diary of Thomas Burton*, vol. 1(as above)

Source 10.56 *The Writings and Speeches of Oliver Cromwell*, vol. 4 (as above)

Source 10.57–10.59 *The Speeches of Oliver Cromwell* (as above)

Source 10.60 *The Writings and Speeches of Oliver Cromwell*, vol. 4 (as above)

Source 10.61 Christopher Hill, *Oliver Cromwell 1658–1958*, Historical Association pamphlet (1984)

Source 10.62 Peter Gaunt, *Oliver Cromwell* (Blackwell, 1996)

Source 10.63 *The Great Rebellion, 1640–60* (as above)

Chapter 11

Source 11.1 Title page of John Taylor's pamphlet, *The Vindication of Christmas*, 1652

Source 11.2 C. H. Firth and R. S. Rait (eds.), *Acts and Ordinances of the Interregnum*, vol. 1 (HMSO, 1911)

Source 11.3 British Library, Thomason Tracts, E.476.41

Source 11.4 British Library, Thomason Tracts, E.619.4

Source 11.5–11.8 *Acts and Ordinances*, vol. 1 (as above)

Source 11.9 *Acts and Ordinances*, vol. 2

Source 11.10 Book of Common Prayer 1559

Source 11.11 *Acts and Ordinances*, vol. 1 (as above)

Source 11.12 Book of Common Prayer 1559

Source 11.13 *Acts and Ordinances*, vol. 1 (as above)

Source 11.14 Book of Common Prayer 1559

Source 11.15 *Acts and Ordinances*, vol. 1 (as above)

Source 11.16–11.18 *Acts and Ordinances*, vol. 2 (as above)

Source 11.19 J. P. Kenyon (ed.), *The Stuart Constitution* (CUP, 1986)

Source 11.20 Parliamentary Act abolishing the celebration of Christmas, 24 December 1652

Source 11.21 British Library, Thomason Tracts, E.422.1

Source 11.22 *Commons Journal*, vol. 6

Source 11.23 British Library, Thomason Tracts, E.684.18

Source 11.24 J. T. Rutt (ed.), *The Diary of Thomas Burton*, vol. 1 (London, 1826)

Source 11.25 C. H. Firth (ed.), *The Clarke Papers*, Camden Society Publs, new series, vol. 60 (1899)

Source 11.26 J. S. Cockburn (ed.), *Somerset Assizes Orders 1640–59*, Somerset Record Society Publs, vol. 71 (1971)

Source 11.27 A. Macfarlane (ed.), *The Diary of Ralph Josselin 1616–83* (London, 1976)

Source 11.28 British Library, Thomason Tracts, E.713.10

Source 11.29–11.31 British Library, Thomason Tracts, E.714.2

Source 11.32 E. A. Wrigley and R. S. Schofield, *The Population History of England 1541–1871* (London, 1981)

Source 11.33 John Loftis (ed.), *Memoirs of Anne, Lady Halket and Anne, Lady Fanshawe* (Oxford, 1979)

Source 11.34 Contemporary woodcut of an alehouse

Source 11.35 L. Fox (ed.), 'The Diary of Robert Beake, mayor of Coventry 1655–6', *Dugdale Miscellany*, Dugdale Society Publs, vol. 31 (1977)

Source 11.36 T. Birch (ed.), *A Collection of the State Papers of John Thurloe Esq*, vol. 5 (London, 1742)

Source 11.37 *Thurloe State Papers*, vol. 5 (as above)

Chapter 12

Source 12.1 W. L. Sachse (ed.), *The Diurnal of Thomas Rugg, 1659–61*, Camden Society Publs, 3rd series, vol. 91 (1961)

Source 12.2 *The Autobiography of Mrs Alice Thornton* (Edinburgh, 1875)

Source 12.3 'The Duke of Newcastle, 1660', Clarendon MS 109 ff. 1920 in J. Thirsk (ed.), *The Restoration* (1976)

Source 12.4 Dorothy White, *A Diligent Search* (1659)

Source 12.5 J. Raine (ed.), *Depositions from the Castle of York Relating to Offences Committed in the Northern Counties in the Seventeenth Century*, Surtees Society, vol. 40 (1861)

Source 12.6 Anti-Quaker pamphlet title page: *The Quakers Dream*, April 1655; the Bodleian Library

Source 12.7 Anti-Quaker pamphlet title page: *The Four-Legg'd Quaker*, 1659; the Bodleian Library

Source 12.8 *A Relation of a Quaker That to the Shame of his Profession Attempted to Bugger a Mare near Colchester* (May 1659)

Source 12.9 J. T. Rutt (ed.), *The Diary of Thomas Burton*, vol. 4 (London, 1826)

Source 12.10 'Sir George Booth's Letter of the 2nd of August, showing the reasons of his present Engagement, 1659', in J. A. Atkinson (ed.), *Tracts Relating to the Civil War in Cheshire, 1641–59*, Chetham Society, new series, vol. 65 (1909)

Source 12.11 'The Uniformity Act, 1662', in J. P. Kenyon (ed.), *The Stuart Constitution* (CUP, 1986)

Source 12.12 A private letter from Monck to Richard Cromwell, 1658, *Thurloe State Papers*, vol. 7

Source 12.13 R. Latham and W. Matthews (eds.), *The Diary of Samuel Pepys*, vol. I (G. Bell and Sons, 1971)

Source 12.14 *The Stuart Constitution* (as above)

Source 12.15 *The Diary of Samuel Pepys*, vol. I (as above)

Source 12.16 E. S. de Beer (ed.), *The Diary of John Evelyn* (1818)

Source 12.17 *The Diurnal of Thomas Rugg, 1659–61* (as above)

Source 12.18 A. Browning (ed.), *English Historical Documents 1660–1714* (Eyre & Spottiswood, 1953)

Source 12.19 J. C. Jeaffreson (ed.), *Middlesex County Records*, Middlesex, County Record Society, 1836–92, vol. 3; D. L. Powell and H. Jenkinson, *Surrey Quarter Sessions Order Book and Sessions Rolls, 1661–63*, Surrey Record Society (1935) in Christopher Hill, *The World Turned Upside Down* (1972)

Source 12.20 John Milton, 'The Readie and Easie Way to Establish a Free Commonwealth' (1660) in R. W. Ayres (ed.), *The Complete Prose Works of John Milton*, vol. 7 (Yale University Press, 1980)

Chapter 13

Source 13.1 Christopher Hill, *Reformation to Industrial Revolution: a Social and Economic History of Britain, 1530–1780* (Weidenfeld and Nicholson, 1967)

Source 13.2 *Reformation to Industrial Revolution* (as above)

Source 13.3 *Reformation to Industrial Revolution* (as above)

Source 13.4 Lawrence Stone, 'The results of the English Revolution' in J. G. A. Pocock (ed.), *Three British Revolutions* (Princeton University Press, 1980)

Source 13.5 John Miller, 'The later Stuart monarchy' in J. R. Jones (ed.), *The Restored Monarchy* (Macmillan, 1979)

Source 13.6 I. M. Green, *The Re-establishment of the Church of England 1660–63* (OUP, 1978)

Source 13.7 Barry Coward, 'Was there an English Revolution in the middle of the seventeenth century?' in C. Jones, M. Newitt and S. Roberts (eds.), *Politics and People in Revolutionary England* (Blackwell, 1986)

Source 13.8 Tim Harris, 'Introduction: revising the Restoration' in Tim Harris *et al* (eds.), *The Politics of Religion in Restoration England* (Blackwell, 1991)

Index